Polish For Dummies®

by Daria Gabryanczyk

A John Wiley and Sons, Ltd, Publication

Polish For Dummies®

Published by
John Wiley & Sons, Ltd
The Atrium
Southern Gate
Chichester
West Sussex
PO19 8SQ
England

Email (for orders and customer service enquires): cs-books@wiley.co.uk

Visit our home page on www.wiley.com

Published by John Wiley & Sons, Ltd, Chichester, West Sussex

For general information on our other products and services, please contact our Customer Care Department within the U.S. at 800-762-2974, outside the U.S. at 317-572-3993, or fax 317-572-4002.

For technical support, please visit www.wiley.com/techsupport.

Wiley also publishes its books in a variety of electronic formats and by print-on-demand. Some content that appears in standard print versions of this book may not be available in other formats. For more information about Wiley products, visit us at www.wiley.com.

British Library Cataloguing in Publication Data: A catalogue record for this book is available from the British Library

ISBN: 978-1-119-97959-3 (paperback), 978-1-119-95120-9 (ebook), 978-1-119-95121-6 (ebook), 978-1-119-95122-3 (ebook)

Printed and bound in Great Britain by TJ International, Padstow, Cornwall
SKY10044825_032123

About the Author

Daria Gabryanczyk has been teaching Polish literature and Polish as a foreign language for almost a decade. She holds an MA in Polish Language and Literature from the University of Łódź. Daria is a teacher and an examiner for the Ministry of Defence Language Examinations Board and the University of Westminster. She has worked as a language teacher for the European High Commission, Foreign and Commonwealth Office, United Kingdom Environmental Law Association and University College, London. Daria provides Polish Business Etiquette and Culture Training for Businesses. She is also an author of the *Polish Easy Readers* series and runs a school of Polish in London.

Author's Acknowledgements

I'd like to thank my husband, Piotr, for hanging in there through the ups and downs of a first-time author, and to my parents for cheering me up and making food for me when I was well and truly lost in writing the book. I'm very grateful to my friends who pre-ordered the book when not a single word had even been written.

Many thanks to all the people at Wiley for making this book possible, especially to my commissioning editor, Kerry Laundon, for finding and selecting me for 'the Polish job'; to Rachael Chilvers, for her coordination, supervision and invaluable help in developing this book; to Kathleen Dobie for her insight, thorough and much-appreciated editing (she made this book a better one!); and to my technical editors, Izabela Mayne and Iwona Dembowska-Wosik, for ensuring that I didn't miss anything.

I owe much gratitude to my student and friend, Simon Williams, for so many scribbling-on-a-napkin conversations about pronunciation and grammar and to Matthew Culver for his help in taking me through the legal aspects of this project.

Publisher's Acknowledgements

We're proud of this book; please send us your comments through our Dummies online registration form located at www.dummies.com/register/.

Some of the people who helped bring this book to market include the following:

Commissioning, Editorial, and Media Development

Project Editor: Rachael Chilvers

Commissioning Editor: Kerry Laundon

Assistant Editor: Ben Kemble

Development Editor: Kathleen Dobie

Technical Editors: Izabela Mayne and Iwona Dembowska-Wosik

Proofreader: Kate O'Leary

Production Manager: Daniel Mersey

Publisher: David Palmer

Cover Photo: © iStock / fotohmmm

Cartoons: Rich Tennant (www.the5thwave.com)

CD Production: David Roper and Davy Nougarede at Heavy Entertainment

Composition Services

Project Coordinator: Kristie Rees

Layout and Graphics: Joyce Haughey, Laura Westhuis, Erin Zeltner

Indexer: Potomac Indexing, LLC

Publishing and Editorial for Consumer Dummies

Kathleen Nebenhaus, Vice President and Executive Publisher

Kristin Ferguson-Wagstaffe, Product Development Director

Ensley Eikenburg, Associate Publisher, Travel

Kelly Regan, Editorial Director, Travel

Publishing for Technology Dummies

Andy Cummings, Vice President and Publisher

Composition Services

Debbie Stailey, Director of Composition Services

Contents at a Glance

Part VI: Appendixes 353

Index 395

Table of Contents

Introduction

Society is becoming ever more international in nature – low-cost airfares make travel abroad a more realistic option, global business environments necessitate overseas travel, friends and neighbours may speak another language. Knowing how to say at least a few words in other languages becomes increasingly useful. You may also want to get in touch with your heritage by learning a little bit of the language that your ancestors spoke.

Whatever your reason for acquiring some Polish, this book can help. *Polish For Dummies* gives you the skills you need for basic communication in Polish. I'm not promising fluency, but if you want to greet someone, purchase a ticket or order something from a menu in Polish, you need look no further than *Polish For Dummies*.

About This Book

This book isn't a class that you have to drag yourself to twice a week for six weeks. You can use *Polish For Dummies* however you want to, whether your goal is to learn some words and phrases to help you get around when you visit Poland, or you simply want to be able to say *Hello* to a Polish-speaking friend. This book can help you reach moments of true understanding in a different language. Use the text as a language and cultural guide for those moments when you really need to know how and why things are done.

Go through this book at your own pace, reading as much or as little at a time as you like. Also, you don't have to trudge through the chapters in order; you can just read the sections that interest you.

The only way to know and love a language is to speak it. Throughout the book are lots of words, phrases and dialogues, complete with pronunciations you can use to practise the language. The audio tracks provide you with a broad sample of spoken dialogues, which you can use to improve your pronunciation and inflection.

Remember that you don't need to chew through this book all at once. So you don't need to read it cover to cover. Just pick a chapter that interests you and you can find cross-references to other parts of the book.

Why I Wrote This Book

Language exposes you to every aspect of the human condition, allowing you to study the past, understand the present and ponder the future. Language sometimes changes the ways in which people express various emotions and conditions. People are connected through their ability to speak, but you can go one step further – to understanding – by being able to communicate in another language. Very few things are as exciting as that!

The best way to discover a new language is to immerse yourself in it. Listen to the way Polish sounds, concentrate on the pronunciation and look at how it's written. By listening and repeating, you enter a new world of ideas and peoples. Acquiring Polish through immersion really does feel like a sort of magic.

Conventions Used in This Book

To make this book easy for you to navigate, I set up a few conventions:

- Polish terms are set in **boldface** to make them stand out.
- Pronunciations, set in brackets in *italics*, follow the Polish terms. The translations, again in parentheses, follow the pronunciations.
- Verb conjugation tables (lists that show you the forms of a verb) follow this order:
  - **ja:** the *I* form
  - **ty:** the singular, informal *you* form
  - **on, ona, ono:** the *he*, *she*, *it* form
  - **my:** the *we* form
  - **wy:** the plural, informal *you* form
  - **oni, one:** the *they* form for a group with at least one man; the *they* form for a group with no man

A typical verb conjugation table has columns for the pronoun forms, the Polish verb, the pronunciation and the translation, as in the following table:

Form	*Polish*	*Pronunciation*	*Translation*
(ja)	czyta-**m**	*(chih-tam)*	I read/am reading
(ty)	czyta-**sz**	*(chih-tash)*	you read/are reading
on/ona/ono	czyta-**ø**	*(chih-ta)*	he/she/it reads/is reading
(my)	czyta-**my**	*(chih-ta-mih)*	we read/are reading
(wy)	czyta-**cie**	*(chih-ta-ch'ye)*	you read/are reading
oni/one	czyta-**ją**	*(chih-ta-yohN)*	they read/are reading

As you may notice, the personal pronouns **ja**, **ty**, **my**, **wy** *(ya, tih, mih, vih)* are in brackets. That's because you don't actually say those pronouns when you're speaking Polish, so I put them in brackets in all conjugation tables in this book. I explain the pronoun issue in detail in Chapter 3.

Unlike English, Polish uses special formal forms to address people in official situations. (I write more about how to address people in Chapter 3.) So, the *you* form has the following formal equivalents in Polish:

- **pan, pani: pan** *(pan)* is the formal *you* to address a man and **pani** *(pa-n'ee)* the formal *you* to a woman (singular).
- **państwo, panowie, panie** *(pan'-stfo pa-no-v'ye pa-n'ye)*: the formal, plural *you* form to address a mixed group, a group of men and a group of women, respectively. **Państwo** also means *ladies and gentlemen*, **panowie** are *gentlemen* and **panie** translates as *ladies* (plural).

When reading verb tables or conjugating verbs, remember that **pan** takes on the same verb form as **on** (he) and **pani** the same verb form as **ona** (she); the third person singular. In the present tense, the plural **państwo**, **panowie** and **panie** take on a verb in the third person plural (the same as **oni** (*they* male or mixed) and **one** (*they* female)). However, in the past tense and the future that uses past tense forms, **państwo** and **panowie** follow **oni**, while **panie** follows **one** in the choice of a verb form. Chapter 2 explains verbs in more detail.

Studying a language is a peculiar beast, and so this book includes a few elements that other *For Dummies* books don't:

- **Talkin' the Talk dialogues:** The best way to improve with a language is to see and hear how it's used in conversation, and so I include dialogues throughout the book. The dialogues come under the heading 'Talkin' the Talk' and show you the Polish words, the pronunciation and the English translation.
- **Words to Know blackboards:** Memorising key words and phrases is also important in language, and so I collect the important words that appear in a chapter (or section within a chapter) and write them on a 'blackboard' under the heading 'Words to Know'.

- **Fun & Games activities:** If you don't have Polish speakers with whom to practise your new language skills, you can use the Fun & Games activities to reinforce what you're discovering. These word games are fun ways to gauge your progress.

Also, because each language has its own ways of expressing ideas, the English translations that I provide for the Polish terms may not be literal. I want you to know the gist of what's being said, not just the words being said. For example, you can translate the Polish phrase **wszystko w porządku** (*fshih-stko fpo-zhon-tkoo*) literally as *everything in order*, but the phrase really means *fine*. This book gives the *fine* translations.

Foolish Assumptions

To write this book, I had to make some assumptions about you and what you want from a book called *Polish For Dummies*:

- You know no Polish.
- You're not looking for a book to make you fluent in Polish; you just want to know some words, phrases and sentence constructions so that you can communicate basic information in Polish.
- You don't want to have to memorise long lists of vocabulary words or a load of boring grammar rules.
- You want to have fun and discover a bit of Polish at the same time.

If these statements apply to you, you've found the right book!

How This Book Is Organised

This book is divided by topic into parts, and then into chapters. The following sections tell you what types of information you can find in each part.

Part I: Getting Started

You get your feet wet in this part as I give you some Polish basics: how to pronounce words, what the accents mean and so on. I even boost your confidence by reintroducing you to some Polish words you probably already know. In addition, I outline the basics of Polish grammar that you may need to know when you turn to the more detailed chapters of the book.

Part II: Polish in Action

In this part, you begin practising and using Polish. Instead of focusing on grammar points, as many language textbooks do, this part focuses on everyday situations in which you may find yourself if you're living in Poland or dealing with your Polish-speaking friends. The chapters in this part hone your small-talk skills and take you on shopping and dining excursions. At the end of this part, you should be able to do some basic navigation in the Polish language.

Part III: Polish on the Go

This part provides the tools you need to take your Polish on the road, whether you're going to a local Polish restaurant or a museum in Warsaw. These chapters help you to survive the Customs process, check into hotels and nab a cab, and have a great time doing it. Sprinkled throughout are cultural titbits that introduce you to people, places and things that are important in Polish culture.

Part IV: Polish in the Workplace

This part transports you to the world of the Polish business, office and work-site cultures and their specialised language.

Part V: The Part of Tens

If you're looking for small, easily digestible pieces of information about Polish, this part is for you. Here, you can find ways to speak Polish quickly, useful Polish expressions to know and celebrations worth joining.

Part VI: Appendixes

This part of the book includes important information that you can use for reference. I give you a mini-dictionary in both Polish-to-English and English-to-Polish formats and provide some brief facts about Poland. I include verb tables that show you how to conjugate a regular verb, and then how to conjugate those verbs that stubbornly refuse to fit the pattern. I also provide a listing of the audio tracks so that you can find out where in the book those dialogues are and follow along.

Icons Used in This Book

You may be looking for particular information while reading this book. To make certain types of information easier for you to find, I place the following icons in the left-hand margins throughout the book:

I use this icon to indicate crucial pieces of information that you need to bear in mind.

This icon highlights tips that can make Polish easier for you.

Languages are full of quirks that may trip you up if you're not prepared for them. This icon points to discussions of these weird grammatical rules.

If you're looking for information and advice about culture and travel, look for this icon.

The audio tracks that come with this book give you the opportunity to listen to real Polish speakers so that you get a better understanding of what Polish sounds like. This icon marks the Talkin' the Talk dialogues that you can find on the audio tracks.

Where to Go from Here

Discovering a new language is all about jumping in and giving it a try (no matter how bad your pronunciation is at first). So make the leap! Never feel at all ashamed when speaking Polish! All your attempts to speak even just a few words will be much appreciated and any language mistakes or cultural faux pas easily forgotten by Poles. What counts is you making an effort to learn and speak the language. Of course, the better your Polish, the more impressed your Polish friends, family or business partners will be.

If you've never taken Polish lessons before, you may want to read the chapters in Part I before tackling the later chapters. Part I gives you some of the basics that you need to know about the language, such as how to pronounce the various sounds.

After that, pick a chapter that interests you or listen to some audio tracks. Above all, make sure that you have fun!

Part I
Getting Started

"The Polish rules of grammar are so easy you can actually begin reading the text without understanding what's being said. You know, like the British tax code."

In this part . . .

Here you can jump right into the Polish language – I start by showing you Polish words whose meaning you can work out without consulting a dictionary; then you discover how to make Polish sounds and how to crack the Polish 'grammar code'. I also give you a few quickie phrases to impress your Polish friends!

Chapter 1

Introducing Polish

In This Chapter

- Identifying some familiar-looking Polish words
- Pronouncing the alphabet and all its vowels and consonants
- Stressing the right syllable
- Using basic expressions

Being able to produce sounds that native speakers can recognise and understand is vital for successful communication. This chapter discusses Polish pronunciation and some of the conventions used in this book.

Spotting the Polish You Already Know

Polish borrows a number of words from English in many different areas, such as computer science, politics, technology, sport, economics and business. The borrowed words have either retained their original spelling or been adapted to the Polish spelling, but they're still easy to recognise (and to remember!) for native English speakers. You won't have much trouble working out the meaning of these words:

- **adres** *(a-dres)* (address)
- **biznes** *(bee-znes)* (business)
- **budżet** *(bood-zhet)* (budget)
- **establishment** *(e-sta-blee-shment)* (establishment)
- **hotel** *(ho-tel)* (hotel)
- **interfejs** *(een-ter-feys)* (interface)
- **kawa** *(ka-va)* (coffee)
- **komputer** *(kom-poo-ter)* (computer)
- **kultura** *(kool-too-ra)* (culture)
- **marketing** *(mar-ke-teenk)* (marketing)

- **mecz** *(mech)* ([football] match)
- **menadżer** *(me-na-djer)* (manager)
- **park** *(park)* (park)
- **telefon** *(te-le-fon)* (telephone)

Of course, you can get into trouble when you're dealing with so-called *false friends* – words that look similar in English and Polish, yet have completely different meanings:

- **Aktualnie** *(a-ktoo-al-n'ye)* means *currently* or *presently* rather than *actually*
- **Data** *(da-ta)* means *date* not *data*
- **Ewentualnie** *(e-ven-too-al-n'ye)* is the English *possibly* rather than *eventually*
- **Hazard** *(ha-zart)* is *gambling* (which can be hazardous to your bank balance)
- **Konfident** *(kon-fee-dent)* doesn't translate to *confident* but rather to *an informer*
- **Ordynarny** *(or-dih-nar-nih)* is *vulgar* rather than *ordinary*
- Someone who is **sympatyczny** *(sihm-pa-tih-chnih)* in Polish is actually *nice* or *friendly*, but not *sympathetic*
- The Polish word **szef** *(shef)* means *boss*, not a *chef*, unless you say **szef kuchni** *(shef koo-hn'ee)* (head chef)
- And the one that can cause you quite a lot of embarrassment if misused: **klozet** *(klo-zet)* is not the English *closet* but colloquially . . . *a toilet*

The Polish Alphabet: Reciting Your ABCs

Next to Polish words throughout this book, you can see their pronunciation in brackets. To make it easier for you to read and say the words, the pronunciations are split into syllables with a hyphen, such as *(al-fa-bet)*. Try to say the underlined syllable more strongly, as it is a stressed syllable. Make your way to the 'Searching for Stress and Blending Prepositions' section later in this chapter to read more about the Polish stress.

When the first writings in Polish appeared, the 26 letters of the Latin alphabet couldn't accommodate the 45 sounds that somehow needed to be represented. As a result, the Polish alphabet consists of 32 letters and uses a variety of consonant clusters such as **ch, cz, dż, dz, dź, sz** and **rz**. ***Note:*** *Q*, *v* and *x* are not Polish letters and appear in foreign words only.

Table 1-1 shows all the Polish letters and how to say them in brackets (listen to audio track 1 to help you).

Table 1-1 The Polish Alphabet

a *(a)*	**ą** *(ohN)*	**b** *(be)*	**c** *(tse)*
ć *(ch'ye)*	**d** *(de)*	**e** *(e)*	**ę** *(ehN)*
f *(ef)*	**g** *(gye)*	**h** *(ha)*	**i** *(ee)*
j *(yot)*	**k** *(ka)*	**l** *(el)*	**ł** *(ew)*
m *(em)*	**n** *(en)*	**ń** *(en')*	**o** *(o)*
ó *(o kreskovane)*	**p** *(pe)*	**q** *(koo)*	**r** *(er)*
s *(es)*	**ś** *(esh')*	**t** *(te)*	**u** *(oo)*
v *(faw)*	**w** *(voo)*	**x** *(eeks)*	**y** *(eegrek)*
z *(zet)*	**ź** *(z'yet)*	**ż** *(zhet)*	

Although the Polish pronunciation may seem pretty daunting, it is in fact regular and once you memorise a couple of patterns, you'll soon notice that you can pronounce every word you come across.

Native speakers find working out how to spell a word from its pronunciation easy (with some exceptions they simply learn by heart). And if in doubt, they just ask for clarification. However, as a foreigner, you may be asked to spell your name or need someone to spell a street name for you, so the following phrases may come in handy:

- **Czy może pan/pani przeliterować?** *(chih mo-zhe pan/pa-n'ee pshe-lee-te-ro-vach')* (Can you spell it, please?) – formal, to a man/woman
- **Proszę przeliterować** *(pro-she pshe-lee-te-ro-vach')* (Please spell it) – formal
- **Czy mam przeliterować?** *(chih mam pshe-lee-te-ro-vach')* (Do you want me to spell it?)
- **Proszę mi to napisać.** *(pro-she mee to na-pee-sach')* (Can you please write it for me?)

When spelling, unlike the English habit of saying, 'A for Alpha', 'B for Bravo' and so on, Polish people often use first names. So you'll hear something like the following: **A jak Anna** *(a yak an-na)*, **Be jak Barbara** *(be yak bar-ba-ra)*, **Ce jak Celina** *(tse yak tse-lee-na)* and so on.

If you're going to Poland, prepare a list of first names you can use to spell your own name so that you won't panic when you need to spell it in Polish.

Checking Out Consonant Pronunciation

Some consonants are pronounced the same way in both Polish and English: **b, d, f, g, k, l, m, n, p, s, t** and **z**. In words with double letters such as **Anna** and **lekki**, each letter is pronounced separately as in *an-na* and *lek-kee*.

For the sake of simplicity, in pronunciation brackets I use **n** before *k* or *g*. Think of how you pronounce **nk** in the English word *bank*. Polish people say *nk* and *ng* in the exactly same way.

The following sections cover the consonants whose pronunciation is different from English.

C

In Polish, **c** is pronounced as *ts* in *tsetse fly* or *Betsy*. Don't confuse it with the English *k* sound as in *car*. In the pronunciation brackets, you'll see the symbol ***ts*** to indicate letter **c**, as in these examples:

- **cebula** *(tse-boo-la)* (onion)
- **co** *(tso)* (what)
- **centrum** *(tsen-troom)* (city centre)

Ć and Ci

These consonants represent exactly the same sound. Unfortunately, that sound doesn't have a direct equivalent in English. You need to think of the word *cheese* and try to say the *chee* part just a touch more softly. Yes, you're in business! In the pronunciation brackets, *ch'* indicates **ć** and **ci**.

The ' in a pronuciation reminds you that it's a soft sound. I add an extra *y* to help you pronounce **ci** when followed by a vowel.

Now, try the sound of these words:

- **ciepło** *(ch'ye-pwo)* (warm)
- **mówić** *(moo-veech')* (to speak, say)

Ć and **ci** are used in different situations. You write **ć** when it appears at the end of a word as in pi**ć** *(peech')* (to drink) or before another consonant as in **ć**ma *(ch'ma)* (moth). The **ci** form is written before a vowel as in **ciocia** *(ch'yo-ch'ya)* (auntie). However, you will see a number of words where **ci** appears before a consonant or at the end of a word. This only happens when **ci**

actually forms a syllable, as in **ci-cho** (*ch'ee-ho*) (quiet) and **ni-ci** (*n'ee-ch'ee*) (sewing threads). Identical rules apply to soft pairs such as **ś** and **si**, **ź** and **zi**, **dź** and **dzi**, **ń** and **ni**, which I cover in upcoming sections.

Cz

Cz shouldn't cause too many pronunciation difficulties. The sound is like the *ch* in *cheddar*, only a touch harder. In the pronunciation brackets you'll see ***ch*** to represent **cz**. Here are some examples:

- **czarny** (*char-nih*) (black)
- **czas** (*chas*) (time)
- **wieczór** (*vye-choor*) (evening)

Dz

The pronunciation of **dz** is like the *ds* in *Leeds* or *goods* and is indicated by ***dz*** in the phonetic script. Practise the following words:

- **dzwon** (*dzvon*) (bell)
- **bardzo** (*bar-dzo*) (very)

Dź and Dzi

Again, the English tongue is unfamiliar with the soft **dź** and **dzi**. Their pronunciation is softer than *je* in *jeans*. To represent them, you'll see ***dj'*** in the pronunciation brackets. I add an extra ***y*** to help you pronounce **dzi** when followed by a vowel and *ee* when **dzi** forms a syllable. Here are some Polish examples:

- **dzień** (*dj'yen'*) (day)
- **godzina** (*go-dj'ee-na*) (hour, time)

You can read about the rules of the **dź** and **dzi** spelling in the 'Ć and Ci' section earlier in this chapter.

Dż

When saying **dż**, think of both of the *g* sounds in the English word *Georgia* and you're in business. To represent **dż**, you'll see ***dj*** in the pronunciation brackets. You're now ready to practise it:

- **dżungla** *(djoon-gla)* (jungle)
- **dżem** *(djem)* (jam)

H and Ch

H and **ch** are identical twins as far as pronunciation is concerned. Think of the *h* in *hat*. Since you say both **h** and **ch** in the same way, in the pronunciation brackets you'll see ***h*** to indicate them both. Now, when practising this sound remember to breathe out gently:

- **historia** *(hee-sto-rya)* (history)
- **hotel** *(ho-tel)* (hotel)
- **chleb** *(hlep)* (bread)
- **ucho** *(oo-ho)* (ear)

Be aware that the **y** sound is represented as ***ih*** – the *i* sound in *pity* – throughout this book, so when you see the ***ih*** combination in the pronunciation brackets, as in **miły** *(mee-wih)*, remember that the *h* is barely breathed. The sound certainly isn't the same as the *h* in the word *hat*. Go to the 'Saying Polish Vowels' section later in this chapter for guidance on pronouncing vowels.

J

The letter **j** is pronounced like the *y* in *yes* and that's how it appears in the pronunciation brackets – ***y***:

- **jeden** *(ye-den)* (one)
- **projekt** *(pro-yekt)* (project)

Ł

This letter may look a bit exotic to you – printed capital **Ł**, small **ł** and handwritten as in Figure 1-1. Luckily, its pronunciation is exactly the same as the English *w* in *water*. **Ł** will be marked as ***w*** in the phonetic script, as in these examples:

- **szkoła** *(shko-wa)* (school)
- **mały** *(ma-wih)* (small)
- **łatwy** *(wa-tfih)* (easy)

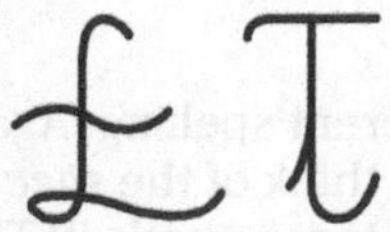

Figure 1-1: The written capital and small ł.

N and Ni

These two consonants, similarly to **ć** and **ci**, are soft and, despite different spellings, they sound exactly the same. Again, they are unfamiliar to the English tongue. When pronouncing **ń** and **ni** think of the English words *onion* or *new*. Throughout this book the soft **ń** and **ni** is presented as ***n'***. I add an extra ***y*** to help you pronounce **ni** before a vowel and ***ee*** when **ni** forms a separate syllable. Read these examples:

- **nie** *(n'ye)* (no)
- **koń** *(kon')* (horse)
- **hiszpański** *(heesh'-pan'-skee)* (Spanish)
- **nisko** *(n'ee-sko)* (low, down)

You can read about the spelling rules for **ń** and **ni** in the 'Ć and Ci' section earlier in this chapter.

R

The letter **r**, although pronounced a bit differently than in English – it's a trilled *r* – is presented as ***r*** in the pronunciation brackets. In fact, it's not a big problem if you pronounce it the English way. Polish native speakers will certainly understand you. However, if you want to perfect it, take a deep breath, oscillate the tip of your tongue just behind your teeth in an up and down motion and say the *r* sound very loudly. Check out audio track 1 for how it actually sounds.

Here are some examples you can use to practise your **r**:

- **rok** *(rok)* (year)
- **rower** *(ro-ver)* (bike)
- **park** *(park)* (park)

Ś and Si

Ś and **si** sound exactly the same, despite their different spelling. Again, you won't find a direct equivalent in English, but if you think of the *shee* part of the English word *sheep*, which you say with a bit of softness, that's it! Throughout this book, theses sounds are represented by ***sh'***. I add an extra ***y*** to help you pronounce **si** when followed by a vowel and ***ee*** when **si** forms a separate syllable. I add an extra ***y*** to help you pronounce **ś** and **si** when followed by a vowel. Here are some examples:

- **siedem** *(sh'ye-dem)* (seven)
- **środa** *(sh'ro-da)* (Wednesday)
- **coś** *(tsosh')* (something)
- **silny** *(sh'eel-nih)* (strong)

For the rules of spelling, refer to the 'Ć and Ci' section earlier in this chapter.

Sz

Sz is pronounced as the *sh* in *shop*, only a bit harder. And, naturally, it appears as ***sh*** in the pronunciation brackets, as in these examples:

- **szansa** *(shan-sa)* (chance)
- **szkoda** *(shko-da)* (shame, pity)
- **wasz** *(vash)* (your [plural])

W

The **w** is pronounced as *v* in *visa* and you'll see ***v*** in the pronunciation brackets to represent **w**, as in these examples:

- **Warszawa** *(var-sha-va)* (Warsaw)
- **woda** *(vo-da)* (water)
- **nazywam się** *(na-zih-vam sh'ye)* (My name is)

Ź and Zi

This is yet another pair of soft sounds that don't exist in English. However, if you pronounce the *s* in the word *Asia* but very, very softly, you'll have a perfect **ź**. In the pronunciation brackets it's indicated as ***z'***. I add an extra ***y*** to help you pronounce **zi** when followed by a vowel and ***ee*** when **zi** forms a separate syllable. Practise these examples:

- **źle** *(z'le)* (wrongly, badly, incorrectly)
- **zima** *(z'ee-ma)* (winter)
- **późno** *(poo-z'no)* (late)

For the rules of the **ź** and **zi** spelling, refer to the 'Ć and Ci' section earlier in this chapter.

Ż and Rz

The somehow exotic looking **ż** and **rz** are easy to say – as *s* in the English words *pleasure* or *vision*. You'll see ***zh*** in the pronunciation brackets to indicate **ż** and **rz**. Practise with:

- **żart** *(zhart)* (joke)
- **rzeka** *(zhe-ka)* (river)
- **marzec** *(ma-zhets)* (March)

Pronouncing Voiced and Silent Consonants

Sometimes some letters are pronounced differently than as described in the previous sections. Welcome to Polish! The difference in pronunciation is because consonants slightly change their personality when surrounded by other consonants. For instance, you learned that *w* is pronounced as *v* as in **w Gdańsku** *(vgdan'-skoo)* (in Gdansk). However:

w Polsce *(fpol-stse)* (in Poland)

Notice that *w* is pronounced here as its silent equivalent *f*. What you're dealing with here are voiced and silent consonants.

The general rule says that a voiced consonant changes to its silent form at the end of a word (**chleb**, bread, is pronounced as *hlep*) or before a silent consonant (po**d**pisać, to sign, is pronounced *pot-pee-sach'*), both within one word or two words as in **w Polsce** (*fpol-stse*). However, consonant clusters are voiced if the last consonant of the cluster is voiced (you pronounce **jest wesoły,** is happy, as *yezd ve-so-wih*). You won't be surprised to know that in some 'special' situations these rules don't quite work.

Instead of going into too much detail (too much theory never helps!), bear in mind the fact that, for the sake of simplicity, words and groups of words are pronounced in a way that doesn't require too much effort from the speaker. For example, say the *dk* in **wódka** (vodka) as *tk (voo-tka)* and the *ż* in **już idę,** *yoosh ee-de* (I'm just coming) as *sh* but as *zh* in **już dzwonię** (*yoozh dzvo-n'ye*) (I'm just calling) because doing so is just easier. In the pronunciation brackets throughout this book, you'll see many examples like this.

Instead of trying to memorise these rules, try to read aloud or converse with a native speaker so that you get used to the sound of Polish. Remember: the less effort you put into pronouncing separate letters, the better result you'll get. Watch Polish native speakers when they speak and you'll soon notice that they do not move their mouths as much as English speakers.

Here are all of the voiced consonants: **b**, **d**, **g**, **w**, **z**, **ź**, **dz**, **dź**, **ż/rz**, **dż**; and their silent equivalents are: **p**, **t**, **k**, **f**, **s**, **ś**, **c**, **ć**, **sz**, **cz**, respectively. Just in case you're terribly interested in what they are!

Saying Polish Vowels

As an English speaker you know that vowels can have more than one sound. For instance, the *a* in *cat* and *Kate* is pronounced very differently. Polish vowels, on the other hand, are very pure and have one and only one pronunciation. Big relief! (The nasal vowels **-ę** and **-ą** are a bit different; I address them in the next sections.)

Table 1-2 presents Polish vowels with examples in both Polish and English, together with phonetic script.

Table 1-2 Polish Vowels (excluding -ą, -ę)

Letter	Symbol	As in English	Comments	Polish Example
A a	*A*	apple		start (*start*)
E e	*E*	yes		element (*e-le-ment*)
I i	*Ee*	meet		idol (*ee-dol*)
O o	*O*	organisation	a short sound *o*	organizacja (*or-ga-n'ee-za-tsya*)
Ó ó	*Oo*	too	Polish **ó** and **u** are pronounced the same	mój (*mooy*)
U u	*Oo*	too	the same as **ó**	tu (*too*) (here)
Y y	*Ih*	pity		syn (*sihn*) (son)

Nasal vowels

Nasal sounds don't exist in English, but Polish has two: **-ą** and **-ę**. They're pretty easy to pronounce. When saying them you just need to imagine you have a cold and your nose is a bit blocked.

The pronunciation of these vowels depends on their position in a word; in other words, what consonants they're followed by. This is somewhat complex and the best way to understand it is to learn one example and, if you come across a word that looks similar, follow that pattern.

Generally speaking, the nasal **ą** can be pronounced as **ohN**, **om**, **on** and **oń**. The other nasal vowel, **ę**, can be pronounced as **ehN**, **em**, **en** and **eń**. Table 1-3 shows some examples.

Table 1-3 Nasal Vowels ą and ę before Consonants

Letter	Symbol	As in English	Polish Example	Pronunciation	Translation
ą	*om*	tomato	kąpać	*kom-pać*	to bathe
			ząb	*zomp*	tooth
	on	bond	mądry	*mon-drih*	wise
			pączek	*pon-chek*	doughnut
	oń		wziąć	*vz'yon'ch'*	to take
	ohN	as in French bon	wąski	*vohN-skee*	narrow
			wąchać	*vohN-hach'*	to sniff
ę	*em*	member	zęby	*zem-bih*	teeth
			tępy	*tem-pih*	blunt
	en	rent	ręce	*ren-tse*	hands
			ręka	*ren-ka*	hand
	eń		dziesięć	*dj'ye-sh'yen'ch'*	ten
	ehN	as in French vin	często	*czehN-sto*	often
			gęsty	*gehN-stih*	thick

The nasal ą and ę in the final position

At the end of a word, the nasal vowel **-ą** is pronounced close to the *an* in *fiance*. If you happen to speak French, the word **bon** as in **bon** *voyage* is very close as well. Remember not to say *n* at the end. In this book, **-ą** is presented as ***ohN*** in the pronunciation brackets. Here are some examples:

- **są** *(sohN)* (they are)
- **idą** *(ee-dohN)* (they go/are going)

The nasal **-ę** in the final position of a word loses its nasal sound and is pronounced like the *e* in *yes*; you'll see ***e*** in the pronunciation brackets. Here are some examples:

- **imię** *(ee-mye)* (first name)
- **idę** *(ee-de)* (I go/am going)

Searching for Stress and Blending Prepositions

Stress is the accent you put on a syllable as you speak – you say that syllable more strongly or loudly than the rest of the word. When pronouncing most Polish words, you emphasise the second from last syllable in a word. Here are some examples:

- **Polska** *(pol-ska)* (Poland)
- **aparat** *(a-pa-rat)* (camera)
- **dyskoteka** *(dih-sko-te-ka)* (disco)

Counting prepositions

Prepositions count as syllables of the words they join with, as if they were one word, so you place the stress accordingly:

- **bez cukru** *(bes tsu-kroo)* (without sugar): Three syllables in total hence you emphasise *tsu*, which is the next to last one.
- **dla nas** *(dla nas)* (for us): Here, you can see two syllables in total and, if you count from the end, the stress falls on *dla*, which is the second to last syllable.

A similar situation happens in the case of negative verbs. If you have **nie** followed by a one-syllable verb, the **nie** part is stressed:

- **nie mam** *(n'ye mam)* (I don't have)
- **nie spał** *(n'ye spaw)* (he wasn't asleep)

In the pronunciation brackets, longer prepositions (consisting of more than just one letter) such as **dla**, **na**, **bez**, **ot** and so on are spelt separately from the words they join, as in: **od Marty** *(ot mar-tih)* (from Marta) and **na lotnisku** *(na lot-n'ee-skoo)* (at the airport). However, short prepositions like **z** and **w** are merged with the next word, as in **w pracy** *(fpra-tsih)* (at work) and **z Anglii** *(zan-glee)* (from England).

Placing unusual stress

The stress is placed on an unusual syllable – the third from last – in the following situations:

- Nouns ending in **-yka** or **-ika**, which were originally taken from Latin or Greek:
  - **gramatyka** *(gra-ma-tih-ka)* (grammar)
  - **muzyka** *(moo-zih-ka)* (music)
  - **botanika** *(bo-ta-n'ee-ka)* (botany)
- Numbers:
  - **czterysta** *(chte-rih-sta)* (400)
  - **siedemset** *(sh'ye-dem-set)* (700)
  - **osiemset** *(o-sh'yem-set)* (800)
  - **dziewięćset** *(dj'ye-vyen'ch'-set)* (900)
- The first and second person plural in the past tense:
  - **lubiliśmy** *(loo-bee-lee-sh'mih)* (we liked)
  - **robiliście** *(ro-bee-lee-sh'ch'ye)* (you [plural, informal] did)

Emphasising the second to last syllable in these verbs accounts for one of the most common sins against Polish grammar, and you may hear numerous native speakers stressing the wrong syllable as it has now become acceptable. Be aware that it still doesn't sound good and don't let your ear pick up that habit! (Read more about verb tenses in Chapter 2.)

For verbs in *we* and *you* (plural) forms of the conditional mood, the stress falls on the fourth from last syllable:

- **chcielibyśmy** (*hch'ye-lee-bihsh'-mih*) (we would like)
- **moglibyście** (*mo-glee-bihsh'-ch'ye*) (you [plural] could)

Some Basic Phrases to Know

These are a couple of very basic phrases useful when taking your first steps into Polish:

- **Nie rozumiem** *(n'ye ro-zoo-myem)* (I don't understand)
- **Słucham?** *(swoo-ham)* (Pardon? Excuse me?)
- **Dziękuję** *(dj'yen-koo-ye)* (Thank you)
- **Przepraszam** *(pshe-pra-sham)* (I'm sorry/Excuse me)
- **Co to znaczy?** *(Tso to zna-chih)* (What does it mean?)
- **Jak się mówi po polsku . . .?** *(yak sh'ye moo-vee po pol-skoo . . .)* (How do you say . . . in Polish?)

Chapter 2

Getting Down to Essential Polish Grammar

In This Chapter

- Discussing cases
- Recognising perfective and imperfective verbs
- Talking tenses

Only young children have the luxury of taking in a new language naturally. A child's brain is like a sponge that soaks up new vocabulary, sentence structure, words stress, pronunciation and everything that makes up language quickly, easily and, most importantly, without explicit grammatical instruction. Unfortunately, when you're an adult, learning a new language takes a bit more effort.

Of course, if you just want to pick up a few expressions so that when you visit Poland you know how to buy a ticket or ask for directions, you can open the appropriate chapter of your *Polish For Dummies*, commit the relevant phrases to memory and leave the whole world of cases, tenses and endings behind. However, knowing how the language works not only helps you master it, but also helps you avoid translations that leave you misunderstood and your Polish listeners confused.

In this chapter, I share the basics of Polish grammar: the cases that nouns and adjectives take in various situations; and the verb conjugations essential in every language.

Lost in translation

Polish works differently to English and word-to-word translation doesn't make sense. Shall we take a small test to prove it? Imagine you've received an email from a Polish learner who isn't really familiar with English grammar or idiomatic norms, and you see the following sentence there:

How I will not find work, this I will must to go to home in Poland.

And one more that appears at the end of this email:

Thank you from the mountain.

Were you able to work out what they mean? They mean 'If I don't find a job, I'll have to return home to Poland' and 'Many thanks in advance'. Funny, isn't it? You certainly don't want to end up with something similar when speaking Polish!

The tables in this chapter use these forms:

- **ja:** the 'I' form
- **ty:** the singular, informal 'you' form
- **on, ona, ono:** the 'he' (masculine), 'she' (feminine), 'it' (neuter) form
- **my:** the 'we' form
- **wy:** the plural, informal 'you' form
- **oni, one:** the 'they' form for a group with at least one man; the 'they form for a group with no man

Remember that you don't actually say the pronouns you see in brackets in the tables when you're speaking Polish.

This chapter makes following the basic Polish grammar rules as natural as putting one foot in front of the other – **krok po kroku** *(krok po kro-koo)* (step by step).

The key to success is to accept that Polish works differently to English. Don't let yourself become frustrated because nouns, pronouns and adjectives change their endings all the time; focus on remembering when and how they change.

The Case of Polish Cases

You may get the impression that Polish nouns, pronouns and adjectives change their endings all the time and that a single noun in English has a number of forms in Polish. Well, that's quite true. In English, you put words in a certain order and can tell by their position in a sentence who or what is doing what to whom. In Polish, however, the order of the words doesn't matter as much as the endings the words use. Take this simple example:

Adam kupił Annie dom *(a-dam koo-peew an-n'ye dom)* (Adam bought Anna a house)

Adam kupił dom Anny *(a-dam koo-peew dom an-nih)* (Adam bought Anna's house)

In both sentences, *Adam* (nominative case) is the subject and *dom* (house) plays the role of the direct object (the thing that is bought, which uses the accusative case). However, in the first sentence Anna is the recipient of the house (*Annie* is in the dative case of Anna and plays the role of an indirect object), while in the second sentence it's Anna's house that has been bought (*Anny* is the genitive case). As you can see, it's the case that tells you what's what in a sentence.

Case refers to the role a noun, adjective or pronoun plays in a sentence. Many of these roles are crucial for everyday communication and this chapter takes you through them all. Polish has seven cases, both singular and plural, and each of them has a set of endings for each gender. (Chapters 5, 8 and 11 explain the endings of the accusative, instrumental and locative cases, respectively.)

Trying to learn isolated endings can give you a real headache. Instead, try to find and memorise a few examples of the cases used in various situations – hobbies, food and familiar places, for example. When you come across a noun or adjective that ends the same way, it will very likely follow the pattern from your example.

Nominative case

The nominative case is the basic case and is the form you see when you look up a noun or an adjective in a dictionary. A noun in the nominative case is the subject of a sentence – the person or thing performing the action of the verb. For example:

Anna pije kawę *(an-na pee-ye ka-ve)* (Anna is drinking a coffee) – Anna is the one performing the action of drinking a coffee and is the subject of this sentence

Nominative is often used after the phrases **To jest . . .** *(to yest)* (This is) or **To są . . .** *(to sohN)* (These are) or their shorter version **To . . .** *(to)*. For example:

To jest Marek *(to yest ma-rek)* or **To Marek** *(to ma-rek)* (This is Marek)

Noun genders

In Polish, each noun has a gender. You can tell a noun's gender from its ending:

- **Masculine nouns end in a consonant:** For example: stół *(stoow)* (table), pies *(pyes)* (dog) and rower *(ro-ver)* (bike). A small number of nouns end in -a: mężczyzna *(mehNsh-chih-zna)* (man), artysta *(art-tih-sta)* (artist) and tata *(ta-ta)* (dad).
- **Feminine nouns usually end in -a:** For example: kobieta *(ko-bye-ta)* (woman), gazeta *(ga-ze-ta)* (newspaper) and Polska *(pol-ska)* (Poland). A few feminine nouns end in -i, such as pani *(pa-n'ee)* (Mrs) and sprzedawczyni *(spshe-daf-chih-n'ee)* (sales assistant).

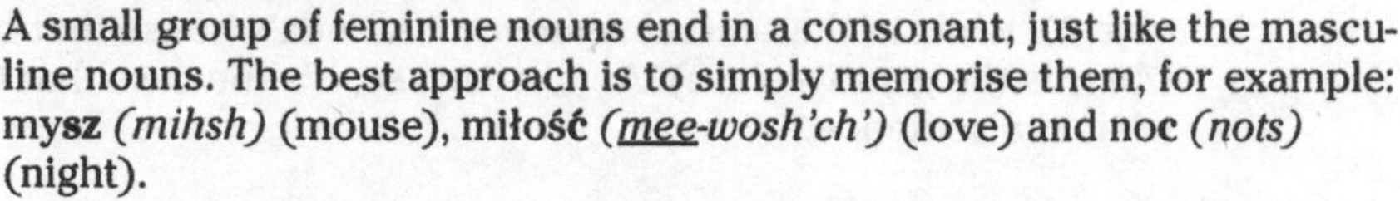
A small group of feminine nouns end in a consonant, just like the masculine nouns. The best approach is to simply memorise them, for example: mysz *(mihsh)* (mouse), miłość *(mee-wosh'ch')* (love) and noc *(nots)* (night).

- **Neuter nouns end in -o, -e, or in -ę or -um:** For example: oko *(o-ko)* (eye), mieszkanie *(mye-shka-n'ye)* (flat), imię *(ee-mye)* (first name) and muzeum *(moo-ze-oom)* (museum).

Adjective endings

Adjectives, used to describe or characterise a noun, agree with their nouns in gender, number and case.

Each adjective has three forms in the nominative singular. For example, 'new' is nowy *(no-vih)* (masculine), nowa *(no-va)* (feminine) and nowe *(no-ve)* (neuter). In some dictionaries, you may see the masculine form in full and then the feminine and neuter endings only: **nowy**, -a, -e. Other dictionaries present the masculine form only. Chapter 4 talks more about adjectives in the nominative case.

Genitive case

This case is the most frequently used case in Polish. While you can check its endings in Chapter 6, here you can familiarise yourself with situations in which it's used:

- **Possession:** To show ownership: samochód **Tomka** *(sa-moo-hoot tom-ka)* (Tomek's car)
- **Negation:** To negate a statement in the accusative case – in other words, use this for the direct object of a negative verb: nie lubię **kawy** *(n'ye loo-bye ka-vih)* (I don't like coffee)

- **After certain verbs such as: uczyć się** *(oo-chihch' sh'ye)* (to learn/study), **szukać** *(shoo-kach')* (to look for), **używać** *(oo-zhih-vach')* (to use), **potrzebować** *(po-tshe-bo-vach')* (to need)
- **Quantity and packaging:** To talk about how much and what it's in: pół **pizzy** *(poow peets-tsih)* (half a pizza), butelka **wody** *(boo-tel-ka vo-dih)* (bottle of water), dużo **ludzi** *(doo-zho loo-dj'ee)* (lots of people), mało **pracy** *(ma-wo pra-tsih)* (little work)
- **Numbers five and above:** pięć **piw** *(pyen'ch' peef)* (five beers) – numbers two, three and four require the nominative plural and one requires the nominative singular
- **To express dates and start and end times: drugiego maja** *(droo-gye-go ma-ya)* (on May 2nd), od **czwartej** do **piątej** *(ot chfar-tey do pyon-tey)* (from four to five a.m.)
- **After the following prepositions: od** *(ot)* (from), **z** *(z)* (from, out, of), **do** *(do)* (to, towards, into), **u** *(oo)* (at someone's place), **bez** *(bes)* (without), **dla** *(dla)* (for), **blisko/koło** *(blee-sko/ko-wo)* (near) [you can use them interchangeably], **obok** *(o-bok)* (beside, next to), **naprzeciwko** *(na-pshe-ch'ee-fko)* (opposite), **w czasie/podczas** *(fcha-sh'ye/pot-chas)* (during) [you can use them interchangeably], **z powodu** *(spo-vo-doo)* (because of, due to).

Table 2-1 lists some prepositions.

Table 2-1 Prepositions

English	*Polish*	*Pronunciation*
at someone's place	u	*oo*
because of, due to	z powodu	*spo-vo-doo*
beside, next to	obok	*o-bok*
during	w czasie/podczas	*fcha-sh'ye/pot-chas*
for	dla	*dla*
from	od	ot
from, out of	z	*z*
into, to, towards	do	*do*
near	blisko/koło	*blee-sko/ko-wo*
opposite	naprzeciwko	*na-pshe-ch'ee-fko*
without	bez	bes

Dative case

Dative isn't the most commonly used case, but you need to change the endings of nouns and adjectives to the dative case in a few situations:

- **Indirect object:** This corresponds to when you want to say that the action is *to* or *for* someone or something – a construction that doesn't exist in Polish. For example:

  Magda daje książkę **Adamowi** *(ma-gda da-ye ksh'ohN-shke a-da-mo-vee)* (Magda [subject] is giving [verb] the book [direct object in the accusative] to Adam [indirect object in the dative])

- **After certain verbs:** Certain verbs require an indirect object in Polish, but not in English:
  - **dziękować** *(dj'yen-ko-vach')* (to thank somebody)
  - **mówić** *(moo-veech')* (to say to/to tell somebody)
  - **odpowiadać** *(ot-po-vya-dach')* (to reply to somebody)
  - **płacić** *(pwa-ch'eech')* (to pay somebody)
  - **podobać się** *(po-do-bach' sh'ye)* (to appeal to somebody)
  - **przypominać** *(pshih-po-mee-nach')* (to remind somebody of something or to resemble somebody)
  - **życzyć** *(zhih-chihch')* (to wish somebody)
- **Impersonal expressions (expressions with no subject):**
  - **Smutno mi** *(smoo-tno mee)* (I feel sad) – literally: It is sad to me
  - **Zimno/Gorąco mi** *(z'ee-mno/go-ron-tso mee)* (I feel cold/hot) – literally: It is cold/hot to me
  - **Jest mi słabo** *(yest mee swa-bo)* (I feel faint)
  - **Głupio mi** *(gwoo-pyo mee)* (I feel stupid)
  - **Nudzi mi się** *(noo-dj'ee mee sh'ye)* (I'm bored)
  - **Łatwo ci mówić** *(wa-tfo ch'ee moo-veech')* (It's easy for you to say)
- **After the following prepositions: dzięki** *(dj'yen-kee)* (thanks to), **przeciwko** *(pshe-ch'eef-ko)* (against, in opposition to), **wbrew** *(vbref)* (contrary to):
  - **Dzięki Annie mam pracę** *(dj'yen-kee an-n'ye mam pra-tse)* (I have a job thanks to Anna)

Almost all masculine nouns take the ending **-owi** in the dative case. Only a few end in **-u** (brat**u**, ojc**u**, chłopc**u**) *(bra-too oy-tsoo hwop-tsoo)* ([to/for] brother, father, boy), which is the ending for most neuter nouns. Adjectives referring to masculine and neuter nouns use the ending **-emu**:

- Pożyczam pieniądze Patryk**owi** *(po-zhih-cham pye-n'yon-dze pa-trih-ko-vee)* (I'm lending money to Patryk)
- Pokaż to młodsz**emu** brat**u**! *(po-kash to mwot-she-moo bra-too)* (Show it to [your] younger brother!)
- Daj to mał**emu** dzieck**u**! *(day to ma-we-moo dj'ye-tskoo)* (Give it to the little child!)

Masculine nouns ending in **-a** are declined like feminine nouns (see Table 2-2 and refer to Chapter 11); for example, Pomagam moj**emu** tacie *(po-ma-gam mo-ye-moo ta-ch'ye)* (I'm helping my dad).

Feminine nouns and adjectives in the dative have exactly the same form as in the locative case (see the 'Locative case' section later in this chapter).

All plural nouns, no matter their gender, end in **-om** in the dative case. Adjectives take the ending **-ym** or **-im** (after *k* or *g*). Table 2-2 shows dative case endings.

Table 2-2 Dative Case Endings

	Dative adjective endings	*Dative noun endings*
Masculine	-emu	-owi (-u) (nouns in -a = locative)
Feminine	= locative	
Neuter	-emu	-u
Plural	***Plural adjective endings***	***Plural noun endings***
	-ym -im (after k, g)	-om

Accusative case

While Chapter 5 presents the accusative case endings, this section explains which situations need the accusative case:

- **For a direct object:** In the example, Adam lubi **Martę** *(a-dam loo-bee mar-te)* (Adam likes Marta), *Adam* is the subject (nominative case), *likes* is the verb and *Martę* is the direct object of the action of liking and is in the accusative case.
- **Duration:** To say how long an event lasts. For example: **całą noc** *(tsa-wohN nots)* (all night)
- **After the following preposition przez** *(pshes)* (through, across, via): **Idę przez park** *(ee-de pshes park)* (I'm walking through the park)

You may see the otherwise locative case prepositions **na** *(na)* (on, to), **o** *(o)* (about), **po** *(po)* (to get something/someone) and **w** *(v)* use the accusative case when they express motion. Similarly, the otherwise instrumental prepositions **między** *(myen-dzih)* (in between), **nad** *(nat)* (above), **pod** *(pot)* (under) and **przed** *(pshet)* (in front of/outside) take the accusative case if you use a verb of motion. (I cover both the locative and instrumental cases in upcoming sections.) For example:

- **Połóż to na stół!** *(po-woosh to na stoow)* (Put it on the table!)
- **Idź po Annę/po zakupy** *(eech' po an-ne/po za-koo-pih)* (Go and get Anna/the shopping)
- **Proszę skręcić w ulicę Norwida** *(pro-she skren'-ch'eech' voo-lee-tse nor-vee-da)* (Please take [turn to] Norwid Street)

Go to Chapter 11 to read more about prepositions.

Instrumental case

You use the instrumental case in the following situations:

- **After the conjugated verb być** *(bihch')* (to be): If you say **jestem** *(yes-tem)* (I am), **jesteś** *(yes-tesh')* (you are), **on/ona/ono jest** *(on o-na o-no yest)* (he/she/it is) and so on, the noun or both the noun and the adjective following this verb need to have instrumental endings:
  - **Jestem lekarzem/lekarką** *(yes-tem le-ka-zhem/le-kar-kohN)* (I'm a [male/female] doctor)
  - **BMW jest szybkim samochodem** *(be em voo yest shihp-keem sa-mo-ho-dem)* (A BMW is a fast car)
- **After the prepositions nad** *(nat)* (above), **pod** *(pot)* (below), **przed** *(pshet)* (in front of), **za** *(za)* (behind), **między . . . a . . .** *(myen-dzih . . . a)* (in between [something] and [something else]) and **z** *(z)* (with): For example, **Spotykamy się z Martą** *(spo-tih-ka-mih sh'ye zmar-tohN)* (We're meeting with Marta)

  (Chapter 11 talks more about prepositions.)

- **For means of transportation:**
  - **Jeżdżę do pracy samochodem lub metrem** *(yezh-dje do pra-tsih sa-mo-ho-dem loob me-trem)* (I go to work by car or tube)
  - **Na lotnisko jedziemy taksówką lub pociągiem** *(na lot-n'ee-sko ye-dj'ye-mih tak-soof-kohN loop po-ch'yon-gyem)* (We're going to the airport by taxi or train)
- **To say that you perform an action using a tool:**
  - **Zupę jem łyżką, a nie widelcem** *(zoo-pe yem wihsh-kohN a n'ye vee-del-tsem)* (I eat soup with a spoon, not with a fork)
  - **Lubię pisać długopisem** *(loo-bye pee-sach' dwoo-go-pee-sem)* (I like to write with a pen)

Make your way to Chapter 8 to see the instrumental case endings.

Locative case

Use this case to specify the position of an object or a person. The following prepositions help you to 'locate' the locative case:

- **na** (on, at, in): **na plaży** *(na pla-zhih)* (on the beach)
- **o** (about, at [time]): **o karierze** *(o ka-rye-zhe)* (about a career), **o pierwszej** *(o pyer-fshey)* (at 1 a.m.)
- **po** (around, along, after [time]): **po parku** *(po par-koo)* (around the park), **po piątej** *(po pyon-tey)* (after 5 a.m.)
- **przy** (near, close to, by): **przy oknie** *(pshih o-kn'ye)* (by the window)
- **w** (in, inside): **w Polsce** *(fpol-stse)* (in Poland)

Vocative case

Polish speakers use the vocative case to address people, animals and objects by name. So, when you want to speak or write to Maria, you should address her as **Mario** *(ma-ryo)* in the vocative case.

However, this case is increasingly replaced by the nominative case, especially in the spoken language. So, you don't really need to worry about it when speaking. If you're writing to someone, on the other hand, your best bet is to ask your Polish friend for help.

Recognising Perfective and Imperfective Verbs

Polish has fewer tenses than English, but it doubles up on verbs. Most Polish verbs have developed two forms:

- The **imperfective** form of a verb refers to an action that is ongoing, repeating or not yet completed.
- The **perfective** form of a verb is used to express a single action or a completed action.

So the bad news is that for (almost) every English verb you have two Polish verbs. The good news is that in most cases the two verbs look very similar. Table 2- 3 shows the difference between the imperfective **pisać** and the perfective **napisać** (both meaning *to write*).

Table 2-3 Imperfective and Perfective Forms of Pisać and Napisać (To Write)

Imperfective	*Perfective*
Repeated/habitual action	***Single action***
Kiedy byłam dzieckiem, regularnie pisałam pamiętnik *(When I was a child, I regularly wrote in my diary)*	Wczoraj napisałam maila *(I wrote an email yesterday)*
Duration	***One moment in time***
Pisałam książkę pół roku *(I was writing the book for half a year)*	Szybko napisałam wypracowanie *(I wrote the essay quickly)*
Simultaneous actions	***Chronological actions***
Pisałam maile i słuchałam muzyki *(I was writing emails and listening to music [at the same time])*	Najpierw napisałam maile, a potem obejrzałam film *(First I wrote emails, then I watched a film)*
Action in progress/Incomplete action	***Completed action***
Wczoraj pisałam maile, ale zostało mi jeszcze kilka *(I was writing emails yesterday but I still have a few left to do)*	Wczoraj napisałam wszystkie maile *(I finished writing all my emails yesterday)*

Since perfective verbs express completed actions (either in the past or in the future), they cannot logically exist in the present tense. If something is still in the process of being completed (in the past, present or future), it's expressed by imperfective verbs.

You form a perfective verb in a couple of ways:

- By adding a prefix to the imperfective form:
  - **czytać – przeczytać** *(chih-tach' pshe-chih-tach')* (to read)
  - **pisać – napisać** *(pee-sach' na-pee-sach')* (to write)
  - **pić – wypić** *(peech' vih-peech')* (to drink)
- By changing the stem:
  - **kupować – kupić** *(koo-po-vach' koo-peech')* (to buy)
  - **pomagać – pomóc** *(po-ma-gach' po-moots)* (to help)

Sometimes, you see two completely different verbs:

- **brać** [imperfective] – **wziąć** [perfective] *(brach' vz'yon'ch')* (to take)
- **mówić** [imperfective] – **powiedzieć** [perfective] *(moo-veech' po-vye-dj'yech')* (to say, to speak, to tell)

The best approach is to learn verbs in pairs and always in the same order so that you know which one is perfective and which one is imperfective.

The following verbs don't have a perfective equivalent: **być** *(bihch')* (to be), **mieć** *(myech')* (to have), **mieszkać** *(mye-shkach')* (to live), **pracować** *(pra-tso-vach')* (to work) and **studiować** *(stoo-dyo-vach')* (to study, be a student).

Finding Your Way in Polish Tenses

The grammar term *tense* translates to the everyday 'time' and identifies when the action you're talking about takes place: in the past, present or future. What's interesting is that the way people understand time varies in different cultures. Hence languages differ.

Being in the now with present tense

The present tense is all about the action happening at the moment of speaking or very close to it.

Be aware that you can translate a Polish sentence in present tense using two English tenses: present simple and present continuous. The question **Co robisz?** *(tso ro-beesh)* can mean 'What do you do [for a living]?' or 'What are you doing [right now]?', depending on the context.

Similarly to English, you can use the present tense to talk about actions that occur frequently:

> **Często chodzę na siłownię** *(chehN-sto ho-dze na sh'ee-wov-n'ye)* (I often go to the gym)

The present tense also describes actions about to happen in the near future, for which you've already made some arrangements:

- **Jutro mam spotkanie** *(yoo-tro mam spot-ka-n'ye)* (I have a meeting tomorrow) – you planned it and it's confirmed
- **W weekend lecę do Polski** *(vwee-kend le-tse do pol-skee)* (I'm flying to Poland over the weekend) – you've probably bought your plane ticket by now

Perhaps surprisingly, the present tense also describes an action that started in the past but has been happening up until now:

> **Pracuję w tej firmie pięć lat** *(pra-tsoo-ye ftey feer-mye pyen'ch' lat)* (I've been working for this company for five years)

Present tense conjugations

Depending on who is performing an action, you need to use the appropriate form of the verb. Grammatically speaking, you conjugate verbs.

Unlike in English, in which you use the same form of the verb for each person (I read, you read, we read), except for he/she/it when you generally add an *s*, in Polish the verb has a different ending for each person. To add to that difficulty, Polish people leave out personal pronouns **ja**, **ty**, **my** and **wy** (I, you [singular], we, you [plural]), so I put these pronouns in brackets in all conjugation tables in this book. With no pronouns to help, you'll have even fewer clues to help you understand the language, so make a point of getting the endings right.

Polish has three types of conjugation. Each type has a separate set of endings. Try to learn one example for each type by heart so that when you come across a new verb, you can conjugate it correctly even if woken up in the middle of the night.

Each conjugation takes its name from the endings of the first **(ja)** and second **(ty)** person singular. Hence, the conjugation in Table 2-4 is called the **-m/-sz** type. It's based on the verb **czytać** *(chih-tach')* (to read).

Table 2-4 Present Tense -m /-sz Type of Conjugation Using czytać (To Read)

	Polish: czyta-ć	*Pronunciation: chih-tach'*	*English: To Read*
(ja)	czyta-**m**	*chih-tam*	I read/I'm reading
(ty)	czyta-**sz**	*chih-tash*	you read/you're reading
on/ona/ono	czyta	*chih-ta*	he/she/it reads/is reading
(my)	czyta-**my**	*chih-ta-mih*	we read/are reading
(wy)	czyta-**cie**	*chih-ta-ch'ye*	you read/are reading *(plural)*
oni/one	czyta-**ją**	*chih-ta-yohN*	they read/are reading

To conjugate a verb you take its basic infinitive (dictionary) form (for example, **czytać** to read), then cut off the infinitive ending **-ć** and what you're left with is called the stem (**czyta-**). The stem is repeated throughout each conjugated form with the endings added.

Table 2-5 shows the **-ę/isz** and **-ę/ysz** type of conjugation based on **myśleć** *(mih-sh'lech')* (to think) and **tańczyć** *(tan'-chihch')* (to dance).

Table 2-5 Present Tense -ę/-isz and -ę/ysz Type of Conjugation Using Myśleć (To Think) and Tańczyć (To Dance)

	Myśl-eć	*Mih-sh'lech'*	*To Think*	*Tańcz-yć*	*Tan'-chihch'*	*To Dance*
(ja)	myśl-**ę**	*mih-sh'le*	I think/I'm thinking	tańcz-**ę**	*tan'-che*	I dance/I'm dancing
(ty)	myśl-**isz**	*mih-sh'leesh*	you think/ you're thinking	tańcz-**ysz**	*tan'-chihsh*	you dance/ you're dancing
on/ ona/ ono	myśl-**i**	*mih-sh'lee*	he/she/it thinks/is thinking	tańcz-**y**	*tan'-chih*	he/she/it dances/is dancing
(my)	myśl-**imy**	*mih-sh'lee-mih*	we think/ are thinking	tańcz-**ymy**	*tan'-chih-mih*	we dance/ are dancing
(wy)	myśl-**icie**	*mih-sh'lee-ch'ye*	you (plural) think/are thinking	tańcz-**ycie**	*tan'-chih-ch'ye*	you dance/ are dancing *(plural)*
oni/ one	myśl-**ą**	*mih-sh'lohN*	they think/ are thinking	tańcz-**ą**	*tan'-chohN*	they dance/ are dancing

Table 2-6 shows the third type of conjugation, called **-ę/-esz**, based on the verb **pracować** *(pra-tso-vach')* (to work).

Table 2-6 Present Tense -ę /-esz Type of Conjugation Using Pracować (To Work)

	Polish: prac-owa-ć	*Pronunciation: pra-tso-vach'*	*English: To Work*
(ja)	prac-uj-**ę**	*pra-tsoo-ye*	I work/I'm working
(ty)	prac-uj-**esz**	*pra-tsoo-yesh*	you work/you're working
on/ona/ono	prac-uj-**e**	*pra-tsoo-ye*	he/she/it works/is working
(my)	prac-uj-**emy**	*pra-tsoo-ye-mih*	we work/are working
(wy)	prac-uj-**ecie**	*pra-tsoo-ye-ch'ye*	you work/are working *(plural)*
oni/one	prac-uj-**ą**	*pra-tsoo-yohN*	they work/are working

Polish has a number of verbs that resemble English words, for example **faksować** *(fa-kso-vach')* (to fax), **mailować** *(mey-lo-vach')* (to send email), **kopiować** *(ko-pyo-vach')* (to copy) and **studiować** *(stoo-dyo-vach')* (to study, to learn). They end in **-ować** in the infinitive and, if you want to conjugate them, you'll need to replace the **-ować** with **-uj-** and then add the **-ę/esz** type endings. Or, you may find it easier to remember the **-uj-** bit together with the ending, as in **-uję, -ujesz, -uje, -ujemy, -ujecie, -ują**.

If you compare all three types of conjugation, you may be able to see a pattern. With the exception of **ja** and **oni/one**, the remaining forms are quite similar. It's not so difficult after all, is it?

You may now wonder how to determine what type of conjugation a particular verb belongs to. Unfortunately, you cannot figure it out on the basis of the infinitive itself. Instead, you need to get yourself a dictionary that shows the type of conjugation a verb belongs to. For instance, if you look up **mieszkać**, you'll see in brackets its conjugation type (**-m, -sz**). If you come across an irregular verb, you'll see the infinitive followed by the first two persons in full, for example **iść (idę, idziesz)** (to go, to walk). Once you know that, you should be able to work out the remaining forms. If you can't remember the pattern, refer to your *Polish For Dummies*.

Irregular verbs

Some verbs, while still following one of the three types of conjugation, change their stem, hence they're called irregular. The rule is that for the **-ę/isz, -ysz** and **-ę/-esz** type, the stem in the first-person singular **(ja)** and the third-person plural (**oni/one**) is always the same. See **iść** (to go, to walk) and **stać** (to stand) in Table 2-7. In the **-m/-sz** type, the stem of the third-person plural shows some irregularities while the remaining persons stay the same. Refer to **wiedzieć** (to know) in the same table.

Table 2-7 Present Tense Conjugations of the Irregular Verbs Wiedzieć (To Know), Stać (To Stand) and Iść (To Go, To Walk)

	Wiedzie-ć (to know)	*Pronunciation*	*Sta-ć (to stand)*	*Pronunciation*	*Iść (to go)*	*Pronunciation*
	-m, -sz		***-ę, -isz***		***-ę, -esz***	
(ja)	wie-m	*vyem*	**stoj-ę**	*sto-ye*	**id-ę**	*ee-de*
(ty)	wie-sz	*vyesh*	sto-isz	*sto-yeesh*	idzi-esz	*ee-dj'yesh*
on/ ona/ ono	wie	*vye*	sto-i	*sto-yee*	idzi-e	*ee-dj'ye*
(my)	wie-my	*vye-mih*	sto-imy	*sto-yoo mih*	idzi-emy	*ee-dj'ye-mih*
(wy)	wie-cie	*vye-ch'ye*	sto-icie	*sto-yee-ch'ye*	idzi-ecie	*ee-dj'ye-ch'ye*
oni/ one	wiedz-ą	*vye-dzohN*	**stoj-ą**	*sto-yohN*	**id-ą**	*ee-dohN*

The best approach to learning irregular verbs is to memorise the first two forms and what type of conjugation they belong to. Try to do so as soon as you come across them.

Remembering the past tense

The past tense in Polish often corresponds to various English past tenses, depending on the context:

- **Kupowałem gazete, kiedy zadzwonił telefon** *(koo-po-va-wem ga-ze-te kye-dih za-dzvo-n'eew te-le-fon)* (I was buying a paper when the telephone rang) – English past continuous
- **Moja firma kupowała polskie produkty** *(mo-ya feer-ma koo-po-va-wa pol-skye pro-doo-ktih)* (My company bought Polish products) – repeated action: simple past

- **Zawsze kupowałem jedzenie w tym sklepie** *(zaf-she koo-po-va-wem ye-dze-n'ye ftihm skle-pye)* (I would always/I used to buy food in this shop) – habitual past: used to/would
- **Już kupiłem mieszkanie** *(yoosh koo-pee-wem mye-shka-n'ye)* (I've bought a flat already) – present perfect

Endings

You'll be relieved to know that to form the past tense, you use just one set of endings in contrast to the three types of conjugation you need for the present tense. To conjugate a verb in the past tense, take the **-ć** off the infinitive (as you do in the present tense) and add past tense endings.

Be aware that Polish past tense distinguishes between three genders – *masculine*, *feminine* and *neuter* – in singular form. With plural nouns, you have two types: *masculine personal nouns* identify a group with at least one man; every other plural noun is part of the second type called non-masculine personal – groups of women, children, objects, animals or any group without a man.

Table 2-8 shows the past tense conjugation of grać *(grach')* (to play).

Table 2-8 Past Tense Conjugation of Gra-ć (To Play)

	Masculine	***Pronunciation***	***Feminine***	***Pronunciation***	***Neuter***	***Pronunciation***	***English***
(ja)	gra-**łem**	*gra-wem*	gra-**łam**	*gra-wam*	-	-	I played
(ty)	gra-**łeś**	*gra-wesh'*	gra-**łaś**	*gra-wash'*	-	-	you played
on/ ona/ ono	gra-**ł**	*graw*	gra-**ła**	*gra-wa*	gra-**ło**	*gra-wo*	he/ she/it played
	Masculine Personal	***Pronunciation***		***Non-Masculine Personal, Feminine and Neuter***		***Pronunciation***	***English***
(my)	gra-**liśmy**	*gra-leesh'-mih*	(my)	gra-**łyśmy**		*gra-wihsh'-mih*	we played
(wy)	gra-**liście**	*gra-leesh'-ch'ye*	(wy)	gra-**łyście**		*gra-wihsh'-ch'ye*	you played (plural)
oni	gra-**li**	*gra-lee*	one	gra-**ły**		*gra-wih*	they played

Watch out for the unusual stress in the **my** and **wy** forms. You need to emphasise the third-to-last syllable – the syllable just before the ending. So, in **graliśmy**, you place more stress on the **gra** syllable. (Chapter 1 has more information on stressing syllables.)

Perfective verbs (which I talk about in the 'Recognising Perfective and Imperfective Verbs' section earlier in this chapter) take the same endings to form the past tense. For example, **zagrać** *(za-grach')* (to play) follows the same pattern as its imperfective equivalent **grać** *(grach')* (to play). Table 2-9 shows the past tense conjugation of **zagrać**.

Table 2-9 Past Tense Conjugation of Zagra-ć (Perfective)

	Masculine	***Pronunciation***	***Feminine***	***Pronunciation***	***Neuter***	***Pronunciation***	***English***
(ja)	zagra-**łem**	*za-gra-wem*	zagra-**łam**	*za-gra-wam*	-	-	I played
(ty)	zagra-**łeś**	*za-gra-wesh'*	zagra-**łaś**	*za-gra-wash'*	-	-	you played
on/ona/ono	zagra-**ł**	*za-graw*	zagra-**ła**	*za-gra-wa*	za-gra-**ło**	*za-gra-wo*	he/she/it played
	Masculine Personal	***Pronunciation***		***Non-Masculine Personal, Feminine and Neuter***		***Pronunciation***	***English***
(my)	zagra-**liśmy**	*za-gra-leesh'-mih*	(my)	zagra-**łyśmy**		*za-gra-wihsh'-mih*	we played
(wy)	zagra-**liście**	*za-gra-leesh'-ch'ye*	(wy)	zagra-**łyście**		*za-gra-wihsh'-ch'ye*	you played (plural)
oni	zagra-**li**	*za-gra-lee*	one	zagra-**ły**		*za-gra-wih*	they played

Irregular verbs

All verbs ending in **-eć** in the infinitive – for example, mie**ć** *(myech')* (to have), rozumie**ć** *(ro-zoo-myech')* (to understand), chcie**ć** *(hch'yech')* (to want) and wiedzie**ć** *(vye-dj'yech')* (to know) – form the past tense in an unusual way. In every form except the masculine personal (plural), you change the **-e-** of the infinitive stem into **-a-** before an ending that starts with **ł**. Table 2-10 shows the conjugation of **mie-ć** *(myech')* (to have), which makes the translation, I, you, he, she, it, we, you and they had.

Table 2-10 Past Tense Conjugation of Mie-ć (To Have)

	Masculine	Pronunciation	Feminine	Pronunciation	Neuter	Pronunciation	English
(ja)	mia-łem	*mya-wem*	mia-łam	*mya-wam*	-	-	I had
(ty)	mia-łeś	*mya-wesh'*	mia-łaś	*mya-wash'*	-	-	you had
on/ ona/ ono	mia-ł	*myaw*	mia-ła	*mya-wa*	mia-ło	*mya-wo*	he/ she/it had

	Masculine Personal	Pronunciation		Non-Masculine Personal, Feminine and Neuter	Pronunciation	English
(my)	mie-liśmy	*mye-leesh'-mih*	(my)	mia-łyśmy	*mya-wihsh'-mih*	we had
(wy)	mie-liście	*mye-leesh'-ch'ye*	(wy)	mia-łyście	*mya -wihsh'-ch'ye*	you had (plural)
oni	mie-li	*mye-lee*	one	mia-ły	*mya -wih*	they had

The irregular verb *to go, to walk* – **iść** in the imperfective form and **pójść** in the perfective form – is used so frequently that memorising all its past tense forms is the best plan.

Table 2-11 shows the past tense conjugation of the imperfective **iść** *(eesh'ch')* as **szedłem, szedłeś, on szedł** *(she-dwem she-dwesh' on shedw)* (I was going/walking, you were going/walking, he was going/walking) and so on. I present its perfective version **pójść** *(pooysh'ch')* in Table 2-12.

Table 2-11 Past Tense Conjugation of Iść (To Go, To Walk) (Imperfective)

	Masculine	Pronunciation	Feminine	Pronunciation	Neuter	Pronunciation	English
(ja)	szed-łem	*shed-wem*	sz-łam	*shwam*	-	-	I was going/ walking
(ty)	szed-łeś	*shed -wesh'*	sz-łaś	*shwash'*	-	-	you were going/ walking

	Masculine	Pronunciation	Feminine	Pronunciation	Neuter	Pronunciation	English
on/ ona/ ono	szed-**ł**	*shedw*	sz-**ła**	*shwa*	sz -**ło**	*shwo*	he/she/ it was going/ walking
	Masculine Personal	**Pronunciation**		**Non-Masculine Personal, Feminine and Neuter**		**Pronunciation**	**English**
(my)	sz-**liśmy**	*shleesh'-mih*	(my)	sz-**łyśmy**		*shwihsh'-mih*	we were going/ walking
(wy)	sz-**liście**	*shleesh'-ch'ye*	(wy)	sz-**łyście**		*shwihsh'-ch'ye*	you were going/ walking (plural)
oni	sz-**li**	*shlee*	one	sz-**ły**		*shwih*	they were going/ walking

Table 2-12 Past Tense Conjugation of Pójść (To Go, To Walk) (Perfective)

	Masculine	Pronunciation	Feminine	Pronunciation	Neuter	Pronunciation	English
(ja)	poszed-**łem**	*po-shed-wem*	posz-**łam**	*po-shwam*	-	-	I went
(ty)	poszed-**łeś**	*po-shed-wesh'*	posz-**łaś**	*po-shwash'*	-	-	you went
on/ ona/ ono	poszed-**ł**	*po-shedw*	posz-**ła**	*po-shwa*	posz -**ło**	*po-shwo*	he/ she/it went
	Masculine Personal	**Pronunciation**		**Non-Masculine Personal, Feminine and Neuter**		**Pronunciation**	**English**
(my)	posz-**liśmy**	*posh-leesh'-mih*	(my)	posz-**łyśmy**		*posh-wihsh'-mih*	we went

(continued)

Table 2-12 *(continued)*

	Masculine Personal	Pronunciation		Non-Masculine Personal, Feminine and Neuter	Pronunciation	English
(wy)	posz-**liście**	*posh-leesh'-ch'ye*	(wy)	posz-**łyście**	*posh-wihsh'-ch'ye*	you went (plural)
oni	posz-**li**	*posh-lee*	one	posz-**ły**	*posh-wih*	they went

Szedłem means *I* [man] *was walking/going/on my way* [when something else happened], while **Poszedłem** means *I* [man] *went* [somewhere once]. The imperfective **szedłem** is not used frequently, but you should definitely memorise **poszedłem**. These examples may help:

- **Kiedy szłam do pracy, spotkałam Karola** *(kye-dih shwam do pra-tsih spot-ka-wam ka-ro-la)* (When I [woman] was walking to work, I met Karol)
- **Wczoraj poszedłem do kina** *(fcho-ray po-she-dwem do kee-na)* (I [man] went to the cinema yesterday)

Looking into the future tense

The Polish future tense corresponds to various English future tenses, as illustrated by these examples:

- **W sobotę będę pisać maile** *(fso-bo-te ben-de pee-sach' mey-le)* (I'll be writing emails on Saturday)
- **W niedzielę napiszę maila do Marka** *(vn'ye-dj'ye-le na-pee-she mey-la do mar-ka)* (I'll write an email to Mark on Sunday)
- **Do jutra przeczytam książkę** *(do yoo-tra pshe-chih-tam ksh'ohN-shke)* (I'll have read the book by tomorrow)
- **Zadzwonię, jak przyjadę** *(za-dzvo-n'ye yak pshih-ya-de)* (I'll call you when I arrive – literally: when I will arrive)

Endings for imperfective verbs

The easiest way to form the future tense of imperfective verbs (which I explain in the 'Recognising Perfective and Imperfective Verbs' section earlier in this chapter), is to use the future form of the verb **być** *(bihch')* (to be), which is shown in Table 2-13, followed by the infinitive of another verb – the same as you do in English. The infinitive I use in Table 2-13 is **pisać** *(pee-sach')* (to write).

Table 2-13 Future Tense Conjugation of Być (To Be) with Pisać (To Write)

Pronoun	*Future*	*Pronunciation*	*Infinitive*	*Translation*
(ja)	**będę**	*ben-de*	**pisać** (*pee-sach'*)	I'll write/be writing
(ty)	**będziesz**	*ben'-dj'yesh*	**pisać** (*pee-sach'*)	you'll write/be writing
on/ona/ono	**będzie**	*ben'-dj'ye*	**pisać** (*pee-sach'*)	he, she, it will write/be writing
(my)	**będziemy**	*ben'-dj'ye-mih*	**pisać** (*pee-sach'*)	we'll write/be writing
(wy)	**będziecie**	*ben'-dj'ye-ch'ye*	**pisać** (*pee-sach'*)	you'll write/be writing
oni/one	**będą**	*ben-dohN*	**pisać** (*pee-sach'*)	they'll write/be writing

You can also form the future tense by conjugating **być** (to be) (*bihch'*) in the future tense (as in Table 2-13) – **będę, będziesz, będzie, będziemy, będziecie, będą** (I, you, he, we, you, they will) – followed by a verb in the third-person singular or plural of the past tense. Don't forget to pick the correct gender form. (Go to the 'Remembering the past tense' section earlier in this chapter for past tense endings.) Check out these examples:

- **Jutro będę czytał książkę** (*voo-tro ben de chih-taw ksh'ohN-shke*) (I [man] will be reading the book tomorrow)
- **W weekend Anna i Marek będą odpoczywali** (*vwee-kent an-na ee ma-rek ben-dohN ot-po-chih-va-lee*) (Anna and Marek will be relaxing over the weekend)

This method is a bit more difficult but since it's very common, try to become familiar enough so that you can recognise, if not use it.

It doesn't really matter which of the two future constructions you use, except when it comes to forming the future tense of modal verbs **chcieć** (*hch'yech'*) (to want), **móc** (*moots*) (can/to be able to/be capable), **musieć** (*moo-sh'yech'*) (to have to) and **umieć** (*oo-myech'*) (can/to know how to). You form the future of these verbs that modify another verb (which is why they're also called *helping verbs* and *auxiliary verbs*) using the **będę** conjugation followed by a verb in the third-person singular or plural of the past tense and the correct gender:

- **On będzie chciał to zrobić** (*on ben'-dj'ye hch'yaw to zro-beech'*) (He wants [literally: will want] to do it)

- **Oni będą mogli pomóc** *(o-n'ee ben-dohN mo-glee po-moots)* (They [mixed group] will be able to help)
- **Jutro będziemy musieli zrobić projekt** *(yoo-tro ben'-dj'ye-mih moo-sh'ye-lee zro-beech' pro-yekt)* (We [mixed/or all-male group] will have to do the project tomorrow)

Endings for perfective verbs

Perfective verbs use the present tense conjugation to form the future (see the 'Being in the now with present tense' section earlier in this chapter). For example, the perfective **pomyśleć** *(po-mih-sh'lech')* (to think) follows the present tense conjugation of the imperfective **myśleć** *(mih-sh'lech')* while keeping its perfective prefix **po-**. Table 2-14 shows future tense conjugations of the perfective verb **pomyśleć**.

Table 2-14 Future Tense Conjugations of Pomyśleć (To Think) (Perfective)

	Myśleć	*Po-mih-sh'lech'*	*To Think*
(ja)	pomyśl-**ę**	*po-mih-sh'le*	I'll think
(ty)	pomyśl-**isz**	*po-mih-sh'leesh*	you'll think
on/ona/on	pomyśl-**i**	*po-mih-sh'lee*	he/she/it will think
(my)	pomyśl-**imy**	*po-mih-sh'lee-mih*	we'll think
(wy)	pomyśl-**icie**	*po-mih-sh'lee-ch'ye*	you'll (plural) think
oni/one	pomyśl-**ą**	*po-mih-sh'lohN*	they'll think

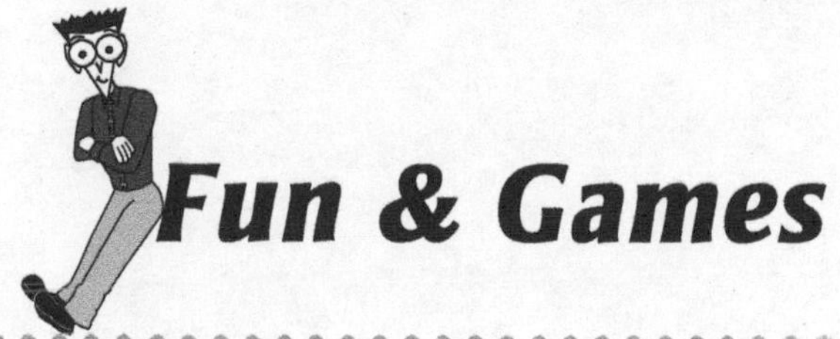

Fun & Games

The verb ***czytać*** meaning ***to read*** got mixed up. Do you think you can match the personal pronouns **ja**, **ty** and so on with the correct form of the verb?

(ja)	czytasz
(ty)	czytają
on/ona/on	czytacie
(my)	czytam
(wy)	czytamy
oni/one	czyta

Answer key:

ja czytam; ty czytasz; on/ona/ono czyta; my czytamy; wy czytacie; oni/one czytają

Part II
Polish in Action

"I can't remember how to say 'Thank you for a lovely meal' in Polish either, but I think we've tried long enough."

In this part . . .

This part focuses on everyday situations in which you may find yourself if you're living in Poland or dealing with your Polish-speaking friends. The chapters in this part hone your small-talk skills and take you on shopping and dining excursions as well as explaining how to enjoy yourself the Polish way. Sprinkled throughout are cultural titbits that introduce you to people, places and things that are important in Polish culture.

Chapter 3

Dzień dobry! Cześć! Greetings and Introductions

In This Chapter

- Addressing people formally and informally
- Introducing yourself and others
- Chatting about learning a new language

Meeting and greeting go hand in hand. Or cheek to cheek, in less formal situations.

Whether you can only say Good day, **Dzień dobry** *(dj'yen' dob-rih)* or already speak quite good Polish, this very first contact can open (Polish) doors (and hearts) for you. Polish is not the easiest language in the world to learn, so if you make an effort to greet someone in it, you've already made a favourable impression. And as a foreigner, you'll generally be excused any language mistakes.

So, if you want to impress your Polish friends, go ahead and dive into greetings and introductions!

Being Formal or Informal

If you're a first-time visitor to Poland, you may get the impression that, in terms of formalities and friendliness, only two extremes exist – Poles seem to be either very friendly or cold and distant. This impression may, to some extent, be created by the distinctions in saying *you* in Polish.

The Polish language has two (or actually seven) ways of saying *you*:

- **Informal: ty** *(tih)* (singular) and **wy** *(vih)* (plural).

- **Formal: pan** *(pan)* (used when you speak to a man), **pani** *(pa-n'ee)* (used when you speak to a woman) or **państwo** *(pan'-stfo)* (plural, mixed group), **panowie** *(pa-no-vye)* (when you speak to a group of men) and **panie** *(pa-n'ye)* (when you speak to a group of women).

If you misuse *you*, people might give you a strange look or, in a worst case scenario, you could end up offending someone.

In general, the informal **ty** is used between family members, friends, children and teenagers. Once a teenager turns 18 and gets their first ID card, they can expect everyone to call them by **pan** or **pani**. In reality, they need to wait a bit longer until they look more mature.

Use the formal *you* in every official situation, such as in business meetings, at the bank, station or airport, or in a shop. Use **pan** or **pani** when you talk to a stranger, everyone middle aged, older than you or your superior at work.

As you get to know people better, you can switch to the less official **ty**. However, in the case of a man and a woman, the man should always wait to be invited to use **ty** – as should a younger person dealing with an older person. The same applies to the workplace. Suggesting to your Polish boss that you switch over to the informal *you* and a first-name basis can be a bit risky, so you had better not!

To initiate less formality, take one of these approaches:

- **Może przejdziemy na 'ty'?** *(mo-zhe pshey-dj'e-mih na tih)* (Shall we switch to first names?) – literally: shall we switch over to using **ty**?
- **Proszę mi mówić po imieniu.** *(pro-she mee moo-veech' po ee-mye-n'yoo)* (Please call me by my first name) – this line enables you both to use **ty**.

If you're on the receiving end of such an invitation, you respond:

Z przyjemnością. *(s-pshih-yem-nosh'-ch'ohN)* (With pleasure).

If you're unsure about whether to use **pan/pani** or somebody's first name, use **pan/pani** to be safe. The easiest way to deal with this situation is to address the person you're speaking to in the same way as they address you. This rule, however, doesn't apply to children and teenagers as they should always show their respect for adults and not call them by their first names but use the formal forms **pan**, **pani** or **państwo**.

Saying 'hi' and 'bye'

The first word you need to know in Polish is the simple *hello*, which isn't so simple in Polish. How you say hello depends on both the situation and time of day:

- **Cześć!** *(chesh'ch')* (Hi!) – an informal greeting used at any time of the day with friends, family and children.
- **Dzień dobry!** *(dj'yen' dob-rih)* (Hello/Good day/morning/afternoon) – use in a formal situation, for example when you enter a shop, meet your older neighbour or greet a ticket collector at the train station; say it at any time during the day until it gets dark.
- **Dobry wieczór!** *(dob-rih vye-choor)* (Good evening) – obviously, the greeting you use in the evening.

The same rules apply to saying *goodbye*:

- **Cześć!** *(chesh'ch')* (Bye!) – no, it's not a mistake that **cześć** is in two lists! You use it to say both *hi* and *bye* informally. So that makes things a bit easier!
- **Do widzenia!** *(do vee-dze-n'ya)* (Goodbye) – use this formal version until it gets dark.
- **Dobranoc!** *(dob-ra-nots)* (Good night) – when it's dark outside, say your formal farewells this way.

Other useful expressions when meeting and leaving people include:

- **Trzymaj się!** *(tshih-may sh'ye)* (Take care) – informal
- **Do jutra!** *(do yoo-tra)* (See you tomorrow) – informal
- **Pa, pa!** *(pa pa)* (Bye-bye!) – very informal, so use it with close friends, family and babies
- **Do zobaczenia!** *(do zo-ba-che-n'ya)* (See you later!) – you can use it in both a formal and informal situation

Avoiding trite greetings

No matter how tempted you are to ask *how are you?* in a formal situation, don't! In Polish the *how are you?* question doesn't belong to the greeting ritual as it does in English. Poles consider this question meaningless and you should avoid it at all costs. Saying **Dzień dobry** *(dj'yen' dob-rih)* or **Dobry wieczór** *(dob-rih vye-choor)* will do.

Superficial pleasantries such as *have a nice day*, **Miłego dnia** *(mee-we-go dn'ya)*, are reserved for contacts with friends and family in informal situations, when you can also ask:

- **Co słychać?** *(tso swih-hach')* (How are things?)
- **Co u ciebie?** *(tso oo ch'ye-bye)* (What's new with you?)
- **Co nowego?** *(tso no-ve-go)* (What's new?)

Don't use these questions with someone you see every day! Use them when you haven't seen or spoken to your friend for some time and you have some catching up to do. And don't be surprised when you hear a long-winded answer, because a Pole will take the question as an opportunity to talk about whatever has happened lately. And that means anything – no matter whether their news is good or bad, you'll hear all about it!

Words to Know

cześć	chesh'ch'	hi/bye
dzień dobry	dj'yen' dob-rih	hello/good day/ morning/afternoon
dobry wieczór	dob-rih vye-choor	good evening
do widzenia	do vee-dze-n'ya	goodbye (formal)
dobranoc	dob-ra-nots	good night (formal)
trzymaj się	tshih-may sh'ye	take care
do jutra	do yoo-tra	see you tomorrow
do zobaczenia	do zo-ba-che-n'ya	see you later
proszę mi mówić po imieniu	pro-she mee moo-veech' po ee-mye-n'yoo	please call me by my first name

Replying to 'How are you?'

When asked **Co słychać?** *(tso swih-hach')* (How are things?) by your friends or family, you can reply quickly with one of the following:

- **Dziękuję, wszystko dobrze** *(dj'yen-koo-ye fshih-stko doh-zhe)* (Fine, thank you)
- **Dziękuję, wszystko w porządku** *(dj'yen-koo-ye fshih-stko fpo-zhon-tkoo)* (Fine, thank you) – literally: thank you, everything is in order
- **Nic nowego** *(neets no-ve-go)* (Much the same) – literally: nothing new
- **Po staremu** *(po sta-re-moo)* (Much the same) – literally: the old way

With time, the better your Polish becomes, the longer your answer to **Co słychać** *(tso swih-hach')* will be.

Talkin' the Talk

Audio track 2: Adam and Magda are friends who have just bumped into each other:

Adam: **Cześć Magda!**
(chesh'ch' mag-da)
Hi Magda!

Magda: **Cześć Adam! Co słychać?**
(chesh'ch' a-dam tso swih-hach')
Hi Adam! How are you?

Adam: **Po staremu. A co u ciebie?**
(po sta-re-moo a tso oo ch'ye-bye)
Much the same. And you?

Magda: **Dziękuję, wszystko w porządku. Trzymaj się!**
(dj'yen-koo-ye fshih-stko fpo-zhon-tkoo tshih-may sh'ye)
Thank you, fine. Take care!

Adam: **Do zobaczenia! Cześć.**
(do zo-ba-che-n'ya chesh'ch')
See you later! Bye!

Meeting and greeting go hand in hand – or cheek to cheek

The gesture that accompanies greetings or introductions depends on the type of situation and who you're dealing with.

In family situations, especially when you see someone after a long time, you can expect a hug and two or three kisses on alternate cheeks. It might sometimes be awkward when you want to kiss twice and the other person three times, or the other way around. Don't worry if it happens to you. Just smile.

The same rule applies between friends, though in the case of two Polish male friends a handshake or simple **cześć** (*chesh'ch'*) will do.

Formal situations are similar to those in Western Europe, where a simple handshake with everyone in the room is sufficient. A man should always wait for a woman to extend her hand first. And if you are a woman meeting a Polish man from an older generation, don't be surprised or even offended if he bows slightly to kiss your hand – doing so is a sign of respect from a perfect gentleman.

Getting Introductions Right

In this section, I cover how to introduce yourself and how to ask people their name. Here, again, different situations require different expressions. Being formal or informal is all about the words and expressions you use; in other words – *how* you ask the question. Phrases you use to talk about yourself remain the same regardless of the type of situation.

Making informal introductions

When meeting a new friend, a child or a teenager, you may find the following expressions handy if you want to start a conversation, especially if your name is Anna. If that's not your name, substitute your own whenever you see *Anna*:

- **Mam na imię Anna** (*mam na ee-mye an-na*) (My first name is Anna)
- **Jestem Anna** (*yes-tem an-na*) (I'm Anna)
- **Jak masz na imię?** (*yak mash na ee-mye*) (What's your [first] name?)
- **A ty?** (*a tih*) (And you/and your name?)
- **Miło cię poznać** (*mee-wo ch'ye poz-nach'*) (Nice to meet you)

- **Miło mi** *(mee-wo mee)* (Nice to meet you) – a shorter version
- **Mnie również** *(mn'ye roov-n'yesh)* (Nice to meet you, too)

In some situations you may need to give your full name, for example if someone is checking your name on a list. The following examples use the verb **nazywam się** *(na-zih-vam sh'ye)*, which literally means *I call myself*. It belongs to the same family of words as **nazwisko** *(naz-vees-ko)*, which means *surname*. A question containing this verb is thus asking about your full name:

- **Nazywam się Anna Nowak** *(na-zih-vam sh'ye an-na no-vak)* (My name is Anna Nowak) – first name and surname
- **Jak się nazywasz?** *(yak sh'ye na-zih-vash)* (What's your name?) – first name and surname, informal
- **Jak się pan/pani nazywa?** *(yak sh'ye pan/pa-n'ee na-zih-va)* (What's your name?) – first name and surname, formal

Talkin' the Talk

Ala and Adrian are teenagers at the same school. Ala's job is to get the names of the students who want to go on a skiing trip.

Adrian: **Cześć. Jestem zainteresowany wyjazdem na narty.**
(chesh'ch' yes-tem za-een-te-re so-va-nih vih-yaz-dem na nar-tih)
Hi. I'm interested in going on the skiing trip.

Ala: **Cześć. Jak się nazywasz?**
(chesh'ch' yak sh'ye na-zih-vash)
Hi. What's your full name?

Adrian: **Adrian Kępa.**
(a-dryan kem-pa)

Ala: **A..d..r..i..a..n. Możesz powtórzyć nazwisko?**
(A d r i a n mo-zhesh pof-too-zhihch' naz-vees-ko)
A..d..r..i..a..n. Can you repeat your surname?

Adrian: **Kępa.**
(kem-pa)

Ala: **Dziękuję. Już. Ja jestem Ala. Ala Karpowska.**
(dj'yen-koo-ye yoosh ya yes-tem a-la a-la kar-pof-ska)
Thank you. Done. I'm Ala. Ala Karpowska.

Adrian: **Miło cię poznać.**
(mee-wo ch'ye poz-nach')
Nice to meet you

Ala: **Mnie również. Do zobaczenia.**
(mn'ye roov-n'yesh do zo-ba-che-n'ya)
And you, too. See you later.

Adrian: **Na razie! Cześć.**
(na ra-z'ye chesh'ch')
See you later/take care! Bye!

Presenting yourself and enquiring about others formally

The way you introduce yourself is always the same, regardless of the type of situation. However, if you want to find out someone's name (first or full name) you have to stick to the right social register. Therefore, if you ask an older person or a client what their name is, you have to use the following formal expressions:

- **Jak ma pan/pani na imię?** *(yak ma pan/pa-n'ee na ee-mye)* (What's your name?) – literally: what's your first name sir/madam?
- **Jak się pan/pani nazywa?** *(yak sh'ye pan/pa-nee na-zih-va)* (What's your name?) – literally: what's your full name sir/madam?
- **Bardzo mi miło pana/panią poznać** *(bar-dzo mee mee-wo pa-na/pa-n'yohN poz-nach')* (Pleased to meet you) – literally: pleased to meet you sir/madam
- **Bardzo mi miło** *(bar-dzo mee mee-wo)* (Pleased to meet you) – a shorter version of the preceding expression

Talkin' the Talk

Audio track 3: Mr Tomasz Wiśniewski approaches a table at a cafe with a person already sitting there and demonstrates how Polish people introduce themselves formally.

Mr Wiśniewski: **Przepraszam!**
(pshe-pra-sham)
Excuse me!

Mrs Smuga: **Tak, słucham?**
(tak swoo-ham)
Yes?

Mr Wiśniewski: **Czy mogę?**
(chih mo-ge)
May I (sit down)?

Mrs Smuga: **Tak, oczywiście. Proszę bardzo.**
(tak o-chih-veesh'-ch'ye pro-she bar-dzo)
Yes, of course. Please do.

Mr Wiśniewski: **Dzień dobry. Nazywam się Tomasz Wiśniewski.**
(dj'yen' dob-rih na-zih-vam sh'ye to-mash veesh'-n'yef-skee)
Hello. My name is Tomasz Wiśniewski.

Mrs Smuga: **Dzień dobry. Bardzo mi miło.**
(dj'yen' dob-rih bar-dzo mee mee-wo)
Hello. Pleased to meet you.

Nazywam się Halina Smuga.
(na-zih-vam sh'ye ha-lee-na smoo-ga)
My name is Halina Smuga.

Mr Wiśniewski: **Miło mi.**
(mee-wo mee)
Nice to meet you.

Presenting other people informally and formally

When it comes to introducing others, in a relaxed situation with your friends you just say:

- **To jest mój kolega Arek** *(to yest mooy ko-le-ga a-rek)* (This is my friend, Arek.)
- **To jest moja koleżanka z pracy, Sylwia** *(to yest mo-ya ko-le-zhan-ka spra-tsih sihl-vya)* (This is my work colleague, Sylwia.)
- **To jest mój znajomy/moja znajoma ze studiów** *(to yest mooy zna-yo-mih/mo-ya zna-yo-ma ze stoo-dyoof)* (This is my male/female friend from university.)

- **Poznaj moją żonę** *(poz-nay mo-yohN zho-ne)* (Meet my wife) – when introducing someone to one person.
- **Poznajcie mojego chłopaka. To jest Rafał** *(po-znay-ch'ye mo-ye-go hwo-pa-ka to yest ra-faw)* (Meet my boyfriend. This is Rafał) – when introducing someone to a group of people.
- **Kto to jest?** *(kto to yest)* (Who is this?)
- **Czy wy się znacie?** *(chih vih sh'ye zna-ch'ye)* (Do you know each other/ Have you met?)

Some situations call for a certain level of formality. If, for example, you are being introduced to a new Polish business partner, you may hear the following:

- **Czy państwo się znają?** *(chih pan'-stfo sh'ye zna-yohN)* (Do you know each other?)
- **Chciałbym/chciałabym przedstawić mojego partnera biznesowego, pana Adama Nowaka** *(hch'yaw-bihm/hch'ya-wa-bihm pshet-sta-veech' mo-ye-go par-tne-ra beez-ne-so-ve-go pa-na a-da-ma no-va-ka)* (Let me introduce my business partner, Mr Adam Nowak.)
- **Bardzo mi miło** *(bar-dzo mee mee-wo)* (Pleased to meet you.)

Chciałbym means *I (a man) would like to. . .*; **Chciałabym** (with the extra *a*) is *I (a woman) would like to . . ..*

Describing Yourself and Others

Chatting in a foreign language is often initiated by someone asking you where you're from. Being able to describe yourself and ask other people questions about themselves can oil the wheels of conversation. This section covers how to communicate using the verb **być** (to be), whether or not to use personal pronouns and how to describe your nationality.

Getting familiar with the verb być, to be

After you know how to introduce yourself, it's time to become familiar with one of the fundamental verbs that let you talk about what country you come from, your nationality and lots more. Get acquainted with the verb **być** *(bihch')* (to be) so that you can tell people where you're from.

As in English, this verb is irregular and your best approach is to learn it by heart. Table 3-1 shows how to conjugate **być**.

Table 3-1 Conjugating Być

Table 3-1	Conjugating Być
(ja) jestem *(ya yes-tem)*	I am
(ty) jesteś *(tih yes-tesh')*	you are
on/ona/ono jest *(on/o-na/o-no yest)*	he/she/it is
pan/pani jest *(pan/ pa-n'ee yest)*	Mr X is, or speaking to a man formally: you (sir) are/ Mrs X is, or speaking to a woman formally: you (madam) are
(my) jesteśmy *(mih yes-tesh'-mih)*	we are
(wy) jesteście *(vih yes-tesh'-ch'ye)*	you are (plural)
oni/one/państwo są *(o-n'ee o-ne pan'-stfo sohN)*	they are

The distinction between **oni** *(o-n'ee)* and **one** *(o-ne)* (both meaning *they*) is pretty straightforward:

- **oni** *(o-nee)* – *they* meaning a mixed group or a male group
- **one** *(o-ne)* – *they* meaning a female group, a group of children or a group of objects
- **państwo** *(pun'-stfo)* – formal, Mr X and Mrs X, or ladies and gentlemen

Examples using the verb **być** *(bihch')*:

- **Kto/Co to jest?** *(kto/co to yest)* (Who/what is this?)
- **To jest . . .** *(to yest)* (This is . . .)
- **Jestem zmęczony/zmęczona** *(yes-tem zmen-cho-nih/zmen-cho-na)* (I'm tired) – male/female
- **Pani Smuga jest z Polski** *(pa-nee smoo-ga yest spol-skee)* (Mrs Smuga is from Poland)
- **To nie jest mój samochód** *(to n'ye yest mooy sa-mo-hoot)* (That's not my car)

Negations in Polish are a piece of cake. You simply put **nie** *(n'ye)* just before the verb, for example:

Być *(bihch')* (to be)
Nie być *(n'ye bihch')* (not to be)

So the whole quote is: **Być albo nie być, oto jest pytanie!** *(bihch' al-bo n'ye bihch' o-to yest pih-ta-n'ye)* (To be or not to be, that is the question!)

Lubię czytać *(loo-bye chih-tach')* (I like to read)

Nie lubię czytać *(n'ye loo-bye chih-tach')* (I don't like reading)

Saying goodbye to personal pronouns – except sometimes

As you may have noticed, in verb conjugations (see Table 3-1 in the preceding section) some of the personal pronouns, such as **ja**, **ty**, **my**, **wy** *(ya, tih, mih, vih)*, are in brackets. That's because you don't actually say those pronouns when you're speaking Polish.

In an English sentence, you always use a noun or pronoun with a verb; for example, you say: *I am . . ., you are . . ., he is . . .* and so on. In Polish, you simply say **jestem** *(yes-tem) I am*, **jesteś** *(yes-tesh'), you are*, **jesteśmy** *(yes-tesh'-mih) we are* and **jesteście** *(yes-tesh'-ch'ye) you are* in plural, instead of **ja jestem**, **ty jesteś** *(ya yes-tem tih yes-tesh')* and so on.

In Polish you omit the pronoun because the verb, and particularly its ending, tells who/what the verb refers to (and to be more grammatically precise, who/what the subject of the sentence is).

There's always an exception, of course, and the exception to the no-pronoun rule is when you use the third person singular – **on**, **ona**, **ono**, **pan**, **pani** *(on o-na o-no pan pa-n'ee)* – or plural – **oni**, **one**, **państwo** *(o-n'ee, o-ne, pan'-stfo)*. When you use the third person, use the personal pronoun with the verb because leaving it out may result in a misunderstanding. For example, if you say:

Mieszka w Paryżu *(myesh-ka fpa-rih-zhoo)* (? lives in Paris.)

the form **mieszka** could mean *he lives*, *she lives*, *it lives*, *you (sir) live*, *you (madam) live*, *Mr X lives* or *Mrs X lives*. A Polish speaker cannot work out exactly what is being said here. So instead you should say:

On mieszka/Ona mieszka w Paryżu *(on myesh-ka/o-na myesh-ka fpa-rih-zhoo)* (He lives/She lives in Paris.)

If you keep talking about the same person/object (in other words, the subject in the next few sentences remains the same), you don't need to repeat the personal pronoun in each sentence (another difference from English).

To jest Maria *(to yest ma-rya)* (This is Maria.)

Ona jest z Polski *(o-na yest spol-skee)* (She's from Poland.)

Mieszka w Krakowie *(myesh-ka fkra-ko-vye)* (She lives in Kraków) – omit the pronoun **ona** here.

Jest wysoka i sympatyczna *(yest vih-so-ka ee sihm-pa-tihch-na)* (She is tall and nice) – omit **ona** again.

You keep the personal pronouns **ja**, **ty**, **my**, **wy** only when you contrast facts about two different subjects. For example:

My jesteśmy z Irlandii, a wy jesteście w Portugalii *(mih yes-tesh'-mih zeer-lan-dee a vih yes-tesh'-ch'ye spor-too-ga-lee)* (We're from Ireland and you [plural] are from Portugal.)

The contrast is that one group of people is from one country, Ireland, and the other people are from Portugal.

Use the personal pronoun together with the verb when you mention two contrasting facts about two separate things.

Talking about countries and nationalities

You're learning a new language and hopefully meeting new people to practise with. A common introductory conversation involves asking new friends and acquaintances where they're from and answering that question yourself. The phrases in the following list can help you to get to know somebody better and have a simple conversation in Polish:

- **Skąd jesteś?** *(skont yes-tesh')* (Where are you from?) – informal.
- **Skąd pan/pani jest?** *(skont pan/pa-n'ee yest)* (Where are you from?) – formal; literally: Where are you from sir/madam?
- **Jestem z Anglii** *(yes-tem zan-glee)* (I'm from England.)
- **Gdzie mieszkasz?** *(gdj'ye myesh-kash)* (Where do you live?)
- **Gdzie pan/pani mieszka?** *(gdj'ye pan/pa-n'ee myesh-ka)* (Where do you live?) – formal.
- **Mieszkam w Londynie** *(myesh-kam vlon-dih -n'ye)* (I live in London.)

- **Ja też mieszkam w Londynie** *(ya tesh myesh-kam vlon-dih-n'ye)* (I live in London, too.)
- **A gdzie dokładnie?** *(a gdj'ye dok-wad-n'ye)* (And whereabouts?)
- **W Notting Hill. To jest bardzo znana dzielnica** *(v Notting Hill to yest bar-dzo zna-na dj'yel-n'ee-tsa)* (In Notting Hill. It's a well-known area.)

In Polish, as in English, you can say 'I come from' as well as 'I am from':

Jestem z Brazylii = **Pochodzę z Brazylii** *(yes-tem zbra-zih-lee = po-ho-dze zbra-zih-lyee)* (I am from Brazil = I come from Brazil)

So, instead of **Skąd jesteś?** *(skont yes-tesh')*, meaning *where are you from*, you can say **Skąd pochodzisz?** *(skont po-ho-dj'eesh)*, meaning *where do you come from*, although this second question is less common in spoken Polish.

As in English, you can either say **Jestem z Anglii** *(yes-tem zan-glee)* (I'm from England) or **Jestem Anglikiem/Angielką** *(yes-tem an-glee-kyem/an-gyel-kohN)* (I'm English [male/female]). The difference is simple: while the first one tells us about the country you come from, the second refers to your nationality. Table 3-2 lists some countries and cities you can use to tell people where you're from.

Table 3-2 Countries and Cities

Skąd jesteś? Jestem . . . (skont yes-tesh' yes-tem) *(Where are you from? I'm . . .)*	*Gdzie mieszkasz? Mieszkam . . . (gdj'ye myesz-kash myesh-kam)* *(Where do you live? I live . . .)*
z Francji *(sfran-tsyee)* (from France)	w Paryżu *(fpa-rih-zhoo)* (in Paris)
z Anglii *(zan-glee)* (from England)	w Londynie *(vlon-dih-n'ye)* (in London)
z USA/ze Stanów *(zoo-es-a/ze sta-noof)* (from the United States)	w Waszyngtonie *(vva-shynk-to-n'ye)* (in Washington)
z Niemiec *(zn'ye-myets)* (from Germany)	w Berlinie *(vber-lee-n'ye)* (in Berlin)
z Włoch *(zvwoh)* (from Italy)	w Rzymie *(vzhih-mye)* (in Rome)
z Rosji *(zros-yee)* (from Russia)	w Moskwie *(vmos-kfye)* (in Moscow)
z Hiszpanii *(s-heesh-pa-n'yee)* (from Spain)	w Barcelonie *(vbar-tse-lo-n'ye)* (in Barcelona)

Table 3-3 provides a list of possible nationalities, with their masculine and feminine forms. You use these nationalities with the proper form of **być** *(bihch')* (to be), as listed in Table 3-1 earlier in this chapter.

Table 3-3 Nationalities

Mężczyzna (mehNsh-chih-zna) (man)	***Kobieta (ko-bye-ta) (woman)***
Polakiem *(po-la-kyem)*	Polką *(pol-kohN)*
Anglikiem *(an-glee-kyem)*	Angielką *(an-gyel-kohN)*
Hiszpanem *(heesh-pa-nem)*	Hiszpanką *(heesh-pan-kohN)*
Włochem *(vwo-hem)*	Włoszką *(vwosh-kohN)*
Niemcem *(n'yem-tsem)*	Niemką *(n'yem-kohN)*
Amerykaninem *(a-me-rih-ka-n'ee-nem)*	Amerykanką *(a-me-rih-kan-kohN)*
Rosjaninem *(ros-ya-n'ee-nem)*	Rosjanką *(ros-yan-kohN)*

Words to Know

ale teraz	*a-le te-ras*	but now
też	*tesh*	also/too
dokładnie	*do-kwad-n'ye*	exactly
możemy	*mo-zhe-mih*	we can
szkoła językowa	*shko-wa yehN-zih-ko-va*	language school
na kawę	*na ka-ve*	for a coffee
mieszkać	*myesh-kach'*	to live

Talkin' the Talk

Audio track 4: Simon and Michelle meet on a train from Kraków to Warszawa. They strike up a conversation.

Simon: **Cześć. Jestem Simon. Jak masz na imię?**
(chesh'ch' yes-tem say-mon yak mash na ee-mye)
Hi. I'm Simon. What's your name?

Michelle: **Cześć. Jestem Michelle. Miło mi.**
(chesh'ch' yes-tem mee-shell mee-wo mee)
Hi. I'm Michelle. Nice to meet you.

Simon: **Mnie również. Skąd jesteś?**
(mn'ye roov-n'yesh skont yes-tesh')
Nice to meet you, too. Where are you from?

Michelle: **Jestem z Francji. Jestem pół Francuzką i pół Polką. A Ty?**
(yes-tem sfran-tsyee yes-tem poow fran-tsoos-kohN ee poow pol-kohN a tih)
I'm from France. I'm half-French and half-Polish. And you?

Simon: **Jestem ze Szkocji, ale teraz mieszkam w Krakowie i uczę się polskiego.**
(yes-tem ze shko-tsyee a-le te-ras myesh-kam fkra-ko-vye ee oo-che sh'ye pol-skye-go)
I'm from Scotland, but at the moment I'm living in Kraków and I'm learning Polish.

Michelle: **Ja też mieszkam w Krakowie!**
(ya tesh myesh-kam fkra-ko-vye)
I live in Kraków, too.

Simon: **A gdzie dokładnie?**
(a gdj'ye dok-wad-n'ye)
And whereabouts?

Michelle: **W centrum!**
(ftsen-troom)
In the centre!

Simon: **To świetnie! Moja szkoła językowa jest w centrum. Możemy się umówić na kawę.**
(to sh'fyet-n'ye mo-ya shko-wa yehN-zih-ko-va yest ftsen-troom mo-zhe-mih sh'ye oo-moo-veech' na ka-ve)
That's great! My language school is in the centre. We can meet up for a coffee.

Michelle: **Chętnie!**
(hen-tn'ye)
I'd love to!

Jumping In to mówię po polsku (Speak Polish)

If you happen to be in a remote place in Poland, far from a big city, you can always ask 'Do you speak English?' in English, though you might get a blank stare in return. But don't worry and don't be afraid; just get stuck in and **mów po polsku** *(moof po pol-skoo)* (speak Polish). Let people know that you only recently started learning Polish with these phrases:

- **Słabo mówię po polsku** *(swa-bo moo-vye po pol-skoo)* (I speak Polish poorly)
- **Tylko trochę mówię po polsku** *(tihl-ko tro-he moo-vye po pol-skoo)* (I speak a little Polish)
- **Dopiero uczę się polskiego** *(do-pye-ro oo-che sh'ye pol-skye-go)* (I'm just learning Polish)
- **Przepraszam, ale w ogóle nie mówię po polsku** *(pshe-pra-sham a-le vo-goo-le n'ye moo-vye po pol-skoo)* (I'm sorry but I don't speak Polish at all)
- **Dobrze mówisz po angielsku** *(dob-zhe moo-veesh po an-gyel-skoo)* (You speak English well)

Notice that the names of languages aren't capitalised in Polish. Grammatically, they're adjectives and, as such, they're not capitalised.

You may have already noticed that in Polish you put the adverb (such as *a little, poor, well, not at all*) before the verb instead of at the end of the sentence. In Polish, you literally say *Very well you speak English.*

As well as talking about languages using **mówić** *(moo-veech')* (to speak), which belongs to the **-ę/isz** conjugation and is very regular (lucky you!), another verb you use is **znać** *(znach')* (to know), which uses what's called the **-m/sz** conjugation. (I talk about both conjugations in Chapter 2.) The following phrases point out situations in which **znać** is appropriate:

- **Znam dobrze angielski, bo moja mama jest z Anglii** *(znam dob-zhe an-gyel-skee bo mo-ya ma-ma yest zan-glee)* (I know English well because my Mum is from England)
- **Jakie znasz języki obce?** *(ya-kye znash yehN-zih-kee op-tse)* (What foreign languages do you know?) – informal
- **Jakie pan/pani zna języki obce?** *(ya-kye pan/pa-n'ee zna yehN-zih-kee op-tse)* (What foreign languages do you know?) – formal

Table 3-4 lists various language forms to use with both **mówić** (to speak) and **znać** (to know).

Table 3-4 Languages to Speak and to Know

Language	*Mówię po . . . (moo-vye po) (I speak . . .)*	*Znam (język) (znam yehN-zihk) (I know (the language of . . .) (You can omit the word język)*
French	francusku *(fran-tsoos-koo)*	francuski *(fran-tsoos-kee)*
Italian	włosku *(vwos-koo)*	włoski *(vwos-kee)*
Spanish	hiszpańsku *(heesh-pan'-skoo)*	hiszpański *(heesh-pan'-skee)*
Russian	rosyjsku *(ro-sihy-skoo)*	rosyjski *(ro-sihy-skee)*
English	angielsku *(an-gyel-skoo)*	angielski *(an-gyel-skee)*
German	niemiecku *(n'ye-myets-koo)*	niemiecki *(n'ye-myets-kee)*
Slovakian	słowacku *(swo-vats-koo)*	słowacki *(swo-vats-kee)*

You can say either **Znam angielski** *(znam an-gyel-skee)* (I know English) or **Znam język angielski** *(znam yehN-zihk an-gyel-skee)* (I know the English language). The first sentence might be a bit easier to pronounce, as saying **język** *(yehN-zihk)* (meaning both a 'language' and 'tongue') is a real tongue twister.

A common mistake foreigners make is mixing things up and saying **Mówię francuski** or **Znam po francusku** instead of the correct versions, **Mówię po francusku** *(moo-vye po fran-tsoos-koo)* (I speak French) and **Znam francuski** *(znam fran-tsoos-kee)* (I know French).

Speaking English in Poland

Although young Poles are eager to learn foreign languages, with English widely spoken in bigger cities, the foreign languages spoken by the older generation are Russian or German (the latter particularly popular in the west of the country).

If you want to practise your Polish, your best bet is to go to a small town or village and simply enjoy being surrounded by Poles and the Polish language. *Polish For Dummies* may come in handy!

Talkin' the Talk

Two young couples meet on a train in Poland. Since they all know some Polish, they decide to put it into practice.

Michał: **Cześć! Mam na imię Michał, a to jest moja koleżanka Isabelle.**
(chesh'ch' mam na ee-mye mee-haw a to yest mo-ya ko-le-zhan-ka ee-sa-bel)
Hi! My name is Michał and this is my (female) friend Isabelle.

Dario: **Cześć! Jestem Dario, a to jest moja żona, Daphne. Ja jestem z Włoch, a Daphne jest z Francji. A wy, skąd jesteście?**
(chesh'ch' yes-tem da-ryo a to yest mo-ya zhu-na daf-ne ya yes-tem zvwoh a daf-ne yest sfran-tsyee a vih skont yes-tesh'-ch'ye)
Hi! I'm Dario and this is my wife, Daphne. I'm from Italy and Daphne is from France. And where are you (plural) from?

Isabelle: **Ja jestem z USA. Jestem Amerykanką.**
(ya yes-tem zoo-es-a yes-tem a-me-rih-kan-kohN)
I'm from the States. I'm American (female).

Daphne: **Świetnie mówicie po polsku!**
(sh'fyet-n'ye moo-vee-ch'ye po pol-skoo)
You (both) speak Polish really well!

Isabelle: **Dziękujemy! Wy też!**
(dj'yen-koo-ye-mih wih tesh)
Thank you! You do, too!

Michał: **Ja jestem pół Polakiem i pół Anglikiem. Moja mama jest Polką i dlatego znam polski, a Isabelle dopiero uczy się polskiego.**
(ya yes-tem poow po-la-kyem ee poow an-glee-kyem mo-ya ma-ma yest pol-kohN ee dla-te-go znam pol-skee a ee-sa-bel do-pye-ro oo-chih sh'ye pol-skye-go)
I'm half-Polish and half-English. My mum is Polish and that's why I know Polish and Isabelle is only just learning Polish.

Isabelle: **Lubię mówić po polsku, ale polski jest bardzo trudny i mam problemy z gramatyką!**
(loo-bye moo-veech' po pol-skoo a-le pol-skee yezd bar-dzo trood-nih ee mam pro-ble-mih zgra-ma-tih-kohN)
I enjoy speaking Polish but Polish is very difficult and I have problems with the grammar!

Daphne: **A ja uczę się włoskiego, bo Dario jest Włochem i jego rodzina mówi tylko po włosku!**
(a ya oo-che sh'ye vwos-kye-go bo da-ryo yezd vwo-hem ee ye-go ro-dj'ee-na moo-vee tihl-ko po vwos-koo)
And I learn Italian because Dario is Italian and his family speaks only Italian.

Isabelle: **Czy włoski jest trudny?**
(chih vwos-kee yest trood-nih)
Is Italian difficult?

Daphne: **Wcale nie! Moim zdaniem jest łatwy.**
(ftsa-le n'ye mo-yeem zda-n'yem yest wat-fih)
Not at all. In my opinion, it's easy.

Words to Know

kolega/koleżanka	*ko-le-ga/ ko-le-zhan-ka*	male/female friend
jestem pół Polakiem, pół Anglikiem	*yes-tem poow po-la-kyem poow an-glee-kyem*	I'm half-Polish and half-English
trudny	*trood nih*	difficult
łatwy	*wat-fih*	easy
na pewno	*na pev no*	certainly/for sure
tylko	*tihl-ko*	only
wcale nie	*ftsa-le n'ye*	not at all
moim zdaniem	*mo-yeem zda-n'yem*	in my opinion

Fun & Games

Some of the words have escaped from this conversation. See if you can find their rightful place.

chętnie, Hiszpanii, mi, trudny, również, z, mam, mieszkam, gdzie, po, do

- Cześć. .... na imię Thomas. A ty?
- Cześć. Jestem Alicja. Miło ....
- Mnie .... Skąd jesteś?
- .... Polski. A ty?
- Moja mama jest z ...., a mój tata z Anglii. Ale teraz .... w Polsce.
- A .... doładnie?
- W Krakowie. W centrum.
- Ja też! To możemy się spotkać na kawę............ !
- Bardzo dobrze mówisz .... polsku!
- Dziękuję! Polski jest bardzo .... !
- To prawda! .... zobaczenia!

Answer key:

mam, mi, również, z, Hiszpanii, mieszkam, gdzie, chętnie, po, trudny, do

Chapter 4

Getting to Know You: Making Small Talk

In This Chapter

- Asking questions
- Giving out your contact information
- Counting
- Talking about family members
- Describing the weather

As you make friends and find more people to talk to in Polish, you want to go beyond introducing yourself (which I cover in Chapter 3) and hold more interesting and serious conversations. Well, maybe not that serious, as the topic can be your family or simply the weather (the latter subject not as popular as in the UK!). Small talk is the best way to start off your first conversation in Polish. You never know, the Polish person sitting next to you on a train or an aeroplane may become your close friend or even your 'better half'! Even if that's unlikely, you should never miss out on an opportunity just to practise your Polish!

Asking Key Questions

In approaching any new subject, you ask a lot of questions. The next sections fill you in on how to form basic questions – and a couple of answers too.

Chit chat

Poles love to talk **o wszystkim i o niczym** *(o fshih-stkeem ee o n'ee-chihm)* (about everything and nothing) and are quick to strike up a conversation. Don't be surprised if you find yourself chatting with a complete stranger while on your way from one city to another or simply over **kufel piwa** *(koo-fel pee-va)* (a glass of beer) in a **bar piwny** *(bar pee-vnih)* (locals' pub) if you choose to discover one. Any topic is good, and with no real taboos you can free your imagination. When it comes to politics, the Polish people often hold strong opinions, and some joke that when two Poles argue over politics, three political parties can be formed!

Finding out who, what, where and 'how do you say . . .?'

In order to request basic information about your Polish-speaking acquaintance, you need to know the following key question words:

- **Kto?** *(kto)* (Who?)
- **Co?** *(tso)* (What?)
- **Gdzie?/Dokąd?/Skąd?** *(gdj'ye/do-kont/skont)* (Where?/Where to?/Where from?)
- **Kiedy?** *(kye-dih)* (When?)
- **Dlaczego?** *(dla-che-go)* (Why?)
- **Ile?** *(ee-le)* (How much/How many?)
- **Jak?** *(yak)* (How?/What?)
- **Jaki/Który?** *(ya-kee/ktoo-rih)* (What type/Which?)

All these words and phrases can be used on their own or in simple sentences, such as the following examples:

- **Kto to jest?** *(kto to yest)* (Who's this?)
- **Co to jest?** *(tso to yest)* (What's this?)
- **Gdzie państwo mieszkają?** *(gdj'ye pan'-stfo myesh-ka-yohN)* (Where do you live?) – formal, speaking to a group of people
- **Dokąd pan/pani jedzie?** *(do-kont pan/pa-n'ee ye-dj'ye)* (Where are you going [in a vehicle]?) – formal, speaking to a man/woman (you can read more about the *to go* verb and means of transportation in Chapter 11)

- **Kiedy ci pasuje?** *(kye-dih ch'ee pa-soo-ye)* (When is good for you?) – informal
- **Dlaczego się pan/pani uczy polskiego?** *(dla-che-go sh'ye pan/pa-n'ee oo-chih pol-skye-go)* (Why are you learning Polish?) – formal, speaking to a man/woman
- **Ile ma pan/pani dzieci?** *(ee-le ma pan/pa-n'ee dj'ye-ch'ee)* (How many children do you have?) – formal, speaking to a man/woman
- **Jaka jest dzisiaj pogoda?** *(ya-ka yest dj'ee-sh'yay po-go-da)* (What's the weather like today?)
- **Który hotel chcesz zarezerwować?** *(ktoo-rih ho-tel htsezh za-re-zer-vo-vach')* (Which hotel do you want to book?) – informal

When you're fairly new to Polish, these few phrases can come in handy:

- **Nie rozumiem** *(n'ye ro-zoo-myem)* (I don't understand)
- **Przepraszam** *(pshe-pra-sham)* (I'm sorry/Apologies/Excuse me)
- **Proszę** *(pro-she)* (Please/Here you are/You're welcome)
- **Proszę mówić wolniej** *(pro-she moo-veedj' vol-n'yey)* (Can you speak more slowly, please?)
- **Proszę powtórzyć/Słucham?** *(pro-she pof-too-zhihch'/swoo-ham)* (Can you repeat that please?/Pardon?) – formal
- **Jak się mówi po polsku . . . ?** *(yak sh'ye moo-vee po pol-skoo)* (How do you say . . . in Polish?)
- **Co to znaczy . . . ?** *(tso to zna-chih)* (What does . . . mean?)

Discovering the secret to forming 'yes'/'no' questions

In English you use auxiliary verbs to form 'yes' or 'no' questions. For example, you say: Have you been . . . ? Did you do . . . ? Are you reading . . . ? Will you go . . . ? and so on. In Polish, yes or no questions and answers are a lot easier than in English (for once!). When speaking Polish, you simply put **czy** *(chih)* in front of every statement to make a question to which the answer can be **tak** *(tak)* (yes) or **nie** *(n'ye)* (no). For example:

Statement	***Question***
Michelle jest z Francji *(mee-shell yest sfran-tsyee)* (Michelle is from France)	**Czy Michelle jest z Francji?** *(chih mee-shell yest sfran-tsyee)* (Is Michelle from France?)

The answer may be positive: **Tak, ona jest z Francji** *(tak o-na yest sfran-tsyee)* (Yes, she's from France); or negative: **Nie, ona nie jest z Francji. Jest z Kanady** *(n'ye o-na n'ye yest sfran-tsyee yest ska-na-dih)* (No, she's not from France. She's from Canada).

When you listen to native speakers, you may notice that Poles often leave out the question word **czy** *(chih)*. Intonation alone indicates the interrogative. As a beginning speaker, you probably want to use **czy** *(chih)*, but as you become more fluent and want to drop it, remember that it's essential to raise your intonation at the end of a question to indicate that it is a question. Otherwise, you'll form a statement, not a question.

Sharing Basic Contact Information

Meeting new people is a great opportunity to practise your Polish. You can find out where people live and exchange addresses, phone numbers and email information.

Living with mieszkać: The verb to live

A common topic for small talk is where you live. The verb **mieszkać** *(myesh-kach')* (to live) belongs to the **-m/-sz** type of conjugation, which you can read more about in Chapters 2 and 3. Some sentences with this verb follow:

- **W której części Nowego Jorku mieszka twoja rodzina?** *(fktoo-rey chehN-sh'ch'ee no-ve-go yor-koo myesh-ka tfo-ya ro-dj'ee-na)* (Which part of New York does your family live in?)
- **Mieszkamy tutaj ponad 10 lat** *(myesh-ka-mih too-tay po-nad dj'ye-sh'yen'ch' lat)* (We've been living here for over 10 years)

Telling people how to reach you

When it comes to requesting the address of a particular venue or somebody's home, you can always say **Proszę mi napisać adres** *(pro-she mee na-pee-sach' a-dres)* (Please write the address down for me), so that you can hand it to a taxi driver later and say, **Tu jest adres** *(too yest a-dres)* (Here is the address) and then sit back and relax. If you want to actually speak Polish, however (and that's why you're reading this, right?), make use of these phrases:

- **Jaki masz adres/Jaki ma pan/pani adres?** *(ya-kee mash a-dres/ya-kee ma pan/pa-n'ee a-dres)* (What's your address?) – informal/formal, speaking to a man/woman

  A shorter version, which is just as proper, is **Jaki adres?** *(ya-kee a-dres)* (What's the address?)

- **Mój adres to . . .** *(mooy a-dres to)* (My address is . . .)

When it comes to giving the address of a particular venue, Polish speakers do it a little differently to English speakers. In Polish, you start with the type of place – **ulica (ul.)** *(oo-lee-tsa)* (street/road/lane), **aleja (al.)** or **Aleje (Al.)** *(a-le-ya/a-le-ye)* (avenue), **osiedle (os.)** *(o-sh'ye-dle)* (estate), **plac (pl.)** (square) – followed by the building number and (if applicable) the flat number, as in:

ulica Nowa 3/7 *(oo-lee-tsa no-va t-shih pshes sh'ye-dem)* (literally: street Nowa, number 3 slash 7, which means Flat 7 at 3 Nowa Street)

Avenue is spelt **aleja (al.)** *(a-le-ya)* when followed by a singular name and you see **Aleje (Al.)** *(a-le-ye)* when the name is in plural. Don't worry too much about it, though. Just follow the spelling on maps and road signs.

The slash (/) is pronounced as either **przez** *(pshes)* (slash/through) or **mieszkania** *(mye-shka-n'ya)* (flat) which is indicated by **m**.

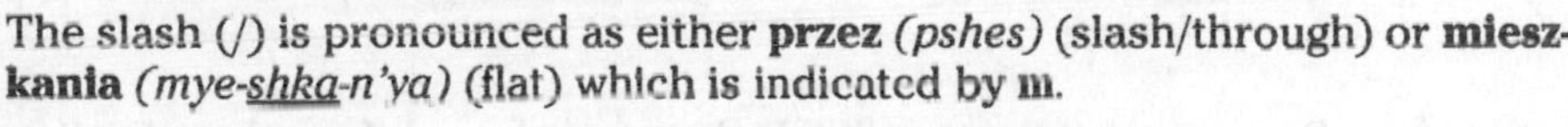

When saying your address use **ulica, aleja/Aleje, osiedle** or **plac** but write **ul., al./Al., os.** or **pl.**

If you want to be in touch with Polish friends and are looking for something more modern and hassle-free, like email rather than traditional letters, use these handy expressions:

- **Jaki masz adres e-mailowy?** *(ya-kee mash a-dres ee-mey-lo-vih)* (What's your email address?) – informal
- **Podaj mi swojego maila!** *(po-day mee sfo-ye-go mey-la)* (Can I have your email address, please?) – informal

- **Mój adres e-mailowy to . . .** *(mooy a-dres ee-mey-lo-vih to)* (My email address is . . .)
- **małpa** *(maw-pa)* (@/monkey) – what you call an *at symbol*, Poles call a monkey!
- **kropka** *(krop-ka)* (dot/full stop)
- **myślnik** *(mihsh'l-n'eek)* (dash)
- **ukośnik** *(oo-kosh'-n'eek)* (forward slash)
- **podkreślenie** *(pot-kre-sh'le-n'ye)* (underscore)

If you'd rather use a phone when getting in touch with people, use these expressions:

- **Jaki masz numer komórki/telefonu komórkowego?** *(ya-kee mash noo-mer ko-moor-kee/te-le-fo-noo ko-moor-ko-ve-go)* (What's your mobile number?) – informal
- **Jaki ma pan/pani numer telefonu służbowego/w pracy?** *(ya-kee ma pan/pa-n'ee noo-mer te-le-fo-noo swoozh-bo-ve-go/fpra-tshih)* (What's your official/work number?) – formal to a man/woman
- **Mój telefon domowy/stacjonarny to . . .** *(mooy te-le-fon do-mo-vy/sta-tsyo-nar-nih to)* (My home/land line number is . . .)
- **Możesz mi podać swój numer telefonu?** *(mo-zhesh mee po-dach' sfooy noo-mer te-le-fo-noo)* (Can you give me your phone number, please?) – informal

Be aware that Poles split telephone numbers differently to English speakers, saying the digits in pairs or triples, for example 0-608-723-733 or 022-602-54-67, saying *zero, six hundred eight, seven hundred twenty three, seven hundred thirty three.* (I talk more about numbers in the next section.)

Counting Numbers

To give new friends your address or leave your phone number for a return call, you need to know your numbers. Table 4-1 shows you how to say the cardinal numbers from 0 to 1,000 in Polish.

Number	Polish (pronunciation)	Number	Polish (pronunciation)	Number	Polish (pronunciation)	Number	Polish (pronunciation)
0	**zero** *(ze-ro)*	10	**Dziesięć** *(dj'ye-sh'yen'ch')*	20	**Dwadzieścia** *(dva-dj'yesh'-ch'ya)*	100	**sto** *(sto)*
1	**jeden** *(ye-den)*	11	**Jedenaście** *(ye-de-nash'-ch'ye)*	30	**Trzydzieści** *(t-shih-dj'yesh'-ch'ee)*	200	**Dwieście** *(dvyesh'-ch'ye)*
2	**dwa** *(dva)*	12	**Dwanaście** *(dva-nash'-ch'ye)*	40	**Czterdzieści** *(chter- dj'yesh'-ch'ee)*	300	**trzysta** *(t-shih-sta)*
3	**trzy** *(t-shih)*	13	**Trzynaście** *(t-shih-nash'-ch'ye)*	50	**Pięćdziesiąt** *(pyen'-dj'ye-sh'ont)*	400	**czterysta** *(chte-rih-sta)*
4	**cztery** *(chte-rih)*	14	**Czternaście** *(chter-nash'-ch'ye)*	60	**Sześćdziesiąt** *(shez'-dj'ye-sh'ont)*	500	**Pięćset** *(pyen'ch'-set)*
5	**Pięć** *(pyen'ch')*	15	**Piętnaście** *(pyet-nash'-ch'ye)*	70	**Siedemdziesiąt** *(sh'ye-dem-dj'ye-sh'ont)*	600	**Sześćset** *(shesh'ch'-set/ shey-set)*
6	**Sześć** *(shesh'ch')*	16	**Szesnaście** *(shes-nash'-ch'ye)*	80	**Osiemdziesiąt** *(o-sh'yem-dj'ye-sh'ont)*	700	**siedemset** *(sh'ye-dem-set)*
7	**siedem** *(sh'ye-dem)*	17	**Siedemnaście** *(sh'ye-dem-nash'-ch'ye)*	90	**Dziewięćdziesiąt** *(dj'ye-vyen'-dj'ye-sh'ont)*	800	**osiemset** *(o-sh'yem-set)*
8	**osiem** *(o-sh'yem)*	18	**Osiemnaście** *(o-sh'yem-nash'-ch'ye)*			900	**Dziewięćset** *(dj'ye-vyen'ch'-set)*
9	**Dziewięć** *(dj'ye-vyen'ch')*	19	**Dziewiętnaście** *(dj'ye-vyet-nash'-ch'ye)*			1,000	**Tysiąc** *(tih-sh'yonts)*

Complaining about Poland – for Poles only

You may notice that Polish people love to complain and make jokes at the same time. Poles will criticise their government or laws, make fun of their bosses, complain about their family or life in general or will laugh about their national traits.

As a foreigner, you may be asked to share your opinion about Poland and its people on numerous occasions. Be careful here! Never join in in criticising Poland or the Polish people. Making jokes about your own country is always a safe way out, or simply focus on the many good things about Poland and its citizens. After all, nobody likes to be criticised!

Number **sześćset** (six hundred) has two possible pronunciations: the proper and accurate *shesh'ch'-set* and the careless (yet grammatically acceptable) *shey-set.*

Combining numbers in Polish works similarly to English: 25 is **dwadzieścia pięć** *(dva-dj'yesh'-ch'ya pyen'ch')* (twenty-five), and for 783 you say **siedemset osiemdziesiąt trzy** *(sh'ye-dem-set o-sh'yem-dj'ye-sh'yont t-shih)* (seven-hundred eighty-three). However, for 1,422, Polish speakers say one thousand, four hundred twenty-two, **tysiąc czterysta dwadzieścia dwa** *(tih-sh'yonts chte-rih-sta dva-dj'yesh'-ch'ya dva)* and never combine it as fourteen hundred twenty-two.

Talkin' the Talk

Audio track 5: Ola *(o-la)* and Tomek *(to-mek)* meet on a plane from London to Warsaw. They are sitting next to each other and seem to be enjoying each other's company. Tomek wants to keep in touch with Ola after they land in Warsaw.

Tomek: **Czy mieszkasz w Warszawie?**
(chih myesh-kazh vvar-sha-vye)
Do you live in Warsaw?

Ola: **Tak, w centrum.**
(tak ftsen-troom)
Yes, in the city centre.

Tomek: **To może spotkamy się kiedyś na dobre polskie piwo albo kolację? Znam świetne miejsce!**
(to mo-zhe spot-ka-mih sh'ye kye-dihsh' na do-bre pol-skye pee-vo al-bo ko-la-tsye znam sh'fyet-ne myeys-tse)
Shall we arrange to meet for a good Polish beer or dinner? I know a great place!

Ola: **Chętnie! A jaki adres?**
(hent-n'ye a ya-kee a-dres)
I'd love to! And what's the address?

Tomek: **Plac Bankowy 2. Jaki masz numer komórki?**
(pladz ban-ko-vih dva ya-kee mash noo-mer ko-moor-kee)
2 Bankowy Square. What's your mobile number?

Ola: **0-604-725-138**
(ze-ro shesh'ch'-set chte-rih sh'ye-dem-sed dva-dj'yesh'-ch'ya pyen'ch' sto t-shih-dj'yesh'-ch'ee o-sh'yem)
Zero six hundred four, seven hundred twenty-five, one hundred thirty-eight.

Tomek: **Ok. Podaj mi też swojego maila, to ci wyślę adres.**
(o-key po-day mee tesh sfo-ye-go mey-la to ch'ee vih-sh'le a-dres)
Okay. Can you also give me your email address so that I can send you the location details.

Ola: **ola@interia.pl**
(o-la maw-pa een-te-rya krop-ka pe el)
ola at interia full stop p l

Tomek: **Dzięki! Bardzo się cieszę!**
(dj'yen-kee bar-dzo sh'ye ch'ye-she)
Thanks! I can't wait! (Literally: I'm very happy.)

Getting to Know People and Families

Poles like to talk about their families and if you want to join the conversation, you need to know the following family members and simple expressions:

- **rodzice** *(ro-dj'ee-tse)* (parents): **mama** *(ma-ma)* (mum) or **matka** *(mat-ka)* (mother) and **tata** *(ta-ta)* (dad) or **ojciec** *(oy-ch'yets)* (father)
- **rodzeństwo** *(ro-dzen'-stfo)* (siblings): **brat** *(brat)* (brother) and **siostra** *(sh'yo-stra)* (sister)
- **dziecko** *(dj'ye-tsko)* (child) or **dzieci** *(dj'ye-ch'ee)* (children): **córka** *(tsoor-ka)* (daughter) and **syn** *(sihn)* (son)
- **wnuki** *(vnoo-kee)* (grandchildren): **wnuk** *(vnook)* (grandson) and **wnuczka** *(vnoo-chka)* (granddaughter)
- **kuzyni** *(koo-zih-n'ee)* (cousins): **kuzyn** *(koo-zihn)* (male cousin) and **kuzynka** *(koo-zihn-ka)* (female cousin)
- **małżeństwo** *(maw-zhen'-stfo)* (married couple): **mąż** *(mohNsh)* (husband) and **żona** *(zho-na)* (wife)
- **bratowa** *(bra-to-va)* (sister-in-law) and **szwagier** *(shfa-gyer)* (brother-in-law)
- **teściowie** *(tesh'-ch'yo-vye)* (in-laws): **teść** *(tesh'ch')* (father-in-law) and **teściowa** *(tesh-ch'yo-va)* (mother-in-law)

Your marital status is often of interest to new friends. Use these phrases to let people know whether you're single or married:

- **jestem żonaty/mężatką** *(yes-tem zho-na-tih/mehN-zhat-kohN)* (I'm married [man/woman])
- **jestem kawalerem/panną** *(yes-tem ka-va-le-rem/pan-nohN)* (I'm single [man/woman]). Recently, a new version is gaining popularity: **Jestem singlem/singielką** *(yestem seen-glem/seen-gyel-kohN)*
- **jestem rozwiedziony/rozwiedziona** *(yes-tem roz-vye-dj'yo-nih/roz-vye-dj'yo-na)* (I'm divorced [man/woman])

Showing ownership with possessive pronouns

If you want to say *my mother* or *his car* you need to use possessive pronouns. *Possessive pronouns* show possession – what belongs to whom or what. Table 4-2 shows you the Polish possessive pronouns in the nominative case.

Table 4-2 Personal and Possessive Pronouns in the Nominative Case

Personal Pronouns	Polish (Pronunciation)	Possessive Pronouns in Singular Masculine	Possessive Pronouns in Singular Feminine	Possessive Pronouns in Singular Neuter	Plural Masculine Personal	Plural Masculine Non-personal, Feminine, Neuter
I	**ja** *(ya)*	**mój** *(mooy)* (my)	**moja** *(mo-ya)* (my)	**moje** *(mo-ye)* (my)	**moi** *(mo-yee)* (my)	**moje** *(mo-ye)* (my)
you (singular)	**ty** *(tih)*	**twój** *(tfooy)* (your)	**twoja** *(tfo-ya)* (your)	**twoje** *(tfo-ye)* (your)	**twoi** *(tfo-yee)* (your)	**twoje** *(tfo-ye)* (your)
he	**on** *(on)*	**jego** *(ye-go)* (his)	**jego** *(ye-go)* (his)	**jego** *(ye-go)* (his)	**jego** *(ye-go)* (his)	**jego** *(ye-go)* (his)
she	**ona** *(o-na)*	**jej** *(yey)* (her)	**jej** *(yey)* (her)	**jej** *(yey)* (her)	**jej** *(yey)* (her)	**jej** *(yey)* (her)
it	**ono** *(o-no)*	**jego** *(ye-go)* (its)	**jego** *(ye-go)* (its)	**jego** *(ye-go)* (its)	**jego** *(ye-go)* (its)	**jego** *(ye-go)* (its)
we	**my** *(mih)*	**nasz** *(nash)* (our)	**nasza** *(na-sha)* (our)	**nasze** *(na-she)* (our)	**nasi** *(na-sh'ee)* (our)	**nasze** *(na-she)* (our)
you (plural)	**wy** *(vih)*	**wasz** *(vash)* (your, plural)	**wasza** *(va-sha)* (your, plural)	**wasze** *(va-she)* (your, plural)	**wasi** *(va-sh'ee)* (your, plural)	**wasze** *(va-she)* (your, plural)
they	**oni/one** *(o-nee/ o-ne)*	**ich** *(eeh)* (their)	**ich** *(eeh)* (their)	**ich** *(eeh)* (their)	**ich** *(eeh)* (their)	**ich** *(eeh)* (their)

The form of the possessive pronoun is determined by the gender of the noun it refers to. (I talk about the gender of nouns in Chapter 2.) For example, *my son* is mój syn *(mooy sihn)* (not moja or moje syn). Because syn is masculine, the possessive pronoun has to have the masculine form mój. Likewise, it's nasza córka *(na-sha tsoor-ka)* (our daughter) instead of nasz or nasze because córka is a feminine noun and nasza is the feminine form of the possessive pronoun.

The forms of **jego** *(ye-go)* (his/its), **jej** *(yey)* (her) and **ich** *(eeh)* (their) are the same for all genders, both in singular and plural.

Unfortunately, possessive pronouns decline in the same way as adjectives, which means they change endings in different cases (not good news!). You can read more about adjective declination in Chapter 2.

Polish speakers tend to replace all possessive pronouns with **swój** *(sfooy)*, **swoja** *(sfo-ya)* and **swoje** *(sfo-ye)* in sentences where the pronoun refers to the subject of the statement, as in the following examples:

- **Adam idzie do kina ze swoją siostrą** *(a-dam ee-dj'ye do kee-na ze sfo-yohN sh'yo-strohN)* (Adam is going to the cinema with his [own] sister)
- **Oni mieszkają ze swoimi rodzicami** *(o-n'ee myesh-ka-yohN ze sfo-yee-mee ro-dj'ee-tsa-mee)* (They live with their [own] parents)

Describing people and objects

Adjectives make your descriptions more interesting and precise. You can use adjectives to compare characteristics as well, as in the following sentences:

- **Mój mąż jest wysoki, a jego brat niski** *(mooy mohNsh yest vih-so-kee a ye-go brat nee-skee)* (My husband is tall but his brother is short)
- **Jaka jest twoja rodzina? Duża czy mała?** *(ya-ka yezd tfo-ya ro-dj'ee-na doo-zha chih ma-wa)* (What is your family like? Big or small?)
- **Ten hotel jest wygodny i luksusowy** *(ten ho-tel yezd vih-god-nih ee loo-ksoo-so-vih)* (This hotel is comfortable and luxurious)
- **Czy twoja teściowa jest sympatyczna?** *(chih tfo-ya tesh'-ch'yo-va yest sihm-pa-tih-chna)* (Is your mother-in-law nice?)
- **Nasze mieszkanie jest przestronne** *(na-she myesh-ka-n'ye yest pshe-stron-ne)* (Our flat is spacious)

Adjectives take different endings depending on the gender of the noun they refer to. So, effectively, each adjective has three different forms. Thus, using the adjective *big* as an example:

Masculine	***Feminine***	***Neuter***
Ends in **–y: duży** *(doo-zhih)*	Ends in **-a: duża** *(doo-zha)*	Ends in **–e: duże** *(doo-zhe)*

If the last letter of the stem (the part of the word just before the ending) is **k** or **g**, masculine adjectives end in **-i**, as in **niski** *(n'ee-skee)* (short) and neuter in **-ie**, as in **niskie** *(n'ee-skye)* (short).

Talkin' the Talk

Audio track 6: Martha (*mar-ta*) is showing her new Polish friend Ela (*e-la*) a photo of her family.

Ela: **Kto to jest?**
(kto to yest)
Who is this?

Martha: **To jest mój mąż, José. Jest Hiszpanem.**
(to yest mooy mohNsh ho-ze yest heesh-pa-nem)
This is my husband, José. He's Spanish.

Ela: **Bardzo przystojny! Wysoki i wysportowany! Czy macie dzieci?**
(bar-dzo pshih-stoy-nih vih-so-kee ee vih-spor-to-va-nih chih ma-ch'ye dj'ye-ch'ee)
Very handsome! Tall and sporty! Do you have any children?

Martha: **Jeszcze nie, ale chcemy mieć syna i córkę. A to jest jego matka, a moja teściowa.**
(yesh-che n'ye a-le htse-mih myech' sih-na ee tsoor-ke a to yest ye-go mat-ka a mo-ya tesh'-ch'yo-va)
Not yet but we want to have a son and a daughter. And this is his mother, my mother-in-law.

Ela: **Jest bardzo młoda. Ile ma lat?**
(yest bar-dzo mwo-da ee-le ma lat)
She's very young. How old is she? [Literally: how many years does she have?]

Martha: **Ma 51 lat.**
(ma pyen'-dj'ye-sh'yont ye-den lat)
She's 51.

Ela: **Czy José ma rodzeństwo czy jest jedynakiem?**
(chih ho-ze ma ro-dzen'-stfo chih yest ye-dih-na-kyem)
Does José have any brothers or sisters or is he an only child?

Martha: **Tak, ma jeszcze młodszego brata i starszą siostrę.**
(tak ma yesh-che mwot-she-go bra-ta ee star-shohN sh'yo-stre)
Yes, he has a younger brother and an older sister.

Words to Know

jeszcze nie	yesh-che n'ye	not yet
czy	chih	or; used to form 'yes' and 'no' questions
rodzeństwo	ro-dzen'-stfo	siblings (brothers and sisters)
jestem jedynakiem/ jedynaczką	ye-stem ye-dih-na-kyem/ ye-dih-nach-kohN	I'm an only child
mam starszego brata	mam star-she-go brat-a	I have an older brother
mam młodszą siostrę	mam mwot-shohN sh'yo-stre	I have a younger sister

Keeping an Eye on the Weather

Polish people don't talk too much about the weather but, if a day is exceptionally good or bad, they'll definitely have their say, as in the following examples:

- **Ale dzisiaj piękna/okropna pogoda!** *(a-le dj'ee-sh'yay pyenk-na/o-krop-na po-go-da)* (What beautiful/awful weather today!)
- **Jest zimno/ciepło/gorąco** *(yest zh'eem-no/ch'ye-pwo/go-ron-tso)* (It's cold/warm/hot)
- **Bardzo wieje** *(bar-dzo vye-ye)* (It's very windy)
- **Pada deszcz/śnieg** *(pa-da deshch/sh'n'yek)* (It's raining/snowing)
- **Jaka będzie jutro pogoda?** *(ya-ka ben'-dj'ye yoo-tro po-go-da)* (What's the weather like for tomorrow?)
- **Świeci słońce/Jest słonecznie** *(sh'fye-ch'ee swon'-tse/yest swo-nech-n'ye)* (The sun is shining/It's sunny)

- **Jest pochmurno** *(yest po-hmoor-no)* (It's cloudy)
- **Lubię wiosnę/lato/jesień/zimę** *(loo-bye vyo-sne/la-to/ye-sh'yen'/z'ee-me)* (I like spring/summer/autumn/winter)

Talkin' the Talk

Katarzyna *(ka-ta-zhih-na)* has moved to Poland and she's visiting her former work colleague Mary *(me-rih)* from New York. They're chatting about the weather in Poland (temperatures are in Celsius).

Mary: **Jaka jest teraz pogoda w Polsce?**
(ya-ka yest te-ras po-go-da fpols-tse)
What's the weather like now in Poland?

Katarzyna: **Teraz jest lato, więc codziennie jest bardzo gorąco. 30 stopni!**
(te-ras yest la-to vyents tso-dj'yen-n'ye yezd bar-dzo go-ron-tso tshih-dj'yesh'-ch'ee stop-n'ee)
It's summer now so every day it's very hot – 30 degrees!

Mary: **A jaka jest pogoda zimą?**
(a ya-ka yest po-go-da z'ee-mohN)
And what's the weather like in winter?

Katarzyna: **Zwykle pada śnieg i jest bardzo zimno. Czasami –20 stopni!**
(zvih-kle pa-da sh'n'yek ee yest bar-dzo z'ee-mno cha-sa-mee mee-nooz dva-dj'yesh'-ch'ya stop-n'ee)
It's usually snowing and very cold. Sometimes minus 20 degrees!

Mary: **Nie lubię, jak jest tak zimno. A jak jest wiosną?**
(n'ye loo-bye yak yest tag z'eem-no a yak yezd vyos-nohN)
I don't like it when it's that cold. And what's the spring like?

Katarzyna: **Pięknie! Świeci słońce, jest ciepło i wszystko się zieleni. Ale ja najbardziej lubię jesień. Czasami pada, to fakt, ale kiedy jest słonecznie, to wszystko jest kolorowe.**
(pyenk-n'ye sfye-ch'ee swon'-tse yest ch'ye-pwo ee fshih-stko sh'ye z'ye-le-n'ee a-le ya nay-bar-dj'yey loo-bye ye-sh'yen' cha-sa-mee pa-da to fakt ale kye-dih yest swo-nech-n'ye to fshih-stko yest ko-lo-ro-ve)
It's beautiful – it's sunny, warm and everything turns green. But I like autumn the most. Sometimes it rains, that's true, but when it's sunny, everything is colourful.

Mary: **Tak, słyszałam – złota polska jesień.**
(tak swih-sha-wam zwo-ta pol-ska ye-sh'yen')
So I've heard – the golden Polish autumn.

Words to Know

lato	*la-to*	summer
jesień	*ye-sh'yen'*	autumn
zima	*z'ee-ma*	winter
wiosna	*vyo-sna*	spring
jest zimno/ciepło/gorąco	*yezd z'ee-mno/ch'ye-pwo/go-ron-tso*	it's cold/warm/hot
pada deszcz/śnieg	*pa-da deshch/ sh'n'yek*	it's raining/snowing
jest słonecznie	*yest swo-ne-chn'ye*	it's sunny
złota polska jesień	*zwo-ta pol-ska ye-sh'yen'*	the golden Polish autumn

The Polish volume

Polish people like to express themselves in a very vocal manner, as they simply like to be heard. Therefore, you shouldn't be surprised or even feel offended if a Polish friend disagrees with you and starts speaking up and gesticulating. That's actually a good sign of you being accepted as an equal in the conversation. **Gratulacje**! *(gra-too-la-tsye)* (congratulations!).

You've undoubtedly mastered the art of small talk in your native language but getting to know someone from another country and doing so in another language can prove difficult. Since practice makes perfect, give it another go. Match the Polish expressions with their English translation.

1. Dlaczego uczysz się polskiego?
2. Skąd jesteś?
3. Jaki masz adres?
4. Kto to jest?
5. To jest moja rodzina.
6. Ile masz lat?
7. Jak się mówi po polsku . . . ?
8. Mój numer komórki to ...
9. Nie rozumiem.
10. Co to znaczy . . . ?
11. Podaj mi swojego maila.

A. This is my family.
B. Give me your email address, please.
C. What does . . . mean?
D. Why are you learning Polish?
E. Where are you from?
F. My mobile number is . . .
G. How old are you?
H. I don't understand.
I. How do you say . . . in Polish?
J. Who's this?
K. What's your address?

Answer key: 1. D; 2. E; 3. K; 4. J; 5. A; 6. G; 7. I; 8. F; 9. H; 10. C; 11. B.

Chapter 5

Dining Out and Going to the Market

In This Chapter

- Covering all the food basics
- Introducing the accusative case
- Enjoying a meal in a restaurant
- Going shopping
- Unpacking the genitive case

This is undoubtedly one of the most appetising chapters as it's all about **jedzenie** *(ye-dze-n'ye)* (food). **Smacznego**! *(smach-ne-go)* (Enjoy your meal!).

Smacznego! Enjoy your Meal!

Polish food was designed to be filling. As a result, it's pretty heavy on the stomach and probably not the most healthy. However, once you try some Polish delights, such as **pierogi** *(pye-ro-gee)* (dumplings) or **kotlet schabowy** *(kot-let s-ha-bo-vih)* (pork cutlet), the Polish cuisine will become one of your favourites. Read on about what awaits you in a Polish kitchen.

Is it time to eat yet? All about meals

Śniadanie *(sh'-n'ya-da-n'ye)* (breakfast) is served between 7 and 10 a.m. and usually consists of a **kanapka** *(ka-nap-ka)* (sandwich), which doesn't look much like the sandwich you know. On a single slice of buttered bread you'll get some **ser** *(ser)* (cheese) and **szynka** *(shihn-ka)* (ham) finished with **pomidor** *(po-mee-dor)* (tomato) or **ogórek** *(o-goo-rek)* (cucumber). Polish people also like eating **jajecznica z cebulą i boczkiem** *(ya-yech-n'ee-tsa stse-boo-lohN ee boch-kyem)* (scrambled eggs with fried onion and diced pork) and **jajko na miękko** *(yay-ko na myenk-ko)* (soft boiled egg). Those watching their cholesterol level go for something lighter like **jogurt z owocami** *(yo-goort zo-vo-tsa-mee)* (yogurt with fruit) or **płatki z mlekiem** *(pwat-kee zmle-kyem)* (cereal with milk).

Obiad *(o-byat)* (lunch) tends to be the main meal of the day. It is usually served between 1 and 4 p.m. It consists of **zupa** *(zoo-pa)* (soup), **drugie danie** *(droo-gye da-n'ye)* (main course) and **deser** *(de-ser)* (desert). However, with long working hours and no time for a three-course meal any more, people tend to grab **sałatka** *(sa-wat-ka)* (salad) or **kanapka** *(ka-nap-ka)* (sandwich) and rush back to the office, putting off the main meal, often called **obiadokolacja** *(o-bya-do-ko-la-tsya)* (lunch-dinner), to the after-work hours.

Kolacja *(ko-la-tsya)* (dinner) is usually a small affair enjoyed between 6 and 10 p.m. It's usually **chleb** *(hlep)* (bread) with some **wędliny** *(ven-dlee-nih)* (cold meat), **śledzie** *(sh'le-dj'ye)* (pickled herring) or **ser** *(ser)* (cheese). It may not sound fun but, with a bewildering variety of **kiełbasa** *(kyew-ba-sa)* (sausages) and **wędliny** *(ven-dlee-nih)* (cold meat), the Polish supper is never boring.

If invited to stay over at your Polish friend's home, you can expect to be offered the biggest room, the most comfortable bed, the best place at the table and the meal will be prepared in your honour. Polish hospitality is famous for being exceptional!

Tackling table terms

When it's time to eat, you need utensils:

- **nóż** *(noosh)* (knife)
- **widelec** *(vee-de-lets)* (fork)
- **łyżka** *(wihsh-ka)* (spoon)
- **kieliszek do wina** *(kye-lee-shek do vee-na)* (wine glass)
- **kieliszek do wódki** *(kye-lee-shek do voot-kee)* (shot glass)
- **łyżeczka** *(wih-zhech-ka)* (teaspoon)
- **kubek** *(koo-bek)* (mug)
- **szklanka** *(shklan-ka)* (glass)
- **filiżanka** *(fee-lee-zhan-ka)* (cup)

At the table, these phrases come into play:

- **Nakryjesz do stołu?** *(na-krih-yezh do sto-woo)* (Will you set the table?)
- **Gdzie są serwetki?** *(gdj'ye sohN ser-vet-kee)* (Where are the napkins?)
- **Jakie sztućce?** *(ya-kye shtooch'-tse)* (What cutlery?)

- **Czy mogę prosić sól?** *(chih mo-ge pro-sh'eech' sool)* (Can I have some salt, please?)
- **Czy możesz mi podać pieprz?** *(chih mo-zhesh mee po-dach' pyepsh)* (Can you pass the pepper, please?) – informal

Eating and drinking phrases

Common phrases connected with meals include:

- **Jestem głodny/głodna** *(yes-tem gwod-nih/gwod-na)* (I'm hungry [man/woman])
- **Chce mi się jeść** *(htse mee sh'ye yesh'ch')* – another way of saying *I'm hungry*
- **Chce mi się pić** *(htse mee sh'ye peech')* (I'm thirsty)
- **Smacznego!** *(smach-ne-go)* (Enjoy your meal!)
- **Dziękuję** *(dj'yen-koo-ye)* (Thank you)
- **Z czym to jest podane?** *(schihm to yest po-da-ne)* (What does it come with?)
- **Czego się napijesz?** *(che-go sh'ye na-pee-yesh)* (What would you like to drink?) – informal
- **Mam ochotę na . . .** *(mam o-ho-te na)* (I feel like having . . .)
- **Na zdrowie!** *(na zdro-vye)* (Cheers!)
- **Uwielbiam polskie jedzenie!** *(oo-vyel-byam pol-skye ye-dze-n'ye)* (I love Polish food!)
- **Danie dnia** *(da-n'ye dn'ya)* (Dish of the day)
- **Dobrze wysmażony/średnio wysmażony/krwisty** *(dob-zhe vih-sma-zho-nih/sh'red-n'yo vih-sma-zho-nih/krfee-stih)* (Well done/medium/rare)
- **Jestem wegetarianinem/wegetarianką** *(yes-tem ve-ge-ta-rya-n'ee-nem/ve-ge-ta-ryan-kohN)* (I'm a vegetarian [man/woman])

Using two verbs at the table: Jeść and pić

When talking about eating and drinking, you use two verbs: **jeść** *(yesh'ch')* (to eat) and **pić** *(peech')* (to drink). Table 5-1 shows the present tense conjugation for each.

Table 5-1 Present Tense Conjugation of Jeść and Pić

	English	Jeść (to eat)	Pić (to drink)
(ja) *(ya)*	I	**jem** *(yem)*	**piję** *(pee-ye)*
(ty) *(tih)*	you	**jesz** *(yesh)*	**pijesz** *(pee-yesh)*
on/ona/ono/pan/pani *(on/o-na/o-no/pan/pa-n'ee)*	he/she/it/you formal to a man/woman	**je** *(ye)*	**pije** *(pee-ye)*
(my) *(mih)*	we	**jemy** *(ye-mih)*	**pijemy** *(pee-ye-mih)*
(wy) *(vih)*	you [plural]	**jecie** *(ye-ch'ye)*	**pijecie** *(pee-ye-ch'ye)*
oni/one/państwo *(o-n'ee/o-ne/pan'-stfo)*	they/formal they	**jedzą** *(ye-dzohN)*	**piją** *(pee-yohN)*

The verb **jeść** belongs to the **-m/-sz** conjugation while **pić** to the **-ę/-esz** type. Both of them are irregular verbs. Head back to Chapter 2 for details on these odd verbs.

The Case of the Accusative Case

You use the accusative case for a direct object of a sentence. When you say *Adam is drinking a coffee*, **Adam pije kawę** *(a-dam pee-ye ka-ve)*, **kawę** is the direct object of this sentence and is in the accusative case. Flip back to Chapter 2 for more details on the function of the accusative case or the basic (dictionary) nominative case.

The accusative case endings are pretty straightforward. The following sections explain how things work.

Neuter nouns and adjectives in the accusative case have endings identical to the nominative (dictionary) case, so you don't need to change any endings. You only have to worry about masculine and feminine nouns and adjectives.

Objectifying masculine nouns and adjectives

For masculine nouns, the choice of ending depends on whether the noun is animate (people and animals) or inanimate (object).

Endings for living things

Animate nouns for living creatures take the ending **-a** in the accusative case. Adjectives referring to animate nouns take the ending **-ego**. Check out these examples:

- **Mam młodszego brata** *(mam mwot-she-go bra-ta)* (I have a younger brother)
- **Lubię Adama** *(loo-bye a-da-ma)* (I like Adam) – yes, people's names change, too – strange, isn't it?
- **Na obiad jem kurczaka** *(na o-byat yem koor-cha-ka)* (I'm eating chicken for lunch)

Endings for inanimate objects (including plants)

Masculine inanimate nouns don't change their endings. They keep their original nominative (dictionary) forms! And remember that plants are treated as inanimate nouns.

- **Kupujemy nowy samochód** *(koo-poo-ye-mih no-vih sa-mo-hoot)* (We're buying a new car)
- **Mam wolny czas** *(mam vol-nih chas)* (I have some free time/I'm free)

Some inanimate nouns (objects) take the animate ending **-a**. These include food, drinks, brand names, games and dances:

- **Jem banana i hot-doga** *(yem ba-na-na ee hod-do-ga)* (I'm eating a banana and a hot dog)
- **Gram w tenisa i w brydża** *(gram fte-n'ee-sa ee vbrih-dja)* (I play tennis and bridge)

Masculine nouns ending in **-a** in the nominative case end in **-ę** in the accusative case; for example, **artysta** *(ar-tih-sta)* (male artist) becomes **artystę** *(ar-tihs-te)*.

- **Uwielbiam tego artystę** *(oo-vyel-byam te-go ar-tihs-te)* (I love this artist)

Most of these nouns are mainly names of male jobs, for example **dentysta** *(den-tih-sta)* (male dentist) and **pianista** *(pya-n'ee-sta)* (male pianist). Remember, the distinction for animate or inanimate nouns doesn't apply here. These odd masculine nouns look feminine and they follow the feminine pattern. Read on to the next section about the feminine nouns.

Changing feminine endings

Feminine nouns ending in a vowel take the ending **-ę** in the accusative case. Those ending in a consonant are identical in the nominative and accusative cases. Feminine adjectives end in **-ą** in the accusative case. The following list offers examples of both:

- **Czytam dzisiejszą gazetę** *(chih-tam dj'ee-sh'yey-shohN ga-ze-te)* (I'm reading today's paper)
- **Piję mocną kawę** *(pee-ye mots-nohN ka-ve)* (I drink strong coffee)
- **Czekam tu całą noc** *(che-kam too tsa-wohN nots)* (I've been waiting here all night)

Tabling the accusative case

Table 5-2 illustrates how the nominative case changes to the accusative and shows a summary of the accusative endings (for everyone who prefers grammatical tables!).

Good news! The accusative plural for all but masculine personal nouns is identical to the nominative plural (I write about it later in this chapter). Masculine personal nouns are identical to the genitive plural, which I cover in 'The Case of the Genitive Case' section later in this chapter.

Eating Out: Trying Polish Food in a Restaurant

In Poland, eating out isn't as popular as it is in other western European countries. That may be partially for economic reasons and partially because Polish food is considered best prepared at home. Therefore, it's mainly young, busy and wealthy people from bigger cities who are regular restaurant-goers. Of course, there are plenty of restaurants with excellent chefs who know all the secrets of **kuchnia polska** *(koo-hn'ya pol-ska)* (Polish cuisine).

Table 5-2 Noun and Adjective Endings for Accusative Case Singular

	English	*Example of Nominative Case*	*English*	*Example of Accusative Case*	*Accusative Adjective Endings*	*Accusative Noun Endings*
Masculine Animate	This is a small cat.	To jest mały kot *(to yest ma-wih kot)*	I have a small cat.	Mam mał**ego** kot**a** *(mam ma-we-go ko-ta)*	-ego	-a
	This is a good dad.	To jest dobry tata *(to yest dob-rih ta-ta)*	I have a good dad.	Mam dobr**ego** tat**ę** *(mam dob-re-go ta-te)*		-ę
Masculine Inanimate	This is a big house.	To jest duży dom *(to yest doo-zhih dom)*	I have a big house.	Mam duży dom *(mam doo-zhih dom)*	Same as nominative case	Same as nominative case
Feminine	This is an older daughter.	To jest starsza siostra *(to yest star-sha sh'yos-tra)*	I have an older daughter.	Mam **starszą siostrę** *(mam star-shohN sh'yos-tre)*	-ą	-ę
Neuter	This is a small child.	To jest małe dziecko *(to yest ma-we dj'yets-ko)*	I have a small child.	Mam małe dziecko *(mam ma-we dj'yets-ko)*	Same as nominative case	Same as nominative case

The (good?) old times

In the 1980s only two types of restaurants existed in Poland: cheap bars serving very simple food and, at the other end of the scale, expensive and posh restaurants which only members of the Communist Party had access to. The service in both was equally poor! You couldn't find either type in smaller towns.

Nowadays, all types of restaurants, serving a variety of food, line the streets of towns of every size. **Jest z czego wybierać** *(yest sche-go vih-bye-rach')* (There is plenty to choose from).

Making reservations

Many restaurants in Poland don't require reservations. You can simply show up and you're seated straight away, and, with a bit of luck, even **przy oknie** (*pshih o-kn'ye*) (by the window).

If you pick a particularly trendy place on a Saturday night, it's safer to call and book a table in advance so as to avoid the big disappointment of hearing **Przykro mi, ale nie mamy wolnego stolika** *(pshih-kro mee a-le n'ye ma-mih vol-ne-go sto-lee-ka)* (I'm really sorry but we have no free tables). Some booking-a-table expressions in action include:

- **Chciałbym zarezerwować stolik dla dwóch osóp na sobotę na 19.00** *(hch'yaw-bihm za-re-zer-vo-vach' sto-leek dla dvooh o-soop na so-bo-te na dj'ye-vyet-nas-tohN)* (I would like to book a table for two people for this Saturday at 7 p.m. [man speaking]).
- **Chciałabym zrobić rezerwację dla czterech osób na przyszły piątek na 7.30** *(hch'ya-wa-bihm zro-beech' re-zer-va-tsye dla chte-reh o-soop na pshih-shwih pyon-tek na fpoow do oos-mey)* (I would like to make a reservation for four people for next Friday at 7.30 p.m. [woman speaking]).

For days of the (Polish) week and the secrets of the (Polish) clock go to Chapter 7.

Talkin' the Talk

Audio track 7: Arek (*a-rek*) wants to take his British friend Anna (*an-na*), who is visiting Poland for the first time, to try out one of the best places in Warsaw serving traditional Polish food. He's phoning the restaurant to make a reservation.

Waiter: **Restauracja Wesele, słucham?**
(re-sta-oo-ra-tsya ve-se-le swoo-ham)
Wesele restaurant, hello?

Arek: **Dzień dobry. Chciałbym zarezerwować stolik na niedzielę.**
(dj'yen' dob-rih hch'yaw-bihm za-re-zer vo-vach' sto-leek na n'ye-dj'ye-le)
Hello. I'd like to book a table for this Sunday.

Waiter: **Dla ilu osób?**
(dla ee-loo o-soop)
How many people?

Arek: **Dla dwóch.**
(dla dvooh)
Two (please).

Waiter: **Na którą godzinę?**
(na ktoo-rohN go-dj'ee-ne)
What time?

Arek: **Na 18.00.**
(na o-sh'yem-nas-tohN)
6 p.m.

Waiter: **Przykro mi, ale o 18.00 nie mamy już wolnego stolika. Może o 20.00?**
(pshih-kro mee a-le o o-sh'yem-nas-tey n'ye ma-mih yoozh vol-ne-go sto-lee-ka mo-zhe o dvoo-dj'yes-tey)
I'm very sorry but we have no table free at 6 p.m. What about 8 p.m.?

Arek: **Może być o 20.00.**
(mo-zhe bihch' o dvoo-dj'yes-tey)
8 p.m. is fine.

Waiter: **Na jakie nazwisko?**
(na ya-kye naz-vees-ko)
What name?

Arek: **Arek Malinowski.**
(a-rek ma-lee-nof-skee)

Waiter: **Gotowe. Czekamy na państwa w niedzielę.**
(go-to-ve che-ka-mih na pan'-stfa vn'ye-dj'ye-le)
[Your booking is] done. We'll be expecting you on Sunday.

Words to Know

zarezerwować stolik	*za-re-zer-vo-vach' sto-leek*	to book a table
dla ilu osób?	*dla ee-loo o-soop*	how many people?
przykro mi	*pshih-kro mee*	I'm very sorry
gotowe	*go-to-ve*	[your booking is] done
czekać	*che-kach'*	to wait

Arriving and being seated

In many restaurants you get to choose where you want to be seated. Don't be surprised if nobody greets you at the door and shows you to your table. Feel free to simply walk in and make yourself comfortable at the best table and a waiter (or a waitress) will bring you the menu immediately.

In more trendy restaurants, you'll be taken very good care of from the moment you step in.

Talkin' the Talk

Audio track 8: Arek and Anna have just arrived at the Wesele restaurant in Warsaw where they have a reservation for tonight.

Arek: **Dobry wieczór. Mamy rezerwację dla dwóch osób.**
(dob-rih vye-choor ma-mih re-zer-va-tsye dla dvooh o-soop)
Good evening. We have a reservation for two people.

Waiter: **Na jakie nazwisko?**
(na ya-kye naz-vees-ko)
Under what name?

Arek: **Malinowski.**
(ma-lee-nof-skee)

Waiter: **Proszę za mną. Zaprowadzę państwa do stolika. Zaraz państwu przyniosę kartę.**
(pro-she za mnohN za-pro-va-dze pan'-stfa do sto-lee-ka za-ras pan'-stfoo pshih-n'yo-se kar-te)
Please follow me. I'll show you to your table. I'll bring the menu right away.

Words to Know

rezerwacja	*re-zer-va-tsya*	booking
dla	*dla*	for
na jakie nazwisko?	*na ya-kye naz-vees-ko*	under what name?
proszę za mną	*pro-she za mnohN*	please follow me
karta/menu	*kar-ta/me-nee*	menu

Smoke-free country

Until late 2010, Poland was one of the countries where smokers could find a welcoming retreat. You were free to light up with a cup of coffee or with your dinner in any restaurant. By law, restaurants were obliged to provide a separate non-smoking section for those who didn't want to light up. And they did, though in many cases, the non-smoking section was in a back corner, close to a toilet or just metres away from those enjoying their cigarettes.

However, since the end of 2010 Poland has been a smoke-free country. Officially, at least, as not all pubs observe the law.

Decoding the menu

When you go to a Polish restaurant, you must try some of the traditional, mouth-watering Polish delights. But don't panic if you can't decode the menu. The rule is that the more sophisticated the restaurant, the more elaborate and difficult to understand is the menu. Don't hesitate to ask the waiter for help in finding one of the following Polish dishes:

- **Zakąski** *(za-kohN-skee)* (starters)
  - **śledź ze śmietaną** *(sh'ledj' ze sh'mye-ta-nohN)* (marinated herring with sour cream)
  - **tatar** *(ta-tar)* (chopped steak tartar served with chopped onion, gherkins and a shot of vodka)
- **Zupy** *(zoo-pih)* (soups)
  - **rosół** *(ro-soow)* (a traditional chicken and beef soup with fine noodles and chopped carrots, sprinkled with parsley eaten in most Polish homes at Sunday **obiad** (lunch))
  - **grzybowa** *(gzhih-bo-va)* (a must-try wild mushroom soup served with a spoon of cream)
  - **żurek** *(zhoo-rek)* (a white sour soup with boiled eggs and sausage sometimes served in a bowl made from bread – **Palce lizać!** *(pal-tse lee-zach')* (finger-licking good))
  - **barszcz z uszkami** *(barshch zoosh-ka-mee)* (a beetroot soup served with ravioli-style dumplings – traditional for Christmas Eve)

- **Dania główne** *(da-n'ya gwoov-ne)* (main courses)
  - **pierogi** *(pye-ro-gee)* (the famous Polish dumplings, served boiled or fried, delicious both ways!) They come with different fillings:

    pierogi z mięsem *(pye-ro-gee zm'yehN-sem)* (with fried mince and fried onions)

    pierogi z kapustą i grzybami *(pye-ro-gee ska-poos-tohN ee gzhih-ba-mee)* (with sauerkraut and wild mushrooms)

    pierogi ruskie *(pye-ro-gee roos-kye)* (made from boiled potatoes, cottage cheese and fried onion)

    pierogi z serem *(pye-ro-gee sse-rem)* (filled with cottage cheese and served sweet – a children's favourite)
  - **gołąbki w sosie pomidorowym** *(go-womp-kee fso-sh'ye po-mee-do-ro-vihm)* (literally: little pigeons! Delicious cabbage rolls stuffed with mince, served with creamy tomato sauce and mashed or boiled potatoes – **Pycha!** *(pih-ha)* (Yummy!))
  - **kaczka z jabłkami** *(kach-ka zyap-ka-mee)* (roast duck with apples, usually served with red cabbage stew and cranberries)
  - **zrazy** *(zra-zih)* (rolled slices of beef, stuffed with pickled cucumber, mushroom and pepper)
  - **placki ziemniaczane** *(plats-kee z'yem-n'ya-cha-ne)* (potato pancakes served with beef goulash, sour cream or simply with sugar)
  - **kotlet schabowy** *(kot-let s-ha-bo-vih)* (a delicious fried thin pork cutlet)
  - **bigos** *(bee-gos)* (traditional Polish hunters' stew – it takes ages to cook!)
- **Desery** *(de-se-rih)* (desserts)
  - **szarlotka z lodami i bitą śmietaną** *(shar-lot-ka zlo-da-mee ee bee-tohN sh'mye ta-nohN)* (warm apple pie served with ice cream and whipped cream)
  - **makowiec** *(ma-ko-vyets)* (poppy-seed cake)
  - **sernik** *(ser-n'eek)* (Polish cheesecake – once you try it, you'll never want to eat any other cake!)

Polish people are not very fond of **owoce morza** *(o-vo-tse mo-zha)* (seafood) and, as a result, you can't get it in many places.

Coffee or tea?

Coffee or tea? If you hear that question, make sure you explain how you drink it. Otherwise, you risk getting **herbata z cytryną** *(her-ba-ta stsih-trih-nohN)* (a light black tea with a slice of lemon). And you can forget the milk! In fact, only children in kindergarden or breast-feeding women drink tea with milk, called **bawarka** *(ba-var-ka)* and for this reason all Poles feel sorry for them! You'll be sure to get a strange look if you ask for a white tea.

Home-made coffee may also be something not to everyone's taste. Imagine a cup with two spoons of regular ground coffee with boiling water. Then just some stirring, possibly some sugar and all done! The last sip can leave you with coffee grounds in your teeth! Better not to smile then! The good news is that all coffee shops serve coffee the way you're used to. Big relief, huh?

Asking for what you want

To ask for Polish delights, use these phrases:

- **Poproszę . . .** *(po-pro-she)* (Can I have . . . please)
- **Dla mnie . . .** *(dla mn'ye)* (For me . . . please)
- **Ja wezmę . . .** *(ya vez-me)* (I'll go for . . .)

If you want to be adventurous, you can ask your server, **Co pan/pani poleca?** *(tso pan/pa-n'ee po-le-tsa)* (What do you recommend?) – formal to a man/woman

Use the accusative case after **Poproszę** *(po-pro-she)* (Can I have), **Wezmę** *(vez-me)* (I'll take), **Lubię** *(loo-bye)* (I like), **Polecam** *(po-le-tsam)* (I recommend) and **Wolę** *(vo-le)* (I prefer).

Talkin' the Talk

Audio track 9: Arek and Anna have just been taken to their table and are placing their order.

Waitress: **Co podać?**
(tso po-dach')
What can I get you?

Arek: **A co pani poleca?**
(a tso pa-n'ee po-le-tsa)
What can you recommend?

Waitress: **Mamy smaczną grzybową, a na drugie danie polecam kaczkę z jabłkami. Jest wyśmienita!**
(ma-mih smach nohN gzhih-bo-vohN a na droo-gye da-n'ye po-le-tsam kach-ke zyap-ka-mee yezd vihsh'-mye-n'ee-ta)
We have a tasty wild mushroom soup and for the main course I suggest duck with apples. It's superb!

Arek: **Hm . . . Niestety, nie jestem fanem kaczki. To ja poproszę grzybową i kotlet schabowy z ziemniakami i surówką z kapusty.**
(hm n'yes-te-tih n'ye yes-tem fa-nem kach-kee to ya po-pro-she gzhih-bo-vohN ee kot-let s-ha-bo-vih zz'yem-n'ya-ka-mee ee soo-roof-kohN ska-poos-tih)
Unfortunately, I'm not a fan of duck. Can I have mushroom soup and pork cutlet with potatoes and cabbage salad, please.

Anna: **Dla mnie rosół i gołąbki z sosem pomidorowym.**
(dla mn'ye ro-soow ee go-womp-kee sso-sem po-mee-do-ro-vihm)
For me, chicken soup and cabbage rolls with tomato sauce [please].

Waitress: **A co do picia?**
(a tso do pee-ch'ya)
What drinks?

Arek: **Butelka wody mineralnej niegazowanej i jakieś polskie piwo.**
(boo-tel-ka vo-dih mee-ne-ral-ney n'ye-ga-zo-va-ney ee ya-kyesh' pol-skye pee-vo)
A bottle of still mineral water and some Polish beer.

Waitress: **Może być Żywiec?**
(mo-zhe bihch' zhih-vyets)
Is Żywiec okay?

Arek: **Tak. Poprosimy duży Żywiec dwa razy.**
(tak po-pro-sh'ee-mih doo-zhih zhih-vyedz dva ra-zih)
Yes. Can we have large [nearly a pint] Żywiec twice.

Waitress: **Czy coś jeszcze?**
(chih tsosh' yesh-che)
Anything else?

Anna: **To wszystko, dziękujemy.**
(to fshih-stko dj'yen-koo-ye-mih)
That's all, thank you.

Words to Know

co podać?	*tso po-dach'*	what can I get you?
polecać	*po-le-tsach'*	to recommend
wyśmienite	*vihsh'-mye-n'ee-te*	superb
na drugie danie	*na droo-gye da-n'ye*	for the main course
dla mnie	*dla mn'ye*	for me
a co do picia?	*a tso do pee-ch'ya*	what drinks?
dwa razy	*dva ra-zih*	twice
kelner/kelnerka	*kel-ner/kel-ner-ka*	waiter/waitress

Preferring, liking and disliking

If you're not a big fan of a particular food or, on the contrary, you absolutely love a particular dish, use the following phrases to express it all in Polish:

- **Wolę ryby niż owoce morza** *(vo-le rih-bih n'eesh o-vo-tse mo-zha)* (I prefer fish to seafood)
- **Nie jem wieprzowiny/wołowiny/baraniny/drobiu** *(n'ye yem vyep-sho-vee-nih/vo-wo-vee-nih/ba-ra-n'ee-nih/dro-byoo)* (I don't eat pork/beef/lamb/poultry)

- **Ale ostre!** *(a-le os-tre)* (It's hot/spicy!)
- **Bardzo smaczne** *(bar-dzo smach-ne)* (Very tasty)
- **To jest pyszne/znakomite!** *(to yest pihsh-ne/zna-ko-mee-te)* (It's yummy/superb!)
- **I jak? Smakuje ci/panu/pani/państwu?** *(ee yak sma-koo-ye ch'ee/pa-noo/pa n'ee/pan'-stfoo)* (And? Do you like it?) – informal/formal to a man/woman/plural
- **Nie za bardzo** *(n'ye za bar-dzo)* (Not really)
- **Jest tłusty/bez smaku/niezły/wyśmienity** *(yest twoos-tih/bes sma-koo/n'ye-zwih/vih-sh'mye-n'ee-tih)* (It's fatty/tasteless/not bad/excellent)
- **To jest za słone/za słodkie/za kwaśne** *(to yest za swo-ne/za swot-kye/za kfash'-ne)* (It's too salty/too sweet/too sour)
- **Nie smakuje mi** *(n'ye sma-koo ye mee)* (I don't like it)
- **Jestem uczulony/uczulona na orzechy** *(yes-tem oo-choo-lo-nih/oo-choo-lo-na na o-zhe-hih)* (I am allergic to nuts [man/woman])
- **Nie mogę jeść . . .** *(n'ye mo-ge yesh'ch')* (I can't eat . . .)
- **Poproszę z/bez . . .** *(po-pro-she z/bes)* (With/without . . . please)

Talkin' the Talk

Audio track 10: It's time for some serious eating now! Arek and Anna are now enjoying their Polish food.

Arek: **I jak? Smakuje ci?**
(ee yak sma-koo-ye ch'ee)
And? Do you like it?

Anna: **Zupa bardzo dobra, a gołąbki są znakomite!**
(zoo-pa bar-dzo dob-ra a go-womp-kee sohN zna-ko-mee-te)
The soup is very good and the cabbage rolls are superb!

Arek: **Mogę spróbować?**
(mo-ge sproo-bo-vach')
Can I try it?

Anna: **Oczywiście. I jak?**
(o-chih-veesh'-ch'ye ee yak)
Of course. And?

Arek: **Pyszne!**
(pihsh-ne)
Yummy!

Audio track 11: Arek and Anna are relaxing after a very good meal when the waitress comes along.

Waitress: **Czy chcą państwo zamówić deser?**
(chih htsohN pan'-stfo za-moo-veedj' de-ser)
Would you like some dessert?

Arek: **Nie, dziękujemy. Może innym razem. Poprosimy rachunek.**
(n'ye dj'yen-koo-ye-mih mo-zhe in-nihm ra-zem po-pro-sh'ee-mih ra-hoo-nek)
No, thank you. Maybe another time. Can we have the bill, please.

Waitress: **Proszę bardzo.**
(pro-she bar-dzo)
You're welcome.

Arek: **Czy można zapłacić kartą?**
(chih mozh-na za-pwa-ch'eech' kar-tohN)
Can we pay by card?

Waitress: **Tak, oczywiście.**
(tak o-chih-veesh'-ch'ye)
Yes, of course.

Tipping tips

Polish waiters and waitresses will make sure you feel comfortable and well taken care of. They'll be discreetly waiting for your sign if you need them. And don't worry; you won't end up with an extra service charge added to your bill! In fact, it's up to you to leave a tip. Many diners leave nothing. So if you tip, you can be sure that doing so will be very much appreciated.

If, on the other hand, you do not intend to tip your waiter, remember to not say **Dziękuję** when paying, as this will be understood as *keep the change.*

Words to Know

smakuje ci?	*sma-koo-ye ch'ee*	do you like it? (food – informal)
spróbować	*sproo-bo-vach'*	to try
zamówić	*za-moo-veech*	to order
może innym razem	*mo-zhe in-nihm ra-zem*	maybe another time
poprosić rachunek	*po-pro-sh'eech' ra-hoo-nek*	to ask for the bill
zapłacić kartą	*za-pwa-ch'eech' kar-tohN*	to pay by card

Finding your way to the 'Ladies' and 'Gents'

Finding the right toilet in Poland may be challenging. The information here could save you a lot of embarrassment!

The gents are marked with a triangle and the ladies with a circle. In some places you can see a letter **'M'** for **mężczyzna** *(mehNsh-chih-zna)* (man) or **'K'** for **kobieta** *(ko-bye-ta)* (woman). Sometimes it could be **'toaleta męska'** *(to-a-le-ta mehN-ska)* (gents room) and **'toaleta damska'** *(to-a-le-ta dam-ska)* (ladies' room).

Seeing the sign **'toaleta nieczynna'** *(to-a-le-ta n'ye-chihn-na)* is never good news. It means *toilet out of order.*

Talkin' the Talk

Audio track 12: At some point everyone needs to ask where the toilets are. Here's how such a conversation may sound.

Anna: **Przepraszam, czy to jest damska toaleta?**
(pshe-pra-sham chih to yest dam-ska to-a-le-ta)
Excuse me, is this the ladies?

Waiter: **Nie, to jest męska toaleta. Damska jest tam.**
(n'ye to yest mehN-ska to-a-le-ta dam-ska yest tam)
No, this is the gents. The ladies is over there.

Here's another scenario:

Simon: **Przepraszam, gdzie jest toaleta?**
(pshe-pra-sham gdj'ye yest to-a-le-ta)
Excuse me, where is the loo?

Waiter: **Tam, na końcu korytarza w prawo.**
(tam na kon'-tsoo ko-rih-ta-zha fpra-vo)
Over there, at the end of the corridor to the right.

Shopping for Food

After you've tried some Polish food in a restaurant or at a Polish friend's home, you may wish to include certain dishes in your menu. Finding recipes on the Internet is easy. Then you need to go and get the ingredients.

Shopping at the supermarket and other grocery shops

Although **hipermarkety** *(hee-per-mar-ke-tih)* (hypermarkets) and their smaller counterparts **supermarkety** *(soo-per-mar-ke-tih)* (supermarkets), where you can buy pretty much everything (and where you don't need to speak a single word of Polish!), are widespread, the best places for food shopping are still the little corner shops or open markets called **targ** *(tark)* or **rynek** *(rih-nek)* known for the high quality of their products. Here are the names of particular shops:

- **sklep spożywczy** *(sklep spo-zhihf-chih)* (grocery shop)
- **sklep mięsny/wędliny** *(sklep myehN-snih/ven-dlee-nih)* (butcher's shop)
- **warzywniak** *(va-zhih-vn'yak)* (shop with fruit and vegetables)
- **piekarnia** *(pye-kar-n'ya)* (bakery)
- **cukiernia** *(tsoo-kyer-n'ya)* (confectionery shop)
- **sklep rybny** *(sklep rihb-nih)* (fish shop)

Finding what you need

Table 5-3 lists items you can purchase in various shops.

Table 5-3 Staple Food Items

baguettes: **bagietki** *(ba-gyet-kee)*	butter: **masło** *(ma-swo)*	beef: **wołowina** *(vo-wo-vee-na)*	bacon: **boczek** *(bo-chek)*
biscuits: **ciastka** *(ch'yas-tka)*	cheese: **ser żółty** *(ser zhoow-tih)*	fish: **ryby** *(rih-bih)*	cold meat: **wędliny** *(ven-dlee-nih)*
bread: **chleb** *(hlep)*	cottage cheese: **ser biały** *(ser bya-wih)*	poultry: **drób** *(droop)*	ham: **szynka** *(shihn-ka)*
bread rolls: **bułki** *(boow-kee)*	cream: **śmietana** *(sh'mye-ta-na)*	pork: **wieprzowina** *(vyep-sho-vee-na)*	sausage: **kiełbasa** *(kyew-ba-sa)*
cake: **ciasto** *(ch'yas-to)*	milk: **mleko** *(mle-ko)*	veal [yes, Polish people eat it!]: **cielęcina** *(ch'ye-len'-ch'ee-na)*	
doughnuts: **pączki** *(pon-chkee)*			

Table 5-4 lists names and pronunciations for a range of fruit and vegetables.

Table 5-4 Fruit and Vegetables

Fruits	***Vegetables***
apple: **jabłko** *(yap-ko)*	broccoli: **brokuły** *(bro-koo-wih)*
banana: **banan** *(ba-nan)*	cabbage: **kapusta** *(ka-poos-ta)*
cherry: **czereśnia** *(che-resh'-n'ya)*	carrot: **marchewka** *(mar-hef-ka)*
currant: **porzeczka** *(po-zhech-ka)*	cauliflower: **kalafior** *(ka-la-fyor)*
grape: **winogrono** *(vee-no-gro-no)*	cucumber: **ogórek** *(o-goo-rek)*
orange: **pomarańcza** *(po-ma-ran'-cha)*	garlic: **czosnek** *(chos-nek)*
peach: **brzoskwinia** *(bzhos-kfee-n'ya)*	lettuce: **sałata** *(sa-wa-ta)*
pear: **gruszka** *(groosh-ka)*	onion: **cebula** *(tse-boo-la)*
plum: **śliwka** *(sh'leef-ka)*	pepper: **papryka** *(pa-prih-ka)*
strawberry: **truskawka** *(troos-kaf-ka)*	spinach: **szpinak** *(shpee-nak)*
mandarin: **mandarynka** *(man-da-rihn-ka)*	
tomato: **pomidor** *(po-mee-dor)*	

Nominative plural

You're much more likely to use the plural *strawberries* than the singular *strawberry*. In this section I tell you how to form plurals.

Masculine nouns (with the exception of masculine personal, which I don't cover in this book to save you a headache) and feminine nouns have these endings in plural: **-y** (the most common one), **-i** (after k or g), **-e** (after hardened *sz, cz, dz, dż, ż, rz,* soft *ś/si, ź/zi, ć/ci, dź/dzi, ń/ni* and c, j and l). Neuter nouns end in **-a** in the nominative plural. All adjectives end in **-e**. Read the following plural examples:

- **To są polskie pomidory** *(to sohN pol-skye po-mee-do-rih)* (These are Polish tomatoes)
- **To są świeże ogórki** *(to sohN sh'fye-zhe o-goor-kee)* (These are fresh cucumbers)
- **To są smaczne truskawki** *(to sohN sma-chne troo-skaf-kee)* (These are tasty strawberries)
- **To są zielone jabłka** *(to sohN z'ye-lo-ne yap-ka)* (These are green apples)

Knowing the measures: Weight, volume and package

Use the following weights, volume and measurements when shopping for food:

- **butelka wina/wody/oliwy** *(boo-tel-ka vee-na/vo-dih/o-lee-vih)* (a bottle of wine/water/olive oil)
- **karton mleka/soku** *(kar-ton mle-ka/so-koo)* (a carton of milk/juice)
- **paczka herbaty/kawy** *(pach-ka her-ba-tih/ka-vih)* (a packet of tea/coffee)
- **słoik dżemu** *(swo-yeek dje-moo)* (a jar of jam)
- **puszka piwa/coli/pomidorów** *(poosh-ka pee-va/ko-lee/po-mee-do-roof)* (a can of beer/cola/a tin of tomatoes)
- **kawałek pizzy/ciasta** *(ka-va-wek peets-tsih/ch'yas-ta)* (a piece of pizza/cake)
- **pięć plasterków szynki/sera** *(pyen'ch pla-ster-koof shihn-kee/se-ra)* (five slices of ham/cheese)
- **zgrzewka piwa** *(zgzhef-ka pee-va)* (a pack of beer)
- **trochę warzyw** *(tro-he va-zhihf)* (some vegetables)
- **dużo/mało sera** *(doo-zho/ma-wo se-ra)* (a lot of/a little cheese)
- **kilka pomidorów** *(keel-ka po-mee-do-roof)* (a few tomatoes)

Kilogram *(kee-lo-gram)* is equivalent to just over two pounds. Poles often say **kilo** *(kee-lo)* instead of **kilogram** and the abbreviation of both is **kg.** Some handy measurements include:

- **pół kilo/kilograma** *(poow kee-lo/kee-lo-gra-ma)* (half a kilogram)
- **ćwierć kilo** *(ch'fyerch' kee-lo)* (quarter of a kilo)
- **20 deka = 200 gramów** *(dva-dj'yesh'-ch'ya de-ka dvyesh'-ch'ye gra-moof)* (200 grams)
- **litr** *(leetr)* (1.7 pints)

When talking about volume, measurements, packaging and numbers over five, remember to use the genitive case, which I talk about in the next section.

Talkin' the Talk

Audio track 13: Simon is buying some products at **rynek** (local market) for tonight's dinner. Here is what this conversation looks like.

Sales assistant: **Co podać?**
(tso po-dach')
What can I get you?

Simon: **Poproszę 30 deka czereśni.**
(po-pro-she tshy-dj'yesh'-ch'ee de-ka che-resh'-n'ee)
Can I have 300 grams of cherries.

Sales assistant: **Może być dziesięć deka więcej?**
(mo-zhe bihdj' dj'ye-sh'yen'dj' de-ka vyen-tsey)
Is another 100 grams more okay?

Simon: **Tak, może być. Po ile są pomidory?**
(tak mo-zhe bihch' po ee-le sohN po-mee-do-rih)
Yes, that's fine. How much are the tomatoes?

Sales assistant: **Siedem złotych za kilo.**
(sh'ye-dem zwo-tihh za kee-lo)
7zł per kilogram.

Simon: **To poproszę pół kilo.**
(to po-pro-she poow kee-lo)
Can I have half a kilo, please.

Sales assistant: **Czy coś jeszcze?**
(chih tsosh' yesh-che)
Anything else?

Simon: **Nie, to wszystko.**
(n'ye to fshih-stko)
No, that's all.

Words to Know

co podać?	tso po-dach'	what can I get you?
tak, może być	tak mo-zhe bihch'	yes, that's fine
czy coś jeszcze?	chih tsosh' yesh-che	anything else?
nie, to wszystko	n'ye to fshih-stko	no, that's all

The Case of the Genitive Case

The genitive case is one of the most commonly used cases in Polish. You use it for possessions (**dom Adama**) *(dom a-da-mu)* (Adam's house); negations of the accusative case (**Nie lubię kawy**) *(n'ye loo-bye ka-vih)* (I don't like coffee); after quantities and packaging (**pół pizzy)** *(poow peets-tsih)* (half a pizza), (**butelka wody**) *(boo-tel-ka vo-dih)* (bottle of water); numbers above five (**pięć piw**) *(pyen'ch' peef)* (five beers) and more. Chapter 2 is the place to go for the details about when to use the genitive case.

Owning masculine nouns and adjectives

In the genitive case, the choice of ending depends on whether the noun is animate (people and animals) or inanimate (object). (I cover the accusative case in 'The Case of the Accusative Case' section earlier in this chapter.) Masculine animate nouns are identical to those in the accusative case and take the ending **-a**. Adjectives referring to animate nouns take the ending **-ego**, as in these examples:

- **Nie mam młodszego brata** *(n'ye mam mwot-she-go bra-ta)* (I don't have a younger brother)
- **Nie jem kurczaka** *(n'ye yem koor-cha-ka)* (I don't eat chicken)

Masculine inanimate nouns in the genitive aren't predictable. The most common ending is **-u**. The ending **-a** is added to names of currencies, fruits, months, games, dances, body parts and tools:

- **Nie mam wolnego czasu** *(n'ye mam vol-ne-go cha-soo)* (I have no free time/I'm not free)
- **Nie umiem tańczyć walca** *(n'ye oo-myem tan'-chihch' val-tsa)* (I can't dance the waltz)

Masculine nouns ending in **-a** in the nominative case change their ending to **-y** in the genitive case: **Nie znam twojego dentysty** *(n'ye znam tfo-ye-go den-tihs-tih)* (I don't know your dentist).

Showing possession of neuters

Changing neuter nouns and adjectives to the genitive case is easy as there are only two endings to remember: **-a** for nouns and **-ego** for adjectives:

- **Nie mam sportowego auta** *(n'ye mam spor-to-ve-go aw-ta)* (I don't have a sports car)
- **Nie lubię ciepłego piwa** *(n'ye loo-bye ch'ye-pwe-go pee-va)* (I don't like warm beer)

Generating feminine genitives

Feminine nouns have the ending **-y** (after hard consonants) or **-i** (after k, g, j, l or soft consonants) in the genitive case. Feminine adjectives end in **-ej**. Here are some examples:

- **Nie piję mocnej kawy** *(n'ye pee-ye mots-ney ka-vih)* (I don't drink strong coffee)
- **Nie lubię tłustej szynki** *(n'ye loo-bye twoos-tey shihn-kee)* (I don't like fatty ham)
- **On nie zna pani** *(on n'ye zna pa-n'ee)* (He doesn't know you) formal to a woman

Tabling the genitive case

Table 5-5 illustrates how the nominative case changes to the genitive and provides a summary of the genitive endings.

Table 5-5 Noun and Adjective Endings for the Accusative Case

	English	*Example of Nominative Case*	*English*	*Example of Genitive Case*	*Genitive Adjective Endings*	*Genitive Noun Endings*
Masculine Animate	This is a small cat.	To jest mały kot *(to yest ma-wih kot)*	I don't have a small cat.	Nie mam mał**ego** kota *(n'ye mam ma-we-go ko-ta)*	-ego	-a
	This is a young dad.	To jest młody tata *(to yest mwo-dih ta-ta)*	I don't have a young dad.	Nie mam młod**ego** taty *(n'ye mam mwo-de-go ta-tih)*		-y
Masculine Inanimate	This is cold juice.	To jest zimny sok *(to yest z'eem-nih sok)*	I don't like cold juice.	Nie lubię zimn**ego** soku *(n'ye loo-bye z'eem-ne-go so-koo)*	-ego	-u
	This is old bread.	To jest stary chleb *(to yest sta-rih hlep)*	I don't like old bread.	Nie lubię star**ego** chleba *(n'ye loo-bye sta-re-go hle-ba)*		-a
Feminine	This is a strong coffee.	To jest mocna kawa *(to yest mo-tsna ka-va)*	I don't like strong coffee.	Nie lubię mocn**ej** kawy *(n'ye loo-bye mots-ney ka-wih)*	-ej	-y
	This is fatty ham.	To jest tłusta szynka *(to yest twoo-sta shih-nka)*	I don't like fatty ham.	Nie lubię tłust**ej** szynki *(n'ye loo-bye twoo-stey shih-nkee)*		-i (after k, g, j, l)
Neuter	This is warm beer.	To jest ciepłe piwo *(to yest ch'ye-pwe pee-vo)*	I don't like warm beer.	Nie lubię ciepł**ego** piw**a** *(n'ye loo-bye ch'ye-pwe-go pee-va)*	-ego	-a

Making plurals

All adjectives in the genitive plural take the ending **-ych** or **-ich** (after k, g).

Feminine and neuter nouns drop their nominative endings and have no ending at all, which is called a zero-ending and marked as **-ø**: Kup pięć zim**nych** piw**-ø** *(koop pyen'ch' z'eem-nihh peef)* (Buy five cold beers).

Sometimes the zero-ending produces consonant clusters, which you break up by inserting **-e-**, as in: Znam dużo mił**ych** student**ek-ø** *(znam doo-zho mee-wihh stoo-den-tek)* (I know many nice [female] students).

Most masculine nouns end in **-ów** in the genitive plural. After hardened consonants such as *sz, cz, dz, dż, ż, rz* and *c*, use the ending **–y**. Use the ending **-i** after soft endings – *ś, ż, ć, dź, ńl* and *j*. Be aware of a few exceptions, such as **owoców** or **krajów**. You need to learn these by heart. Here are some examples:

- Nie znam **tych** student**ów** *(n'ye znam tihh stoo-den-toof)* (I don't know these students)
- Nie mam drobn**ych** pienię**dzy** *(n'ye mam drob-nihh pye-n'yen-dzih)* (I have no small change)
- Nie lubię nasz**ych** nauczyciel**i** *(n'ye loo-bye na-shihh na-oo-chih-ch'ye-lee)* (I don't like our teachers)

Fun & Games

Hungry? Before you head off to a Polish meal, try to name the food in Figure 5-1 (more than one option is possible).

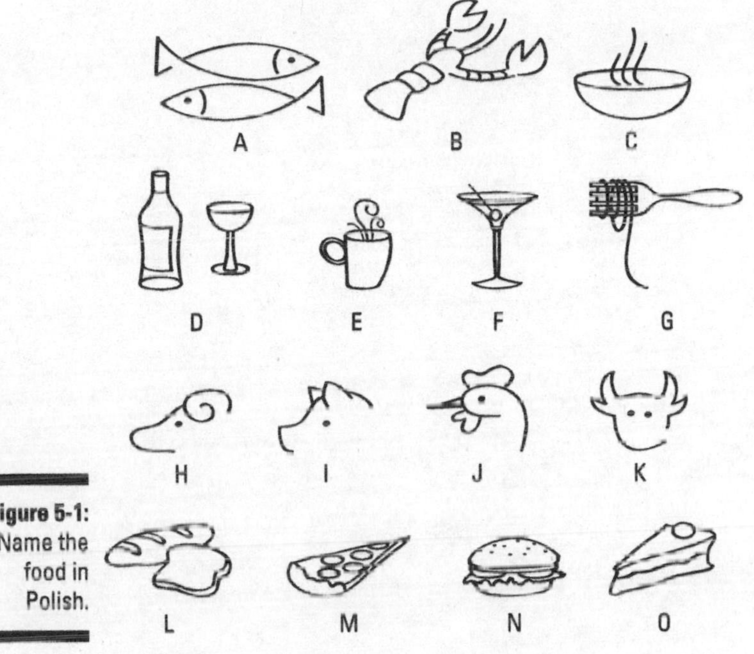

Figure 5-1: Name the food in Polish.

Answer key: A. ryba/ryby; B. homar/owoce morza; C. zupa/zupy; D. wino/kieliszek czerwonego wina; E. herbata/kawa/gorąca czekolada; F. drink; G. spagetti; H. baranina; I. wieprzowina; J. drób/kurczak; K. wołowina; L. chleb; M. pizza/kawałek pizzy; N. hamburger/kanapka; O. ciasto

Chapter 6

Shopping Made Easy

In This Chapter

- Identifying shops
- Buying clothes in various colours, materials and patterns
- Comparing items
- Complimenting your choices

Skleping *(skle-peenk)* is a new word that combines the Polish word **sklep** *(sklep)*, which means *a shop* and the English word *shopping*. Not many Poles know this funny new word **skleping** so seize the opportunity to teach them something fun!

So, **Idziemy na skleping?** or to speak proper Polish, **Idziemy na zakupy?** *(ee-dj'ye-mih na za-koo-pih)* (Shall we go shopping?).

Introducing Places to Shop

As in every country in the European Union (EU), big cities in Poland have large shopping centres, often called **galeria handlowa** *(ga-le-rya han-dlo-va)*, with a myriad of shops, restaurants, cafes, playgrounds for children, cinemas and clubs, all under one roof. (You use the word **galeria** for an art gallery as well. After all, the ability to put different clothes together so that they can speak for your personality is certainly an art form!) In smaller towns, shops are cosy and carry merchandise that feels unique and exotic. Very popular are **rynek** *(rih-nek)* or **targ** *(tark)* (open-air markets) where you can search for both food and clothes, the latter not necessarily from the latest collections, though.

Other types of shops in which you can spend money include:

- **apteka** *(ap-te-ka)* (pharmacy)
- **kiosk** *(kyosk)* (newsagent, where you can get a lot more than a paper – bus tickets, postcards, toiletries, laundry products, tights and so on)
- **księgarnia** *(ksh'yen-gar-n'ya)* (book shop)

- **kwiaciarnia** *(kfya-ch'yar-n'ya)* (flower shop)
- **optyk** *(op-tihk)* (optician)
- **sklep AGD** *(sklep a gye de)* (home appliance shop)
- **sklep RTV** *(sklep er te faw)* (a small appliance shop selling TVs, radios, CD players and so on)
- **sklep jubilerski** *(sklep yoo-bee-ler-skee)* (jeweller's shop)
- **sklep obuwniczy** *(sklep o-boov-n'ee-chih)* (shoe shop)
- **sklep papierniczy** *(sklep pa-pyer-n'ee-chih)* (stationery shop)

You can find **godziny otwarcia** *(go-dj'ee-nih ot-far-ch'ya)* (opening hours) of every shop on the Internet but on some occasions you may find it useful to know how to ask the following:

- **Jakie są godziny otwarcia?** *(ya-kye sohN go-dj'ee-nih ot-far-ch'ya)* (What are your hours?)
- **Czy jest otwarte w niedzielę?** *(chih yest ot-far-te vn'ye-dj'ye-le)* (Are you open on Sundays?)

Once you decide on where you want to go shopping, here are some expressions worth knowing:

- **Przepraszam, gdzie jest . . . ?** *(pshe-pra-sham gdj'ye yest)* (Excuse me, where is . . . ?)
- **Gdzie znajdę sklepy z bielizną?** *(gdj'ye znay-de skle-pih zbye-lee-znohN)* (Where can I find lingerie shops?)
- **Szukam apteki** *(shoo-kam ap-te-kee)* (I'm looking for a pharmacy)
- **Na którym piętrze są buty?** *(na ktoo-rihm pyen-tshe sohN boo-tih)* (Which floor for shoes?)
- **Na parterze** *(na par-te-zhe)* (On the ground floor)
- **Na pierwszym/drugim piętrze** *(na pyer-fshihm/droo-geem pyen-tshe)* (On the first/second floor)

  You may want to refer to Chapter 7 to check out all the forms of ordinal numbers. Be aware that the endings here are in the locative case, which is covered in Chapter 11.
- **Wejście/Wyjście** *(vey-sh'ch'ye/vihy-sh'ch'ye)* (entrance/exit)
- **Otwarte/Zamknięte** *(o-tfar-te/zam-kn'yen-te)* (open/closed)
- **Schody/Schody ruchome** *(sho-dih/sho-dih roo-ho-me)* (stairs/escalator)
- **Winda** *(veen-da)* (lift)

The verb **szukać** *(shoo-kach')* (to look for/search) is followed by nouns in the genitive case. You can read more about the genitive case in Chapter 5.

Words to Know

iść na zakupy	*eesh'ch' na za-koo-pih*	to go shopping
pasuje ci . . . ?	*pa-soo-ye ch'ee*	is . . . good for you?
pewnie	*pev-n'ye*	sure
możemy pójść do	*mo-zhe-mih pooyz'dj' do*	we can go to
dobry pomysł	*dob-rih po-mihsw*	good idea
wszystko	*fshihs-tko*	everything

Talkin' the Talk

Anna *(an-na)* and Natalia *(na-ta-lya)* have a party to attend and they've just realised they have nothing to wear! They have no other choice but to go shopping (not that they don't enjoy it!).

Anna: **Nie mam się w co ubrać!**
(n'ye mam sh'ye ftso oo-brach')
I have nothing to wear!

Natalia: **Ja też. Kiedy idziemy na zakupy?**
(ya tesh kye-dih ee-dj'ye-mih na za-koo-pih)
Me neither! When are we going shopping?

Anna: **Pasuje ci w piątek?**
(pa-soo-ye ch'ee fpyon-tek)
Can you do Friday? [Literally: does Friday suit you?]

Natalia: **Pewnie. Możemy pójść do tej nowej galerii.**

	(pev-n'ye mo-zhe-mih pooyz'dj' do tey no-vey ga-le-ryee) Sure! We can go to the new shopping centre.
Anna:	**Dobry pomysł! Tam można kupić wszystko.** *(dob-rih po-mihsw tam mozh-na koo-peech' fshihs-tko)* Good idea. You can get everything there.

Shopping for Clothes

In this section I tell you about different pieces of the Polish wardrobe, including colours, patterns and fabrics – how to enquire about them, find them and try them on – all you need to know to successfully browse the shelves.

Table 6-1 offers a short list of **ubrania** *(oo-bra-n'ya)* (clothes) you may want to purchase.

Table 6-1 Clothing Items

Item	Polish	Pronuciation	Item	Polish	Pronuciation
swimming costume/ trunks	**kostium kąpielowy/ kąpielówki**	*kos-tyoom kom-pye-lo-vih/kom-pye-loof-kee*	skirt	**spódnica**	*spoo-dn'ee-tsa*
blouse	**bluzka**	*bloos-ka*	slippers	**kapcie**	*kap-ch'ye*
coat	**płaszcz**	*pwashch*	socks	**skarpetki**	*skar-pet-kee*
dress	**sukienka**	*soo-kyen-ka*	suit jacket (man)	**marynarka**	*ma-rih-nar-ka*
stilettos	**szpilki**	*shpeel-kee*	suit jacket (woman)	**żakiet**	*zha-kyet*
jacket	**kurtka**	*koor-tka*	sweater	**sweter**	*sfe-ter*
jeans	**dżinsy**	*djeen-sih*	trousers	**spodnie**	*spod-n'ye*
sandals	**sandały**	*san-da-wih*	T-shirt	**koszulka/ T-shirt**	*ko-shool-ka/ tee-shert*
shirt	**koszula**	*ko-shoo-la*	underwear	**bielizna**	*bye-leez-na*
shoes	**buty**	*boo-tih*			

Getting assistance and trying clothes on

In large shopping centres you can simply dive in and enjoy the shopping without being interrupted. In smaller shops, the minute you walk in, you'll be offered help by **sprzedawczyni** *(spshe-daf-chih-nee)* (female sales assistant) or **sprzedawca** *(spshe-daf-tsa)* (male sales assistant).

- **Czy mogę w czymś pomóc?** *(chih mo-ge fchihmsh' po-moots)* (How can I help you?)
- **Nie, dziękuję. Tylko się rozglądam** *(n'ye dj'yen-koo-ye tihl-ko sh'ye roz-glon-dam)* (No, thank you. I'm just looking around)
- **Proszę mi powiedzeć, jak będzie pan/pani czegoś potrzebować** *(pro-she mee po-vye-dj'yech' yag ben'-dj'ye pan/pa-n'ee che-gosh' pot-she-bo-vach')* (Please let me know if you need any help) – formal, to a man/woman
- **Jaki rozmiar?** *(ya-kee roz-myar)* (What size?)
- **Czy chce pan/pani przymierzyć?** *(chih htse pan/pa-n'ee pshih-mye-zhi-hch')* (Do you want to try it on?) – formal, to a man/woman

In shopping situations, you need to speak formally so as not to risk offending someone. You need to use **pan** *(pan)*, **pani** *(pa-n'ee)* or **państwo** *(pan'-stfo)* to address a man, a woman or a group of people, respectively. You can find more on speaking formally and informally in Chapter 3.

Sometimes you may require some help and here is how you can ask for it:

- **Przepraszam, czy może mi pan/pani pomóc?** *(pshe-pra-sham chih mo-zhe mee pan/pa-n'ee po-moots)* (Excuse me, can you help me?) – formal, to a man/woman
- **Czy mogę przymierzyć?** *(chih mo-ge pshih-mye-zhihch')* (Can I try it on?)
- **Czy mogę prosić większy/mniejszy rozmiar?** *(chih mo-ge pro-sh'eech' vyenk-shih/mn'yey-shih roz-myar)* (Can I have a bigger/smaller size, please?)
- **Czy może mi pani przynieść inny kolor?** *(chih mo-zhe mee pa-n'ee pshih-n'yesh'ch' in-nih ko-lor)* (Can you bring me a different colour?) – formal, to a woman
- **Gdzie jest przymierzalnia?** *(gdj'ye yest pshih-mye-zhal-n'ya)* (Where is the fitting room?)
- **Ten sweter jest za duży/za mały** *(ten sfe-ter yezd za doo-zhih/za ma-wih)* (This sweater is too big/small)
- **Ta spódnica jest za ciasna/za luźna** *(ta spoo-dn'ee-tsa yezd za ch'ya-sna/za looz'-na)* (This skirt is too tight/loose)

Shopping now and then

In most shops the sales assistants are very friendly and helpful. They'll offer you their advice if you can't make up your mind or gladly bring you yet another pair of jeans to try on. Indeed, the whole experience can feel like personal shopping! With one major difference – all that service at no extra cost! So, take this opportunity and shop till you drop!

In some shops, however, you may notice that the sales assistants are not exceptionally helpful or friendly and hardly ever smile. This attitude to clients is an old relic of the Communist era when all goods were very limited and shop shelves stayed virtually empty. It was the salespeople who had access to goods and having such power in their hands they felt no need to go out of their way to be nice to anyone.

Talkin' the Talk

Audio track 14: Anna (*an-na*) has just found a nice dress for the party. She goes to ask the shop assistant for the right size.

Sales assistant: **Czy mogę w czymś pomóc?**
(chih mo-ge fchihmsh' po-moots)
Can I help you?

Anna: **Tak. Podoba mi się ta sukienka. Czy jest rozmiar 38?**
(tak po-do-ba mee sh'ye ta soo-kyen-ka chih yest roz-myar tshih-dj'yesh'-ch'ee o-sh'yem)
Yes. I like this dress. Do you have [it in] size 38?

Sales assistant: **Już sprawdzam.**
(yoosh sprav-dzam)
Let me check.

Po chwili *(po hfee-lee)* (After a while)

Jest. Proszę bardzo.
(yest pro-she bar-dzo)
Yes, we have it [in stock]. Here it is.

Anna: **Czy mogę przymierzyć?**
(chih mo-ge pshih-mye-zhihch')
Can I try it on?

Sales assistant: **Ależ oczywiście.**
(alesh o-chih-veesh'-ch'ye)
But of course.

Anna: **A gdzie jest przymierzalnia?**
(a gdj'ye yest pshih-mye-zhal-n'ya)
And where is the fitting room?

Sales assistant: **Tam, po prawej stronie.**
(tam po pra-vey stro-n'ye)
There, on the right-hand side.

A few minutes later Anna comes out of the fitting room with the dress on.

Sales assistant: **I jak?**
(ee yak)
And? How is it?

Anna: **Niestety, jest za duża.**
(n'yes-te-tih yezd za-doo-zha)
Unfortunately, it's too big.

Sales assistant: **Podać mniejszy rozmiar?**
(po-dach' mn'yey-shih roz-myar)
Would you like a smaller size?

Anna: **Tak, poproszę.**
(tak po-pro-she)
Yes, please.

A few minutes later:

Anna: **Ten rozmiar pasuje idealnie. Biorę ją.**
(ten roz-myar pa-soo-ye ee-de-al-n'ye byo-re yohN)
This size fits perfectly. I'll take it.

Words to Know

pomóc	*po-moots*	to help
rozglądać się	*roz-glon-dach' sh'ye*	to look around/to browse
potrzebować	*po-tshe-bo-vach'*	to need
podoba mi się . . .	*po-do-ba mee sh'ye*	I like . . .
już sprawdzam	*yoosh sprav-dzam*	let me check
przymierzyć	*pshih-mye-zhihch'*	to try on
przymierzalnia	*pshih-mye-zhal-n'ya*	fitting room
i jak?	*ee yak*	and how is it?
za mały	*za ma-wih*	too small
za duży	*za doo-zhih*	too big
mniejszy rozmiar	*mn'yey-shih roz-myar*	smaller size
większy rozmiar	*vyenk-shih roz-myar*	bigger size
pasować	*pa-so-vach'*	to fit/suit
biorę go/ją/je	*byo-re go/yohN/ye*	I'll take it (masculine/feminine/plural)

Colour me Polish

When picking out new clothes, what's more important than finding the right colour? Table 6-2 gives you the basic **kolory** *(ko-lo-rih)* (colours) in Polish.

Table 6-2 Colours

Colour	*Polish*	*Pronunciation*
black	czarny	*char-ny*
blue	niebieski	*n'ye-byes-kee*
brown	brązowy	*brohN-zo-vih*
grey	szary	*sha-rih*
green	zielony	*z'ye-lo-nih*
light blue	błękitny	*bwen-keet-nih*
navy blue	granatowy	*gra-na-to-vih*
orange	pomarańczowy	*po-ma-ran'-cho-vih*
pink	różowy	*roo-zho-vy*
red	czerwony	*cher-vo-nih*
violet	fioletowy	*fyo-le-to-vih*
white	biały	*bya-wih*
yellow	żółty	*zhoow-tih*

If you think that the green of your new blouse is a bit too green and you want something lighter, you simply add the prefix **jasno-** *(yas-no)* (light) to have *light green*: **jasnozielony** *(ya-sno-z'ye-lo-nih)*. Add **ciemno-** *(ch'yem-no)* to form *dark green*: **ciemnozielony** *(ch'yem-no-z'ye-lo-nih)*. You can use **jasno** or **ciemno** for: *It's dark/light in here*, **Ciemno/Jasno tutaj** *(chyem-no/yas-no too-tay)* as well.

Colours are adjectives. Chapter 2 tells you how to fit them into sentences.

Checking fabrics and patterns

Whether you're buying a scarf or an expensive suit, it's always good to know what fabric it's made from. See some vocabulary in action:

- **Czy te buty są skórzane?** *(chih te boo-tih sohN skoo-zha-ne)* (Are these leather shoes?)
- **Z czego jest ta sukienka? Z jedwabiu?** *(sche-go yest ta soo-kyen-ka zyed-va-byoo)* (What is this dress made from? Is it silk?)

- **Z bawełny i poliestru** *(zba-vew-nih ee po-lee-es-troo)* (It's [made from] cotton and polyester)
- **Czy te spodnie są wełniane?** *(chih te spod-n'ye sohN vew-n'ya-ne)* (Are these woollen trousers?)
- **Jest 80 procent wełny i 20 procent nylonu** *(yest o-sh'yem-dj'ye-sh'yont pro-tsend vew-nih ee dva-dj'yesh'-ch'ya pro-tsent nih-lo-noo)* (There's 80 per cent wool and 20 per cent nylon [in this material])

You can talk about patterns using these terms:

- Checkered: **w kratkę** *(fkrat-ke)*
- Dotted: **w groszki** *(vgrosh-kee)* (literally: in big dots)
- Flowered: **w kwiaty** *(fkfya-tih)* (literally: in flowers)
- Plain, no pattern: **gładki** *(gwat-kee)*
- Polka dots: **w kropki** *(fkrop-kee)* (literally: in polka dots)
- Striped: **w paski** *(fpas-kee)* (literally: in stripes)

Identifying yourself by what you're wearing

If you arrange to meet up in a busy place with somebody you've never seen face to face, the verb **mieć na sobie** *(myech' na so-bye)* (to be wearing) can come in handy: **Mam na sobie dżinsy i czarną skórzaną kurtkę** *(mam na so-bye djeen-sih ee char-nohn skoo-zha-nohN koor-tke)* (I'm wearing jeans and a black leather jacket).

Also useful is the verb *to wear*, which is **nosić** *(no-sh'eech')*. Here are some examples:

- **Do pracy zwykle noszę garnitur i koszulę** *(do pra-tsih zvih-kle no-she gar-n'ee-toor ee ko-shoo-le)* (I usually wear a suit and a shirt to work)
- **W domu zawsze noszę coś na luzie** *(vdo-moo zaf-she no-she tsosh' na loo-z'ye)* (At home I always wear something casual)

Both **nosić** and **mieć na sobie** are followed by the accusative case. You can go back to Chapter 5 for more details on the noun and adjective endings.

Making Comparisons: Good, Better, Best and More

Polish, just like English, has three degrees of adjectival comparison: positive, comparative and superlative: for example, **młody**, **młodszy** and **najmłodszy** *(mwo-dih mwot-shih nay-mwot-shih)* (young, younger and youngest).

Comparing with the comparative degree

To form the comparative degree of a word, you insert the suffix **-sz-** in between the stem (the main part of a word) and the adjectival ending (**-y**/**-i** for masculine, **-a** for feminine, **-e** for neuter):

- nowy becomes now**sz**y *(no-vih nof-shih)* (new, newer)
- gruba becomes grub**sz**a *(groo-ba groop-sha)* (fat/thick, fatter/thicker)
- bogate becomes bogat**sz**e *(bo-ga-te bo-gat she)* (rich, richer)

All the following examples present the masculine form only. Remember, feminine and neuter adjectives follow exactly the same pattern.

When the stem ends in two consonants, you use the longer suffix **-iejsz**, which breaks the consonant cluster and helps you to pronounce it:

- ład**n**y becomes ładn**iejsz**y *(wad-nih wad-n'yey-shih)* (pretty, prettier)
- trud**n**y becomes trudn**iejsz**y *(trood-nih trood-n'yey-shih)* (difficult, more difficult)
- smut**n**y becomes smutn**iejsz**y *(smoot-nih smoot-n'yey-shih)* (sad, sadder)

Adjectives with their stem ending in **-k-**, **-ek-** or **-ok-** lose these suffixes before adding the **-sz-** comparative:

- krót**k**i becomes krót**sz**y *(kroot-kee kroot-shih)* (short, shorter)
- szer**ok**i becomes szer**sz**y *(she-ro-kee sher-shih)* (wide, wider)

You may also see some irregularities within the stem itself. These are called alternations and here are the most common ones:

- miły becomes milszy (**ł** changes to **l**) *(mee-wih meel-shih)* (nice, nicer)
- dro**g**i becomes dro**ż**szy (**g** changes to **ż**) *(dro-gee drosh-shih)* (expensive, more expensive)

- **tani** becomes **tańszy** (**n** changes to **ń**) *(ta-n'ee tan'-shih)* (cheap, cheaper)
- **niski** becomes **niższy** (**s** changes to **ż**) *(n'ees-kee n'eesh-shih)* (short, shorter [to describe a person])

For many adjectives, you need to use **bardziej** *(bar-dj'yey)* (more) or **mniej** *(mn'yey)* (less) to form the comparative:

- **zajęty, bardziej zajęty** *(za-yen-tih bar-dj'yey za-yen-tih)* (busy, busier) – literally: more busy
- **interesujący, mniej interesujący** *(een-te-re-soo-yon-tsih mn'yey een-te-re-soo-yon-tsih)* (interesting, less interesting)

This pattern works for borrowings (words that are taken from other languages, many of which you'll recognise from the English), longer adjectives and adjectives formed from verbs. Unfortunately, no rule can help you to determine which adjective is long enough to use this pattern. Your best bet is to try it yourself and see whether it works.

Besting the superlative degree

The superlative is formed by adding the prefix **naj-** to the comparative degree:

- **ładniejszy** becomes **najładniejszy** *(wad-n'yey-shih nay-wad-n'yey-shih)* (prettier, prettiest)
- **milszy** becomes **najmilszy** *(meel-shih nay-meel-shih)* (nicer, nicest)
- **bardziej zajęty** becomes **najbardziej zajęty** *(bar-dj'yey za-yen-tih nay-bar-dj'yey za-yen-tih)* (busier, busiest)

Dealing with irregular comparatives and superlatives

Following are the most-used irregular adjectives.Your best bet is to learn them by heart:

- **dobry, lepszy, najlepszy** *(dob-rih lep-shih nay-lep-shih)* (good, better, best)
- **zły, gorszy, najgorszy** *(zwih gor-shih nay-gor-shih)* (bad, worse, worst)

- **duży, większy, największy** *(doo-zhih vyenk-shih nay-vyenk-shih)* (big, bigger, biggest)
- **mały, mniejszy, najmniejszy** *(ma-wih mn'yey-shih nay-mn'yey-shih)* (small, smaller, smallest)

Here are some of these adjectives in action:

- **Ten sweter jest lepszy niż mój** *(ten sfe-ter yest lep-shih n'eesh mooy)* (This sweater is better than mine)
- **Ten hotel jest najgorszy ze wszystkich** *(ten ho-tel yest nay-gor-shih ze fshih-stkeeh)* (This hotel is the worst of all)

Paying Compliments

It's always good to have someone to advise you when you're not sure whether **kupić czy nie kupić** *(koo-peech' chih n'ye koo-peech')* (to buy or not to buy). The following phrases are ones you may hear or offer when trying on clothes:

- **Bardzo ładnie wyglądasz w tej sukience** *(bar-dzo wad-n'ye vih-glon-dash ftey soo-kyen-tse)* (You look very nice in that dress)
- **Do twarzy ci w tym kolorze** *(do tfa-zhih ch'ee ftihm ko-lo-zhe)* (This colour suits you)
- **Masz świetne dżinsy** *(mash sh'fyet-ne dj'een-sih)* (You have great jeans)
- **Podoba mi się twój krawat** *(po-do-ba mee sh'ye tfooy kra-vat)* (I like your tie)

The last sentence uses **podobać się** *(po-do-bach' sh'ye)* (to like). In Chapter 8, I talk about **lubić** *(loo-beech')*, which also means *to like*. Unfortunately, although they mean the same, you can't use these verbs interchangeably. You use **lubić** for food, people and places you know quite well or have known for quite some time (and like, of course):

- **Lubię pierogi** *(loo-bye pye-ro-gee)* (I like Polish dumplings)
- **Lubię Alicję** *(loo-bye a-lee-tsye)* (I like Alicja)
- **Lubię Kraków** *(loo-bye kra-koof)* (I like Kraków) [It's a city you know well]

However, if you're sharing your first impression of something, such as a new film, book or city, or you're saying that you fancy someone, you use **podobać się** *(po-do-bach' sh'ye)*:

- **Podoba mi się ta wystawa** *(po-do-ba mee sh'ye ta vih-sta-va)* (I like this exhibition) [One you've never seen before]
- **Podoba mi się tutaj** *(po-do-ba mee sh'ye too-tay)* (I like it in here)
- **Podoba ci się Arek?** *(po-do-ba ch'ee sh'ye a-rek)* (Do you like/fancy Arek?)
- **Podoba mi się Kraków** *(po-do-ba mee sh'ye kra-koof)* (I like Kraków) [Sharing your first impression of the city]

Talkin' the Talk

At last, Natalia *(na-ta-lya)* has found a nice blouse which she's trying on.

Anna: **I jak?**
(ee yak)
And? How is it?

Natalia: **Sama nie wiem . . . Jak myślisz?**
(sa-ma n'ye vyem yak mihsh'-leesh)
I'm not sure . . . What do you think?

Anna: **Moim zdaniem wyglądasz super!**
(mo-yeem zda-n'yem vih-glon-dash soo-per)
In my opinion, you look great!

Natalia: **A kolor ci się podoba?**
(a ko-lor ch'ee sh'ye po-do-ba)
And do you like the colour?

Anna: **Bardzo dobrze ci w tym kolorze!**
(bar-dzo dob-zhe ch'ee ftihm ko-lo-zhe)
That colour suits you very well!

Natalia: **Dobrze, to idę do kasy!**
(dob-zhe to ee-de do ka-sih)
Good, I'm going to the checkout then.

Words to know

sam/sama nie wiem	*sam/sa-ma n'ye vyem*	I'm not sure (man/woman)
jak myślisz?	*yak mihsh'-leesh*	what do you think?
moim zdaniem	*mo-eem zda-n'yem*	in my opinion
podoba ci się?	*po-do-ba ch'ee sh'ye*	do you like it?
kasa	*ka-sa*	checkout

You arrange to meet a client in a busy place. You've never seen this client face-to-face. With so many people around you, you're struggling to find each other and you have no other choice but to call him/her and describe what you're wearing. Look at Figure 6-1 and start with the following:

Mam na sobie (I'm wearing) . . .

Figure 6-1: Describe what you're wearing.

Answer key:

Mężczyzna: Mam na sobie marynarkę, koszulę, spodnie, krawat, skórzane buty i skórzany pasek. (The man: I'm wearing a jacket, shirt, trousers, tie, leather shoes and leather belt)

Kobieta: Mam na sobie żakiet, bluzkę, spódnicę i skórzane szpilki. (The woman: I'm wearing a jacket, blouse, skirt and leather stilettos)

Chapter 7

Going Out on the Town

In This Chapter

- Telling the time and describing parts of the day
- Introducing the days of the week
- Responding to and proffering invitations
- Getting out and enjoying yourself

In this chapter, you find out how to enjoy yourself the Polish way. Whether you like dancing and drinking until the wee hours, touring museums and galleries or catching a concert or play, you can find it all in Poland – at least in the bigger cities. You won't stand a chance of getting bored. Take every opportunity to explore Polish theatres, cinemas, galleries, comedy shows and parties and you won't regret it!

Understanding that Timing Is Everything

When it comes to telling the time in Polish, you can use two systems: the 'old-fashioned' way (also called *unofficial*) that uses the 12-hour clock, or the official 24-hour format (commonly known as *military time* in English). The 12-hour format dominates informal situations, while the 24-hour clock is used for airline, train and bus timetables as well as theatre and cinema schedules.

The time-telling method you adopt is a matter of personal choice. However, it makes sense to familiarise yourself with both systems so that you can use and understand each one of them.

Counting ordinal numbers

Polish speakers use ordinal numbers to tell the time. For instance, they call 3 a.m. 'the 3rd hour' (**trzecia**) *(t-she-ch'ya)* and 3 p.m. is actually 'the 15th hour' (**piętnasta**) *(pyet-nas-ta)*. Table 7-1 shows the ordinal numbers you need to know to become a master in telling the time the Polish way. (Chapter 4 lists the cardinal numbers – basic counting numbers.)

Table 7-1 Ordinal Numbers for Telling Time

Hour	*To tell the time, use . . .*	*To say at what time, use . . .*	*Hour*	*To tell the time, use . . .*	*To say at what time, use . . .*
1	pierwsza *(pyer-fsha)*	o pierwszej *(o pyer-fshey)*	13	trzynasta *(t-shih-nas-ta)*	o trzynastej *(o t-shih-nas-tey)*
2	druga *(droo-ga)*	o drugiej *(o droo-gyey)*	14	czternasta *(chter-nas-ta)*	o czternastej *(o chter-nas-tey)*
3	trzecia *(t-she-ch'ya)*	o trzeciej *(o t-she-ch'yey)*	15	piętnasta *(pye-tnas-ta)*	o piętnastej *(o pye-tnas-tey)*
4	czwarta *(chfar-ta)*	o czwartej *(o chfar-tey)*	16	szesnasta *(shes-nas-ta)*	o szesnastej *(o shes-nas-tey)*
5	piąta *(pyon-ta)*	o piątej *(o pyon-tey)*	17	siedemnasta *(sh'ye-dem-nas-ta)*	o siedemnastej *(o sh'ye-dem-nas-tey)*
6	szósta *(shoos-ta)*	o szóstej *(o shoos-tey)*	18	osiemnasta *(o-sh'yem-nas-ta)*	o osiemnastej *(o o-sh'yem-nas-tey)*
7	siódma *(sh'ood-ma)*	o siódmej *(o sh'ood-mey)*	19	dziewiętnasta *(dj'ye-vyet-nas-ta)*	o dziewiętnastej *(o dj'ye-vyet-nas-tey)*
8	ósma *(oos-ma)*	o ósmej *(o oos-mey)*	20	dwudziesta *(dvoo-dj'yes-ta)*	o dwudziestej *(o dvoo-dj'yes-tey)*

Hour	To tell the time, use . . .	To say at what time, use . . .	Hour	To tell the time, use . . .	To say at what time, use . . .
9	dziewiąta *(dj'ye-vyon-ta)*	o dziewiątej *(o dj'ye-vyon-tey)*	21	dwudziesta pierwsza *(dvoo-dj'yes ta p'yer-fsha)*	o dwudziestej pierwszej *(o dvoo-dj'yes-tey p'yer-fshey)*
10	dziesiąta *(dj'ye-sh'yon-ta)*	o dziesiątej *(o dj'ye-sh'yon-tey)*	22	dwudziesta druga *(dvoo-dj'yes-ta droo-ga)*	o dwudziestej drugiej *(o dvoo-dj'yes-tey droo-gyey)*
11	jedenasta *(ye-de-nas-ta)*	o jedenastej *(o ye-de-nas-tey)*	23	dwudziesta trzecia *(dvoo-dj'yes-ta t-she-ch'ya)*	o dwudziestej trzeciej *(o dvoo-dj'yes-tey t-she-ch'yey)*
12	dwunasta *(dvoo-nas-ta)*	o dwunastej *(o dvoo-nas-tey)*	24	dwudziesta czwarta *(dvoo-dj'yes ta chfar-ta)*	o dwudziestej czwartej *(o dvoo-dj'yes-tey chfar-tey)*

On the hour

Table 7-1 shows you how to say both *it's 4 o'clock*, which is **czwarta** *(chfar-ta)*, and *at 4 o'clock*, which is **o czwartej** *(o chfar-tey)*. To say *at . . . o'clock* you just need to put **o** at the very beginning and replace the ending **-a** *(a)* of the hour with **-ej** *(ey)*:

> **Jadę do Paryża o piętnastej trzydzieści** *(ya-de do pa-rih-zha o pyet-nas-tey t-shih -dj'yesh'-ch'ee)* (I'm going to Paris at fifteen (hundred hours) thirty)

Note: **Druga** *(droo-ga)* (2) becomes **o drugiej** *(o droo-gyey)* with an extra **i** just before the ending **-ej**.

- **Która godzina? (Jest) dokładnie dziesiąta** *(ktoo-ra go-dj'ee-na yest do-kwad-n'ye dj'ye-sh'yon-ta)* (What time is it? It's 10 a.m. on the dot)

- **O której godzinie idziemy na basen? O dziesiątej rano** *(o ktoo-rey go-dj'ee-n'ye ee-dj'ye-mih na na-ba-sen o dj'ye-sh'yon-tey ra-no)* (What time are we going to the pool? At 10 a.m.)

If you want to be clear about whether the time is a.m. or p.m., you can clarify by adding **rano** *(ra-no)*, **wieczorem** *(vye-cho-rem)* or **w nocy** *(vno-tsih)* (literally: in the morning, in the evening, at night). In the case of 1 p.m. to 5 p.m., you can say **po południu** *(po po-wood-n'yoo)* (in the afternoon).

A few minutes after

Sometimes you need to express time that isn't directly on the hour.

In the case of minutes past the hour, you just say the cardinal (basic counting) number to express minutes followed by the preposition **po** (after/past) and add the ordinal hour with the ending **-ej:**

- **Spotykamy się dziesięć po czwartej** *(spo-tih-ka-mih sh'ye dj'ye-sh'yen'ch' po chfar-tey)* (We're meeting at ten [minutes] past four; 4:10 p.m.)
- **Film jest dwadzieścia po piątej** *(feelm yest dva-dj'yesh'-ch'ya po pyon-tey)* (The film is at twenty [minutes] past five; 5:20 p.m.)
- **Sztuka kończy się kwadrans/piętnaście po dziewiątej** *(shtoo-ka kon'-chih sh'ye kfa-drans/pyet-nash'-ch'ye po dj'ye-vyon-tey)* (The play finishes at quarter past nine; fifteen [minutes]/9:15 p.m.) – you can add **wieczorem** *(vye-cho-rem)* here to mean p.m.
- **Spektakl zaczyna się piętnaście po ósmej wieczorem** *(spek-takl za-chih-na sh'ye pyet-nash'-ch'ye po oos-mey vye-cho-rem)* (The play starts at fifteen [minutes] past eight in the evening; 8:15 p.m.)

You don't say *twenty past seventeen* but *twenty past five*. After all, this is the informal way of telling the time. So you can stick to the 12-hour clock. I talk about the 24-hour clock in the later section 'Using the 24-hour clock'.

On the half hour

The half hour gets a little complicated, but as long as you remember that Polish speakers are truly forward thinking you'll be all right. For example, when it's 5:30 a.m., you say that it's half an hour before 6 a.m. rather than half an hour after 5 a.m. A new phrase for you to learn is **o wpół do** *(o fpoow do)* – literally: at half to (the next hour).

- **Idę do teatru o wpół do siódmej** *(ee-de do te-a-troo o fpoow do sh'yood-mey)* (I'm going to the theatre at half to seven; 6:30 p.m.)
- **Możemy pójść na siłownię o wpół do ósmej wieczorem** *(mo-zhe-mih pooysh'ch' na sh'ee-wov-n'ye o fpoow do oos-mey vye-cho-rem)* (We can go to the gym at half to eight in the evening; 7:30 p.m.)

A few minutes before

To say minutes before the hour, Polish speakers say **za** (in) followed by the number of minutes (basic counting number) and then say the hour (ordinal number ending in **-a**); for example, **za pięć dziewiąta** *(za pyen'ch' dj'ye-vyon-ta)* (in five [minutes to] nine o'clock; 8:55 a.m.).

- **Spotykamy się za dziesięć piąta** *(spo-tih-ka-mih sh'ye za dj'ye-sh'yen'ch' pyon-ta)* (We're meeting at ten to five; 4:50 p.m.)
- **Możesz za piętnaście/kwadrans ósma?** *(mo-zhezh za pyet-nash'-ch'ye/kfa-drans oo-sma)* (Can you make it at fifteen/quarter to eight; 7.45 a.m.?)
- **Pasuje ci za dwadzieścia trzecia?** *(pa-soo-ye ch'ee za dva-dj'yesh'-ch'ya t-she-ch'ya)* (Does twenty to three suit you; 2.40 p.m.?)

Talkin' the Talk

Dominika *(do-mee-n'ee-ka)* is a bit nervous because she's been waiting for her husband, **Tomasz** *(to-mash)*, for a good 30 minutes, and the concert starts in five minutes. Finally she sees him coming

Dominika: **No jesteś nareszcie!**
(no yes-tesh' na-resh-ch'ye)
You're here at last!

Tomasz: **Przepraszam za spóźnienie.**
(pshe-pra-sham za spooz'-n'ye-n'ye)
I'm sorry for being late.

Dominika: **Czy wiesz, która jest godzina? Czekam tu już pół godziny!**
(chih vyesh ktoo-ra yezd go-dj'ee-na che-kam too yoosh poow go-dj'ee-nih)
Do you know the time? I've been waiting here for half an hour!

Tomasz: **Przepraszam, ale nie mam zegarka i nie wiedziałem, że już jest tak późno.**
(pshe-pra-sham ale n'ye mam ze-gar-ka ee n'ye vye-dj'ya-wem zhe yoosh yest tak pooz'-no)
I'm sorry but I don't have a watch and I didn't know it was so late already.

Dominika: **Koncert zaczyna się za pięć minut, ale na szczęście mamy już bilety.**
(kon-tserd za-chih-na sh'ye za pyen'ch' mee-noot a-le na shchehN-sh'ch'ye ma-mih yoozh bee-le-tih)
The concert starts in five minutes but, luckily, we already have tickets.

Tomasz: **Gdzie jest szatnia?**
(gdj'ye yest shat-n'ya)
Where is the cloakroom?

Dominika: **Na parterze po prawej stronie.**
(na par-te-zhe po pra-vey stro-n'ye)
On the ground floor on the right.

Words to Know

no jesteś nareszcie	*no yes-tesh' na-resh-ch'ye*	you're here at last
przepraszam za spóźnienie	*pshe-pra-sham za spooz'-n'ye-n'ye*	sorry I'm late
czekam tu już pół godziny	*che-kam too yoosh poow go-dj'ee-nih*	I've been waiting here for half an hour
już tak późno?	*yoosh tak pooz'-no*	is it that late already?
na szczęście	*na shchehN-sh'ch'ye*	luckily
szatnia	*shat-n'ya*	cloakroom
na parterze	*na par-te-zhe*	on the ground floor

Using the 24-hour clock

The 24-hour clock is used for airline, train and bus timetables, as well as theatre and cinema schedules, where it's crucial to avoid any chance of misunderstanding.

In this system everything is expressed in terms of minutes after the hour, with no room for phrases like half past or quarter to or after the hour. You always need to start with the hour, followed by the minutes:

- **Jest czternasta piętnaście** *(yest chter-nas-ta pyet-nash'-ch'ye)* (It's fourteen [hundred hours] fifteen; 14:15), which corresponds to 2:15 p.m.
- **Jest trzecia trzydzieści** *(yest t-she-ch'ya t-shih-dj'yesh'-ch'ee)* (It's three thirty; 3:30), which is 3:30 a.m.
- **Jest piętnasta trzydzieści** *(yest pyet-nas-ta t-shih-dj'yesh'-ch'ee)* (It's fifteen [hundred hours] thirty; 15:30), which is 3:30 p.m.

When talking about events happening at a certain hour, you just need to add an **o** *(o)* before the hour and change the hour's ending to **-ej** *(ey)*, as shown in Table 7-1 earlier in this chapter.

- **Jadę do Paryża o piętnastej trzydzieści** *(ya-de do pa-rih-zha o pyet-nas-tey t-shih-dj'yesh'-ch'ee)* (I'm going to Paris at fifteen [hundred hours] thirty), which is 3.30 p.m.

Splitting the day and talking about the future

Here is how a day gets split in Polish:

- **rano** *(ra-no)* (in the morning)
- **przed południem** *(pshet po-wood-n'yem)* (before midday) – it's more or less between 11 a.m. and 12 p.m.
- **w południe** *(fpo-wood-n'ye)* (at midday)
- **po południu** *(po po-wood-n'yoo)* (in the afternoon)
- **wieczorem** *(vye-cho-rem)* (in the evening)
- **w nocy** *(vno-tsih)* (at night)
- **o północy** *(o poow-no-tsih)* (at midnight)

Sometimes, you may need to say the approximate time, as in the following examples:

- **w przyszłym/w następnym tygodniu** *(fpshih-shwihm/vnas-tem-pnihm tih-god-n'yoo)* (next week)
- **w zeszłym/w ubiegłym miesiącu** *(vzesh-wihm/voo-byeg-wihm mye-sh'yon-tsoo)* (last month)
- **w tym roku** *(ftihm ro-koo)* (this year)
- **dzisiaj wieczorem** *(dj'ee-sh'yay vye-cho-rem)* (tonight) – literally: today in the evening
- **jutro/wczoraj rano** *(yoo-tro/fcho-ray ra-no)* (tomorrow/yesterday in the morning)

Listing the Days of the Week

Being able to read a theatre or cinema timetable is all well and good, but if you're meeting friends for a film on Thursday, you need to get yourself acquainted with the names of **dni tygodnia** *(dn'ee tih-god-n'ya)* (days of the week).

Polish **dni tygodnia** don't look similar to their English equivalents at all but you may notice some similarities to Polish numbers and other words:

- **w poniedziałek** *(fpo-n'ye-dj'ya-wek)* (on Monday) – Monday is the day after – **po** *(po)* (after) – Sunday – **niedzieli** *(n'ye-dj'ye-lee)*
- **we wtorek** *(ve-fto-rek)* (on Tuesday)
- **w środę** *(fsh'ro-de)* (on Wednesday) – the word of the middle day of the week is related to the expression **w środku** *(fsh'rot-koo)* (inside, in the middle)
- **w czwartek** *(fchfar-tek)* (on Thursday) – **cztery** *(chte-rih)* is the number 4 and Thursday is the fourth day of the week!
- **w piątek** *(fpyon-tek)* (on Friday) – similar to **pięć** *(pyen'ch')*, which is the number 5 in Polish
- **w sobotę** *(fso-bo-te)* (on Saturday)
- **w niedzielę** *(vn'ye-dj'ye-le)* (on Sunday)

Unlike in English, days of the week in Polish are not capitalised.

Inviting and Being Invited

Never miss an opportunity to explore a Polish city with a Polish friend as your guide. Use these phrases to invite someone to accompany you:

- **Może pójdziemy dzisiaj do kina na jakiś dobry film?** *(mo-zhe pooy-dj'ye-mih dj'ee-sh'yay do kee-na na ya-keesh' dob-rih feelm)* (Why don't we go to the cinema to see a good film today?)
- **Proponuję kawę i lody** *(pro-po-noo-ye ka-ve ee lo-dih)* (I suggest [we go for] a coffee and ice cream)
- **Masz ochotę na piwo?** *(mash o-ho-te na pee-vo)* (Do you fancy a beer?)
- **Chcesz pójść na koncert?** *(htsesh pooysh'ch' na kon-tsert)* (Do you want to go to a concert?)
- **Co robisz w piątek wieczorem?** *(tso ro-beesh fpyon-teg vye-cho-rem)* (What are you doing on Friday night?)
- **Masz już jakieś plany na weekend?** *(mash yoosh ya-kyesh' pla-nih na wee-kent)* (Do you have any plans for the weekend yet?)

Whether you're delighted with the idea of dancing the night away or too tired to go to yet another museum, the following expressions can be handy when it comes to accepting or refusing invitations:

- **To dobry pomysł!** *(to dob-rih po-mihsw)* (That's a good idea!)
- **Świetnie! Dlaczego nie?** *(sh'fyet-n'ye dla-che-go n'ye)* (Great! Why not?)
- **Chętnie! Dziękuję za zaproszenie** *(hent-n'ye dj'yen-koo-ye za za-pro-she-n'ye)* (I'd love to! Thank you for the invitation)
- **Jasne!** *(yas-ne)* (Sure!)
- **Niestety, nie mam czasu** *(n'yes-te-tih n'ye mam cha-soo)* (Unfortunately, I don't have time)
- **Dzięki, ale nie mogę** *(dj'en-kee a-le n'ye mo-ge)* (Thanks, but I can't)
- **Jeszcze nie wiem** *(yesh-che n'ye vyem)* (I don't know yet)
- **Może** *(mo-zhe)* (Maybe)

Talkin' the Talk

Audio track 15: Marek *(ma-rek)* wants to go to see a new Polish film. He calls Agata *(a-ga-ta)* to ask her to join him.

Agata: **Słucham?**
(swoo-ham)
Hello?

Marek: **Cześć, tu Marek.**
(chesh'ch' too ma-rek)
Hi! It's Marek.

Agata: **A, cześć! Co słychać?**
(a chesh'ch' tso swih-hach')
Oh, hi! How are you?

Marek: **Wszystko w porządku. Co robisz w piątek wieczorem?**
(fshih-stko fpo-zhont-koo tso ro-beesh fpyon-teg vye-cho-rem) Fine. What are you doing on Friday?

Agata: **Nic specjalnego. Nie mam jeszcze planów. A dlaczego pytasz?**
(n'eets spe-tsyal-ne-go n'ye mam yesh-che pla-noof a dla-che-go pih-tash)
Nothing special. I have no plans as yet. Why do you ask?

Marek: **Może pójdziemy do kina?**
(mo-zhe pooy-dj'ye-mih do kee-na)
Why don't we go to the cinema?

Agata: **Chętnie! A na co?**
(hent-n'ye a na tso)
I'd love to. And what are we going to see? [Literally: and for what?]

Marek: **Proponuję 'Och, Karol!' To świetna polska komedia.**
(pro-po-noo-ye oh ka-rol to sh'fyet-na pol-ska ko-me-dya)
I suggest 'Och, Karol!' That's a great Polish comedy.

Agata: **To dobry pomysł. Gdzie i o której się spotkamy?**
(to dob-rih po-mihsw gdj'ye ee o ktoo-rey sh'ye spot-ka-mih)
Good idea. When and where shall we meet?

Marek: **Film zaczyna się o 19.30, więc może spotkamy się o 18:00 przed kinem? Kupimy bilety, a potem pójdziemy na piwo.**
(feelm za-chih-na sh'ye o dj'ye-vyet-nas-tey t-shih-dj'yesh'-ch'ee vyents mo-zhe spot-ka-mih sh'ye o o-sh'yem-nas-tey pshet kee-nem koo-pee-mih bee-le-tih a po-tem pooy-dj'ye-mih na pee-vo)
The film starts at 7:30 p.m., so shall we meet at 6 p.m. in front of the cinema? We can buy the tickets and then go for a beer.

Agata: **Świetnie! To do zobaczenia w piątek!**
(sh'fyet-n'ye to do zo-ba-che-n'ya fpyon-tek)
Great! See you Friday, then!

Words to Know

może pójdziemy . . .	mo-zhe pooy dj'ye-mih	shall we go . . .
masz ochotę na kino?	mash o-ho-te na kee-no	do you feel like going to the cinema?
nie mam jeszcze planów	n'ye mam yesh-che pla-noof	I have no plans as yet.
gdzie i o której ?	gdj'ye ee o ktoo-rey	when and where?

Making the Most of the Nightlife

If you're not **zbyt zmęczony** *(zbihd zmen-cho-nih)*/**zbyt zmęczona** *(zbihd zmen-cho-na)* (too tired [male/female]) after a whole day of rushing from one museum to another must-see building, you may want get a taste of how Poles entertain themselves at night. If so, you'd better prepare yourself as Polish people love **imprezować** *(eem-pre-zo-vach')* (partying), both in nightclubs and at home.

Polish partying

Much has changed for the better since the end of Communism in Poland in 1989, including a massive growth in possibilities for spending your free time.

However, even today, if you're in a small town or in the countryside, finding a restaurant or a pub open after 10 p.m. might be a challenge. If you're lucky, there may be one cinema, though showing the same film for a number of days! Therefore, if you fancy clubs, galleries or concerts and don't want to risk being stuck at home, go for a bigger city such as **Kraków** *(kra-koof)* or **Warszawa** *(var-sha-va)* when planning your stay in Poland.

Of course, in smaller towns, you may have more luck in finding a private party. During the Communist era, the limited number of pubs, restaurants and social events was mostly reserved for party members. As a result, Polish people became masters of home entertaining. This custom is still very much alive. So make sure you don't miss out on an opportunity for a grand feast at a Polish home!

If you go to a nightclub, be sure to dress smartly. Sports shoes are definitely not acceptable but jeans are just fine in many places. Polish pubs are open **do ostatniego gościa** *(do os-tat-n'ye-go gosh'-ch'ya)* (till the last guest leaves).

If you're invited to a Polish house party (see the nearby sidebar 'Polish partying'), it's customary to take a bottle of vodka or wine. With the drinking goes a lot of eating (very sensible!), so you may want to ask your host **Czy mam coś przynieść?** *(chih mam tsosh' pshih-n'yesh'ch')* (Do you want me to bring anything?) to ensure you don't take something nobody wants to eat or, in the worst case scenario, be the only one arriving empty-handed.

Here are some phrases worth memorising:

- **Dziś wieczorem idziemy do klubu** *(dj'eez' vye-cho-rem ee-dj'ye-mih do kloo-boo)* (Tonight we're going to a club)
- **Idziesz z nami?** *(ee-dj'yezh zna-mee)* (Do you want to join us?) – literally: are you going with us?
- **Mam ochotę potańczyć** *(mam o-ho-te po-tan'-chihch')* (I feel like going to dance)
- **W sobotę organizujemy u nas imprezę. Przyjdziecie?** *(fso-bo-te or-ga-n'ee-zoo-ye-mih oo-nas eem-pre-ze pshihy-dj'ye-ch'ye)* (We're organising a party this Saturday at our place. Will you [plural] come?)
- **Bawimy się do samego rana!** *(ba-vee-mih sh'ye do sa-me-go ra-na)* (We're going to party all night!) – literally: until early morning

Uwaga! Wódka! (Attention! Vodka!)

Although the time when the Polish people drank large quantities of **wódka** *(voot-ka)* (vodka) has all but gone, take it easy if you indulge in Polish vodka – it's 40 per cent alcohol!

Remember, the more you drink, the more you'll be offered to drink! And if you try to refuse, you may find yourself facing **karniak** *(kar-n'yak)*, which is not a single shot, but rather a big glass of vodka!

Common toasts that accompany vodka tasting are **na zdrowie** *(na zdro-vye)* (to your health, also meaning bless you) or **sto lat** *(sto lat)* (100 years, implying that you should live to be 100 years old).

Baw się dobrze! *(baf sh'ye dob'-zhe)* (Have fun!).

Talkin' the Talk

Audio track 16: Paweł *(pa-vew)* has just bought a new flat and decides to throw a party. He invites his best friend, Sylwia *(sihl-vya)*.

Paweł: **W tę sobotę organizuję parapetówkę. Przyjdziesz?**
(fte so-bo-te or-ga-nee-zoo-ye pa-ra-pe-toof-ke pshihy-dj'yesh)
I'm organising a house-warming party. Will you come?

Sylwia: **Oczywiście! Co mam przynieść?**
(o-chih-veesh'-ch'ye tso mam pshih-n'yesh'ch')
Of course! What do you want me to bring?

Paweł: **Może butelkę wina?**
(mo-zhe boo-tel-ke vee-na)
How about a bottle of wine?

Sylwia: **A kto będzie?**
(a kto ben'-dj'ye)?
And who is coming? [Literally: Who will be there?]

Paweł: **Znajomi ze studiów i z pracy. Dużo ludzi. Będzie super zabawa!**
(zna-yo-m'ee ze stoo-dyoof ee spra-tsih doo-zho loo-dj'ee ben'-dj'ye soo-per za-ba-va)
My friends from the uni and from work. Lots of people. It's going to be a great party!

Sylwia: **Będą tańce?**
(ben-dohN tan'-tse)
Are we going to dance?

Paweł: **No pewnie!**
(no pev-n'ye)
Sure!

Sylwia: **A mogę przyjść z kolegą?**
(a mo-ge pshihysh'ch' sko-le-gohN)
And can I come with a [male] friend?

Paweł: **Jasne!**
(yas-ne)
Sure!

Sylwia: **Będziemy na pewno! Już się nie mogę doczekać, kiedy zobaczę twoje nowe mieszkanie!**
ben'-dj'ye-mih na pev-no yoosh sh'ye n'ye mo-ge do-che-kach' kye-dih zo-ba-che tfo-ye no-ve myesh-ka-n'ye)
We'll be there for sure! I can't wait to see your new flat!

Enjoying yourself at shows and events

Before you head out for a day of fun, you need to be able to say and understand when an event is going to take place. Here are a couple of questions you may find useful when arranging outings in Poland:

- **Przepraszam, która (jest) godzina?** *(pshe-pra-sham ktoo-ra yezd go-dj'ee-na)* (Excuse me, what time is it?)
- **Niestety, nie mam zegarka** *(n'yes-te-tih n'ye mam ze-gar-ka)* (Unfortunately, I don't have a watch)
- **O której (godzinie) zaczyna się film?** *(o ktoo-rey go-dj'ee-n'ye za-chih -na sh'ye feelm)* (What time does the film start?)
- **Od której do której jest otwarte muzeum?** *(ot ktoo-rey do ktoo-rey yest ot-far-te moo-ze-oom)* (What are the opening hours of the museum? – literally: from what time to what time is the museum open?)
- **Na którą godzinę mamy rezerwację?** *(na ktoo-rohN go-dj'ee-ne ma-mih re-zer-va-tsye)* (What time is the reservation for?)

Words to Know

imprezować	eem-pre-zo-vach'	to party
baw się dobrze!	baf sh'ye dob'-zhe	have fun!
organizuję parapetówkę	or-ga-nee-zoo-ye pa-ra-pe-toof-ke	I'm throwing a house-warming party
przyjdziesz?	pshihy-dj'yesh	will you (singular) come?
co mam przynieść?	tso mam pshih-n'yesh'ch'	what do you want me to bring?
no pewnie/jasne!	no pev-n'ye/yas-ne	sure
już się nie mogę doczekać	yoosh sh'ye n'ye mo-ge do-che-kach'	I can't wait
będę na pewno	ben-de na pev-no	I'll be there for sure

Whether you're a classical music lover, a film addict or can't live without exhibition openings, theatres or comedy shows, Poland has it all, and more, on offer. The easiest way to find out what's on is by checking local newspaper listings or the Internet. Poland has world-renowned film directors **Polański** *(po-lan'skee)*, **Kieślowski** *(kye-sh'lof-skee)* and **Wajda** *(vay-da)*, and the **Łódzka Szkoła Filmowa** *(woots-ka shko-wa feel-mo-va)* (the Łódź Film School) attracts students from all over the world. If you haven't had a chance to see any Polish films as yet, you can fix that with a visit to a Polish cinema.

Here are some phrases to help you:

- **W którym teatrze grają 'Hamleta'?** *(fktoo-rihm te-a-t-she gra-yohN ha-mle-ta)* (Which theatre is now showing 'Hamlet'?)
- **Ile kosztuje bilet na wieczorne przedstawienie?** *(ee-le kosh-too-ye bee-let na vye-chor-ne pshet-sta-vye-n'ye)* (How much is the ticket for tonight's show?)

- **Mam dwa zaproszenia do galerii** *(mam dva za-pro-she-n'ya do ga-le-ryee)* (I have two invitations to the gallery)
- **Jaki strój obowiązuje?** *(ya-kee strooy o-bo-vyohN-zoo-ye)* (What's the dress code?)
- **Co grają w tym tygodniu w kinie 'Bałtyk'?** *(tso gra-yohN ftihm tih-go-dn'yoo fkee-n'ye baw-tihk)* (What's on in the Baltic cinema this week?)
- **W którym rzędzie siedzimy?** *(fktoo-rihm zhen'-dj'ye sh'ye-dj'ee-mih)* (Which row are we sitting in?)

If speaking Polish all day long gives you a real headache, you'll undoubtedly be happy to know that Polish cinemas screen foreign language films with their original soundtracks, with Polish subtitles. What a nice treat!

Purchasing tickets

You may be pleasantly surprised with the inexpensive ticket prices for the theatre, opera, concerts and other shows in Poland. This is one positive cultural heritage remaining from Communism, when factory workers were taken on compulsory and cheap outings to the opera.

When buying tickets in Polish, these phrases will be useful:

- **Poproszę dwa bilety normalne i jeden ulgowy na sobotę** *(po-pro-she dva bee-le-tih nor-mal-ne ee ye-den ool-go-vih na so-bo-te)* (Can I have two full-price tickets and one discounted ticket for this Saturday)
- **Czy mogę prosić program?** *(chih mo-ge pro-sh'eech' pro-gram)* (Can I have the [show] programme?)
- **Niestety, nie ma już biletów na dzisiejszy wieczór** *(n'yes-te-tih n'ye ma yoozh bee-le-toof na dj'ee-shey-shih vye-choor)* (Unfortunately, we have no tickets left for tonight's show)
- **Czy są jeszcze wolne miejsca na dzisiejszy spektakl?** *(chih sohN yesh-che vol-ne myey-stsa na dj'ee-sh'yey-shih spek-takl)* (Do you have any seats left for tonight's play?)
- **Ile trwa przedstawienie?** *(ee-le trfa pshet-sta-vye-n'ye)* (How long is the show?)

Dressing well and behaving well

When going to a theatre or opera in Poland, you should dress smartly. Don't worry, nobody expects you to wear a dinner-jacket or evening gown, but save your jeans and T-shirts for less formal occasions, such as going to a pop concert or the cinema.

Taking snacks or drinks into a play or opera is unacceptable. Such behaviour is seen as disrespectful to the actors and the people sitting next to you. They won't hesitate to tell you off at the slightest crackling of sweets or crisps. Even a short exchange of opinions with your neighbour about the play should be avoided and you may be given an annoyed look and hear 'Shhh'.

Talkin' the Talk

Audio track 17: Simon is at the **kasa biletowa** *(ka-sa bee-le-to-va)* (ticket office) **w Teatrze Wielkim w Warszawie** *(fte-a-t-she vyel-keem vvar-sha-vye)* (the Great Theatre in Warsaw). He wants to purchase two tickets for this Saturday from the **kasjerka** (female cashier).

Simon: **Poproszę dwa bilety normalne na 'Madame Butterfly'.**
(po-pro-she dva bee-le-tih nor-mal-ne na ma-dam ba-ter-flay)
Can I have two full-price tickets for 'Madame Butterfly', please.

Cashier: **Na kiedy?**
(na kye-dih)
When for?

Simon: **Na tę sobotę o dwudziestej (20:00).**
(na te so-bo-te o dvoo-dj'yes-tey)
For this Saturday at 8 p.m., please.

Cashier: **Bardzo mi przykro, ale wszystkie bilety są już wyprzedane. Ale mamy jeszcze wolne miejsca na przedstawienie o siedemnastej trzydzieści (17:30).**
(bar-dzo mee pshih-kro ale fshihs-tkye bee-le-tih sohN yoozh vih-pshe-da-ne a-le ma-mih yesh-che vol-ne myeys-tsa na pshet-sta-vye-n'ye o sh'ye-dem-nas-tey tshih-dj'yesh'-ch'ee)
I'm really sorry but all tickets are sold out. However, we still have seats available for the 5:30 p.m. show.

Simon: **W którym rzędzie?**
(fktoo-rihm zhen'-dj'ye)
In which row?

Cashier: **W czwartym, na samym środku.**
(fchfar-tihm na sa-mihm sh'rot-koo)
Row four, right in the middle.

Simon: **Dobrze, to poproszę dwa bilety na to wcześniejsze przedstawienie. Czy mogę zapłacić kartą?**
(dob-zhe to po-pro-she dva bee-le-tih na to fchesh'-n'yey-she pshet-sta-vye-n'ye chih mo-ge za-pwa-ch'eech' kar-tohN)
Okay. I'll take two tickets for the earlier show. Can I pay by card?

Cashier: **Tak, oczywiście. Tu są pana bilety. Spektakl zaczyna się punktualnie o wpół do szóstej (17.30).**
(tak o-chih-veesh'-ch'ye too sohN pa-na bee-le-tih spek-takl za-chih-na sh'ye poon-ktoo-al-n'ye o fpoow do shoos-tey)
Yes, of course. Here are your tickets. The show starts at 5:30 p.m. on the dot.

Words to Know

na kiedy	*na kye-dih*	for when
bardzo mi przykro	*bar-dzo mee pshih-kro*	I'm really sorry
mamy jeszcze wolne miejsca	*ma-mih yesh-che vol-ne myeys-tsa*	we still have some seats available
w którym rzędzie	*fktoo-rihm zhen'-dj'ye*	in which row
zaczyna się	*za-chih-na sh'ye*	it starts
punktualnie	*poon-ktoo-al-n'ye*	on the dot

Discussing the show

After attending a good party or enjoying a new exhibition, you may want to share your opinion with your friends. Here are some useful phrases:

- **Bawiłem się/Bawiłam się doskonale!** *(ba-wee-wem sh'ye/ba-wee-wam sh'ye dos ko-na-le)* (I had a really good time!) – male/female
- **Ta wystawa była znakomita** *(ta vihs-ta-va bih-wa zna-ko-mee-ta)* (This exhibition was superb)
- **Aktorzy grali wspaniale** *(a-kto-zhih gra-lee fspa-n'ya-le)* (The actors were excellent)
- **Naprawdę warto to zobaczyć** *(na-prav-de var-to to zo-ba-chihch')* (It's really worth seeing)
- **W ogóle mi się nie podobało** *(vo-goo-le mee sh'ye n'ye po-do-ba-wo)* (I didn't like it at all)
- **Nudziło mi się** *(noo-dj'ee-wo mee sh'ye)* (I was bored)
- **Strata czasu** *(stra-ta cha-soo)* (A waste of time)
- **I jak ci się podobało?** *(ee yak ch'ee sh'ye po-do-ba-wo)* (And how did you like it?)

Talkin' the Talk

Magda *(mag-da)* went to a concert last night. She loves classical music, Chopin in particular. Today, at the office, she's talking to her colleague Adam *(a-dam)* about the concert. The dialogue is formal.

Adam: **Słyszałem, że była pani wczoraj na koncercie w Filharmonii Narodowej.**
(swih-sha-wem zhe bih-wa pa-n'ee fcho-ray na kon-tser-ch'ye ffeel-har-mo-n'ee na-ro-do-vey)
I heard you were at a concert at the National Philharmonic Concert Hall yesterday.

Magda: **Tak, to był koncert chopinowski.**
(tak to bihw kon-tsert sho-pe-nof-skee)
Yes, that was the Chopin concert.

Adam: **I jak się pani podobało?**
(ee yak sh'ye pa-n'ee po-do-ba-wo)
How did you like it?

Magda: **Bardzo! Muzycy byli fantastyczni. Naprawdę warto zobaczyć.**
(bar-dzo moo-zih-tsih bih-lee fan-tas-tih-chn'ee na-pra-vde var-to zo-ba-chihch')
Very much! The musicians were fabulous. It's really worth seeing.

Adam: **Czy można jeszcze dostać bilety?**
(chih mo-zhna yesh-che do-stadj' bee-le-tih)
Is it still possible to get tickets?

Magda: **Musi pan zadzwonić do filharmonii i zapytać.**
(moo-sh'ee pan za-dzvo-n'eech' do feel-har-mo-n'ee ee za-pih-tach')
You need to call the Philharmonic Concert Hall and ask them.

It's been a while since you fell in love with Poland and its culture and decided to settle down in this beautiful country. You were so busy with finding a job and a place to live that you neglected your friends! They've decided to email you to let you know they're coming over for a week and you've got to show them around! That's great news but it also means that you need to plan a whole week of great entertainment for them! Use the chart below to plan what you're going to do each day. Translate each day and event. Use the dictionary if you need to.

Day	*What you're going to do*
poniedziałek	Idziemy do polskiej restauracji na kolację. Mamy rezerwację o 19.30.
wtorek	Robimy w domu imprezę. Zapraszamy znajmomych z Polski. Pijemy polską wódkę i tańczymy.
środa	Uprawiamy sport – biegamy, pływamy, jeździmy na rowerze.
czwartek	Idziemy do galerii na wystawę.
piątek	Idziemy do kina na film (po angielsku, oczywiście!).
sobota	Zwiedzamy miasto cały dzień.
niedziela	Rano odpoczywamy, a potem idziemy na obiad o 14:00.

Answer key:

Monday: We're going to a Polish restaurant for dinner. We have a reservation at 7.30 p.m. / Tuesday: We're throwing a house party. We invite Polish friends. We drink vodka and dance. / Wednesday: We play sport – we run, swim and ride a bike. / Thursday: We are going to a gallery for an exhibition. / Friday: We're going to the cinema for a film (in English, of course!). / Saturday: We're visiting/sightseeing in the town all day. / Sunday: We relax in the morning and then go for lunch at 2 p.m.

Chapter 8

Enjoying Yourself: Recreation

In This Chapter

- Talking about what you like
- Considering the reflexive case
- Exploring the instrumental case
- Taking adverbs of frequency on board
- Enjoying the great outdoors

Most Poles are stuck indoors for long hours, and when they get a chance to escape work and enjoy the outdoors they never hesitate. Of course, some people are perfectly happy with spending their time off at home; the majority, however, go for outdoor activities. And there are plenty to choose from!

Liking the Verb Lubić

The verb **lubić** *(loo-beech')* (to like) belongs to the **-ę/-isz** type of conjugation. Go to Chapter 2 to read more about present tense verbs.

If you're asked **Co lubisz robić?** *(tso loo-beesh ro-beech')* (What do you like to do?), you can reply by saying **Lubię . . .** *(loo-bye)* (I like . . .) followed by something like this:

- **czytać książki** *(chih-tach' ksh'ohN-shkee)* (to read books)
- **śpiewać** *(sh'pye-vach')* (to sing)
- **tańczyć w klubie** *(tan'-chihch' fkloo-bye)* (to dance in a club)
- **chodzić do kina/do teatru/do pubu/do klubu/do kawiarni** *(ho-dj'eedj' do kee-na/do te-a-troo/do pa-boo/do kloo-boo/do ka-vyar-n'ee)* (to go to the cinema/theatre/pub/club/coffee shop)

- **jeździć na rowerze/na nartach/na rolkach** *(yez'-dj'eech' na ro-ve-zhe/ na nar-tah/na rol-kah)* (to ride a bike/to ski/to roller-skate)
- **grać w tenisa/w piłkę nożną/w siatkówkę** *(grach' fte-n'ee-sa/fpeew-ke nozh-nohN/fsh'yat-koof-ke)* (to play tennis/football/volleyball)
- **grać na gitarze/na pianinie** *(grach' na gee-ta-zhe/na pya-n'ee-nye)* (to play the guitar/piano)
- **spotykać się ze znajomymi** *(spo-tih-kach' sh'ye ze zna-yo-mih-mee)* (to meet up with friends)
- **rozmawiać przez telefon** *(roz-ma-vyach' pshes te-le-fon)* (to talk on the phone)
- **odpoczywać w ogrodzie/robić grilla** *(ot-po-chih-vach' vo-gro-dj'ye/ ro-beedj' gree-la)* (to relax in the garden/to barbecue)
- **żeglować** *(zhe-glo-vach')* (to sail)
- **podróżować** *(po-droo-zho-vach')* (to travel)
- **pływać** *(pwih-vach')* (to swim)
- **chodzić na siłownię** *(ho-dj'eech' na sh'ee-wov-n'ye)* (to go to the gym)
- **uprawiać sport** *(oo-pra-vyach' sport)* (to play sport)

The following list shows the verb **lubić** *(loo-beech')* (to like) in action. Note that the verb that follows **lubić** is in basic infinitive (not conjugated) form.

In English you say, *I like/enjoy singing.* In Polish, however, you literally say *I like to sing*: **Lubię śpiewać** *(loo-bye sh'pye-vach')*.

- **W wolnym czasie lubię spotykać się ze znajomymi** *(vvol-nihm cha-sh'ye loo-bye spo-tih-kach' sh'ye ze zna-yo-mih-mee)* (I like to meet up with my friends in my spare time)
- **Mój brat lubi grać na gitarze** *(mooy brat loo-bee grach' na gee-ta-zhe)* (My brother likes to play the guitar)
- **Lubisz jeździć na rowerze?** *(loo-beesh yez'-dj'eech' na ro-ve-zhe)* (Do you like to ride a bike?)
- **Latem uwielbiam żeglować** *(la-tem oo-vyel-byam zhe-glo-vach')* (I love sailing in the summer)
- **Nie lubisz chodzić na siłownię?** *(n'ye loo-beesh ho-dj'eech' na sh'ee-wov-n'ye)* (Don't you like going to the gym?)

Podobać się *(po-do-bach' sh'ye)* is another verb that means 'to like'. I cover it in Chapter 6, so go there for examples and details. Just keep in mind that **lubić** is for food, people and places you're familiar with. Use **podobać się** to share first impressions of things you like (but not food) and people you fancy.

Note that other verbs followed by infinitives include: **umieć** *(oo-myech')* (can/to know how to [do something]), **móc** *(moots)* (can/to be able to [do something]), **chcieć** *(hch'yech')* (want) and **musieć** *(moo-sh'yech)* (have to/must). Grammatically speaking, they are *modal verbs* (also called *auxiliary verbs*) and they modify the verb that accompanies them. Read the following list to see how to use modal verbs:

- **Umiesz grać w tenisa?** *(oo-myezh grach' fte-nee-sa)* (Can you play tennis?)
- **Nie chcę robić grilla w ten weekend** *(n'ye htse ro-beech' gree-la ften wee-kent)* (I don't want to have a barbecue this weekend)
- **Nie mogę w tym roku pojechać na urlop** *(n'ye mo-ge ftihm ro-koo po-ye-hach' na oor-lop)* (I can't go on holiday this year)
- **Muszę regularnie chodzić na siłownię** *(moo-she re-goo-lar-n'ye ho-dj'eech' na sh'ee-wov-n'ye)* (I have to go to the gym regularly)

Being Interested in the Reflexive Verb

When talking about your hobbies, you can use another verb: **interesować się** *(een-te-re-so-vach' sh'ye)* (to be interested in). All the secrets of its conjugation type are revealed in Chapter 2, where I talk about verbs ending in -ować.

This verb consists of two parts: the **interesować** (to be interested in) verb itself and the reflexive pronoun **się** (oneself). If you translate this expression literally, it means to interest oneself (in something) and is followed by the object of your interest directly (there is no word *in*). In English, many verbs are reflexive: *to wash oneself, to introduce oneself,* to name just a couple. But, unlike in English, where you change *oneself* to *myself, yourself, himself* and so on to fit the situation, in Polish, the reflexive **się** stays the same.

Some verbs are reflexive in one language but not in another! There's no easy way out, you just have to memorise them.

It's time to pose the question: **Czym się interesujesz?** *(chihm sh'ye een-te-re-soo-yesh)* (What are you interested in?) – informal.

The answer can be **Interesuję się** *(een-te-re-soo-ye sh'ye)* followed by one of these (or more if you have extensive interests!): **sportem** *(spor-tem)* (sport), **muzyką klasyczną/rockową** *(moo-zih-kohN kla-sihch-nohN/ro-ko-vohN)* *(classical/rock music)*, **filmem** *(feel-mem)* (film), **teatrem** *(te-a-trem)* (theatre), **literaturą** *(lee-te-ra-too-rohN)* (literature), **sztuką** *(shtoo-kohN)* (art), **piłką nożną** *(peew-kohN nozh-nohN)* (football), **ekonomią** *(e-ko-no-myohN)* (economics), **ogrodnictwem** *(o-grod-n'eets-tfem)* (gardening), **żeglarstwem** *(zhe-glar-stfem)* (sailing), **narciarstwem** *(nar-ch'yar-stfem)* (skiing), **tenisem** *(te-n'ee-sem)* (tennis), **gotowaniem** *(go-to-va-n'yem)* (cooking) or **komputerami** *(kom-poo-te-ra-mee)* (computers/Internet technology).

Talkin' the Talk

Audio track 18: Dominika *(do-mee-n'ee-ka)* is reading a book. Her new class mate, Marek *(ma-rek)*, wants to get to know her better:

Marek: **Co robisz?**
(tso ro-beesh)
What are you doing?

Dominika: **Czytam książkę. Jest bardzo ciekawa!**
(chih-tam ksh'ohN-shke yezd bar-dzo ch'ye-ka-va)
I'm reading a book. It's very interesting!

Marek: **Dużo czytasz?**
(doo-zho chih-tash)
Do you read much?

Dominika: **Tak, interesuję się literaturą współczesną. A ty? Lubisz czytać?**
(tak een-te-re-soo-ye sh'ye lee-te-ra-too-rohN fspoow-ches-nohN a tih loo-beesh chih-tach')
Yes, I'm interested in contemporary literature. And you? Do you like reading?

Marek: **Nie za bardzo. Wolę kino. Lubię oglądać filmy. Ale najbardziej interesuję się sportem.**
(n'ye za bar-dzo vo-le kee-no loo-bye o-glon-dach' feel-mih a-le nay-bar-dj'yey een-te-re-soo-ye sh'ye spor-tem)
Not really. I prefer the cinema. I like watching films. But I'm mostly interested in sport.

Dominika: **A jakim konkretnie?**
(a ya-keem kon-kret-n'ye)
Which one in particular?

Marek: **Lubię grać w tenisa i w piłkę nożną, pływać i żeglować. A zimą często jeżdżę na nartach.**
(loo-bye grach' fte-nee-sa ee fpeew-ke nozh-nohN pwy-vach' ee zhe-glo-vach' a z'ee-mohN chehN-sto yezh-dje na nar-tah)
I like to play tennis, football, to swim and sail. And in winter I often go skiing.

Dominika: **Mój brat jest fanem futbolu!**
(mooy brat yest fa-nem foot-bo-loo)
My brother is a fan of football!

Marek: **Świetnie! Może razem pójdziemy na jakiś mecz!**
(sh'fyet-n'ye mo-zhe ra-zem pooy-dj'ye-mih na ya-keesh' mech)
Great! Maybe we should go and watch a match together.

Dominika: **Na pewno się ucieszy!**
(na pev-no sh'ye oo-ch'ye-shih)
I'm sure he'll be delighted!

Words to Know

nie za bardzo	n'ye za bar dzo	not really
konkretnie	kon-kret-n'ye	in particular
jest fanem fulbolu	yest fa-nem foot-bo-loo	she/he's a football fan
mecz	mech	match
na pewno się ucieszy	na pev-no sh'ye oo-ch'ye-shih	I'm sure he/she'll be delighted

The Case of the Instrumental Case

What's interesting about the verb **interesować się** *(een-te-re-so-vach' sh'ye)* (to be interested in) is that it requires a change in the endings of the noun, or both the noun and the adjective that follow it, to the *instrumental case*. (While I talk more about other situations when you use this case in Chapter 2, here I focus on the **interesować się** verb.)

In the statement **Interesuję się sportem i muzyką klasyczną** *(een-te-re-soo-ye sh'ye spor-tem ee moo-zih-kohN kla-sihch-nohN)* (I'm interested in sport and classical music), the dictionary forms **sport** *(sport)* and **muzyka klasyczna** *(moo-zih-ka kla-sihch-na)* get changed into the instrumental case: **sportem** *(spor-tem)* and **muzyką klasyczną** *(moo-zih-kohN kla-sihch-nohN)*. You won't find the instrumental case in a dictionary! (More rules for the instrumental case and the basic nominative case are in Chapter 2.)

You may have already worked out the endings of the instrumental case from the preceding paragraph, but it's always good to summarise:

- **Masculine nouns:** Masculine nouns take the ending **-em** or **-iem** (after k or g) and masculine adjectives replace the nominative **-y/-i** (after k or g) with **-ym/-im**, accordingly. For example:
  - **To jest nowy autobus** *(to yest no-vih aw-to-boos)* (This is a new bus) in nominative case becomes **Jadę nowym autobusem** *(ya-de no-vihm aw-to-boo-sem)* (I'm going by a new bus) in instrumental case.
  - **To jest wysoki budynek** *(to yezd vih-so-kee boo-dih-nek)* (This is a high building) in nominative case is **Stoję przed wysokim budynkiem** *(sto-ye pshed vih-so-keem boo-dihn-kyem)* (I'm standing outside/in front of a high building) in instrumental case.
- **Masculine nouns ending in -a:** Some masculine nouns end in **-a** (**poeta** *(po-e-ta)* [male poet], for example) and therefore look like feminine nouns. With these nouns, you replace the nominative ending **-a** with the instrumental **-ą** as you do with the feminine nouns they resemble. However, any adjectives keep the masculine ending **-ym/-im** (after k or g), as in:
  - **To jest młody poeta** *(to yest mwo-dih po-e-ta)* (This is a young [male] poet) in nominative case becomes **Spotykam się z młodym poetą** *(spo-tih-kam sh'ye zmwo-dihm po-e-tohN)* (I'm meeting/going out with a young [male] poet) in instrumental case.
- **Feminine nouns:** With feminine nouns, you replace the nominative **-a** with the instrumental ending **-ą** as you do with the feminine adjectives, too:

- **Anna to piękna kobieta** (*an-na to pyen-kna ko-bye-ta*) (Anna is a beautiful woman) in nominative case becomes **Anna jest piękną kobietą** (*an-na yest pyen-knohN ko-bye-tohN*) (Anna is a beautiful woman) in instrumental case.

These two sentences translate into English in the same way. However, as far as Polish grammar is concerned, the first one is in the nominative case (which is easy to spot by the word **to** or **to jest**). The latter is in the instrumental case and you have to remember to add the instrumental endings here.

- **Neuter nouns:** Neuter nouns follow the rules for masculine nouns in the instrumental case. You just need to remember to add **-em/-iem** (after k or g) to nouns and **-ym/-im** (after k or g) to adjectives, as in these examples:
  - **To jest nowe pióro** (*to yest no-ve pyoo-ro*) (This is a new pen) in nominative case is **Piszę nowym piórem** (*pee-she no-vihm pyoo-rem*) (I'm writing with a new pen) in instrumental case.
  - **To jest małe dziecko** (*to yest ma-we dj'yets-ko*) (This is a small child) in nominative case is **Nie jesteś już małym dzieckiem** (*n'ye yes-tesh' yoosh ma-wihm dj'yets-kyem*) (You're not a small child any more) in instrumental case.

For tips on how to determine whether a noun is neuter in Polish (it won't necessarily be neuter in English as in the above example including the word *child*), go to Chapter 2.

- **Plural nouns:** Again, plural nouns are very easy, as only one ending exists for all nouns, which is **-ami.** Adjectives end in **-ymi/-imi** (after k or g). For example:
  - **To jest włoski samochód** (*to yest vwos-kye sa-mo-hoot*) in nominative case singular becomes **Interesujemy się włoskimi samochodami** (*een-te-re-soo-ye-mih sh'ye vwos-kee-mee sa-mo-ho-da-mee*) (We're interested in Italian cars) in the instrumental case plural.

Using 'Often' Often: Adverbs of Frequency

When talking about how often you get a chance to do the things you like to do, knowing some adverbs of frequency is handy. (You can also use these adverbs to describe how often you have to do things you don't like to do!) The following sentences use various frequency terms, many of them sports-related:

- **Od czasu do czasu gram z kolegami w piłkę nożną** *(ot cha-soo do cha-soo gram sko-le-ga-mee fpeew-ke-nozh-nohN)* (From time to time I play football with my friends)
- **Sylwia często chodzi na basen** *(sihl-vya chehN-sto ho-dj'ee na ba-sen)* (Sylwia often goes to the swimming pool)
- **Nigdy nie jeżdżę na rowerze, kiedy pada deszcz** *(n'ee-gdih n'ye yezh-dje na ro-ve-zhe kye-dih pa-da deshch)* (I never ride a bike when it's raining)

You may be surprised to see that a sentence with **nigdy** *(n'ee-gdih)* (never) has a double negation. In Polish, you say **Nigdy nie śpiewam** *(n'ee-gdih n'ye sh'pye-vam)*, which literally translates to *I never [don't] sing*. Funny, isn't it?

- **Moja siostra rzadko chodzi na siłownię, bo nie lubi** *(mo-ya sh'yo-stra zhat-ko ho-dj'ee na sh'ee-wov-n'ye bo n'ye loo-bee)* (My sister rarely goes to the gym, because she doesn't like it)
- **Czasami, kiedy mam wolne, chodzę po górach** *(cha-sa-mee kye-dih mam vol-ne ho-dze po goo-rah)* (Sometimes, when I have a day off, I walk in the mountains)
- **Regularnie uprawiam sport** *(re-goo-lar-n'ye oo-pra-vyam sport)* (I regularly play sports)
- **Jak często chodzisz do teatru?** *(yak chehN-sto ho-dj'eezh do te-a-troo)* (How often do you go to the theatre?)
- **We wtorek zawsze trenujemy judo** *(ve fto-reg zaf-she tre-noo-ye-mih djoo-do)* (We always do judo on Tuesday)
- **Powinieneś codziennie biegać** *(po-vee-n'ye-nesh' co-dj'yen-n'ye bye-gach')* (You [male] should run every day)

Exploring the Outdoors

It doesn't matter whether you're a professional climber, off-piste skier or simply enjoy walking in the mountains or swimming in a lake, it all counts as being active and liking the outdoors. And with the fresh air, taking on board new Polish phrases gets a lot easier!

Hiking in the mountains

Polish people like **chodzić po górach** *(ho-dj'eech' po goo-rah)* (walking in the mountains) and the mountains can get a bit crowded in July and August when lots of Poles are on holiday. Whether you want to take things easy and prefer lower mountains, or, at the other end of the scale, you're a fan of **wspinaczka** *(fspee-nach-ka)* (rock climbing), the whole southern part of Poland has it all on offer. You just need to choose what place you want to go to and take some useful vocabulary with you:

- **W ten weekend jadę w góry** *(ften wee-kent ya-de vgoo-rih)* (I'm going to the mountains this weekend)
- **Masz ochotę pochodzić po górach?** *(mash o-ho-te po-ho-dj'eech' po goo-rah)* (Do you fancy hiking in the mountains?)
- **Bardzo lubię się wspinać** *(bar-dzo loo-bye sh'ye fspee-nach')* (I really enjoy rock climbing)

Talkin' the Talk

Marek *(ma-rek)* plans to go to the Tatra Mountains. He knows that Bartek *(bar-tek)* loves hiking and he suggests that he comes along, too. Here's what they say:

Marek: **W lipcu jedziemy ze znajomymi na kilka dni w góry. Jedziesz z nami?**
(vlee-ptsoo ye-dj'ye-mih ze zna-yo-mih-mee na keel-ka dn'ee vgoo-rih ye-dj'yezh zna-mee)
We're going to the mountains with friends for a few days in July. Do you want to come with us?

Bartek: **Pewnie! A jaki jest plan?**
(pev-n'ye a ya-kee yest plan)
Sure! What's the plan?

Marek: **Jedziemy pociągiem do Zakopanego. Będziemy nocować w schronisku.**
(ye-dj'ye-mih po-ch'yon-gyem do za-ko-pa-ne-go ben'-dj'ye-mih no-tso-vach' fs-hro-n'ees-koo)
We're taking a train to Zakopane. We'll be staying in a hostel.

Bartek: **A, czyli chcecie chodzić z plecakami?**
(a chih-lee htse-ch'ye ho-dj'eech' sple-tsa-ka-mee)
So you want to hike with rucksacks?

Marek: **Tak, ale nie bierzemy dużo rzeczy - tylko śpiwór, latarkę i coś ciepłego, bo wieczorem może być zimno. No i trochę jedzenia.**
(tak a-le n'ye bye-zhe-mih doo-zho zhe-chih tihl-ko sh'pee-voor la-tar-ke ee tsosh' ch'ye-pwe-go bo vye-cho-rem mo-zhe bihdj' z'ee-mno no ee tro-he ye-dze-n'ya)
Yes, but we're not taking many things – just a sleeping bag, torch and something warm [to wear] as the evenings can get cold. And some food.

Bartek: **A macie już wybraną trasę?**
(a ma-ch'ye yoozh vih-bra-nohN tra-se)
Have you already decided on a route?

Marek: **Tak, tu jest mapa. Zobacz, chcemy chodzić łatwymi szlakami.**
(tak too yest ma-pa zo-bach htse-mih ho-dj'eech' wat-fih-mee shla-ka-mee)
Yes, here is the map. Look, we want to hike the easy trails.

Bartek: **Widoki będą wspaniałe! Jadę z wami!**
(vee-do-kee ben-dohN fspa-n'ya-we ya-de zva-mee)
The views will be spectacular! I'm going with you!

Words to Know

pewnie	*pe-vn'ye*	sure
w schronisku	*fs-hro-nees-koo*	in a hostel
śpiwór	*sh'pee-voor*	sleeping bag
latarka	*la-tar-ka*	torch
szlaki/trasy	*shla-kee/tra-sih*	trails/routes
widoki	*vee-do-kee*	the views

Polish mountain-climbing etiquette

When walking in the mountains in Poland, you always give way to people climbing up. It's also customary to greet everyone with **dzień dobry** *(dj'yen' dob-rih)* or **cześć** *(chesh'ch')* when they go past you. In the summer, when the paths are packed with hikers, greeting everyone might be a bit tiring, but it's a custom worth cultivating.

Sunbathing on the beach

Polish beaches are long and sandy. All the sea resorts have plenty of beach restaurants that serve **świeża ryba** *(sh'fye-zha rih-ba)* (fresh fish) or **gofry** *(go-frih)* (waffles). **Palce lizać** *(pal-tse lee-zach')* (finger-licking good)! The only disadvantage may be the fact that the Baltic Sea is pretty cold, even in the summer, at only around 18–19 degrees Centigrade (about 65 degrees Fahrenheit) – Brrr!

Some expressions you may find useful at the beach include:

- **Są duże fale/Nie ma fal** *(sohN doo-zhe fa-le/n'ye ma fal)* (The waves are big/There are no waves)
- **Gdzie są moje okulary przeciwsłoneczne?** *(gdj'ye sohN mo-ye o-koo-la-rih pshe-ch'eef-swo-nech-ne)* (Where are my sunglasses?)
- **Zaraz idziemy na plażę** *(za-ras ee-dj'ye-mih na pla-zhe)* (We're about to leave for the beach)
- **Lubię się opalać** *(loo-bye sh'ye o-pa-lach')* (I like sunbathing)
- **Idziemy popływać?** *(ee-dj'ye-mih po-pwih-vach')* (Shall we go for a swim?)
- **Nie umiem pływać** *(n'ye oo-myem pwih-vach')* (I can't swim)
- **Pływam kraulem/żabką/na plecach** *(pwih-vam kraw-lem/zhap-kohN/na ple-tsah)* (I can swim crawl/breaststroke [literally: 'froggy style'!] /backstroke style)
- **Nie zapomnij kremu do opalania!** *(n'ye za-pom-n'eey kre-moo do o-pa-la-n'ya)* (Don't forget the sun cream!)

Talkin' the Talk

Sylwia *(sihl-vya)* and Rafał *(ra-faw)* are talking about their holiday plans.

Sylwia: **Bardzo lubię jeździć nad polskie morze.**
(bar-dzo loo-bye yez'-dj'eech' nat pol-skye mo-zhe)
I really like going to the Polish seaside.

Rafał: **Bałtyk jest piękny, ale według mnie woda jest trochę za zimna. Poza tym, wolę aktywny wypoczynek.**
(baw-tihk yest pyen-knih a-le ve-dwook mn'ye vo-da yest tro-he za z'eem-na po-za tihm vo-le a-ktihv-nih vih-po-chih-nek)
The Baltic Sea is beautiful but I think the water is a bit too cold. Besides, I prefer active recreation.

Sylwia: **Ale nad morzem też można aktywnie spędzać czas! Mój mąż gra w siatkówkę na plaży, dzieci pływają na desce (windsurfingowej), a ja dużo spaceruję, opalam się i pływam.**
(a-le nat mo-zhem tesh mozh-na a-ktihv-n'ye spen-dzach' chas mooy mohNzh gra fsh'yat-koof-ke na pla-zhih dj'ye-ch'ee pwih-va-yohN na des-tse (weent-ser-feen-go-vey) a ya doo-zho spa-tse-roo-ye o-pa-lam sh'ye ee pwih-vam)
But you can still be active by the sea! My husband plays beach volleyball, the kids windsurf and I walk a lot, sunbathe and swim.

Rafał: **Ja w tym roku nie mam już urlopu!**
(ya ftihm ro-koo n'ye mam yoosh oor-lo-poo)
I've run out of holiday this year already.

Words to Know

trochę za zimna	*tro-he za z'eem-na*	a bit too cold
poza tym	*po-za tihm*	besides
aktywny wypoczynek	*a-ktihv-nih vih-po-chih-nek*	active recreation
grać w siatkówkę na plaży	*grach' fsh'yat-koof-ke na pla-zhih*	to play beach volleyball
pływać na desce (windsurfingowej)	*pwih-vach' na des-tse (weent-ser-feen-go-vey)*	to windsurf
nie mam już urlopu	*n'ye mam yoosh oor-lo-poo*	I've run out of holiday

Going to the countryside

Each year more and more people go for **urlop w gospodarstwie agroturystycznym** *(oor-lob vgos-po-dar-stfye a-gro-too-rih-stih-chnihm)* (a farm holiday). This may not be to everyone's taste but this type of holiday has definite advantages, especially for children. The children have plenty of space to play, can eat organic food and learn how to look after animals – and may even become experts in milking cows!

Some of the questions and expressions you may want to use in the country include:

- **Można pić świeże mleko prosto od krowy** *(mo-zhna peech' sfye-zhe mle-ko pro-sto ot kro-vih)* (You can drink fresh milk straight from the cow)
- **Idziemy na grzyby** *(ee-dj'ye-mih na gzhih-bih)* (We're going to pick mushrooms)
- **Strasznie mnie gryzą komary!** *(stra-shn'ye mn'ye grih-zohN ko-ma-rih)* (I keep getting bitten by mosquitoes!)
- **Masz coś na komary?** *(mash tsosh' na ko-ma-rih)* (Have you got anything to stop mosquitos from biting?) – informal
- **Na wsi jest zdrowe jedzenie** *(na fsh'ee yezd zdro-ve ye-dze-n'ye)* (The food in the countryside is healthy)
- **W mieście tego nie ma** *(vmyesh'-ch'ye te-go n'ye ma)* (You won't get that in a city)

Skiing in the mountains

Skiing is a popular activity in Poland and in other countries with mountains and snow. Even though the Polish mountains are not as impressive as the Alps, you can still find plenty of skiing opportunities. Resorts like **Zakopane** *(za-ko-pa-ne)* and **Szczyrk** *(shchihrk)* (this city is real tongue-twister!) offer traditional accommodation, delicious food and a constantly-improving skiing infrastructure. However, Polish slopes are shorter and very crowded compared to the resorts in the Alps, and queuing for ski lifts is unavoidable. **Nic nie jest idealne!** *(n'eets n'ye yest ee-de-al-ne)* (Nothing is perfect!).

Phrases to use on the slopes include:

- **Kup karnety na cały tydzień!** *(koop kar-ne-tih na tsa-wih tih-dj'yen')* (Buy ski passes for the whole week!) – informal
- **Idę wypożyczyć narty** *(ee-de vih-po-zhih-chihch' nar-tih)* (I'm going to rent skis)
- **Muszę oddać narty do renowacji** *(moo-she od-dach' nar-tih do re-no-va-tsyee)* (I have to take my skis in for servicing)
- **Jakie są warunki narciarskie?** *(ya-kye sohN va-roon-kee nar-ch'yar-skye)* (What are the skiing conditions like?)
- **Bardzo długa kolejka do wyciągu** *(bar-dzo dwoo-ga ko-ley-ka do vih-ch'yon-goo)* (The ski lift queue is very long)
- **Mam ochotę na grzane wino** *(mam o-ho-te na gzha-ne vee-no)* (I fancy some mulled wine)
- **Proszę zostawić narty w narciarni** *(pro-she zo-sta-veech' nar-tih vnar-ch'yar-n'ee)* (Please leave your skis in the ski room) – formal

Talkin' the Talk

Sylwek *(sihl-vek)* and Tomek *(to-mek)* have gone to Zakopane *(za-ko-pa-ne)* on a skiing holiday. They've just got up and are looking out of the window.

Sylwek: **Pogoda idealna! Zimno, ale słonecznie!**
(po-go-da ee-de-al-na z'eem-no a-le swo-nech-n'ye)
The weather is perfect! Cold but sunny!

Tomek: **Tak, całą noc padał śnieg, więc warunki na stoku są fantastyczne!**
(tak tsa-wohN nots pa-daw sh'n'yek vyents va-roon-kee na sto-koo sohN fan-tas-tih-chne)
Yes, it snowed all night, so the skiing conditions are superb!

Sylwek: **Lubię jeździć w puchu!**
(loo-bye yez'-dj'eech' fpoo-hoo)
I like skiing in powder!

Tomek: **A ja wolę, kiedy trasy są wyratrakowane.**
(a ya vo-le kye-dih tra-sih sohN vih-ra-tra-ko-va-ne)
And I prefer when the slopes are groomed.

Sylwek: **Zaraz po śniadaniu ja idę kupić karnety, a ty możesz iść wypożyczyć sprzęt narciarski.**
(za-ras po sh'n'ya-da-n'yoo ya ee-de koo-peech' kar-ne-tih a tih mo-zhesh eesh'ch' vih-po-zhih-chihch' spshent nar-ch'yar-skee)
Straight after breakfast, I'll go to get the ski passes and you can go to hire skis.

Tomek: **Dobrze. Spotykamy się przy wyciągu.**
(dob-zhe spo-tih-ka-mih sh'ye pshih vih-ch'yon-goo)
Okay. I'll see you at the ski lift.

Words to Know

warunki na stoku	*va-roon-kee na sto-koo*	skiing conditions
jeździć w puchu	*yez'-dj'eech' fpoo-hoo*	skiing in powder
wyratrakowane trasy	*vih-ra-tra-ko-va-ne tra-sih*	groomed slopes
zaraz po śniadaniu	*za-ras po sh'n'ya-da-n'yoo*	straight after breakfast
wypożyczyć sprzęt narciarki	*vih-po-zhih-chihch' spshent nar-ch'yar-skee*	to rent skis
przy wyciągu	*pshih vih-ch'yon-goo*	at the ski lift

Sailing in the summertime

If you're a sailing enthusiast, the Masuria lakeside has everything you need to get onboard. For thrill-seekers, the Baltic Sea with its winds and short but stiff waves can be a great challenge. Chartering a yacht is easy and don't worry if you're not a skipper, you can always hire a boat with a crew. All you need to know are a few Polish verbs:

- **zacumować łódkę** *(za-tsoo-mo-vach' woot-ke)* (to moor the boat)
- **postawić żagle** *(po-sta-veech' zha-gle)* (to set the sails)
- **rzucić kotwice** *(zhoo-ch'eech' ko-tfee-tse)* (to anchor)
- **żeglować z wiatrem** *(zhe-glo-vadj' zvya-trem)* (to sail with the wind)
- **płynąć pod wiatr** *(pwih-non'ch pod vyatr)* (to sail close to the wind)
- **wyczarterować jacht/łódkę** *(vih-char-te-ro-vach' yaht/woot-ke)* (to charter a yacht/boat)
- **mieć patent** *(myech' pa-tent)* (to be a certified skipper)
- **spać na jachcie** *(spach' na yah-ch'ye)* (to sleep on the boat)

Talkin' the Talk

Norbert *(nor-bert)* is an experienced skipper and he's organising a sailing trip. He stayed at work a bit longer to do some research. His work colleague, Rysiek *(rih-sh'yek)*, is interested.

Norbert: **Jadę na żagle na Mazury i szukam firmy czarterującej jachty.**
(ya-de na zha-gle na ma-zoo-rih ee shoo-kam feer-mih char-te-roo-yon-tsey yah-tih)
I'm going to sail to Mazury and I'm looking for a yacht chartering company.

Rysiek: **A jaką łódkę chcesz wyczarterować?**
(a ya-kohN woot-ke htsezh vih-char-te-ro-vach')
And what type of boat do you want to charter?

Norbert: **Nie za dużą i nie za małą. Dla czterech osób.**
(n'ye za doo-zhohN ee n'ye za ma-wohN dla chte-reh o-soop)
Neither too big nor too small. For four people.

Rysiek: **Gdzie będziecie cumować?**
(gdj'ye ben'-dj'ye-ch'ye tsoo-mo-vach')
Where are you going to moor?

Norbert: **W portach albo na kotwicy. Oczywiście będziemy spać na jachcie.**
(fpor-tah al-bo na ko-tfee-tsih o-chih-veesh'-ch'ye ben'-dj'ye-mih spach' na yah-ch'ye)
In ports, or we'll drop anchor. Of course, we will sleep on the boat.

Rysiek: **A macie sternika?**
(a ma-ch'ye ster-n'ee-ka)
Do you have a skipper?

Norbert: **Tak, ja mam patent.**
(tak ya mam pa-tent)
Yes, I'm a certified skipper.

Rysiek: **Fajnie. Ja nie umiem pływać i w ogóle boję się wody!**
(fay-n'ye ya n'ye oo-myem pwih-vach' ee vo-goo-le bo-ye sh'ye vo-dih)
Cool. I can't swim and I'm afraid of water in general!

Words to Know

jadę na żagle	ya-de na zhag-le	I'm going sailing
szukam	shoo-kam	I'm looking for
na jachcie	na yah-ch'ye	on the yacht/boat
sternik	ster-neek	skipper
boję się wody	bo-ye sh'ye vo-dih	I'm afraid of water

Going camping

Camping is always fun and a great way to escape the city. Here are some useful camping-related expressions:

- **Jedziemy pod namiot** *(ye-dj'ye-mih pot na-myot)* (We're going camping)
- **Pomóż mi rozbić namiot!** *(po-moosh mee roz-beech' na-myot)* (Can you help me to pitch the tent!)
- **Prysznice są płatne** *(prih-shn'ee-tse sohN pwat-ne)* (You have to pay for the showers)
- **Umiesz rozpalić ognisko?** *(oo-myesh ros-pa-leech' og-n'ee-sko)* (Do you know how to start a campfire?)
- **Jadę na ryby** *(ya-de na rih-bih)* (I'm going fishing)
- **Lubię piec kiełbaski przy ognisku** *(loo-bye pyets kyew-bas-kee pshih og-n'ee-skoo)* (I like cooking sausages on a bonfire)

Check your vocabulary with this crossword. Fill in the correct Polish words.

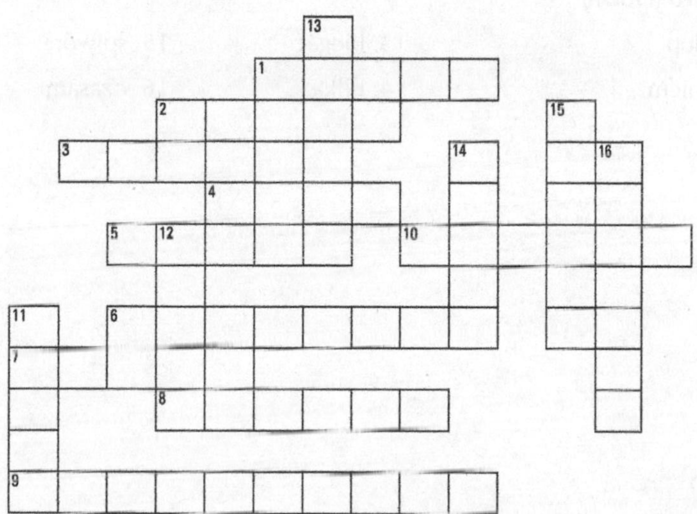

Poziomo (Across)

1. never
2. snow
3. ski lift
4. to play
5. to like
6. gym
7. a bike
8. city
9. to travel
10. to swim

Pionowo (Down)

11. holiday
12. I can/I know how to
13. to run
14. ball
15. sleeping bag
16. sometimes

Answer key:

Poziomo (Across)

1. nigdy
2. śnieg
3. wyciąg
4. grać
5. lubić
6. siłownia
7. rower
8. miasto
9. podróżować
10. pływać

Pionowo (Down)

11. urlop
12. umiem
13. biegać
14. piłka
15. śpiwór
16. czasami

Chapter 9

Talking on the Phone

In This Chapter

- Introducing yourself and checking who's on the other end
- Leaving the necessary details in a message
- Arranging meetings and appointments on the phone

Not long ago Poles had to be on a waiting list for ten years or more before getting phone service. For the lucky ones who got connected, getting a clear line for calls even within one city proved difficult! Connections between two cities required an hour-long wait and, when the call finally came, the line would break. **A to pech!** *(a to peh)* (What bad luck!). Those days are all but gone now (thank heaven)! Everyone has a mobile phone now, even the kids.

Dealing with the Preliminaries

When Polish people answer the phone, they say **halo** *(ha-lo)* or **słucham** *(swoo-ham)* with rising intonation. Sometimes, to your confusion, they say **tak** *(tak)*, which normally means *yes*, and occasionally *really* or **proszę** *(pro-she)* meaning *please/you're welcome/there you go*. Then it's your turn to greet the other party and introduce yourself:

- **Cześć! Mówi Adam** *(chesh'ch' moo-vee a-dam)* (Hi! It's Adam speaking) – informal
- **Cześć. Tu Michał** *(chesh'ch too mee-haw)* (Hi! It's Michał) – informal
- **Dzień dobry. Wiktor Nowak z tej strony** *(dj'yen' dob-rih vee-ktor no-vak stey stro-nih)* (Hello. Wiktor Nowak at this end) – formal
- **Dobry wieczór. Mówi Agata Wiśnia** *(dob-rih vye-choor moo-vee a-ga-ta vee-sh'n'ya)* (Good evening. Agata Wiśnia speaking) – formal

A company receptionist would answer the phone by stating the name of the company, then their name followed by **słucham** *(swoo-ham)* (hello) or **w czym mogę pomóc?** *(fchihm mo-ge po-moots)* (How can I help?).

To finish a phone call, you simply say **do usłyszenia** *(do oo-swih-she-n'ya)*, which is the phone equivalent of **do zobaczenia** *(do zo-ba-che-n'ya)* (see you later) – literally: 'hear you later'! or **do widzenia** *(do vee-dze-n'ya)* (goodbye).

Asking who you're talking to

You may not always be sure who you're speaking to, so double checking before you share the details of your last date with your . . . friend's mother is always a good idea!

CULTURAL WISDOM

Don't forget to introduce yourself before you ask who you're speaking to. Not doing so is considered impolite.

- **Czy to Ania?** *(chih to a-n'ya)* (Is this Ania?)
- **Przepraszam, czy rozmawiam z Tomkiem?** *(pshe-pra-sham chih roz-ma-vyam stom-kyem)* (Excuse me, am I speaking to Tomek?)
- **Z kim rozmawiam?** *(skeem roz-ma-vyam)* (To whom am I speaking?)
- **Kto mówi?** *(kto moo-vee)* (Who's speaking?)

If indeed your friend's mother answers the phone, you may need to express that you want to speak to your friend (or someone else in a different situation):

- **Czy jest Arek?** *(chih yest a-rek)* (Is Arek in?)
- **Czy mogę rozmawiać z Magdą?** *(chih mo-ge roz-ma-vyadj' zmag-dohN)* (Can I speak to Magda, please?)

If you're calling a company, you can say the following:

- **Czy może mnie pan/pani połączyć z gabinetem dyrektora?** *(chih mo-zhe mn'ye pan/pa-n'ee po-won-chihdj' zga-bee-ne-tem dih-re-kto-ra)* (Can you put me through to the director's office, please?) – formal, to a man/woman
- **Proszę mnie połączyć z pokojem 4** *(pro-she mn'ye po-won-chihch' spo-ko-yem chte-rih)* (Please put me through to room 4)
- **Chciałbym/Chciałabym rozmawiać z panią Aliną Kowal** *(hch'yaw-bihm/hch'ya-wa-bihm roz-ma-vyach' spa-n'yohN a-lee-nohN ko-val)* (I would like to speak to Mrs Alina Kowal) – man/woman

Talkin' the Talk

Audio track 19: Emilia *(e-mee-lya)* is calling her friend Patrycja *(pa-trih-tsya)* to remind her about a new Polish course starting today. Emilia has called several times but the line was busy. She got lucky this time.

Patrycja: **Słucham?**
(swoo-ham)
Hello?

Emilia: **Cześć! W końcu odebrałaś! Cały czas było zajęte!**
(chesh'ch' fkon'-tsoo o-de-bra-wash' tsa-wih chas bih-wo za-yen-te)
Hi! You answered at last! It was busy all the time!

Patrycja: **A kto mówi?**
(a kto moo-vee)
And who's speaking?

Emilia: **To ja, Emilia!**
(to ya e-mee-lya)
It's me, Emilia!

Patrycja: **A! Emilia! Nie poznałam cię! Rozmawiałam z rodzicami.**
(a e-mee-lya n'ye po-zna-wam ch'ye roz-ma-vya-wam zro-dj'ee-tsa-mee)
Emilia! I didn't recognise your voice! I was on the phone with my parents.

Emilia: **Tak myślałam. Zostawiłam Ci wiadomość, ale dla pewności dzwonię jeszcze raz, żeby ci przypomnieć o kursie.**
(tak mih-sh'la-wam zos-ta-vee-wam ch'ee vya-do-mosh'ch' a-le dla pev-nosh'-ch'ee dzvo-n'ye yesh-che ras zhe-biy ch'ee pshih-pom-n'yech' o koor-sh'ye)
That's what I thought. I left you a message but to be sure I'm calling again to remind you about the course.

Words to Know

w końcu	fkon'-tsoo	at last
odebrać	o-de-brach'	to answer (phone)
nie poznałem/ poznałam cię	n'ye po-zna-wem/ po-zna-wam ch'ye	I didn't recognise your voice (man/woman)
tak myślałem/ myślałam	tak mih-sh'la-wem/ mih-sh'la-wam	that's what I thought (man/woman)
zostawić wiadomość	zos-ta-veedj' vya-do-mosh'ch'	to leave a message

Making the connection

How unlucky you are! The person you want to speak to isn't there (or not available to talk). Here's what you'll hear in such a situation:

- **Nie ma go/jej** *(n'ye ma go/yey)* (He's/She's not here)
- **Niestety, właśnie wyszedł/wyszła** *(n'yes-te-tih vwash'-n'ye vih-shedw/ vih-shwa)* (Unfortunately, he/she just left)
- **Nie odbiera** *(n'ye od-bye-ra)* (He/She doesn't answer)
- **Jest na drugiej linii** *(yest na droo-gyey lee-n'ee)* (He/She is on another line right now)
- **Nie może teraz rozmawiać** *(n'ye mo-zhe te-ras roz-ma-vyach')* (He/She can't talk right now)
- **Jest zajęte** *(yezd za-yen-te)* (It is busy [the line])

Leaving Messages

If you can't get through to someone, you may want to leave a message. The following expressions can come in handy:

- **Czy coś przekazać?** *(chih tsosh' pshe-ka-zach')* (Can I pass on a message?)
- **Czy mogę zostawić dla niego/dla niej wiadomość?** *(chih mo-ge zos-ta-veedj' dla n'ye-go/dla n'yey vya-do-mosh'ch')* (Can I leave a message for him/her?)
- **Czy może mu/jej pani przekazać, żeby do mnie oddzwonił/oddzwoniła?** *(chih mo-zhe moo/yey pa-n'ee pshe-ka-zach' zhe-bih do mn'ye od-dzvo-n'eew/od-dzvo-n'ee-wa)* (Can you ask him/her to call me back, please?) – formal, to a woman
- **Proszę mu/jej przekazać, że dzwoniłem/dzwoniłam** *(pro-she moo/yey pshe-ka-zach' zhe dzvo-n'ee-wem/dzvo-n'ee-wam)* (Please tell him/her that I called) – to a man/woman
- **Zadzwonię poźniej** *(za-dzvo-n'ye pooz'-n'yey)* (I'll call later)
- **Spróbuję jeszcze raz jutro** *(sproo-boo-ye yesh-che ras yoo-tro)* (I'll try to reach him/her again tomorrow)
- **Będę czekać na telefon** *(ben-de che-kach' na te-le-fon)* (I'll be waiting for [his/her] call)
- **Oddzwoń do mnie, jak znajdziesz chwilę** *(od-dzvon' do mn'ye yag znay-dj'yesh hfee-le)* (Call me back when you have a moment) – informal
- **Zadzwoń do mnie na komórkę** *(za-dzvon' do mn'ye na ko-moor-ke)* (Call me on my mobile)

Talkin' the Talk

Audio track 20: Mrs Lewis wants to speak to Mr Nowak at the Winiarek company about a meeting on Friday, but he's not in the office. She leaves a message for him with Mrs Gałązka, his secretary.

Mrs Gałązka: **Winiarek, Maria Gałązka, słucham?**
(vee-n'ya-rek ma-rya ga-wohN-ska swoo-ham)
Winiarek, Maria Gałązka, hello?

Mrs Lewis: **Dzień dobry, mówi Martha Lewis. Chciałabym rozmawiać z panem Nowakiem.**
(dj'yen' dob-rih moo-vee mar-ta loo-wees hch'ya-wa-bihm roz-ma-vyach' spa-nem no-va-kyem)
Good day, Martha Lewis speaking. I'd like to talk to Mr Nowak.

Mrs Gałązka: **Niestety, nie ma go teraz w biurze.**
(n'yes-te-tih n'ye ma go te-raz vbioo-zhe)
Unfortunately, he's not in the office.

Mrs Lewis: **A kiedy będzie?**
(a kye-dih ben'-dj'ye)
And when will he be back?

Mrs Gałązka: **Może za pół godziny. Czy coś przekazać?**
(mo-zhe za poow go-dj'ee-nih chih tsosh' pshe-ka-zach')
Probably in half an hour. Can I pass on a message?

Mrs Lewis: **Tak, proszę przekazać, że dzwoniłam i proszę o telefon w sprawie spotkania w ten piątek. Niestety, nie mogę w piątek, ale proponuję czwartek o tej samej godzinie.**
(tak pro-she pshe-ka-zach' zhe dzvo-n'ee-wam ee pro-she o te-le-fon fspra-vye spot-ka-n'ya ften pyon-tek n'yes-te-tih n'ye mo-ge fpyon-tek a-le pro-po-noo-ye chfar-tek o tey sa-mey go-dj'ee-n'ye)
Yes, please tell him that I called and I would appreciate a phone call back regarding the meeting this Friday. Unfortunately, I can't make Friday but would suggest Thursday at the same time instead.

Mrs Gałązka: **Dobrze. Proszę przeliterować swoje nazwisko.**
(dob-zhe pro-she pshe-lee-te-ro-vach' sfo-ye naz-vees-ko)
Okay. Please spell your surname.

Mrs Lewis: **Tak, oczywiście, Lewis: el, e, wu, i, es.**
(tak o-chih-veesh'-ch'ye loo-wees el e voo ee es)
Yes, of course, L, E, W, I, S.

Mrs Gałązka: **Telefon kontaktowy?**
(te-le-fon kon-tak-to-vih)
Your contact number?

Mrs Lewis: **022-701-03-18. Dziękuję i do usłyszenia.**
(ze-ro dva-dj'yesh'-ch'ya dva sh'ye-dem-set ye-den ze-ro t-shih o-sh'yem-nash'-ch'ye dj'yen-koo-ye ee do oo-swih-she-n'ya)
022-701-03-18. Thank you and goodbye.

Words to Know

nie ma go/jej	_n'ye_ ma go/yey	he/she is not here
czy coś przekazać?	chih tsosh' pshe-_ka_-zach'	can I take a message?
proszę o telefon	_pro_-she o te-_le_-fon	I'd appreciate a call back
proszę przekazać, że . . .	pro-she pshe-_ka_-zach' zhe	please tell (him/her) that . . .
do usłyszenia	do oo-swih-_she_-n'ya	goodbye (on the phone)

Asking someone to repeat themselves

Especially if you're new to the Polish language, native speakers may speak too quickly for you to understand. While in a face-to-face conversation, you can use body language to help work out meanings, but in a phone conversation you don't have these clues. On top of that, the line may also be bad or you may be on a busy street. Don't get too stressed, though! Asking the person on the other end to slowly repeat what they said isn't being rude in the least. Also, be patient when people ask you to repeat your message again and again. They may have similar difficulties understanding you!

These expressions should help you if you can't make out the words:

- **Przepraszam, nie słyszę** *(pshe-_pra_-sham n'ye _swih_-she)* (I'm sorry, I can't hear you)
- **Proszę mówić głośniej/Mów głośniej** *(_pro_-she _moo_-veedj' _gwosh'_-n'yey/ moov _gwosh'_-n'yey)* (Please speak up) – formal/informal
- **Możesz powtórzyć?** *(_mo_-zhesh pof-_too_-zhihch')* (Can you repeat that, please?) – informal
- **Słucham?** *(_swoo_-ham)* (Pardon?/Excuse me?)

- **Nie dosłyszałem/dosłyszałam** *(n'ye do-swih-sha-wem/do-swih-sha-wam)* (I didn't hear you)
- **Proszę przeliterować** *(pro-she pshe-lee-te-ro-vach')* (Please spell it) – formal
- **Proszę powtórzyć wolniej i innymi słowami, bo nie rozumiem** *(pro-she pof-too-zhihch' vol-n'yey ee een-nih-mee swo-va-mee bo n'ye ro-zoo-myem)* (Please say it slowly and in different words because I don't understand)
- **Słabo cię/pana/panią słyszę** *(swa-bo ch'ye/pa-na/pa-n'yohN swih-she)* (I can't hear you very well) – informal/formal to a man/formal to a woman

Setting up your voicemail greetings

Poland is a beautiful country, the people are friendly and in no time you may realise that this is the place where you want to settle down. If you do, you definitely need to get a phone and set up the message for your answering machine. Here's how it can be done:

- **Tu numer 07. . . Po usłyszeniu sygnału proszę zostawić wiadomość** *(too noo-mer ze-ro sh'ye-dem po oo-swih-she-n'yoo sih-gna-woo pro-she zos-ta-veedj' vya-do-mosh'ch')* (You've reached number 07. . . Please leave a message after the tone)
- **Cześć. Tu Marek. Zostaw wiadomość. Oddzwonię** *(chesh'ch' too ma-rek zos-tav vya-do-mosh'ch' od-dzvo-n'ye)* (Hi. It's Marek. Leave me a message. I'll call you back)

Making Appointments

In the old days people would show up at an official's office and wait at the reception for hours in the hope of getting an appointment. Nowadays, time is money and you hardly get to see anyone without making a prior appointment. Here's how you make an appointment:

- **Chciałbym się umówić na spotkanie na jutro rano** *(hch'yaw-bihm sh'ye oo-moo-veech' na spot-ka-n'ye na yoo-tro ra-no)* (I would like to arrange a meeting for tomorrow morning) – a man speaking
- **Chciałabym się umówić na wizytę do dentysty** *(hch'ya-wa-bihm sh'ye oo-moo-veech' na vee-zih-te do den-tihs-tih)* (I would like to make an appointment to see a dentist) – a woman speaking

- **Czy możemy przesunąć jutrzejsze spotkanie?** *(chih mo-zhe-mih pshe-soo-non'ch' yoo-tshey-she spot-ka-n'ye)* (Can we postpone tomorrow's meeting?)
- **Pasuje ci/panu/pani?** *(pa-soo-ye ch'ee/pa-noo/pa-n'ee)* (Is that okay for you?) – informal/formal to a man/formal to a woman
- **Może być** *(mo-zhe bihch')* (That's fine)
- **Dzisiaj to niemożliwe** *(dj'ee-sh'yay to n'ye-mo-zhlee-ve)* (It's impossible today)

Talkin' the Talk

Audio track 21: Mr Radosław Kowalik *(ra-dos-waf ko-va-leek)* is calling the 'Lingua' school. The school secretary answers the phone.

Secretary: **Szkoła 'Lingua', Anita Siedlarska, słucham?**
(shko-wa leen gwa a-n'ee-ta sh'yed-lar-ska swoo-ham)
Lingua school, Anita Siedlarska, hello?

Mr Kowalik: **Dzień dobry. Czy może mnie pani połączyć z panią Eweliną Michnik? Mówi Radosław Kowalik.**
(dj'yen' dob-rih chih mo-zhe mn'ye pa-n'ee po-won-chihch' spa-n'yohN e-ve-lee-nohN meeh-n'eek moo-vee ra-dos-waf ko-va-leek)
Hello. Can you please put me through to Mrs Ewelina Michnik? Radosław Kowalik speaking.

Secretary: **Chwileczkę. Już łączę.**
(hfee-lech-ke yoosh won-che)
Just a moment. I'm putting you through.

Po chwili *(po hfee-lee)* (after a while)

Secretary: **Niestety, pani Michnik nie może teraz rozmawiać.**
(n'yes-te-tih pa-nee meeh-n'eek n'ye mo-zhe te-ras roz-ma-vyach')
Unfortunately, Mrs Michnik can't talk right now.

Mr Kowalik: **Przepraszam, słabo panią słyszę. Proszę mówić głośniej.**
(pshe-pra-sham swa-bo pa-n'yohN swih-she pro-she moo-veedj' gwosh'-n'yey)
I'm sorry, I can't hear you very well. Can you speak up, please?

Secretary: **Pani Michnik jest na drugiej linii. Może coś przekazać?**
(pa-n'ee meeh-n'eek yest na droo-gyey lee-n'ee mo-zhe tsosh' pshe-ka-zach')
Mrs Michnik is on another line. Can I take a message?

Mr Kowalik: **Proszę powiedzieć, że dzwoniłem.**
(pro-she po-vye-dj'yech' zhe dzvo-n'ee-wem)
Can you please tell her that I called.

Words to Know

połączyć z	*po-won-chihdj' z*	to put through to
już łączę	*yoosh won-che*	I'm putting you through
proszę mówić głośniej	*pro-she moo-veedj' gwosh'-n'yey*	please speak up (formal)
słabo pana/ panią słyszę	*swa-bo pa-na/ pa-n'yohN swih-she*	I can't hear you very well (formal to a man/woman)
jest na drugiej linii	*yest na droo-gyey lee-n'ee*	is on another line

Fun & Games

Before you make your first serious phone call in Polish, you may want to practise. Fill in the dialogues with the phone-related expressions.

Dialogue 1

Szkoła językowa 'Lingua'. Słucham?

Dzień dobry. .... (1) [your name]. **Czy może mnie pani ....** (2) **z panią Salwach?**

Niestety, Pani Salwach nie może teraz .... (3). **Czy coś ....** (4)?

Tak, proszę jej powiedzieć, że dzwoniłem/dzwoniłam i proszę o .... (5).

Oczywiście. Przekażę. Do .... (6).

Dialogue 2

Halo?

Cześć [your name]**! Co robisz dziś wieczorem?**

Przepraszam, a .... (7) **mówi?**

To ja! Anka!

A! Nic .... (8).

Answer:

(1) **mówi** (speaking); (2) **połączyć** (connect, put through); (3) **rozmawiać** (talk); (4) **przekazać** (pass on); (5) **telefon** (phone call back); (6) **do usłyszenia** (see you; literally: hear you later); (7) **kto** (who); (8) **poznałem cię** (I didn't recognise your voice)

Part III
Polish on the Go

In this part . . .

I give you the tools you need to take your Polish on the road, whether you're going to a Polish restaurant or a museum in the capital. These chapters cover all aspects of travel from tips on how to get through the customs process, check into hotels, nab a cab, exchange your currency, ask for directions and even get help in case of emergency.

Chapter 10

Money, Money, Money

In This Chapter

- Paying by card or cash
- Withdrawing money from cash machines
- Working out currency exchanges

According to the Polish saying, **Pieniądze szczęścia nie dają** *(pye-n'yon-dze shchehN-sh'ch'ya n'ye da-yohN)*, money can't buy you happiness. However, without money you wouldn't be able to afford the holiday you've waited all year for, or get the newest gadget you crave or that pair of shoes you've dreamed of wearing! The reason you get up and go to work every day is because you love your job, naturally! But it's also (and you must agree!) for the money that provides all the things that make you smile. Since **Czas to pieniądz** *(chas to pye-n'yondz)* (Time is money), it's time to get to the money business.

Cashing In with Some Basic Info about Money

Wherever you're going, it's always a good thing to have some cash in the form of **banknoty** *(ban-kno-tih)* (notes) and **monety** *(mo-ne-tih)* (coins) on you, along with some basic cash-related expressions:

- **Masz pieniądze?** *(mash pye-n'yon-dze)* (Do you have any money?) – informal
- **Nie mam przy sobie pieniędzy** *(n'ye mam pshih so-bye pye-n'yen-dzih)* (I've got no money on me)
- **Mamy wystarczająco dużo pieniędzy** *(ma-mih vih-star-cha-yon-tso doo-zho pye-n'yen-dzih)* (We've got enough money)
- **Nie mam drobnych** *(n'ye mam drob-nihh)* (I have no small change)
- **Czy może mi pan/pani rozmienić 100 złotych?** *(chih mo-zhe mee pan/pa-n'ee ro-zmye-n'eech' sto zwo-tihh)* (Can you change 100 PLN for me, please?) – speaking to a man/woman

- **Jaka cena?/Ile to kosztuje?** *(ya-ka tse-na/ee-le to kosh-too-ye)* (What's the price/How much is it?)
- **Mamy złotówki** *(ma-mih zwo-toof-kee)* (We have Polish currency)
- **Płacę gotówką/kartą** *(pwa-tse go-toof-kohN/kar-tohN)* (I'm paying by cash/card)

When travelling in Poland, always make sure you have some cash on you – preferably in small notes, **niskie nominały** *(n'ee-skye no-mee-na-wih)*. Giving you change, **drobne** *(drob-ne)*, could be a problem for vendors, especially early in the day. Forget being able to get some chewing gum with a 100-złotych note! You'll hear: **Drobne, proszę!** *(drob-ne pro-she)* (Small change, please!) or **Nie mam wydać** *(n'ye mam wih-dach')* (I have no change).

If you live in an area where using a credit card (or any payment card, for that matter) is so easy and comfortable that you can hide your wallet full of cash deep down in a drawer and still be able to get whatever you want, be prepared for money-culture shock when you visit Poland. Despite a growing number of restaurants and shops that take most credit and debit cards, paying cash is still very common and may be the only payment option, especially in the markets or smaller shops.

Talkin' the Talk

Audio track 22: Simon enjoys shopping in Poland, but knows he can't always use a credit card.

Simon: **Czy można zapłacić kartą?**
chih mo-zhna za-pwa-ch'eech' kar-tohN
Is it possible to pay by card?

Cashier: **Niestety, nie. Tylko gotówką.**
n'ye-ste-tih n'ye tihl-ko go-toof-kohN
Unfortunately, no. Cash only.

Simon: **Nie mam tyle pieniędzy. A gdzie jest najbliższy bankomat?**
n'ye mam tih-le pye-n'yen-dzih a gdj'ye yest nay-bleesh-shih ban-ko-mat
I don't have enough cash. Where is the nearest cash machine?

Cashier: **Po wyjściu z budynku w lewo jakieś 200 metrów.**
po vihy-sh'ch'yoo zboo-dihn-koo vle-vo ya-kyesh' dvyesh'-ch'ye me-troof
At the exit of the building turn left and it's about 200 metres.

Spending złoty and grosz

The Polish currency is called **złoty** *(zwo-tih)* (in everyday usage: **złotówki** *(zwo-toof-kee)* and is abbreviated to PLN for Polish New Zloty. The Polish government plans on switching to the euro in the near future, but until then, you should have a wallet full of **złotówki** when you travel to Poland – or some cash at least. Otherwise you may not be very successful when trying to pay by card for . . . a toilet!

One złoty consists of 100 **groszy** *(gro-shih)*. It's like pounds and pence or euro and eurocents. Złoty notes come in denominations of 10, 20, 50, 100 and 200; coins in 10, 20 and 50 groszy and 1, 2 and 5 złoty. The notes vary in colour and each but one has a king on it. The coins are in different sizes, too, but they don't necessarily grow in proportion to the denomination.

As with everything in the Polish language, the endings of złoty and grosz change with the numbers they go with. Just remember to say **złote** *(zwo-te)* and **grosze** *(gro-she)* when a number ends in 2, 3 or 4 and **złotych** *(zwo-tihh)* or **groszy** *(gro-shih)* after any other number ending between 5 and 9 or 0 and 1. For example:

- **2, 23, 164**: złote/grosze
- **5, 16, 51, 97, 128, 329, 10**: złotych/groszy

A small exception: 12, 13 and 14 use złotych/groszy.

When you read the prices or do your banking, remember that Polish and English present numbers differently. Polish uses commas, not full stops, to separate decimal groups, and full stops between hundreds and thousands. So 2,35 zł (read it as **dwa złote, trzydzieści pięć groszy**) *(dva zwo-te t-shih-dj'yesh'-ch'ee pyen'ch' gro-shih)* in English would be 2.35, and 5.234 zł is 5,234 in English.

Talkin' the Talk

Simon wants to see what's going on in the city this weekend and he goes to a newsagent, **kiosk** *(kyosk)*, to get today's paper.

Simon: **Poproszę gazetę z dodatkiem kulturalnym.**
po-pro-she ga-ze-te zdo-dat-kyem kool-too-ral-nihm
Can I have a paper with cultural information, please.

Cashier: **Proszę bardzo. 5 złotych 50 groszy (5,50 zł).**
pro-she bar-dzo pyen'ch' zwo-tihh pyen'-dj'ye-sh'yont gro-shih
Here you are. It's 5.50 PLN.

Simon hands over a 100-PLN note.

Cashier: **Ale nie mam wydać. Ma pan drobne?**
a-le n'ye mam vih-dach' ma pan drob-ne
But I have no change. Do you have any small change?

Simon: **Niestety, nie.**
n'ye-ste-tih n'ye
Unfortunately, no.

Operating cash machines

If you run out of cash, simply make your way to the nearest **bankomat** *(ban-ko-mat)* (cash machine/ATM) (Chapter 11 tells you how to ask for and understand directions). In this section, I tell you how to use the Polish buttons on the cash machine's display panel. However, to be perfectly honest, all you need to know is **Wybierz język** *(vih-byesh yehN-zihk)*, which means choose the language, click on English and then you're . . . home again.

For those who'd rather practise their Polish, here are the instructions in the order they appear on the screen. Be aware that instructions aren't standardised, though, and they may vary slightly from the following:

- **Włóż kartę** *(vwoosh kar-te)* (Please insert your card)
- **Proszę czekać. Trwa sprawdzanie karty** *(pro-she che-kach' trfa sprav-dza-n'ye kar-tih)* (Please wait. Your card is being checked)
- **Wybierz język** *(vih-byesh yehN-zihk)* (Select language)
- **Wprowadź PIN** *(fpro-vach' peen)* (Enter your PIN)
- **Wypłata** *(vih-pwa-ta)* (Cash withdrawal)
- **Stan konta** *(stan kon-ta)* (Balance)
- **Doładuj telefon** *(do-wa-dooy te-le-fon)* (Top up your phone)
- **Wybierz kwotę** *(vih-byesh kfo-te)* (Select amount)
- **Inna kwota** *(een-na kfo-ta)* (Other amount)
- **Czy wydrukować potwierdzenie transakcji?** *(chih vih-droo-ko-vach' po-tfyer-dze-n'ye tran-zak-tsyee)* (Do you want to print out your receipt?)
- **Odbierz kartę** *(od-byesh kar-te)* (Please take your card)
- **Odbierz pieniądze** *(od-byesh pye-n'yon-dze)* (Please take your money)

You may see the following buttons on the screen:

- **Akceptuj/Zatwierdź** *(ak-tsep-tooy/za-tfyerch')* (Accept)
- **Popraw** *(po-praf)* (Correct)
- **Anuluj/Stop** *(a-noo-looy/stop)* (Cancel)

Talkin' the Talk

Simon is about to pay for his new camera. He has no cash and wants to pay by card. He talks to the cashier.

Simon: **Czy przyjmują państwo karty?**
chih pshihy-moo-yohN pan'-stfo kar-tih
Do you take cards?

Cashier: **Oczywiście.**
o-chih-veesh'-ch'ye
Certainly.

Simon: **Świetnie! Proszę bardzo. (Tu jest moja karta.)**
sh'fye-tn'ye pro-she bar-dzo too yest mo-ya kar-ta
Great. Here you are. (Here is my card.)

Cashier: **Proszę wprowadzić PIN.** [Or] **Proszę podpisać.**
pro-she fpro-va-dj'eech' peen pro-she pot-pee-sach'
Please enter your PIN. [Or] Please sign.

Dziekuję. Proszę kartę i paragon.
dj'yen-koo-ye pro-she kar-te ee pa-ra-gon
Thank you. Here is your card and receipt.

Words to Know

przyjmować karty	*pshihy-mo-vach' kar-tih*	to take cards
wprowadzić PIN	*fpro-va-dj'eech' peen*	enter (your) PIN
podpisać	*pot-pee-sach'*	to sign
paragon	*pa-ra-gon*	receipt
można	*mozh-na*	one can/ it's possible
zapłacić	*za-pwa-ch'eech'*	to pay
kartą/gotówką	*kar-tohN/go-toof-kohN*	by card/cash
bankomat	*ban-ko-mat*	cash machine
wyjście	*vihy-sh'ch'ye*	exit

Using travellers' cheques

Don't take travellers' cheques, **czeki podróżne** *(che-kee po-droo-zhne)*, to Poland as you won't be able to cash them. You risk being sent from one bank to another and still ending up with no cash in your hand. Some hotels accept travellers' cheques as a means of payment for your stay, but you'll struggle to cash them.

If you find it difficult to believe or are already on your way to Poland with travellers' cheques in your pocket, here are some expressions that can come in handy:

- **Gdzie mogę zrealizować czeki podróżne?** *(gdj'ye mo-ge zre-a-lee-zo-vach' che-kee po-droo-zhne)* (Where can I cash my travellers' cheques?)
- **Czy mogę tutaj zrealizować czeki podróżne?** *(chih mo-ge too-tay zre-a-lee-zo-vach' che-kee po-droo-zhne)* (Can I cash my travellers' cheques here?)

Cheques in general, not only travellers' cheques, are not very popular in Poland. Unlike in other countries, wages are paid directly to a person's bank account or occasionally in cash. Shops don't take cheques at all – cash payment or credit card only.

Exchanging Currency

You go to either a **bank** *(bank)* or **kantor** *(kan-tor)* (currency exchange bureau) to change your money, **wymienić pieniądze** *(vih-mye-n'eech' pye-n'yon-dze)*. To get to one or the other, ask these questions:

- **Gdzie mogę wymienić pieniądze?** *(gdj'ye mo-ge vih-mye-n'eech' pye-n'yon-dze)* (Where can I exchange money?)
- **Gdzie jest najbliższy kantor/bank/bankomat?** *(gdj'ye yest nay-bleesh-shih kan-tor/bank/ban-ko-mat)* (Where is the nearest currency exchange bureau/bank/cash machine?)

Chain hotels offer currency exchange services, **kantor**, to save you trouble. If you're thinking about exchanging a larger amount of money, it's worth checking the **kurs** *(koors)*, exchange rate, in different banks and currency exchange offices as it may vary from place to place. Generally speaking, **kantory** tend to offer more favourable rates than banks. And they don't charge a commission, either.

All the currency exchange offices display the rates and the rates are split into two groups: **Skup** *(skoop)* (We buy) and **Sprzedaż** *(spshe-dash)* (We sell). You can always ask the following questions to find out the exchange rate:

- **Jaki jest kurs złotówki/funta/euro/dolara?** *(ya-kee yest koors zwo-toof-kee/foon-ta/ew-ro/do-la-ra)* (What's the rate for PLN/GBP/EUR/USD?)
- **Ile złotówek dostanę za 200 funtów?** *(ee-le zwo-too-vek do-sta-ne za dvyesh'-ch'ye foon-toof)* (How many PLN will I get for 200 GBP?)

Try these expressions to help practise changing money:

- **Chciałbym/Chciałabym wymienić funty/euro/dolary na złotówki** *(hch'yaw-bihm/hch'ya-wa-bihm vih-mye-n'eech' foon-tih/ew-ro/do-la-rih na zwo-toof-kee)* (I'd like to change GBP/EUR/USD into PLN) – a man/woman speaking
- **Czy jest jakaś prowizja?** *(chih yest ya-kash' pro-vee-zya)* (Is there any commission rate?)
- **Jaka jest prowizja?** *(ya-ka yest pro-vee-zya)* (What's the commission rate?)
- **Czy mogę prosić mniejsze nominały?** *(chih mo-ge pro-sh'eech' mn'yey-she no-mee-na-wih)* (Can I have smaller notes, please?)

Talkin' the Talk

Audio track 23: Simon is in a currency exchange bureau trying to change British pounds for Polish złoty.

Simon: **Dzień dobry. Chciałbym wymienić funty brytyjskie na złotówki.**
dj'yen' dob-rih hch'yaw-bihm vih-m'ye-n'eech' foon-tih brih-tihy-skye na zwo-toof-kee
Hello. I'd like to exchange British pounds for złoty.

Kasjer: **Proszę bardzo.**
pro-she bar-dzo
Yes, no problem.

Simon: **Jaki jest dzisiaj kurs funta?**
ya-kee yezd dj'yee-sh'yay koors foon-ta
What's the exchange rate for the [British] pound today?

Kasjer: **4,20 (4 złote 20 groszy za 1 funt).**
chte-rih zwo-te dva-dj'yesh'-ch'ya gro-shih za ye-den foont
4.20 PLN [4 złote and 20 groszy for 1 pound]

Simon: **Czy jest jakaś prowizja przy wymianie?**
chih yest ya-kash' pro-vee-zya pshih vih mya-n'ye
Do you charge commission?

Kasjer: **Nie, nie ma prowizji.**
n'ye n'ye ma pro-vee-zyee
No, we don't charge commission.

Simon: **Dobrze, to wymieniam 200 funtów.**
dob-zhe to vih-mye-n'yam dvyesh'-ch'ye foon-toof
Good, so I [want to] exchange 200 pounds.

Kasjer: **Proszę 840 zł (złotych) I pokwitowanie.**
pro-she o-sh'yem-set chter-dj'ye-sh'ch'ee zwo-tihh ee po-kfee-to-va-n'ye
Here is your 840 PLN and your receipt.

Words to Know

kantor	*kan-tor*	currency exchange bureau
wymienić	*vih-m'ye-n'eech'*	to change
funty na złotówki	*foon-tih na zwo-toof-kee*	pounds for złoty (GBP for PLN)
kurs funta	*koors foon-ta*	the GBP exchange rate
prowizja przy wymianie	*pro-vee-zya pshih vih-mya-n'ye*	commission
pokwitowanie	*po-kfee-to-va-n'ye*	receipt

Here is where you can put your money-related knowledge to the test. Match the Polish expressions to their English equivalents.

1. Kantor	*kan-tor*	A. Currency exchange rate
2. Kurs wymiany	*koors vih-mya-nih*	B. Cash machine
3. Przyjmować karty	*pshihy-mo-vach' kar-tih*	C. Currency exchange bureau
4. Pieniądze	*pye-n'yon-dze*	D. Money
5. Bankomat	*ban-ko-mat*	E. Take/accept cards
6. Gotówka	*go-toof-ka*	F. Receipt
7. Drobne	*drob-ne*	G. Polish currency
8. Paragon	*pa-ra-gon*	H. To change British pounds
9. Złotówki	*zwo-toof-kee*	I. Small change
10. Wymienić funty	*vih-mye-n'eech foon-tih*	J. Cash

Answer key:

1. C; **2.** A; **3.** E; **4.** D; **5.** B; **6.** J; **7.** I; **8.** F; **9.** G; **10.** H

Chapter 11
Asking Directions

In This Chapter

- Finding your way around
- Getting help when you're lost
- Looking into the locative case and location prepositions

Whenever and wherever you travel, sooner or later you'll need to ask how to get where you're going. Understanding directions can prove difficult in your native language, let alone in Polish. Don't worry, though. This chapter helps get you back on the map.

Finding Your Way Around

Just strolling through an unfamiliar city can be an adventure – and a great way to experience the place and the people who live there – but sometimes you need a little help in reaching your destination. You can approach the nearest helpful-looking person and say **Chyba się zgubiłem/zgubiłam** *(hih-ba sh'ye zgoo-bee-wem/zgoo-bee-wam)* (I think I'm lost [man/woman speaking]), and then ask a question from the following list (I help you understand probable answers in the next section):

- **Gdzie jest najbliższy bankomat?** *(gdj'ye yest nay-bleesh-shih ban-ko-mat)* (Where is the nearest cash machine?)
- **Przepraszam, gdzie jest dworzec główny?** *(pshe-pra-sham gdj'ye yezd dvo-zhedz gwoo-vnih)* (Excuse me, where is the main train station?)
- **Czy może mi pan/pani powiedzieć, gdzie znajduje się . . . ?** *(chih mo-zhe mee pan/pa-n'ee po-vye-dj'yech' gdj'ye znay-doo-ye sh'ye)* (Could you please tell me where . . . is? [speaking formally to a man/woman])
- **Jak dojść do centrum?** *(yag doyz'dj' do tsen-troom)* (How do I get [on foot] to the city centre?)

- **Jak dojechać do rynku?** *(yag do-ye-hach' do rihn-koo)* (How do I get [by a means of transportation] to the town square?)
- **Czy może mi pan/pani pokazać na mapie?** *(chih mo-zhe mee pan/pa-n'ee po-ka-zach' na ma-pye)* (Can you show me on the map, please?)

If you ask the question **Jak dojść do . . . ?** *(yag doyz'dj' do)* or **Jak dojechać do . . . ?** *(yag do-ye-hadj' do)* (How do I get [on foot/with a means of transportation] to . . . ?) or **Szukam . . .** *(shoo-kam)* (I'm looking for . . .), the place you're enquiring about has to take the genitive ending. Make your way to Chapter 7 to learn how the endings work. If you're a bit lost in the labyrinth of endings, simply stick to the easy question **Gdzie jest . . . ?** *(gdj'ye yest)* (Where is . . . ?) – no change to the ending is required.

Some of the places you may want to get to are listed in Table 11-1.

Table 11-1 Destinations in the City

English	*Polish*	*Pronunciation*
airport	**lotnisko**	*lot-n'ee-sko*
bank/cash machine	**bank/bankomat**	*bank/ban-ko-mat*
bus station	**dworzec autobusowy**	*dvo-zhets aw-to-boo-so-vih*
bus/tram stop	**przystanek**	*pshih-sta-nek*
city centre	**centrum**	*tsen-troom*
hospital/A&E	**szpital/pogotowie**	*shpee-tal/po-go-to-vye*
hotel	**hotel**	*ho-tel*
Internet café	**kawiarenka internetowa**	*ka-vya-ren-ka een-ter-ne-to-va*
museum	**muzeum**	*moo-ze-oom*
nearest park	**najbliższy park**	*nay-bleesh-shih park*
pharmacy	**apteka**	*a-pte-ka*
post office	**poczta**	*po-chta*
taxi stand	**postój taksówek**	*po-stooy ta-ksoo-vek*
tourist information	**informacja turystyczna**	*een-for-ma-tsya too-rih-stih-chna*
train station	**dworzec kolejowy**	*dvo-zhets ko-le-yo-vih*
tube/tube station	**metro/stacja metra**	*me-tro/sta-tsya me-tra*

Understanding the Answer

Asking how to find a place is only the beginning of getting on your way to your destination. You're then faced with understanding an answer that may include a lot of vocabulary you're not familiar with. Don't expect to be able to understand everything. Instead, sharpen your focus on recognising basic directions such as those in Table 11-2, and rely on the international language of hand gestures for the rest.

Table 11-2 Directions

English	*Polish*	*Pronuciation*
at the crossroads (intersection)	**na skrzyżowaniu**	*na skshih-zho-va-n'yoo*
at the roundabout	**na rondzie**	*na ron'-dj'ye*
at the traffic lights	**na światłach**	*na sh'fya-twah*
here/in here	**tu/tutaj**	*too/too-tay*
on the other side	**po drugiej stronie**	*po droo gyey stro-n'ye*
on the right-/ left-hand side	**po prawej stronie/ po lewej stronie**	*po-pra-vey stro-n'ye/ po le-vey stro-n'ye*
opposite	**naprzeciwko/ na wprost**	*na-pshe-ch'eef-ko/ na fprost*
over there	**tam**	*tam*
straight ahead	**prosto**	*pro-sto*
to the end of this road	**do końca tej ulicy**	*do kon'-tsa tey oo-lee-tsih*
to the right/left	**w prawo/w lewo**	*fpra-vo/vle-vo*
turn right/left	**proszę skręcić w prawo/ w lewo**	*pro-she skren'-ch'eech' fpra-vo/vle-vo*

Some of the answers to get you on the move may include the following phrases:

- **Proszę iść prosto do końca tej ulicy** (*pro-she eesh'ch' pro-sto do kon'-tsa tey oo-lee-tsih*) (Go straight to the end of this road)
- **Proszę skręcić w pierwszą (ulicę) w lewo** (*pro-she skren'-ch'eech' fpyer-fshohN oo-lee-tse vle-vo*) (Take the first [road on the] left)

- **Proszę przejść przez skrzyżowanie** *(pro-she psheysh'ch' pshes skshih-zho-va-n'ye)* (Go straight through the intersection)
- **Dworzec PKS jest po prawej stronie** *(dvo-zhets pe ka es yest po pra-vey stro-n'ye)* (The bus station is on the right-hand side)
- **Proszę iść dalej prosto** *(pro-she eez'dj' da-ley pro-sto)* (Carry on straight ahead)
- **Musi pan/pani pojechać autobusem, bo to daleko** *(moo-sh'ee pan/pa-n'ee po-ye-hach' aw-to-boo-sem bo to da-le-ko)* (You need to take a bus because it's far away) – formal to a man/woman
- **Musi pan/pani przejść na drugą stronę ulicy** *(moo-sh'ee pan/pa-n'ee psheysh'ch' na droo-gohN stro-ne oo-lee-tsih)* (You need to cross the road) – formal
- **Minie pan/pani pocztę** *(mee-n'ye pan/pa-n'ee po-chte)* (You'll go past the post office) – formal
- **Bank jest naprzeciwko kościoła** *(bank yest na-pshe-ch'eef-ko kosh'-ch'yo-wa)* (The bank is opposite the church)
- **Trzeba iść w tamtą stronę** *(tshe-ba eesh'ch' ftam-tohN stro-ne)* (You need to go that way)
- **To jest tam, na rogu** *(to yest tam na ro-goo)* (It's there, on the corner)

When talking about taking the first or second right, you need to use ordinal numbers, which I cover in detail in Chapter 7. You won't be surprised to hear that you need to alter all the cardinal numbers that are provided in Table 7-1 (Chapter 7) by changing the ending **-a** to **-ą** – for example, **pierwsza** becomes **w pierwszą, druga** becomes **w drugą, trzecia** becomes **w trzecią** and so on *(pyer-fsha fpyer-fshohN droo-ga vdroo-gohN t-she-ch'ya ft-she-ch'yohN)* – followed by **ulicę w prawo/w lewo** *oo-lee-tse fpra-vo/vle-vo)* ([take the] first, second, third right). If you want to practise first or second floor, go to Chapter 13.

Talkin' the Talk

Audio track 24: Anna arrived in Gdańsk last night and today she's on her way to see the Old Town, Starówka. The trouble is, she's got a bit lost. She's just stopped a Polish woman to ask her for directions. Because she's talking to a stranger, the conversation is formal.

Anna: **Przepraszam panią. Chyba się zgubiłam.**
pshe-pra-sham pa-n'yohN hih-ba sh'ye zgoo-bee-wam
Excuse me. I think I'm lost.

Woman: **Gdzie pani chce dojść?**
gdj'ye pa-n'ee htse doysh'ch'
Where do you want to go [literally: get to]?

Anna: **Nie wiem, jak dojść do Starówki.**
n'ye vyem yag doyz'dj' do sta-roof-kee
I don't know how to get to the Old Town.

Woman: **To niedaleko stąd. Dziesięć minut pieszo.**
to n'ye-da-le-ko stont dj'ye-sh'yen'ch' mee-noot pye-sho
It's not far from here. Ten minutes on foot.

Proszę iść prosto i skręcić w trzecią ulicę w lewo. Dalej proszę iść prosto do końca.
pro-she eesh'ch' pro-sto ee skren'-ch'eech' ft-she-ch'yohN oo-lee-tse vle-vo da-ley pro-she eesh'ch' pro-sto do kon'-tsa
Go straight on and take the third left. Then carry on walking straight ahead to the end [of that road].

Words to Know

chyba	*hih-ba*	I think/maybe/probably
zgubić się	*zgoo-beech' sh'ye*	to get lost
chcieć	*hch'yech'*	want
dojść do	*doyz'dj' do*	to get to (by foot)
niedaleko stąd	*n'ye-da-le-ko stont*	not far from here
pieszo	*pye-sho*	on foot
prosto	*pro-sto*	straight on
skręcić w lewo/ w prawo	*skren'-ch'eedj' vle-vo/fpra-vo*	turn left/right
dalej	*da-ley*	carry on
do końca	*do kon'-tsa*	to the end

Knowing How Far You Go

If you're not the biggest fan of long walks, finding out how far away your place of interest is might save you some time and hassle. Use these questions to gauge the distance:

- **Jak to daleko stąd?** *(yak to da-le-ko stont)* (How far is it from here?)
- **Czy to daleko stąd?** *(chih to da-le-ko stont)* (Is it far from here?)
- **Czy to niedaleko?** *(chih to n'ye-da-le-ko)* (Is it not far away?)
- **Czy da się tam dojść na nogach?** *(chih da sh'ye tam doysh'ch' na no-gah)* (Is it possible to walk there?)

And here is what you might hear in reply:

- **Nie, to niedaleko stąd** *(n'ye to n'ye-da-le-ko stont)* (No, it's not far from here)
- **To bardzo blisko** *(to bar-dzo blee-sko)* (It's very close)
- **Bankomat jest tutaj** *(ban-ko-mat yest too-tay)* (The cash machine [ATM] is right here)
- **Jeszcze 300 metrów i będzie pan/pani na miejscu** *(yesh-che t-shih-sta me-troof ee ben'-dj'ye pan/pa-n'ee na myey-stsoo)* (Another 300 metres and you'll be right there) – formal to a man/woman
- **Jakieś dziesięć10 minut na nogach** *(ya-kyez' dj'ye-sh'yen'ch' mee-noot na no-gah)* (About ten minutes on foot)
- **To dosyć daleko** *(to do-sihdj' da-le-ko)* (It's pretty far away)
- **Lepiej wziąć taksówkę albo pojechać autobusem** *(le-pyey vz'yon'ch' tak-soof-ke al-bo po-ye-hach' aw-to-boo-sem)* (It's better to take a cab or bus)

Talkin' the Talk

Audio track 25: Simon is unlucky. He's caught a cold while on a weekend break in Poland. He needs to get some medicine but first he has to find out where the pharmacy is. He talks to the receptionist at his hotel.

Simon: **Przepraszam, jak daleko stąd jest apteka?**
pshe-pra-sham yag da-le-ko stont yest ap-te-ka
Excuse me, how far away is the pharmacy?

Receptionist: **Dosyć daleko.**
do-sihdj' da-le-ko
It's pretty far away.

Simon: **Czy da się tam dojść na nogach?**
chih da sh'ye tam doysh'ch na no-gah
Is it possible to get there on foot?

Receptionist: **Tak, ale to jakieś dwadzieścia minut. Ale można pojechać autobusem numer 7.**
tak a-le to ya-kyez' dva-dj'yesh'-ch'ya mee-noot a-le mozh-na po-ye-hach' aw-to-boo-sem noo-mer sh'ye-dem
Yes, but it's about twenty minutes away. But you can take bus number 7.

Mapping the Place

Nowadays, you can easily save yourself the hassle of walking or driving with a map by hiring a car with a satnav or getting a smartphone that has a map application. With those, you'll never get lost. Nor will you need to read this chapter!

However, if you're more traditional and actually enjoy moving your finger along the surface of a map, here are some phrases worth mastering:

- **Bałtyk jest na północy Polski** *(baw-tihk yest na poow-no-tsih pol-skee)* (The Baltic Sea is in the north of Poland)
- **Na południu są góry** *(na po-woo-dn'yoo sohN goo-rih)* (The mountains are in the south)
- **Nigdy nie byłem na wschodzie Europy** *(n'ee-gdih n'ye bih-wem na fsho-dj'ye ew-ro-pih)* (I've never been to Eastern Europe) – literally: to the East of Europe
- **Mieszkam na zachodzie Londynu** *(mye-shkam na za-ho-dj'ye lon-dih-noo)* (I live in West London)
- **Ta ulica jest w centrum/na obrzeżach miasta** *(ta oo-lee-tsa yest ftsen-troom/na o-bzhe-zhah mya-sta)* (This road is in the city centre/suburbs)
- **Proszę jechać na południe** *(pro-she ye-hach' na po-woo-dn'ye)* (Drive south)

Words to Know

na północy	*na poow-no-tsih*	in the north
na południu	*na po-woo-dn'yoo*	in the south
na zachodzie	*na za-ho-dj'ye*	in the west
na wschodzie	*na fsho-dj'ye*	in the east
na północnym zachodzie	*na poow-no-tsnihm za-ho-dj'ye*	in the north-west
na północnym wschodzie	*na poow-no-tsnihm fsho-dj'ye*	in the north-east
na południowym zachodzie	*na po-woo-dn'yo-vihm za-ho-dj'ye*	in the south-west
na południowym wschodzie	*na po-woo-dn'yo-vihm fsho-dj'ye*	in the south-east
północny	*poow-nots-nih*	Northern
południowy	*po-woo-dn'yo-vih*	Southern
zachodni	*za-ho-dn'ee*	Western
wschodni	*fsho-dn'ee*	Eastern

Going with the Four Verbs 'To Go'

You won't be able to go anywhere without knowing the verb *to go*. Actually, all four of them: **iść** *(eesh'ch')*, **chodzić** *(ho-dj'eech')*, **jechać** *(ye-hach')* and **jeździć** *(yez'-dj'eech')*. Before you master their conjugation, it's worth getting familiar with where they actually go.

The following sentences highlight the differences between **iść** and **chodzić**. **Iść** is used for a one-off action of going somewhere and translates to the English present continuous tense (I'm going), whereas **chodzić** is used for an action you do repeatedly (I go):

- **Iść**: ***Dzisiaj*** **idę na siłownię** *(dj'ee-sh'yay ee-de na sh'ee-wov-n'ye)* (I'm going to the gym *today*)
- **Chodzić**: ***Regularnie*** **chodzę na siłownię** *(re-goo-lar-n'ye ho-dze na sh'ee-wov-n'ye)* (I go to the gym *regularly*)

Adverbs of frequency including **często** *(chehN-sto)* (often), **rzadko** *(zhat-ko)* (rarely), **od czasu do czasu** *(ot cha-soo do cha-soo)* (from time to time) and **nigdy** *(n'ee-gdih)* (never) all go with **chodzić** as they imply a repeated action. **Teraz** *(te-ras)* (now), **jutro** *(yoo-tro)* (tomorrow) and **właśnie** *(vwa-sh'n'ye)* (right now/just), on the other hand, are one-off situations and as such go with **iść**. (For more adverbs of frequency, head to Chapter 8.)

Now, if you plan on going to a place you need a car, train or bus to get to, **jechać** and **jeździć** come into play. Again, you use one verb for a single action of going somewhere by a means of transportation – **jechać** – and another – **jeździć** – for repeated actions:

- **Jechać**: ***Właśnie*** **jadę do Warszawy** *(vwa-sh'n'ye ya-de do var-sha-vih)* (I'm *just* on my way [literally: going] to Warsaw)
- **Jeździć**: ***Często*** **jeżdżę do Stanów** *(chehN-sto yezh-dje do sta-noof)* (I *often* go to the States)

Check out Table 11-3 for the present tense conjugation of *to go* in all its verb forms.

Table 11-3 Present Tense Conjugations of Iść, Chodzić , Jechać and Jeździć

Iść – to go (on foot) [single action]		***Chodzić – to go (on foot) [repeated action]***	
idę	*ee-de*	chodzę	*ho-dze*
idziesz	*ee-dj'yesh*	chodzisz	*ho-dj'eesh*
idzie	*ee-dj'ye*	chodzi	*ho-dj'ee*
idziemy	*ee-dj'ye-mih*	chodzimy	*ho-dj'ee-mih*
idziecie	*ee-dj'ye-ch'ye*	chodzicie	*ho-dj'ee-ch'ye*
idą	*ee-dohN*	chodzą	*ho-dzohN*
Jechać – to go (by a vehicle) [single action]		***Jeździć – to go (by a vehicle) [repeated action]***	
jadę	*ya-de*	jeżdżę	*yezh-dje*
jedziesz	*ye-dj'yesh*	jeździsz	*yez'-dj'eesh*
jedzie	*ye-dj'ye*	jeździ	*yez'-dj'ee*
jedziemy	*ye-dj'ye-mih*	jeździmy	*yez'-dj'ee-mih*
jedziecie	*ye-dj'ye-ch'ye*	jeździcie	*yez'-dj'ee-ch'ye*
jadą	*ya-dohN*	jeżdżą	*yezh-djohN*

If you plan on taking a plane, another two verbs come into play: **lecieć** *(le-ch'yech')* (an irregular verb following the **-ę/-isz** type conjugated as **ja lecę, ty lecisz** *(ya le-tse tih le-ch'eesh)* and **latać** (find the **-m/-sz** conjugation in Chapter 2).

- **W tym tygodniu lecę do Paryża** *(ftihm tih-go-dn'yoo le-tse do pa-rih-zha)* (I'm going [literally: flying] to Paris this week) – a one-off action
- **Często latam do Londynu** *(chehN-sto la-tam do lon-dih-noo)* (I often go [literally: fly] to London) – repeated time action

Travelling by Car or another Vehicle

When taking a bus or train, you mustn't forget to take the right noun and adjective cases along. When you're travelling, you need the instrumental case, which you can read more about in Chapter 8.

The following examples include means of transportation in the instrumental case, a selection of verbs of motion (details of which you can find in the preceding section) and adverbs of frequency (covered in Chapter 8):

- **Rzadko jeżdżę do pracy taksówką** *(zhat-ko yezh-dze do pra-tsih tak-soof-kohN)* (I rarely take a cab to work) – literally: go by taxi
- **Jedziemy samochodem** *(ye-dj'ye-mih sa-mo-ho-dem)* (We're going by car)
- **Boję się latać samolotem** *(bo-ye sh'ye la-tach' sa-mo-lo-tem)* (I'm afraid of flying [by plane])
- **Jadę na lotnisko autobusem** *(ya-de na lot-n'ee-sko aw-to-boo-sem)* (I'm taking [literally: going by] a bus to the airport)
- **Nigdy nie jeżdżę pociągiem** *(n'ee-gdih n'ye yezh-dje po-ch'yon-gyem)* (I never go by train)
- **Rzadko jeżdżę do pracy rowerem, bo mieszkam za daleko** *(zhat-ko yezh-dze do pra-tsih ro-ve-rem bo myesh-kam za da-le-ko)* (I rarely bike to work as I live too far away)
- **Do Dover płyniemy promem** *(do dow-ver pwih-n'ye-mih pro-mem)* (We're taking a ferry to Dover)
- **Często jeździsz metrem do biura?** *(chehN-sto yez'-dj'eesh me-trem do byoo-ra)* (Do you often commute to the office by tube?)
- **Czym jeździsz do pracy?** *(chihm yez'-dj'eesh do pra-tsih)* (How do you commute [literally: go] to work?)

Talkin' the Talk

Michael and Tom are talking about their holiday arrangements. You can practise along with them.

Michael: **W tym roku spędzamy urlop w Polsce, a konkretnie na południowym-wschodzie Polski.**
ftihm ro-koo spen-dza-mih oor-lop fpol-stse a kon-kre-tn'ye na po-woo-dn'yo-vihm fsho-dj'ye pol-skee
We're going to spend our holiday in Poland, in the south-east to be more precise.

Tom: **A czym tam jedziecie?**
a chihm tam ye-dj'ye-ch'ye
And how are you going to get there?

Michael: **Lecimy samolotem do Lublina, a potem wynajmujemy samochód i jedziemy w góry.**
le-ch'ee-mih sa-mo-lo-tem do loo-blee-na a po-tem vih-nay-moo-ye-mih sa-mo-hoot ee ye-dj'ye-mih vgoo-rih
We're flying to Lublin and then hiring a car to get to the mountains.

Tom: **Czy to daleko?**
chih to da-le-ko
Is it far away?

Michael: **Z lotniska jakieś trzy, może cztery godziny samochodem.**
zlot-n'ee-ska ya-kyesh' tshih mo-zhe chte-rih go-dj'ee-nih sa-mo-ho-dem
From the airport about three, maybe four hours by car.

Tom: **Będziecie podróżować z mapą?**
ben'-dj'ye-ch'ye po-droo-zho-vadj' zma-pohN
Are you taking a map?

Michael: **Wypożyczamy samochód z nawigacją.**
vih-po-zhih-cha-mih sa-mo-hood zna-vee-ga-tsyohN
We're hiring a car with satellite navigation.

Words to Know

spędzać urlop	*spen-dzach' oor-lop*	to spend a holiday
czym jedziecie?	*chihm ye-dj'ye-ch'ye*	how? (by what means of transportation)
lecieć samolotem	*le-ch'yech' sa-mo-lo-tem*	to go by plane (literally: fly)
jechać samochodem	*ye-hach' sa-mo-ho-dem*	to go by car
daleko	*da-le-ko*	far away
podróżować	*po-droo-zho-vach'*	to travel
mapa	*ma-pa*	map
nawigacja satelitarna	*na-vee-ga-tsya sa-te-lee-tar-na*	satellite navigation

Describing a Position or Location

Imagine you're home from work (in Poland) but can't find your house keys anywhere. You've checked all your bags and pockets, but the keys aren't there. You need to call your colleague and ask him to check in your desk. In order to explain where you think you left your keys, you need to be familiar with the locative case and prepositions expressing location.

Locating the locative case

The main usage of the *locative case* is to say where a person or an object is or when you use a preposition **o** (about). For example:

- **Gdzie jest Adam? W pracy** *(gdj'ye yest a-dam fpra-tsih)* (Where is Adam? At work) – **w pracy** is in the locative case
- **Myślę o Adamie** *(mih-sh'le o a-da-m'ye)* (I'm thinking about Adam) – **o Adamie** is in the locative case

Chapter 2 has more detailed information about when to use this case; here, I focus on the endings. And although this case may look a bit complicated at first, with a few examples and a little bit of practice, your locative case will be perfectly 'located'.

The general rule is that masculine and neuter nouns have only two endings, **-e** or **-u**, and three for feminine nouns, **-e, -y** or **-i**. However, the tricky part is that some letters of the stem itself change to other letters (called an *alternation* in grammar terms).

To master this case, try to memorise at least one example for each group and then, if you come across a noun that ends in the same letters (sounds similar), it will most likely (although not always) follow the same pattern. For example, try to say the following words out loud: **asystent** *(a-sih-stent)* (assistant), **student** *(stoo-dent)* (student) and **kontynent** *(kon-tih-nent)* (continent). They end in the same group of letters (**ent**) and sound similar so they follow the same pattern when changing to the locative case.

Making changes to consonant stems

For nouns in all genders (masculine, feminine and neuter) whose last syllable ends in **-b**, **-f**, **-m**, **-n**, **-p**, **-s**, **-w** and **-z** (or ends in these letters before a final vowel), the locative changes the ending to **-bie**, **-fie**, **mie**, **-nie**, **-pie**, **-sie**, **-wie** and **-zie**, respectively (the very last letter **-e** is the actual locative ending). Table 11-4 shows some examples of the basic nominative (dictionary form) and the locative case. Say them out loud a couple of times so that your ear gets used to the sound!

Table 11-4 Alternations of Words Ending in -b, -f, -m, -n, -p, -s, -w and -z

Nominative Case	*Pronunciation*	*English*	*Locative Case*	*Pronunciation*	*English*
pub	*pap*	pub	w pubie	*fpa-bye*	in a pub
szef	*shef*	boss	o szefie	*o she-fye*	about a boss
program	*pro-gram*	programme	w programie	*fpro-gra-mye*	in a programme
telefon	*te-le-fon*	phone	w telefonie	*fte-le-fo-n'ye*	in a phone
sklep	*sklep*	shop	w sklepie	*fskle-pye*	in a shop
klasa	*kla-sa*	classroom	w klasie	*fkla-sh'ye*	in a classroom
staw	*staf*	pond	w stawie	*fsta-vye*	in a pond
Warszawa	*var-sha-va*	Warsaw	w Warszawie	*vvar-sha-vye*	in Warsaw
wyraz	*vih-ras*	word	o wyrazie	*o vih-ra-z'ye*	about a word

Table 11-5 shows alternations in all genders for words ending in **-d**, **-ł**, **-r**, **-sł**, **-st** and **-t**.

Table 11-5 Alternations of Words Ending in -d, -ł, -r, -sł, -st and -t

Nominative Case	*Pronunciation*	*English*	*Locative Case*	*Pronunciation*	*English*
samochód	*sa-mo-hoot*	car	w samochodzie	*fsa-mo-ho-dj'ye*	in the car
artykuł	*ar-tih-koow*	article	w artykule	*var-tih-koo-le*	in an article
biuro	*byoo-ro*	office	w biurze	*vbyoo-zhe*	in the office
krzesło	*kshe-swo*	chair	na krześle	*na kshe-sh'le*	on a chair
turysta	*too-rih-sta*	tourist	o turyście	*o too-rihsh'-ch'ye*	about a tourist
student	*stoo-dent*	student	o studencie	*o stoo-den-ch'ye*	about a student

These three consonant changes appear in feminine nouns only:

- **g** changes to **dze: droga** *(dro-ga)* (road) changes to **na drodze** *(na dro-dze)* (on the road)
- **k** changes to **ce: Polska** *(pol-ska)* (Poland) changes to **w Polsce** *(fpol-stse)* (in Poland)
- **ch** changes to **sze** (this one not terribly frequent): **mucha** *(moo-ha)* (fly) changes to **o musze** *(o moo-she)* (about a fly)

Changing vowel stems

Some words change vowels that are part of their stem:

- **ó** changes to **o/e: stół** *(stoow)* (table) changes to **na stole** *(na sto-le)* (on a table), **ogród** *(o-groot)* (garden) changes to **w ogrodzie** *(vo-gro-dj'ye)* (in a garden), **kościół** *(kosh'-ch'yoow)* (church) changes to **w kościele** *(fkosh'-ch'ye-le)* (in a church)
- **a** changes to **e: sąsiad** *(sohN-sh'yat)* (neighbour) changes to **o sąsiedzie** *(o sohN-sh'ye-dj'ye)* (about a neighbour), **miasto** *(mya-sto)* (town) changes to **w miescie** *(vmye-sh'ch'ye)* (in a town)

Finding easy (no alternation) endings

If you're dealing with a masculine or neuter noun that ends in a different letter from the ones in the preceding sections, simply add the ending **-u**:

- **fotel** *(fo-tel)* (armchair) becomes **w fotelu** *(ffo-te-loo)* (in an armchair)
- **jabłko** *(yap-ko)* (apple) changes to **w jabłku** *(vyap-koo)* (in an apple)
- **lekarz** *(le-kash)* (doctor) changes to **o lekarzu** *(o le-ka-zhoo)* (about a doctor)
- **maj** *(may)* (May) changes to **w maju** *(vma-yoo)* (in May)
- **Polak** *(po-lak)* (a Pole) changes to **o Polaku** *(o po-la-koo)* (about a Pole)
- **róg** *(rook)* (corner) changes to **na rogu** *(na ro-goo)* (on the corner)
- **słońce** *(swon'-tse)* (the sun) changes to **w słońcu** *(fswon'-tsoo)* (in the sun)

Feminine nouns whose stems end in **-c**, **-cz**, **-dz**, **-rz/ż** and **-sz** take the **-y**. For example:

- **praca** *(pra-tsa)* (work) changes to **w pracy** *(fpra-tsih)* (at work)
- **dacza** *(da-cha)* (holiday house) changes to **w daczy** *(vda-chih)* (in a holiday house)
- **władza** *(vwa-dza)* (authority) changes to **o władzy** *(o vwa-dzih)* (about the authority)

- **róża** *(roo-zha)* (rose) changes to **na róży** *(na roo-zhih)* (on the rose)
- **cisza** *(ch'ee-sha)* (quiet) changes to **w ciszy** *(fch'ee-shih)* ([sitting] in the quiet)

Those feminine nouns whose stem ends in a soft letter **-ć/ci, -dź/dzi, -j, -l, -ń/ni, -ś/si** and **-ź/zi** take the ending **-i**, as in the following examples:

- **restauracja** *(res-taw–ra-tsya)* (restaurant) changes to **w restauracji** *(vres-taw-ra-tsyee)* (in a restaurant)
- **Łódź** *(wooch')* (city of Łódź) changes to **w Łodzi** *(vwo-dj'ee)* (in Łódź)
- **Ola** (*o-la*) (Ola/female name Alex) changes to **o Oli** (*o o-lee*) (about Ola)
- **babcia** *(bap-ch'ya)* (grandmother) changes to **o babci** *(o bap-ch'ee)* (about grandmother)
- **kuchnia** *(koo-hn'ya)* (kitchen) changes to **w kuchni** *(fkoo-hn'ee)* (in the kitchen)
- **Kasia** *(ka-sh'ya)* (Kate) becomes **o Kasi** *(o ka-sh'ee)* (about Kate)
- **więź** (link, bond, connection) *(vyehNsh')* becomes **o więzi** *(o vyehN-z'ee)* (about a link, bond, connection)

Addressing adjectives

Single masculine and neuter adjectives take the ending **-ym** or **-im** (after k or g) and feminine adjectives take **-ej**. For example:

- **duże miasto** *(doo-zhe mya-sto)* (big city) becomes **w dużym mieście** *(vdoo-zhihm myesh'-ch'ye)* (in a big town)
- **wysoki budynek** *(vih-so-kee boo-dih-nek)* becomes **w wysokim budynku** *(vvih-so-keem boo-dihn-koo)* (in a tall building)
- **mała sala** *(ma-wa sa-la)* (small room) becomes **w małej sali** *(vma-wey sa-lee)* (in a small room)

Locative plural

When it comes to dealing with plural locatives, you can breathe a big sigh of relief. Absolutely all nouns have only one ending – **-ach**! With plural locative adjectives, you have just two endings to choose from: use **-ych** for almost everything and **-ich** after k or g. What could be easier!

- o zagraniczn**ych** podróż**ach** *(o za-gra-n'eech-nihh po-droo-zhah)* (about foreign travels)
- na wysok**ich** obcas**ach** *(na vih-so-keeh op-tsa-sah)* (with [literally: on] high heels)

Locative case exceptions

Of course, there are exceptions to every grammatical rule (probably every rule in general)! You simply have to memorise a couple of words that break the locative case rules by inventing their own endings instead. Learn these words as you come across them:

- **dom** *(dom)* (home) changes to **w domu** *(vdo-moo)* (at home)
- **pan** *(pan)* (Mr) changes to **o panu** *(o pa-noo)* (about Mr)
- **syn** *(sihn)* (son) changes to **o synu** *(o sih-noo)* (about a son)
- **wieś** *(vyesh')* (countryside) changes to **na wsi** *(na fsh'ee)* (in the countryside)
- **mąż** *(mohNsh)* (husband) changes to **o mężu** *(o mehN-zhoo)* (about a husband)
- **ksiądz** *(ksh'yonts)* (priest) changes to **o księdzu** *(o ksh'yen-dzoo)* (about a priest)
- **Włochy** *(vwo-hih)* (Italy) changes to **we Włoszech** *(ve vwo-sheh)* (in Italy)
- **Niemcy** *(n'yem-tsih)* (Germany) changes to **w Niemczech** *(vn'yem-cheh)* (in Germany) – Italy and Germany are plural nouns in Polish!

Exploring prepositions of location and position

When talking about location, position or spatial relations, a number of prepositions come into play.

Every Polish preposition can have many different meanings in English. For example, **od** means *from* but can also mean *since* and *than* to name a couple. To add to the difficulty, the same preposition can use different cases, as **na** *(na)* (at, to) reveals in these examples:

- **Jestem na spotkaniu** *(yes-tem na spo-tka-n'yoo)* (I'm at a meeting) – locative case
- **Idę na spotkanie** *(ee-de na spot-ka-n'ye)* (I'm going to a meeting) – accusative case

To avoid being totally confused, learn prepositional phrases, not prepositions as separate words. Table 11-6 offers a number of examples to help you to remember prepositions, their meaning and how they're used in a sentence.

Table 11-6 Prepositions Expressing Locations

Preposition	Pronunciation	Meaning	Example
Genitive Case Prepositions			
obok koło	o-bok ko-ło	next to, beside	**Usiądź obok/koło mnie.** *oo-sh'yon'ch' o-bok/ko-wo mn'ye* Sit next to me.
na wprost naprzeciwko	na fprost na-pshe-ch'eef-ko	opposite	**Siedzę na wprost okna.** *sh'ye-dze na fprost o-kna* I'm sitting opposite the window.
Instrumental Case Prepositions			
nad	*nat*	above, over	**Lampa wisi nad stołem.** *lam-pa vee-sh'ee nat sto-wem* The lamp hangs above the table.
pod	*pot*	under, below	**Kot siedzi pod stołem.** *kot sh'ye-dj'ee pot sto-wem* The cat is sitting under the table.
przed	*pshet*	in front of, earlier than	**Jestem przed pubem.** *yes-tem pshet pa-bem* I'm in front of [outside] the pub.
za	*za*	behind, beyond	**Park jest za pocztą.** *park yezd za poch-tohN* The park is behind the post office.
między	*myen-dzih*	between, among	**Bank jest między apteką a sklepem.** *bank yest myen-dzih ap-te-kohN a skle-pem* The bank is between the pharmacy and the shop.

Preposition	*Pronunciation*	*Meaning*	*Example*
Locative Case Prepositions			
na	*na*	on, at, in [open area]	**Gazeta jest na stole.** *ga-ze-ta yest na sto-le* The newspaper is on the table.
w	*v*	in, inside	**Mieszkam w Londynie.** *myesh-kam vlon-dih-n'ye* I live in London.
przy	*pshih*	by, near, close by	**Lubię siedzieć przy oknie.** *loo-bye sh'ye-dj'yech' pshih o-kn'ye* I like to sit by the window.

Go to Chapter 2 for the rules of usage of each case and a list of common prepositions.

You're visiting a small Polish city and need to ask for directions to the park. Look at the map in Figure 11-1 and try to translate, from Polish to English, the following directions:

Proszę iść prosto.

Na światłach proszę skręcić w lewo.

Dalej prosto do końca tej ulicy i potem proszę skręcić w prawo.

Po prawej stronie minie pani bank.

Na rondzie proszę skręcić w pierwszą ulicę.

Po lewej stronie jest kościół.

Park jest naprzeciwko kościoła.

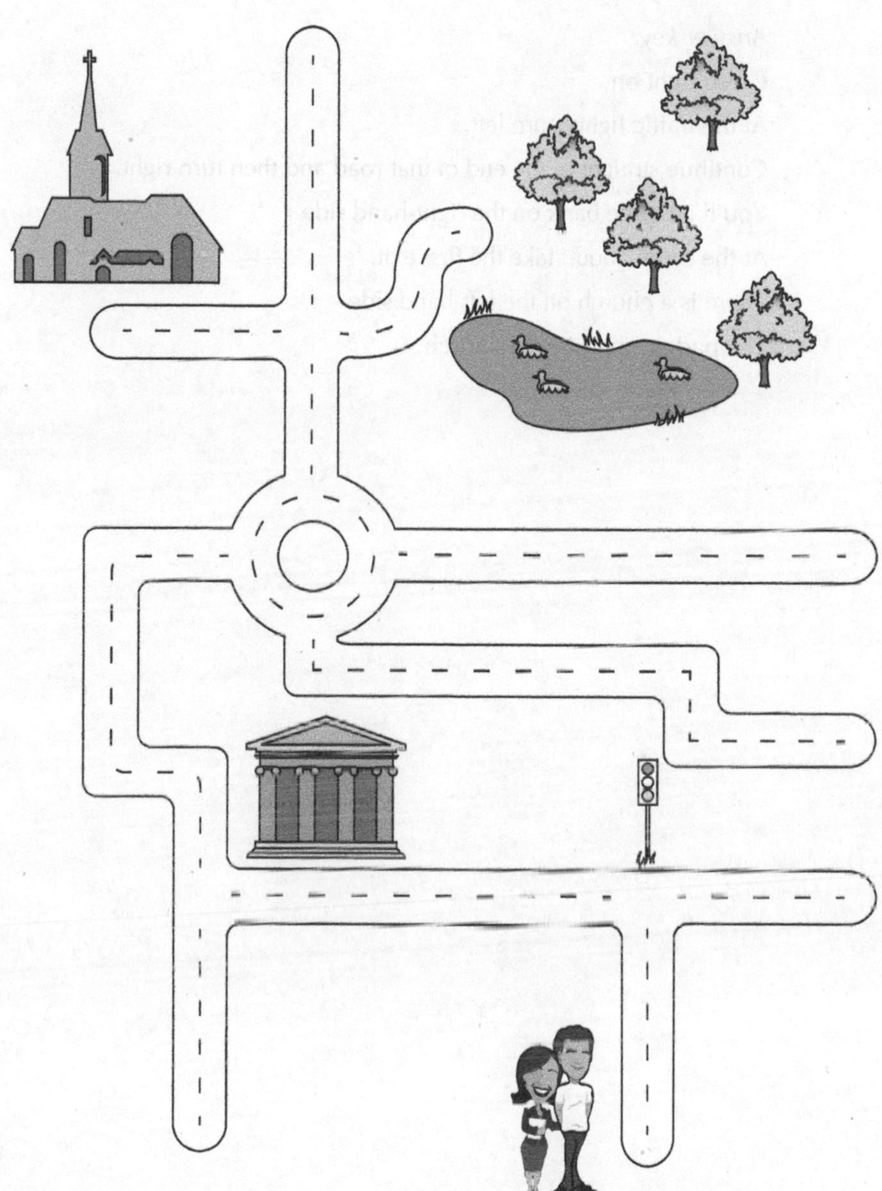

Figure 11-1: A map to the park.

Answer key:

Go straight on.

At the traffic lights, turn left.

Continue straight to the end of that road and then turn right.

You'll pass the bank on the right-hand side.

At the roundabout, take the first exit.

There is a church on the left-hand side.

The park is opposite the church.

Chapter 12

Checking into a Hotel

In This Chapter

- Finding a hotel and making a reservation
- Checking in and out

This chapter will help you find your home away from home – a place to stay while on holiday or a business trip in Poland.

Choosing a Hotel

The choice of accommodation in Poland is wide, ranging from luxurious Western hotel chains, **hotele** *(ho-te-le)*, top-class Polish hotels, where you can experience some of the culture too, through to relatively inexpensive **pensjonaty** *(pen-syo-na-tih)* (boarding houses) with a friendly atmosphere, **kwatery prywatne** *(kfa-te-rih prih-vat-ne)* (private rooms), also called **pokoje gościnne** *(po-ko-ye gosh'-ch'een-ne)*, to the mountain hostels, **schroniska górskie** *(shro-n'ees-ka goor-skye)* or student hostels called **akademiki** *(a-ka-de-mee-kee)*. Gaining in popularity is a stay at a **gospodarstwo agroturystyczne** *(gos-po-dar-stfo a-gro-too-rih-stih-chne)* tourist farm – check out Chapter 8 to find out what awaits you there.

Describing the room you want

After you get an affirmative answer to **Czy mają państwo wolne pokoje?** *(chih ma-yohN pan'-stfo vol-ne po-ko-ye)* (Do you have any rooms available [formal]?), you can start discussing what size room you need and what amenities you prefer. Table 12-1 shows some common options.

Table 12-1 Hotel Room Sizes and Amenities

English	*Polish*	*Pronunciation*
single room	**pokój jednoosobowy**	*po-kooy ye-dno-o-so-bo-vih*
double room	**pokój dwuosobowy**	*po-kooy dvoo-o-so-bo-vih*
three-person room	**pokój trzyosobowy**	*po-kooy t-shih-o-so-bo-vih*
with bathroom	**z łazienką**	*zwa-z'yen-kohN*
with shower	**z prysznicem**	*sprih-shn'ee-tsem*
with air-conditioning	**z klimatyzacją**	*sklee-ma-tih-za-tsyohN*
without air-conditioning	**bez klimatyzacji**	*bes klee-ma-tih-za-tsyee*
lift	**winda**	*veen-da*
television	**telewizor**	*te-le-vee-zor*
with breakfast	**ze śniadaniem**	*ze sh'n'ya-da-n'yem*
without breakfast	**bez śniadania**	*bes sh'n'ya-da-n'ya*
half board	**z obiadokolacją**	*zo-bya-do-ko-la-tsyohN*
full board	**z pełnym wyżywieniem**	*spew-nihm vih-zhih-vye-n'yem*
for non-smokers	**dla niepalących**	*dla n'ye-pa-lon-tsihh*
for smokers	**dla palących**	*dla pa-lon-tsihh*
with a sea view	**z widokiem na morze**	*zvee-do-kyem na mo-zhe*
with a mountain view	**z widokiem na góry**	*zvee-do-kyem na goo-rih*
with a lake view	**z widokiem na jezioro**	*zvee-do-kyem na ye-z'yo-ro*
overlooking the street	**z widokiem na ulicę**	*zvee-do-kyem na oo-lee-tse*

Making a reservation

When you're ready to book a room, say, **Chciałbym zarezerwować pokój . . .** *(hch'yaw-bihm za-re-zer-vo-vach' po-kooy)* (I'd like to book a room . . .) if you're a man; if you're a woman, use **chciałabym** *(hch'ya-wa-bihm)* instead. Then use the following phrases to talk about timing:

- **Od tego piątku** *(ot te-go pyont-koo)* (from this Friday)
- **Od przyszłej niedzieli** *(ot psih-shwey n'ye-dj'ye-lee)* (from next Sunday)
- **Od następnego tygodnia** *(ot nas-tem-pne-go tih-go-dn'ya)* (from next week)

- **Na weekend** *(na wee-kent)* (for a weekend)
- **Na dwa dni** *(na dva dn'ee)* (for two nights) – literally: for two days
- **Na tydzień** *(na tih-dj'yen')* (for a week)
- **Na dwa tygodnie** *(na dva tih-god-n'ye)* (for two weeks)

Now, you can start talking money:

- **Ile to kosztuje?** *(ee-le to kosh-too-ye)* (How much is it?) or **Jaka jest cena?** *(ya-ka yest tse-na)* (What's the price?)
- **Czy można płacić kartą?** *(chih mozh-na pwa-ch'eech' kar-tohN)* (Is it possible to pay by card?)

Discussing services and facilities

Checking the services and facilities your hotel offers is always worth it, especially if you're looking for more than just a room with a bed. Start your question with **Czy w hotelu jest . . .** *(chih fho-te-loo yest)* (Does the hotel have . . .) and choose the extras you're interested in from Table 12-2.

Table 12-2 Hotel Services and Facilities

English	*Polish*	*Pronunciation*
currency exchange	**kantor**	*kan-tor*
guest parking	**parking dla gości**	*par-keeng dla gosh'-ch'ee*
gym	**siłownia**	*sh'ee-wov-n'ya*
Internet	**Internet**	*een-ter-net*
Internet café	**kafejka internetowa**	*ka-fey-ka een-ter-ne-to-va*
mini-bar	**barek**	*ba-rek*
restaurant	**restauracja**	*res-taw-ra-tsya*
safe	**sejf**	*seyf*
sauna	**sauna**	*saw-na*
swimming pool	**basen**	*ba-sen*
television	**telewizor**	*te-le-vee-zor*
WiFi	**internet bezprzewodowy/ WiFi**	*een-ter-net bes-pshe-vo-do-vih/vee-fee*

If you need one of those things foreign travellers often need, use **Czy mogę prosić o . . .** *(chih mo-ge pro-sh'eech' o)* (Can I have . . .) and add the appropriate item:

- **Przejściówkę** *(pshey-sh'ch'yoof-ke)* (an adapter)
- **Suszarkę** *(soo-shar-ke)* (a hairdryer)
- **Żelazko** *(zhe-las-ko)* (an iron)

Ask a helpful hotel employee for information you want:

- **Na którym piętrze jest sauna?** *(na ktoo-rihm pyent-she yest saw-na)* (Which floor is the sauna on?)
- **Do której godziny jest czynny basen?** *(do ktoo-rey go-dj'ee-nih yest chihn-nih ba-sen)* (What time is the swimming pool open until?)

Talkin' the Talk

Audio track 26: Anna Daniels calls a hotel in Zakopane (*za-ko-pa-ne*) to check their room availability and hopefully book a room for herself and her husband.

Hotel clerk: **Hotel Tatry. W czym mogę pomóc?**
ho-tel ta-trih fchihm mo-ge po-moots
Tatry Hotel. How can I help you?

Anna: **Dzień dobry. Czy mają państwo wolne pokoje?**
dj'yen' dob-rih chih ma-yohN pan'-stfo vol-ne po-ko-ye
Good day. Do you have any rooms available?

Hotel clerk: **Od kiedy i na jak długo?**
ot kye-dih ee na yag dwoo-go
From when and for how long?

Anna: **Od następnego piątku na tydzień.**
od nas-tem-pne-go pyon-tkoo na tih-dj'yen'
From next Friday, for a week.

Hotel clerk: **Jaki pokój?**
ya-kee po-kooy
What [sort of] room?

Anna: **Dwuosobowy z łazienką.**
dvoo-o-so-bo-vih zwa-z'yen-kohN
Double room with a bathroom.

Hotel clerk: **Tak, mamy jeszcze wolne takie pokoje.**
tak ma-mih yesh-che vol-ne ta-kye po-ko-ye
Yes, we still have such rooms available.

Anna: **Bardzo się cieszę. Jaka jest cena?**
bar-dzo sh'ye ch'ye-she ya-ka yest tse-na
That's great [I'm very happy]. What's the price?

Hotel clerk: **215 złotych ze śniadaniem.**
dvyesh'-ch'ye pyet-nash'-ch'ye zwo-tihh ze sh'n'ya-da-n'yem
215 PLN with breakfast.

Anna: **A ile kosztuje pełne wyżywienie?**
a ee-le kosh-too-ye pew-ne vih-zhih-vye-n'ye
And how much is full board?

Hotel clerk: **Dodatkowo 50 złotych.**
do-dat-ko-vo pyen'-dj'ye-sh'yond zwo-tihh
50 PLN extra.

Anna: **Świetnie. Chciałabym zarezerwować jeden pokój.**
sh'fyet-n'ye hch'ya-wa-bihm za-re-zer-vo-vach' ye-den po-kooy
Perfect. I'd like to book one room, please.

Hotel clerk: **Oczywiście. Na jakie nazwisko ma być rezerwacja?**
o-chih-veesh'-ch'ye na ya-kye naz-vee-sko ma bihch' re-zer-va-tsya
Of course. Under what name [Is the reservation to be]?

Anna: **Anna Daniels.**

Hotel clerk: **Czy mogę prosić o telefon kontaktowy i adres emailowy?**
Przyślemy pani potwierdzenie rezerwacji mailem.
chih mo-ge pro-sh'eech' o te-le-fon kon-tak-to-vih ee a-dres ee-mey-lo-vih
pshih-sh'le-mih pa-n'ee po-tfyer-dze-n'ye re-zer-va-tsyee mey-lem
Can I have your contact telephone number and email address?
We will send your booking confirmation by email.

Words to Know

wolne pokoje	*vol-ne po-ko-ye*	available rooms
od kiedy	*ot kye-dih*	from when?
na jak długo	*na yag dwoo-go*	how long for?
cena	*tse-na*	price
ze śniadaniem	*ze sh'n'ya-da-n'yem*	with breakfast
pełne wyżywienie	*pew-ne vih-zhih-vye-n'ye*	full board
potwierdzenie rezerwacji	*po-tfyer-dze-n'ye re-zer-va-tsyee*	booking confirmation

Checking into a Hotel

When you arrive at your hotel, you need to complete just a little bit of paperwork before you're on the way to your room. **Nareszcie!** *(na-resh-ch'ye)* (At last!) You'll probably encounter some or all of the following phrases:

- **Mam rezerwację na nazwisko . . .** *(mam re-zer-va-tsye na na-zvee-sko)* (I have a booking under the name . . .)
- **Tu jest mój paszport** *(too yest mooy pash-port)* (Here is my passport)
- **Proszę wypełnić formularz** *(pro-she vih-pew-n'eech' for-moo-lash)* (Please fill out this form)
- **Tu są klucze** *(too sohN kloo-che)* (Here are the keys)
- **Na którym piętrze jest pokój?** *(na ktoo-rihm pyen-tshe yest po-kooy)* (Which floor is the room on?)
- **Czy mogę prosić o dodatkowe łóżko?** *(chih mo-ge pro-sh'eech o do-dat-ko-ve woosh-ko)* (Can I have an extra bed, please?)
- **Chciałbym zamówić budzenie na 7 rano** *(hch'yaw-bihm za-moo-veedj' boo-dze-n'ye na sh'ood-mohN ra-no)* (I'd like [a man speaking] to book a wake up call for 7 a.m.)

Go to Chapter 7 to practise ordinal numbers so that you can say the floor your room is on. Remember to add the ending **-ym**, as in **na pierwszym**, **drugim**, **trzecim piętrze** *(na pyer-fshihm, droo-geem, t-she-ch'eem pyent-she)* (on the first, second, third floor).

Talkin' the Talk

Audio track 27: Anna Daniels has arrived at the hotel where she made a reservation a couple of days ago.

Anna: **Dzień dobry. Mam rezerwację na nazwisko Daniels.**
dj'yen' dob-rih mam re-zer-va-tsye na na-zvee-sko da-n'yels
Good morning. I have a reservation under the name of Daniels.

Hotel clerk: **Już, chwileczkę... Tak, pokój jednoosobowy od dzisiaj na 5 dni.**
yoosh hfee-lech-ke tak po-kooy ye-dno-o-so-bo-vih od dj'ee-sh'yay na pyen'dj' dn'ee
Just a minute . . . Yes, it's a single room from today for five days.

Anna: **Zgadza się.**
zga-dza sh'ye
That's correct.

Hotel clerk: **Poproszę pani dokument tożsamości.**
po-pro-she pa-n'ee do-koo-ment tosh-sa-mosh'-ch'ee
Can I see your ID, please.

Proszę wypełnić formularz - imię, nazwisko, adres, numer paszportu i podpisać na końcu.
pro-she vih-pew-n'eech' for-moo-lash ee-mye naz-vee-sko a-dres noo-mer pash-por-too ee pot-pee-sach' na kon'-tsoo
Please fill out this form – your first name, surname, address and passport number – and sign at the bottom.

Proszę bardzo. Tu są klucze. Pokój jest na trzecim piętrze. Winda jest za rogiem. Czy pomóc pani z bagażem?
pro-she bar-dzo too sohN kloo-che po-kooy yest na t-she-ch'eem pyent-she veen-da yezd za ro-gyem chih po-moots pa-n'ee zba-ga-zhem
No problem. Here are your keys. Your room is on the third floor. The lift is around the corner. Do you need help with your luggage?

Anna: **Nie dziękuję. Mam tylko jedną małą torbę.**
n'ye dj'yen-koo-ye mam tihl-ko yed-nohN ma-wohN tor-be
No, thank you. I've only got one small bag.

Words to Know

mam rezerwację	*mam re-zer-va-tsye*	I have a reservation
zgadza się	*zga-dza sh'ye*	that's correct
dokument tożsamości	*do-koo-ment tosh-sa-mosh'-ch'ee*	ID
podpisać	*pot-pee-sach'*	to sign
klucze	*kloo-che*	keys
bagaż	*ba-gash*	luggage

Talkin' the Talk

Anna has taken a refreshing shower and she's now back at the reception desk to ask about the hotel's facilities.

Anna: **Czy w pokoju jest internet bezprzewodowy?**
chih fpo-ko-yoo yest een-ter-net bes-pshe-vo-do-vih
Is there WiFi in the room?

Hotel clerk: **Tak. Tutaj jest hasło.**
tak too-tay yest ha-swo
Yes. Here is the password.

Anna: **O której godzinie jest śniadanie?**
o ktoo-rey go-dj'yee-n'ye yest sh'n'ya-da-n'ye
What time is breakfast?

Hotel clerk: **Śniadanie serwujemy od 7 do 11 rano w restauracji na parterze.**
sh'n'ya-da-n'ye ser-voo-ye-mih ot sh'yood-mey do ye-de-nas-tey ra-no vres-taw-*ra-tsyee na par-te-zhe*
We serve breakfast from 7 till 11 a.m. in the ground floor restaurant.

Anna: **Czy rachunek za kolację można wziąć na pokój?**
chih ra-hoo-neg za ko-la-tsye mozh-na vz'yon'ch' na po-kooy
Can I add the restaurant bill to the room, please?

Hotel clerk: **Nie ma problemu.**
n'ye ma pro-ble-moo
No problem.

Anna: **Na którym piętrze jest spa?**
na ktoo-rihm pyen-tshe yest spa
Which floor is the spa on?

Hotel clerk: **Na poziomie minus 1. Tam też jest basen i bar.**
na po-z'yo-mye mee-noos ye-den tam tesh yest ba-sen ee bar
It's minus 1. The swimming pool and bar are there, too.

Words to Know

internet bezprzewodowy/WiFi	*een-ter-net bes-pshe-vo-do-vih/vee-fee*	WiFi
login i hasło	*lo-geen ee ha-swo*	login and password
sejf	*seyf*	safe
barek	*ba-rek*	mini-bar
basen	*ba-sen*	swimming pool

Checking Out

Well, all good things have to come to an end. So must your holiday in Poland. Now it's time to check out of a hotel and head to the airport.

If you have an early flight to catch, it might be easier to sort out the bill the night before your departure or ask for it to be ready in the morning. You can say the following:

- **Wyjeżdżam jutro rano** *(vih-yezh-djam yoo-tro ra-no)* (I'm leaving tomorrow morning)
- **Czy mogę teraz uregulować rachunek?** *(chih mo-ge te-ras oo-re-goo-lo-vach' ra-hoo-nek)* (Could I sort out the bill now, please?)
- **Czy mogę prosić o przygotowanie rachunku na jutro rano?** *(chih mo-ge pro-sh'eech' o pshih-go-to-va-n'ye ra-hoon-koo na yoo-tro ra-no)* (Could I please have the bill ready for tomorrow morning?)

Of course, you have to pay for any extra services that you've used, such as the mini-bar, phone calls or the Internet. You can also ask the receptionist to book a taxi for you. Here is how you do it:

- **Korzystałem/Korzystałam z barku/z Internetu w pokoju** *(ko-zhih-sta-wem/ko-zhih-sta-wam zba-rkoo/zeen-ter-ne-too fpo-ko-yoo)* (I [man/woman] used the mini-bar/Internet)
- **Wziąłem/wzięłam piwo i wodę mineralną z barku** *(vz'yo-wem/vz'ye-wam pee-vo ee vo-de mee-ne-ral-nohN zba-rkoo)* (I've taken one beer and a mineral water from the mini-bar)
- **Ile wynosi mój rachunek za telefon?** *(ee-le vih-no-sh'ee mooy ra-hoo-neg za te-le-fon)* (How much is my telephone bill?)
- **Proszę mi zamówić taksówkę na lotnisko na siódmą rano** *(pro-she mee za-moo-veech' tak-soof-ke na lot-n'ee-sko na sh'yood-mohN ra-no)* (Please book a cab to the airport for 7 a.m.)

If you have plenty of time on your hands before you leave the city, you certainly want to know by what time you need to check out of the room so that you can plan your day accordingly. Be aware, that if you miss your check-out time, you may be charged for an extra night. Ask these questions:

- **O ktorej godzinie muszę zwolnić pokój?** *(o ktoo-rey go-dj'ee-n'ye moo-she zvol-n'eech' po-kooy)* (What time is the check-out?) – literally: What time do I need to vacate the room?
- **Czy mogę zostawić swój bagaż w hotelu?** *(chih mo-ge zos-ta-veech' sfooy ba-gash fho-te-lu)* (Can I leave my luggage in the hotel?)

Once you return to pick it up, you can say:

- **Czy mogę wziąć swój bagaż?** *(chih mo-ge vz'yon'ch' sfooy ba-gash)* (Can I take my luggage, please?)

Talkin' the Talk

Audio track 28: Anna has had a lovely stay in Poland but now she has to go back to the UK. She's checking out of her hotel.

Anna: **Dzień dobry. Chciałabym zwolnić pokój. Tu są klucze.**
dj'yen' dob-rih hch'ya-wa-bihm zvol-n'eech' po-kooy too sohN kloo-che
Hello. I'd like to check-out. Here are the keys.

Hotel clerk: **Tutaj jest faktura za pokój ze śniadaniem za 5 dni, 3 rachunki z restauracji i barek.**
too-tay yest fa-ktoo-ra za po-kooy ze sh'n'ya-da-n'yem za pyen'ch' dn'ee t-shih ra-hoon-kee zres-taw-ra-tsyee ee ba-rek
Here is the invoice for your room with breakfast, 5 nights, 3 restaurant bills and the mini-bar.

Anna: **Tak, wszystko się zgadza. Czy mogę zapłacić kartą?**
tak fshih-stko sh'ye zga-dza chih mo-ge za-pwa-ch'eech' kar-tohN
Yes, all correct. Can I pay by card?

Hotel clerk: **Proszę bardzo.**
pro-she bar-dzo
No problem.

Anna: **Czy mogę gdzieś zostawić bagaż?**
chih mo-ge gdj'yez' zo-sta-veedj' ba-gash
Can I leave my luggage somewhere?

Hotel clerk: **Oczywiście. Tutaj proszę.**
o-chih-veesh'-ch'ye too-tay pro-she
Certainly. In here, please.

Anna: **Chciałabym też zamówić taksówkę na lotnisko na 18.00.**
hch'ya-wa-bihm tezh za-moo-veech' tak-soof-ke na lot-n'ees-ko na o-sh'yem-nas-tohN
I'd also like to book a taxi to the airport for 6 p.m.

Words to Know

zwolnić pokój	*zvol-n'eech' po-kooy*	to check-out
faktura	*fa-ktoo-ra*	invoice
wszystko	*fshih-stko*	everything
zapłacić kartą	*za-pwa-ch'eech' kar-tohN*	to pay by card
bagaż	*ba-gash*	luggage
zamówić taksówkę	*za-moo-veech' tak-soof-ke*	to book a cab

Unscramble words 1–13 and write them in the middle column provided. You can find their English translation in the right-hand column.

1. okpój jednoosobwoy		A. single room
2. z łanzieką		B. with a bathroom
3. bażag		C. luggage
4. od kediy		D. from when?
5. cerepcja		E. reception desk
6. z widokime an romez		F. with a sea view
7. wyełnipć orfmularz		G. to fill out the form
8. na ajk długo?		H. for how long?
9. an kórytm piętzre?		I. on which floor?
10. złapacić arktą		J. to pay by card
11. baerk		K. mini-bar
12. słoniaw		L. gym
13. iel kozstuje?		M. how much?

Answer key:

pokój jednoosobowy (single room); *z łazienką* (with bathroom); *bagaż* (luggage); *od kiedy* (from when?); *recepcja* (reception desk); *z widokiem na morze* (with a sea view); *wypełnić formularz* (to fill out the form); *na jak długo?* (for how long?); *na którym piętrze?* (on which floor?); *zapłacić kartą* (to pay by card); *barek* (mini-bar); *siłownia* (gym); *ile kosztuje?* (how much?)

Chapter 13

Getting Around: Planes, Trains, Taxis and More

In This Chapter

- Getting through the airport
- Making your way around the city
- Staying on time

What's more exciting than taking some time off and getting on a plane to one of the well-known Polish cities such as Kraków *(kra-koof)*, Gdańsk *(gdan'sk)* or Warszawa *(var-sha-va)*. And you don't need to limit yourself to typical tourist destinations. Get on a train, take a bus or hit the roads by car and discover the real Poland. This chapter will definitely get you safely to your destination, so, off you go!

Arriving in Poland by Air

With so many low-budget airlines – **tanie linie lotnicze** *(ta-n'ye lee-n'ye lot-n'ee-che)* – frequently flying to quite a number of Polish cities, getting yourself to Poland has never been easier, even if just for a long weekend.

Since all airline personnel speak English and the signs at the airports are in both Polish and English, you don't have to worry about speaking the language to get there. You can get through **port lotniczy** *(port lot-n'ee-chih)* (airport), commonly called **lotnisko** *(lot-n'ees-ko)*, without saying a single word of Polish. But that's certainly not what you want, is it?

Dealing with customs

When you get off the plane – **samolot** *(sa-mo-lot)* – you need to go to passport control, **kontrola paszportowa** *(kon-tro-la pash-por-to-va)*, to show your **paszport** *(pash-port)*. Or, if you're arriving from the European Union, **dowód osobisty** *(do-voot o-so-bees-tih)*, an ID card will do. Be prepared to answer some simple questions:

- **Jakim lotem pan/pani przyleciał/przyleciała?** *(ya-keem lo-tem pan/pa-n'ee pshih-le-ch'ya-w/pshih-le-ch'ya-wa)* (What flight did you come on?) – formal to a man/woman
- **Jak długo zamierza pan/pani zostać w kraju?** *(yag dwoo-go za-m'ye-zha pan/pa-n'ee zos-tach' fkra-yoo)* (How long do you intend to stay in the country?) – formal to a man/woman

Then, you'll hear: **Życzę miłego pobytu** *(zhih-che mee-we-go po-bih-too)* (Have a nice stay).

Are you a joker? Better hold your horses when talking to Polish customs officers. They're serious people dealing with serious business.

Once you've cleared passport control, you can head to **odbiór bagażu** *(od-byoor ba-ga-zhoo)* (baggage collection) and then go to one of the exits:

- **Nic do oclenia** *(n'eedz do o-tsle-n'ya)* (Nothing to declare) – if you don't have goods exceeding the customs limits
- **Towary do oclenia** *(to-va-rih do o-tsle-n'ya)* (Goods to declare) – check the customs regulations beforehand to avoid an unnecessary rise in blood pressure!

Sorting out check-in and boarding

On the way out of Poland, you first need to go to the right **terminal** *(ter-mee-nal)* in the appropriate **hala odlotów** *(ha-la od-lo-toof)* (departure hall) for **odprawa bagażowa** *(ot-pra-va ba-ga-zho-va)* (check-in). Get ready to show your **bilet lotniczy** *(bee-let lot-n'ee-chih)* (plane ticket) or **potwierdzenie rezerwacji** *(po-tfyer-dze-n'ye re-zer-va-tsyee)* (booking confirmation) and answer questions about your baggage:

- **Czy ma pan/pani bagaż do nadania?** *(chih ma pan/pa-n'ee ba-gazh do na-da-n'ya)* (Do you have any luggage to check in?) – formal to a man/woman
- **Ile sztuk bagażu ma pan/pani do nadania**? *(ee-le shtoog ba-ga-zhoo ma pan/pa-n'ee do na-da-n'ya)* (How many pieces of luggage do you have to check in?) – formal to a man/woman

You'll then get your **karta pokładowa** *(kar-ta po-kwa-do-va)* (boarding card) and can head to **kontrola paszportowa** *(kon-tro-la pash-por-to-va)* (passport control) and **kontrola bezpieczeństwa** *(kon-tro-la bes-pye-chen'-stfa)* (security control). It's a good idea to check when your flight starts boarding, **wejście na pokład samolotu** *(vey-sh'ch'ye na po-kwat sa-mo-lo-too)*, so that you don't miss your plane, **spóźnić się na samolot** *(spooz'-n'eech' sh'ye na sa-mo-lot)* while enjoying the duty free zone.

Talkin' the Talk

Audio track 29: Anna has enjoyed a holiday in Wrocław *(vro-tswaf)* and is heading home again. She is at the airport's check-in desk:

Agent: **Poproszę bilet lotniczy i dokument ze zdjęciem.**
po-pro-she bee-let lot-n'ee-chih ee do-koo-mend ze zdyen'-ch'yem
Can I see your ticket and photo ID, please?

Anna: **Proszę bardzo.**
pro-she bar-dzo
Here you are.

Agent: **Dokąd pani leci?**
do-kont pa-n'ee le-ch'ee
Where are you flying to?

Anna: **Do Londynu.**
do lon-dih-noo
To London.

Agent: **Ile ma pani sztuk bagażu?**
ee-le ma pa-n'ee shtoog ba-ga-zhoo
How many pieces of luggage do you have?

Anna: **Jedną walizkę do nadania i jeden bagaż podręczny.**
yed-nohN va-lees-ke do na-da-n'ya ee ye-den ba-gash pod-rench-nih
One bag to check in and one piece of hand luggage.

Agent: **Czy sama pani pakowała walizkę?**
chih sa-ma pa-n'ee pa-ko-va-wa va-lees-ke?
Did you pack your bag by yourself?

Anna: **Tak.**
tak
Yes.

Agent: **Jakieś płyny w bagażu podręcznym?**
ya-kyesh' pwih-nih vba-ga-zhoo pod-rench-nihm
Any liquids in your hand luggage?

Anna: **Nie.**
n'ye
No.

Agent: **Proszę, tu jest pani karta pokładowa i potwierdzenie nadania bagażu.**
pro-she too yest pa-n'ee kar-ta po-kwa-do-va ee po-tfyer-dze-n'ye na-da-n'ya ba-ga-zhoo
Here is your boarding card and baggage receipt.

Wejście na pokład zaczyna się o 9:05, wyjście numer 2.
vey-sh'ch'ye na po-kwad za-chih-na sh'ye o dj'ye-vyon-tey pyen'ch' vihy-sh'ch'ye noo-mer dva
Boarding starts at 9:05, gate 2.

Words to Know

port lotniczy/ lotnisko	*port lot-n'ee-chih/ lot-n'ees-ko*	airport
bilet lotniczy	*bee-let lot-n'ee-chih*	airline ticket
odprawa bagażowa	*ot-pra-va ba-ga-zho-va*	check in
wejście na pokład	*vey-sh'ch'ye na po-kwat*	boarding
przyloty/hala przylotów	*pshih-lo-tih/ha-la pshih-lo-toof*	arrivals
odloty/hala odlotów	*od-lo-tih/ha-la od-lo-toof*	departures
opóźniony	*o-pooz'-n'yo-nih*	delayed
wylądował	*vih-lon-do-vaw*	landed
odwołany	*od-vo-wa-nih*	cancelled
wyjście	*vihy-sh'ch'ye*	exit/gate

Travelling Around in the City

Large Polish cities have well-oiled and relatively inexpensive public transport, which consists of **autobusy** *(aw-to-boo-sih)* (buses), **minibusy** *(mee-n'ee-boo-sih)* (mini-buses), **tramwaje** *(tram-va-ye)* (trams) and, in Warsaw, **metro** *(me-tro)* (the tube). The next sections explain how to buy tickets, enquire about schedules and so on.

Finding a taxi

To save yourself the hassle of finding the right train or bus that will take you to your hotel, the easiest and quickest way out of the airport is to take a taxi, **taksówka** *(ta-ksoo-fka)*. Some of the phrases you may need include:

- **Gdzie jest postój taksówek?** *(gdj'ye yest po-stooy ta-ksoo-vek)* (Where is the taxi rank?)
- **Proszę do hotelu Mariott** *(pro-she do ho-te-loo ma-ryot)* ([to the] Marriott Hotel, please)
- **Jaki adres?** *(ya-kee a-dres)* (What address?)
- **Tu jest adres** *(too yest a-dres)* (Here is the address)
- **Ile płacę?** *(ee-le pwa-tse)* (How much do I owe?)

Sometimes, if you don't want to risk being late, booking a taxi in advance is sensible. Some handy expressions in that situation are:

- **Poproszę taksówkę na adres ul. Nowa 3** *(po-pro-she ta-ksoo-fke na a-dres oo-lee-tsa no-va tshih)* (I'd like to book a cab from Nowa Street 3)
- **Na kiedy?** *(na kye-dih)* (When for?)
- **Jutro o szóstej rano** *(yoo-tro o shoo-stey ra-no)* (Tomorrow at 6 a.m.)
- **Dokąd będzie kurs?** *(do-kond ben'-dj'ye koors)* (Where are you going?)
- **Kurs na lotnisko** *(koors na lot-n'ees-ko)* (To the airport)
- **Poproszę o telefon kontaktowy** *(po-pro-she o te-le-fon kon-tak-to-vih)* (Can I have your contact number, please?)

Although taxi drivers are generally very honest, keeping your eyes and ears open is sensible. Take taxis that clearly display their company name and phone number together with their fares. At airports and train stations, go to taxi information desks.

Taking a train or bus

If you plan to hop from city to city during your visit to Poland, taking a **pociąg** *(po-ch'yonk)* (train) is comfortable, relatively inexpensive and fast. When it comes to getting to smaller places train travel can prove more difficult, but taking a bus, **autobus** *(aw-to-boos)*, or the increasingly popular **mini-bus** *(mee-n'ee-boos)*, can save you a lot of time and hassle. Use these phrases:

- **Przepraszam, gdzie jest dworzec autobusowy/kolejowy?** *(pshe-pra-sham gdj'ye yezd dvo-zhets aw-to-boo-so-vih/ko-le-yo-vih)* (Excuse me, where is the train station?)
- **Na dworzec PKS/PKP, poproszę** *(na dvo-zhets pe ka es/pe ka pe po-pro-she)* ([To the] bus/train station, please)

A railway station has two names in Polish: **dworzec kolejowy** *(dvo-zhets ko-le-yo-vih)* or **dworzec PKP** *(dvo-zhets pe ka pe)* (abbreviation of *Polskie Koleje Państwowe*, the Polish National Railway). Similarly, you'll hear **dworzec autobusowy** *(dvo-zhets aw-to-boo-so-vih)* or **dworzec PKS** *(dvo-zhets pe ka es)* for a bus station.

- **Jak dojść do dworca autobusowego/kolejowego?** *(yag doyz'dj' do dvor-tsa aw-to-boo-so-ve-go/ko-le-yo-ve-go)* (How do I get to the train station?)

You may have the option of several types of train:

- **Pociąg pospieszny** *(po-ch'yonk pos-pyesh-nih)* (fast train)
- **Pociąg osobowy** *(po-ch'yonk o-so-bo-vih)* (local train)
- **Ekspres** *(eks-pres)* (express)
- **Intercity** *(in-ter-see-tih)* (intercity)

Talkin' the Talk

Adam *(a-dam)* wants to get to Stare Miasto *(sta-re mya-sto)* (Old Town) but he's too tired to walk and wants to take a bus or tram. He asks a woman on the street for help:

Adam:	**Przepraszam, jak dojechać do centrum?** *pshe-pra-sham yag do-ye-hadj' do tsen-troom* Excuse me, how can I get to the city centre?

Woman: **Autobusem sto dwa lub tramwajem numer pięć.**
aw-to-boo-sem sto dva loop tram-va-yem noo-mer pyen'ch'
Bus 102 or tram number 5.

Adam: **Czy to daleko stąd?**
chih to da-le-ko stont
Is it far from here?

Woman: **Nie, blisko. Jakieś dziesięć minut.**
n'ye blees-ko ya-kyez' dj'ye-sh'yen'ch' mee-noot
No, it's very close. About ten minutes.

Adam: **A z którego przysta n ku?**
a sktoo-re-go pshih-stan-koo
And what bus stop?

Woman: **Z tamtego.**
stam-te-go
The one over there.

Adam: **Gdzie można kupić bilet?**
gdj'ye mozh-na koo-peedj' bee-let
Where can I buy a ticket?

Woman: **W kiosku lub w automacie.**
fkyo-skoo loob vaw-to-ma-ch'ye
At a newsagent or from a ticket machine.

Adam: **Na którym przystanku muszę wysiąść?**
na ktoo-rihm pshih-stan-koo moo-she vih-sh'yohNsh'ch'
Which bus stop do I need to get off at?

Woman: **Zaraz, sprawdzę... Raz, dwa, trzy... Na trzecim.**
za-ras sprav-dze ras dva t-shih na t-she-ch'eem
Let me check . . . one, two, three . . . At the third one.

Words to Know

metro/stacja metra	me-tro/sta-tsya me-tra	tube/tube station
tramwaj	tram-vay	tram
kiosk	kyosk	newsagent
automat z biletami	aw-to-mat zbee-le-ta-mee	ticket machine
jak dojechać?	yag do-ye-hach'	how do I get there (by transport)?
przystanek tramwajowy	pshih-sta-nek tram-va-yo-vih	tram stop
zaraz sprawdzę	za-ras sprav-dze	let me check

Checking the timetable

If you have Internet access, go to www.pkp.pl *(voo voo voo krop-ha po ka pe krop ka pe el)* to check train connections and book tickets for your journeys in Poland. This website is available in a number of languages.

Some useful expressions you may need for reading a **rozkład jazdy** *(ros-kwat yaz-dih)* (timetable) include:

- **Przyjazdy/Odjazdy** *(pshih-yaz-dih/od-yaz-dih)* (arrivals/departures)
- **Przyjeżdżać/Odjeżdżać** *(pshih-yezh-djach'/od-yezh-djach')* (to arrive/to depart)
- **Stacja/Przystanek/Stanowisko** *(sta-tsya/pshih-sta-nek/sta-no-vees-ko)* (station/stop/bus stop)
- **Przez** *(pshes)* (via)
- **Tor/Peron** *(tor/pe-ron)* (track/platform)

Getting information and buying tickets

Go to **informacja** *(een-for-ma-tsya)* to get details about train or bus connections and to **kasa biletowa** *(ka-sa bee-le-to-va)* to purchase a ticket:

- **O której godzinie odjeżdża pociąg/autobus do Krakówa?** *(o ktoo-rey go-dj'ee-n'ye od-yezh-dja po-ch'yong/aw-to-booz do kra-ko-va)* (What time does the train/bus to Kraków leave?)
- **Z którego peronu/stanowiska?** *(sktoo-re-go pe-ro-noo/sta-no-vees-ka)* (From which platform/bus stop?)
- **Czy to jest pociąg bezpośredni czy z przesiadką?** *(chih to yest po-chyong bes-po-sh'red-n'ee chih spshe-sh'yat-kohN)* (Is this a direct train or do I have to change?)
- **Czy trzeba się przesiadać?** *(chih tshe-ba sh'ye pshe-sh'ya-dach')* (Do I need to change?)
- **O której będzie na miejscu?** *(o ktoo-rey ben'-dj'ye na myey-stsoo)* (What time will it arrive?)
- **Czy jest jakiś pociąg . . .** *(chih yest ya-keesh' po-ch'yonk)* (Is there a train . . .)
  - **z** *(z)* (from)
  - **do** *(do)* (to)
  - **o** *(o)* (at [time])
- **Czy jest jakieś bezpośrednie połączenie?** *(chih yest ya-kyez' bes-po-sh'red-n'ye po-won-che-n'ye)* (Is there a direct [train/bus] connection?)
- **Na którym przystanku muszę wysiąść?** *(na ktoo-rihm pshih-stan-koo moo-she vih-sh'yohNsh'ch')* (Which stop do I need to get off at?)
- **Ile kosztuje bilet normalny/ulgowy?** *(ee-le kosh-too-ye bee-let nor-mal-nih/ool-go-vih)* (How much is the full price/reduced fare ticket?)
- **Poproszę bilet w jedną stronę/powrotny?** *(po-pro-she bee-led vyed-nohN stro-ne/po-vrot-nih)* (Can I have a single/return ticket, please?)
- **Pierwsza/druga klasa** *(pyer-fsha/droo-ga kla-sa)* (first/second class)
- **Rezerwacja miejsc/Miejscówka** *(re-zer-va-tsya myeysts/myeys-tsoof-ka)* (reserved seat)

The numbering of Polish platforms works a bit differently from what you may be familiar with. When enquiring about the platform number, you'll hear something like this:

- **Tor drugi przy peronie pierwszym** *(tor droo-gee pshih pe-ro-n'ye pyer-fshihm)* (Track 2 at platform 1)
- **Tor piąty przy peronie trzecim** *(tor pyon-tih pshih pe-ro-n'ye t-she-ch'eem)* (Track 5 at platform 3)

Use ordinal numbers (first, second and so on) for track and platform numbers (you can find more on ordinal numbers in Chapter 7).

Different cities have different ticketing systems. In some cities, you can buy a travel card, **bilet miesięczny** *(bee-let mye-sh'yen-chnih)*, for a week or a month. Some tickets are for a single journey on a particular line, while others allow you to change between trams and buses. Time-based tickets are good for as little as 10 minutes through to 30, 60 and 120 minutes; you can even get a 24-hour ticket, **bilet dobowy** *(bee-led do-bo-vih)*, which can be very convenient. Check out the public transport information point of a particular city, for details.

Talkin' the Talk

Audio track 30: Michał *(mee-haw)* is at the ticket office at the Warszawa Centralna *(var-sha-va tsen-tral-na)* train station buying a ticket to Zakopane *(za-ko-pa-ne)*.

Michał: **Poproszę bilet normalny w jedną stronę na pociąg pospieszny z Warszawy Centralnej do Zakopanego.**
po-pro-she bee-let nor-mal-nih vyed-nohN stro-ne na po-ch'yonk pos-pyesh-nih z var-sha-vih tsen-tral-ney do za-ko-pa-ne-go
Can I have a single, full-price ticket for the fast train from Central Warsaw station to Zakopane, please?

Cashier: **Która klasa?**
ktoo-ra kla-sa
Which class?

Michał: **Pierwsza. Z którego peronu?**
pyer-fsha sktoo-re-go pe-ro-noo
First class. What platform?

Cashier: **Tor czwarty przy peronie drugim.**
tor chfar-tih pshih pe-ro-n'ye droo-geem
Track 4 at platform 2.

Michał: **Czy to jest pociąg bezpośredni?**
chih to yest po-ch'yong bes-po-sh'red-n'ee
Is this a direct train?

Cashier: **Niestety nie, trzeba się przesiąść w Krakowie.**
n'yes-te-tih n'ye tshe-ba sh'ye pshe-sh'yohNsh'ch' fkra-ko-vye
Unfortunately, no; you need to change at Kraków.

Michał:	**O której godzinie odjeżdża pociąg z Krakowa?** *o ktoo-rey go-dj'yee-n'ye od-yezh-dja po-ch'yonk skra-ko-va* What time does the train leave Kraków?
Cashier:	**O szesnastej. Ma pan trzydzieści minut na przesiadkę.** *o shes-nas-tey ma pan t-shih-dj'yesh'-ch'ee mee-noot na pshe-sh'yat-ke* At 4 p.m. You'll have 30 minutes to change.

Words to Know

w jedną stronę	*vyed-nohN stro-ne*	single (ticket)
powrotny/ w obie strony	*po-vrot-nih/vo-bye stro-nih*	return (ticket)
odjeżdżać	*od-yezh-djach'*	to depart
stacja	*sta-tsya*	station
przystanek autobusowy	*pshih-sta-nek aw-to-boo-so-vih*	bus stop
miejscówka	*myeys-tsoof-ka*	reserved seat

When entering a compartment on a train, it's customary to greet other passengers with **dzień dobry** *(dj'yen' dob-rih)* (hello) and to say **do widzenia** *(do vee-dze-n'ya)* (goodbye) when leaving. If you haven't reserved a seat, it's polite to double-check whether the one you're about to take is actually free by saying **wolne?** *(vol-ne)* (may I?) (with rising intonation). Don't be surprised if a complete stranger starts a conversation with you. Take it as an opportunity to practise your Polish!

Tickets for inspection

When taking a bus or a tram, remember to validate your ticket as soon as you get on. Different cities have different validation machines installed on buses and trams but using any of them is always straightforward.

Ticket inspections are common and it can be both pricey and embarrassing to hear **Bilety do kontroli** *(bee-le-tih do kon-tro-lee)* (tickets for inspection) when you don't actually have a validated ticket.

Renting a car

If you want to explore smaller towns or the countryside, or simply want the freedom and flexibility that come with travelling by car, renting one is a sensible option.

Renting a car when you arrive can be a pricey business and you also risk not getting the type of car you want. Booking a car in advance via the Internet makes sense.

Here are some expressions to get you on the road:

- **Gdzie jest wypożyczalnia samochodów?** *(gdj'ye yezd vih-po-zhih-chal-n'ya sa-mo-ho-doof)* (Where is the car rental?)
- **Chciałbym wypożyczyć samochód** *(hch'yaw-bihm vih po-zhih-chihch' sa-mo-hoot)* (I'd like to rent a car) – a man speaking
- **Chciałabym odebrać samochód** *(hch'ya-wa-bihm o-de-bruch' sa-mo-hoot)* (I'd like to pick up the car [I booked]) – a woman speaking
- **Tutaj jest potwierdzenie rezerwacji** *(too-tay yest po-tfyer-dze-n'ye re-zer-va-tsyee)* (Here's the booking confirmation)
- **Ile kosztuje ubezpieczenie?** *(ee-le kosh-too-ye oo-bes-pye-che-n'ye)* (How much is the insurance?)
- **Czy są opony zimowe?** *(chih sohN o-po-nih z'ee-mo-ve)* (Does [the car] have winter tyres?)
- **Ile pali?** *(ee-le pa-lee)* (What's the fuel consumption?)
- **Gdzie mam oddać samochód?** *(gdj'ye mam od-dach' sa-mo-hoot)* (Where do I return the car?)

- **Mam oddać z pełnym czy z pustym bakiem?** *(mam od-dach' spew-nihm chih spoos-tihm ba-kyem)* (Do I return the car with the tank full or empty?)
- **Proszę, tu jest moje prawo jazdy** *(pro-she too yest mo-ye pra-vo yaz-dih)* (Here is my driving licence)
- **Czy jest jakiś limit kilometrów?** *(chih yest ya-keesh' lee-meet kee-lo-me-troof)* (Is there a mileage limit?)
- **Czy ten samochód ma nawigację satelitarną?** *(chih ten sa-mo-hoot ma na-vee-ga-tsye sa-te-lee-tar-nohN)* (Does this car have satellite navigation?)

Poles drive on the right-hand side and they measure distance in kilometres, not miles. Slow down when you see a road sign with a number 50 on it; that's actually only 30 miles per hour! But if you hire a car in Poland, the speedometer will be in kilometres anyway, so no worries.

Driving in Poland can be quite an experience. With not so many motorways (lots of them are being built), you may need to use narrow lanes and those, especially after the winter months, may have potholes. Be careful when overtaking and beware of drivers overtaking you, as they tend to force their way through.

Expressions you may need on the road include:

- **Autostrada/Droga ekpresowa** *(aw-to-stra-da/dro-ga eks-pre-so-va)* (Motorway/expressway)
- **Gdzie jest stacja benzynowa?** *(gdj'ye yest sta-tsya ben-zih-no-va)* (Where is the petrol station?)
- **Mapa Polski** *(ma-pa pol-skee)* (road map of Poland)
- **Benzyna bezołowiowa (PB95/PB98)/gaz/olej napędowy** *(ben-zih-na bez-o-wo-v'yo-va (pe be dj'ye-vyen'-dj'ye-sh'yont pyen'ch'/pe be dj'ye-vyen'-dj'ye-sh'yont o-sh'yem)/gas/o-ley na-pen-do-vih)* (unleaded/gas/diesel fuel)

If you have a petrol car, look out for the symbols **PB 98** or **PB 95** (which is slightly cheaper than the PB 98) for unleaded petrol at the petrol station.

Police road patrols are common in Poland, especially in the holiday period, **święta** *(sh'fyen-ta)*. You can see the patrols on the side roads checking speed and breathalysing drivers.

Scheduling Issues: Running Late, Being Early or Arriving on Time

Since time is money, **czas to pieniądz** *(chas to pye-n'yonts)*, reaching your destination **na czas** *(na chas)* (on time) is crucial. This vocabulary comes into play when talking about being late, on time or ahead of schedule:

- **Samolot wylądował przed czasem** *(sa-mo-lod vih-lon-do-vaw pshet cha-sem)* (The plane landed early) – literally: ahead of time
- **Nasz lot jest opóźniony/odwołany** *(nash lot yest o-pooz'-n'yo-nih/ od-vo-wa-nih)* (Our flight is delayed/cancelled)
- **Spóźnimy się na pociąg!** *(spooz'-n'ee-mih sh'ye na po-ch'yonk)* (We're going to miss the train!)
- **Nie zdążę na lotnisko!** *(n'ye zdohN-zhe na lot-n'ees-ko)* (I'm not going to make it to the airport!)
- **Autobus przyjechał punktualnie/na czas** *(aw-to-boos pshih-ye-haw poon-ktoo-al-n'ye/na chas)* (The bus arrived on time)
- **Jesteś w samą porę** *(ye-stesh' fsa-mohN po-re)* (You're just in time)
- **Zgodnie z rozkładem/Planowo** *(zgod-n'ye zros-kwa-dem/pla-no-vo)* (According to the timetable/As planned)

Fun & Games

Before you head off to the station to get your first ticket, try to arrange the sentences of the following dialogue in the correct order:

Sentence	Correct Order Number
Czy ten pociąg rano jest bezpośredni?	
Niestety, to jest pociąg z przesiadką w Krakowie.	
Która klasa?	
Druga.	
Dziękuję bardzo za informację, do widzenia.	
Tak, jest pociąg pospieszny o jedenastej i Intercity o dziewiętnastej.	
A ile kosztuje bilet normalny?	
Dzień dobry. Czy jest jakieś połączenie z Zakopanego do Warszawy?	
85 zł.	

Answer key:

Dzień dobry. Czy jest jakieś połączenie z Zakopanego do Warszawy? (Hello. Is there any [train] connection from Zakopane to Warsaw?)

Tak, jest pociąg pospieszny o 11.00 i Intercity o 19.00. (Yes, there is a fast train at 11 a.m. and an Intercity at 7 p.m.)

Czy ten pociąg rano jest bezpośredni? (Is the morning train direct?)

Niestety, to jest pociąg z przesiadką w Krakowie. (Unfortunately, you will have to change in Kraków.)

A ile kosztuje bilet normalny? (And how much is an adult ticket?)

Która klasa? (Which class?)

Druga. (Second [please].)

85 zł. (85 PLN.)

Dziękuję bardzo za informację, do widzenia. (Thank you for your information; goodbye.)

Chapter 14

Planning a Trip

In This Chapter

- Talking to a travel agent
- Checking the calendar
- Sorting out travel documents
- Packing your luggage
- Considering adaptors

Planning a trip, **planowanie podróży** *(pla-no-va-n'ye po-droo-zhih)*, can be as exciting as the trip itself. After all, you need to make important decisions on where to go, where to stay, what to do, how to get around when you're there and much more.

Check out `www.poland.gov.pl` to get ideas of places to go and things to do in Poland.

Whatever you desire, you'll be spoilt for choice in Poland – traditional and modern cities dotted around the breath-taking and varying landscape; the higher and lower mountains covering the southern part of Poland; the low-lands of central Poland with their marvellous hills and thousands of vivid lakes, rivers and canals; and, in the very north, the coast with wide and beautiful sandy beaches. Name any activity, and most likely, you'll be able to do it in Poland!

Earlier chapters in this Part put you in practice hotel, restaurant and train station situations; use them and this chapter to help you to fully enjoy Poland.

Making Travel Plans with a Travel Agent

If you don't really have time to look for a flight, organise accommodation or do the research on what to visit, your best bet is to go to a **biuro podróży** *(byoo-ro po-droo-zhih)* (travel agent), and leave it all to them.

You may still, however, need to get ready for some questions and practise the answers to them, as shown in the following examples:

- **Jakie mają państwo oferty wycieczek do Polski?** *(ya-kye ma-yohN pan'-stfo o-fer-tih vih-ch'ye-chek do pol-skee)* (What kind of trips to Poland do you have on offer?) – formal
- **Dokąd chce pan/pani pojechać na urlop?** *(do-kont htse pan/pa-n'ee po-ye-hach' na oo-rlop)* (Where would you like to go on holiday?) – formal to a man/woman
- **Która część Polski?** *(ktoo-ra chehNsh'ch' pol-skee)* (Which part of Poland?)
- **Nie byłem jeszcze nad morzem** *(n'ye bih-wem yesh-che nad mo-zhem)* (I've never been to the seaside)
- **Chcę pojechać w góry/nad jeziora** *(htse po-ye-hadj' vgoo-rih nad ye-z'yo-ra)* (I want to go to the mountains/lake district)
- **Może Kraków?** *(mo-zhe kra-koof)* (What about Kraków?)
- **Chciałbym wykupić wycieczkę** *(hch'yaw-bihm vih-koo-peedj' vih-ch'yech-ke)* (I'd like to book [literally: buy] a trip) – a man speaking
- **Od kiedy i na jak długo?** *(ot kye-dih ee na yag dwoo-go)* (From when and for how long?)
- **Mamy specjalną ofertę** *(ma-mih spe-tsyal-nohN o-fer-te)* (We have a special offer)
- **Co jest wliczone w cenę?** *(tso yezd vlee-cho-ne ftse-ne)* (What's included in the price?)
- **W cenie są wyżywienie i zakwaterowanie** *(ftse-n'ye sohN vih-zhih-vye-n'ye ee za-kfa-te-ro-va-n'ye)* (Food and accommodation are included in the price)

Go to Chapter 13 if you want the challenge of booking accommodation yourself.

Talkin' the Talk

Simon comes from a Polish background but he's never had the chance to go to see the country of his grandfather. He goes to a Polish travel agent to book a trip to Poland.

Simon: **Chciałbym wykupić wycieczkę do Polski.**
hch'yaw-bihm vih-koo-peedj' vih-ch'yech-ke do pol-skee
I'd like to book a trip to Poland.

Agent: **W jakim terminie?**
vya-keem ter-mee-n'ye
What dates?

Simon: **W przyszły weekend. Na tydzień. Dla dwóch osób.**
fpshih-shwih wee-kent na tih-dj'yen' dla dvooh o-soop
Next weekend. For a week. For two people.

Agent: **Mamy jeszcze wolne miejsca.**
ma-mih yesh-che vol-ne myeys-tsa
We still have places available.

Chce pan lecieć samolotem czy jechać autokarem?
htse pan le-ch'yech' sa-mo-lo-tem chih ye-hach' aw-to-ka-rem
Do you want to go by plane or coach?

Simon: **Wolę samolotem, bo będzie szybciej.**
vo-le sa-mo-lo-tem bo ben'-dj'ye shihp-ch'yey
I prefer flying because it's quicker.

Agent: **Mamy ofertę promocyjną: lot, zakwaterowanie w hotelu trzygwiazdkowym ze śniadaniem oraz transport z lotniska i na lotnisko.**
ma-mih o-fer-te pro-mo-tsihy-nohN lot za-kfa-te-ro-va-n'ye fho-te-loo t-shih-gvyast-ko-vihm ze sh'n'ya-da-n'yem o-ras tran-spord zlot-n'ees-ka ee na lot-n'ees-ko
We have this special offer: the flight, 3-star hotel accommodation with breakfast and airport transfers.

Simon: **Jaki jest plan wycieczki?**
ya-kee yest plan vih-ch'yech-kee
What's the itinerary?

Agent: **Tu jest broszura ze szczegółami.**
too yezd bro-shoo-ra ze shche-goo-wa-mee
Here is a brochure with more details.

Simon: **Świetnie. Proszę zarezerwować dwa miejsca.**
sh'fyet-n'ye pro-she za-re-zer-vo-vadj' dva myeys-tsa
Great! Please book two places.

Words to Know

podróż	*po-droosh*	travel/trip
wycieczka	*vih-ch'yech-ka*	trip/excursion
w jakim terminie?	*vya-keem ter-mee-n'ye*	what dates?
w przyszły weekend	*fpshih-shwih wee-kent*	next weekend
autokarem	*aw-to-ka-rem*	by coach
samolotem	*sa-mo-lo-tem*	by plane
zakwaterowanie	*za-kfa-te-ro-va-n'ye*	accommodation
transport	*tran-sport*	(airport) transfers
zobaczyć	*zo-ba-chihch'*	to see
tu	*too*	here
broszura	*bro-shoo-ra*	brochure
proszę zarezerwować	*pro-she za-re-zer-vo-vach'*	please book

Timing Your Trip

The four seasons in Poland are: **wiosna** *(vyos-na)* (spring – mid-March to mid-June), **lato** *(la-to)* (summer – mid-June to mid-September), **jesień** *(ye-sh'yen')* (autumn – mid-September to mid-December) and **zima** *(z'ee-ma)* (winter – mid-December to mid-March). And each one of them paints the landscape with different colours, so if you've seen the white winter, you'll be surprised when you come to see the Polish golden autumn, **polska złota jesień** *(pol-ska zwo-ta ye-sh'yen')*.

Unfortunately, the **pogoda** *(po-go-da)* (weather) in Poland is pretty unpredictable. The summer can get hot and dry one year, yet be chilly and wet the next. You may experience bitter cold and a pile of snow or, if you're unlucky, dark, wet and foggy winter days. Always check the **prognoza pogody** *(pro-gno-za po-go-dih)* (weather forecast) and make sure you bring something to wear for both rainy and sunny days.

Whether you're planning your next summer holiday in Poland, want to arrange a business meeting or schedule a doctor's appointment, knowing the Polish calendar, **kalendarz** *(ka-len-dash)*, will help you to schedule it more easily.

First, try to memorise the months of the year. When talking about the months, you'll probably use them in a phrase – *in March*, for example – as shown in the following list:

- **w styczniu** *(fstih-chn'yoo)* (in January)
- **w lutym** *(vloo-tihm)* (in February)
- **w marcu** *(vmar-tsoo)* (in March)
- **w kwietniu** *(fkfye-tn'yoo)* (in April)
- **w maju** *(vma-yoo)* (in May)
- **w czerwcu** *(fcher-ftsoo)* (in June)
- **w lipcu** *(vleep-tsoo)* (in July)
- **w sierpniu** *(fsh'yer-pn'yoo)* (in August)
- **we wrześniu** *(ve vzhe-sh'n'yoo)* (in September)
- **w październiku** *(fpaz'-dj'yer-n'ee-koo)* (in October)
- **w listopadzie** *(vlee-sto-pa-dj'ye)* (in November)
- **w grudniu** *(vgroo-dn'yoo)* (in December)

Unlike in English, names of the Polish months, **miesiące** *(mye-sh'yon-tse)*, are spelt with small letters and they don't have much to do with the names of months in other European languages you may be familiar with, **niestety**! *(n'ye-ste-tih)* (unfortunately!). To add to this difficulty, the pronunciation of some of them can be real tongue-twisters! Simply try to relax your mouth muscles and gently whisper all the consonant clusters. That always works!

- **W grudniu jadę do Polski** *(vgroo-dn'yoo ya-de do pol-skee)* (In December I'm going to Poland)
- **Lecę do Sopotu w maju** *(le-tse do so-po-too vma-yoo)* (I'm flying to Sopot in May)
- **W sierpniu będziemy na urlopie** *(fsh'yer-pn'yoo ben'-dj'ye-mih na oor-lo-pye)* (We'll be on holiday in August)

Make your way to Chapter 16 for information on dates and to Chapter 7 for days of the week and parts of the day.

The best way to remember the Polish months and days of the week is by getting a Polish calendar. Don't be surprised that the endings of the names of the months don't exactly match those in the preceding list. After all, this is Polish – you'll get used to the endings getting changed all the time!

Talkin' the Talk

Audio track 31: Simon Harvey phones a travel agent to book his flight to Poland for the coming Christmas.

Agent: **Dzień dobry. W czym mogę pomóc?**
dj'yen' dob-rih fchihm mo-ge po-moots
Good afternoon. How can I help you?

Simon: **Czy może mi pan zarezerwować bilet lotniczy do Warszawy?**
chih mo-zhe mee pan za-re-zer-vo-vadj' bee-let lot-n'ee-chih do var-sha-vih
Could you please book a flight to Warsaw for me?

Agent: **Oczywiście. Na kiedy?**
o-chih-veesh'-ch'ye na kye-dih
Certainly. When [literally: for when?])

Simon: **Na święta w grudniu.**
na sh'fyen-ta vgroo-dn'yoo
For the [Christmas] holiday in December.

Agent: **Jaki termin pana interesuje?**
ya-kee ter-meen pa-na een-te-re-soo-ye
What dates are you interested in?

Simon: **Od dwudziestego grudnia na dwa tygodnie.**
od dvoo-dj'yes-te-go groo-dn'ya na dva tih-god-n'ye
From 20 December for two weeks.

Agent: **Mamy kilka lotów do wyboru. O której godzinie chce pan lecieć?**
ma-mih keel-ka lo-toov do vih-bo-roo o ktoo-rey go-dj'ee-n'ye htse pan le-ch'yech'

We have a couple of flights to choose from. What time do you want to depart [literally: fly]?

Simon: **Może jest jakiś lot rano?**
mo-zhe yest ya-keesh' lot ra-no
Is there a flight in the morning?

Agent: **Jest o 9:15 z lotniska City. Lądowanie w Warszawie o 12:00 czasu lokalnego.**
yest o dj'ye-vyon-tey pyet-nash'-ch'ye zlot-n'ees-ka see-tih lon-do-va-n'ye vvar-sha-vye o dvoo-nas-tey cha-soo lo-kal-ne-go
There is one at 9:15 from City Airport. It lands in Warsaw at 12:30 local time.

Simon: **Pasuje mi. Proszę zarezerwować jeden bilet.**
pa-soo-ye mee pro-she za-re-zer-vo-vach' ye-den bee-let
That suits me. Please book one ticket for me.

Words to Know

pomóc	*po-moots*	to help
zarezerwować	*za-re-zer-vo-vach'*	to reserve
bilet lotniczy	*bee-let lot-n'ee-chih*	flight ticket
do	*do*	to
na święta	*na sh'fyen-ta*	for the holiday period
jaki termin?	*ya-kee ter-meen*	what dates?
lot	*lot*	flight
do wyboru	*do vih-bo-roo*	to choose from
czas lokalny	*chas lo-kal-nih*	local time
pasuje mi	*pa-soo-ye mee*	(that) suits me

Mastering Visas and Passports

Whatever your destination, check what documents you need to have ready well ahead of the trip, so as not to risk an unnecessary rise in blood pressure when you find out at the airport that your passport has expired or you need a visa.

If you're going to Poland, you may not need a **wiza** *(vee-za)* (visa) if you're from any of a number of countries and plan to stay 90 days or less. Go to the Polish Ministry of Foreign Affairs' website at `www.msz.gov.pl` to check the latest requirements (the website is in Polish, so you can practise your Polish as you discover travel requirements but if you want to be sure you understand everything correctly, click on the *International Version* link at the top of that page).

Here are some document-related expressions you may want to remember:

- **Czy masz ważny paszport?** *(chih mazh vazh-nih pash-port)* (Is your passport valid?) – informal
- **Do kiedy masz ważny paszport?** *(do kye-dih mazh vazh-nih pash-port)* (How long is your passport valid for?)
- **Biorę prawo jazdy** *(byo-re pra-vo yaz-dih)* (I'm taking my driving licence)
- **Musisz mieć międzynarodowe prawo jazdy** *(moo-sh'eesh myech' myen-dzih-na-ro-do-ve pra-vo yaz-dih)* (You need [to have] an international driving licence)
- **Czy do Polski potrzebna jest wiza?** *(chih do pol-skee pot-sheb-na yezd vee-za)* (Is it necessary to have a visa to visit Poland?)
- **Zgubiłem/Zgubiłam paszport** *(zgoo-bee-wem/zgoo-bee-wam pash-port)* (I've [man/woman] lost my passport)

To work out visa or passport issues, you may need to visit the **konsulat** *(kon-soo-lat)* (consulate) or **ambasada** *(am-ba-sa-da)* (embassy).

Since Poland joined the Schengen Area in 2007, Polish citizens and citizens of the other Schengen Area countries such as Germany, France, Spain, Italy, Austria, Portugal, Belgium, the Netherlands and many more may travel freely within a vast area of Europe. There are no physical borders to cross or tiring and time-consuming border checks! The member countries of the Schengen Area incorporate specific rules and cooperate with regard to border security and citizens' personal data protection and engage in reciprocal law enforcements services.

The UK and Ireland are beyond the Schengen Area, so if you're a citizen of those countries, or are travelling from or through those countries, you need to have a passport or ID card to enter the Schengen Area.

Packing For Your Visit

The time of the year you plan your trip to Poland, the region you're going to visit and the type of activities you're going to do all determine what you need to take with you.

Don't take too much and don't worry if you realise you left behind your favourite pair of jeans. You can find plenty of amazing shopping centres all over Poland! (Chapter 6 talks extensively about clothing and the pleasure of shopping.)

While packing your suitcase, you may want to practise these expressions:

- **Mam ciężką walizkę/torbę podróżną** *(mam ch'yehN-shkohN va-lees-ke/ tor-be po-droozh-nohN)* (My suitcase/travel bag is heavy)
- **Mam mały bagaż podręczny** *(mam ma-wih ba-gash po-dren-chnih)* (I have small hand luggage)
- **Gdzie jest moja torebka?** *(gdj'ye yest mo-ya to-rep-ka)* (Where is my handbag?)
- **Musimy się jeszcze spakować** *(moo-sh'ee-mih sh'ye yesh-che spa-ko-vach')* (We still have to pack)
- **Ciekawe, czy zabrałam wszystko** *(ch'ye-ka-ve chih za-bra-wam fshih stko)* (I wonder if I've packed everything) – a woman speaking
- **Chyba czegoś zapomniałem** *(hih-ba che-goz' za-po-mn'ya-wem)* (I might have left something behind) – a man speaking
- **Mamy ubezpieczenie na bagaż** *(ma-mih oo-bes-pye-che-n'ye na ba-gash)* (We have luggage insurance)
- **Zgubili mój bagaż** *(zgoo-bee-lee mooy ba-gash)* (They lost my luggage)

Remember that Poles tend to dress smartly for theatres, art galleries and other cultural events. If you plan on visiting the Mariacki Church in Kraków (or any other religious place), avoid wearing sleeveless T-shirts, short dresses or shorts. In Poland, not dressing inappropriately is very much a matter of respect for the people and their culture.

Talkin' the Talk

Patricia and Kelly are leaving for Poland tomorrow. They need to do the packing now so that everything is ready for the trip and they can sit down and relax.

Patricia: **Spakowałaś się już?**
spa-ko-va-wash' sh'ye yoosh?
Have you packed already?

Kelly: **No właśnie dopiero zaczynam.**
no vwash'-n'ye do-pye-ro za-chih-nam
I'm just about to start it.

Patricia: **Ja też jeszcze nie miałam czasu.**
ya tesh yesh-che n'ye mya-wam cha-soo
I haven't had the time either.

Kelly: **Co bierzesz?**
tso bye-zhesh
What are you taking with you?

Patricia: **Na pewno coś ciepłego, jakby była brzydka pogoda.**
na pe-vno tsosh' ch'ye-pwe-go yag-bih bih-wa bzhi-tka po-go-da
Certainly something warm in case of bad weather.

Kelly: **Jasne. Ja biorę ubrania na luzie i coś eleganckiego na wieczór.**
ya-sne ya byo-re oo-bra-n'ya na loo-zh'ye ee tsosh' e-le-gants-kye-go na vye-choor
Sure. I'm taking casual clothes and something smart for the evening.

Jakieś wygodne buty i oczywiście kostium kąpielowy na plażę.
ya-kyez' vih-go-dne boo-tih ee o-chih-veesh'-ch'ye ko-styoom kom-pye-lo-vih na pla-zhe
Some comfortable shoes and, of course, a swimsuit for the beach.

Patricia: **No i nie zapomnij spakować dokumentów, biletu i pieniędzy!**
no ee n'ye za-pom-n'eey spa-ko-vadj' do-koo-men-toof bee-le-too ee pye-n'yen-dzih
And don't forget to pack your documents, the tickets and money!

Kelly: **Już spakowane.**
yoosh spa-ko-va-ne
I packed them already.

Words to Know

spakować (się)	*spa-ko-vach' (sh'ye)*	to pack
już	*yoosh*	already
dopiero	*do-pye-ro*	only
zaczynać	*za-chih-nach'*	to start
nie mieć czasu	*n'ye m'yech' cha-soo*	to not have time
brać	*brach'*	to take
coś ciepłego	*tsosh' ch'ye-pwe-go*	something warm
na luzie	*na loo-z'ye*	casual
coś eleganckiego	*tsosh' e-le-gants-kye-go*	something smart
wygodny	*vih-god-nih/a/e*	comfortable
nie zapomnij!	*n'ye za-pom-n'eey*	don't forget
dokumenty	*do-koo-men-tih*	documents
pieniądze	*pye-n'yon-dze*	money
spakowany	*spa-ko-va-nih/a/e*	packed

Taking Your Computer Along

Electrical devices come with different plugs depending on the country of purchase. If you're going on a business trip to Poland or simply can't live without your laptop or phone, make sure you take the right adaptor. Airports sell international adaptors that work in most countries.

Sockets in Poland are the two-pronged, 220-volt European standard. If you're coming from the UK, United States or a country with different sockets, you need to get an adaptor – **przejściówka** *(pshey-sh'ch'yoof-ka)*. Otherwise, no straightening your hair or charging your mobile!

Practise the following expressions as they may come in handy if you forget your charger or the right adaptor:

- **Masz ładowarkę do laptopa?** *(mash wa-do-var-ke do lap-to-pa)* (Do you have a charger for your laptop?) – informal
- **Jaką masz ładowarkę do telefonu?** *(ya-kohN mash wa-do-var-ke do te-le-fo-noo)* (What type of charger do you have for your mobile?) – informal
- **Czy ma pan/pani przejściówkę?** *(chih ma pan/pa-n'ee pshey'-sh'ch'yoof-ke)* (Do you have an adaptor?) – formal to a man/woman
- **Mam złą przejściówkę** *(mam zwohN pshey-sh'ch'yoof-ke)* (I've got the wrong adaptor)
- **Gdzie jest kontakt?** *(gdj'ye yest kon-takt)* (Where is the socket?)

Fun & Games

Ten travel-related words are hidden in the grid below. Look for the Polish words for *passport, ticket, travel, insurance, visa, adaptor, dates, brochure, documents* and *money* reading down and across. Try to find them!

R B X Z A P A S Z P O R T A P

B R P K B I L E T A M T E X Y

D O K U M E N T Y Y X R R Ę I

I S A N L N F A I B G A M W E

A Z B F Ę I Ą W I Z A Ą I E R

S U Z R E Ą Ę Z G L Q A N S T

S R X P O D R Ó Ż M B V C X Y

Z A U B E Z P I E C Z E N I E

U A P R Z E J Ś C I Ó W K A I

Answer key:

R **B** X Z A **P** **A** **S** **Z** **P** **O** **R** **T** A P

B **R** P K **B** **I** **L** **E** **T** A M T **E** X Y

D **O** **K** **U** **M** **E** **N** **T** **Y** Y X R **R** Ę I

I **S** A N L **N** F A I B G A **M** W E

A **Z** B F Ę **I** Ą **W** **I** **Z** **A** Ą **I** E R

S **U** Z R E **Ą** Ę Z G L Q A **N** S T

S **R** X **P** **O** **D** **R** **Ó** **Ż** M B V C X Y

Z **A** **U** **B** **E** **Z** **P** **I** **E** **C** **Z** **E** **N** **I** **E**

U A **P** **R** **Z** **E** **J** **Ś** **C** **I** **Ó** **W** **K** **A** I

paszport, bilet, podróż, ubezpieczenie, wiza, przejściówka, termin, broszura, dokumenty, pieniądze

Chapter 15

Help! Handling Emergencies

In This Chapter

- Raising the alarm
- Sorting out medical problems
- Coping with road accidents
- Getting help for legal and domestic incidents

Hope for the best, prepare for the worst. If you find yourself in an emergency situation, you won't have time to flick through a dictionary in search of the right expression to call an ambulance or catch a thief. So, make the most of this chapter to get ready for emergency situations – language-wise, at least.

Shouting for Help – Pomocy!

When faced with a situation you can't handle on your own, start by asking:

Czy ktoś tu mówi po angielsku? *(chih ktosh' too moo-vee po an-gyel-skoo)* (Does anybody here speak English?)

Although English is widely spoken by the younger generation of Poles, in smaller places you may have to count on yourself and on your Polish. **Pomocy!** *(po-mo-tsih)* (Help!) is the most general and common word to signal distress. Here are some more shouting-for-help expressions:

- **Na pomoc!/Pomocy!** *(na po-mots/po-mo-tsih)* (Help!)
- **Proszę mi pomóc!** *(pro-she mee po-moots)* (Help me, please!) – formal
- **Pomóż mi!** *(po-moosh mee)* (Help me!) – informal
- **Złodziej!** *(zwo-dj'yey)* (Thief!)
- **Pożar!** *(po-zhar)* (Fire!)
- **Szybko!** *(shihp-ko)* (Quickly!)

- **Jak najszybciej!** *(yak nay-shihp-ch'yey)* (As soon as possible!)
- **Pospiesz się/Proszę się pospieszyć!** *(pos-pyesh sh'ye/pro-she sh'ye pos-pye-shihch')* (Hurry up!) – informal/formal

If you know what type of help you need, you can use these requests:

- **Proszę zadzwonić po karetkę** *(pro-she za-dzvo-neech' po ka-ret-ke)* (Call an ambulance, please!)
- **Proszę zadzwonić po straż pożarną!** *(pro-she za-dzvo-neech' po strash po-zhar-nohN)* (Call the fire brigade, please!)
- **Proszę zadzwonić po policję!** *(pro-she za-dzvo-neech' po po-lee-tsye)* (Call the police, please!)
- **Dzwoń po lekarza!** *(dzvon' po le-ka-zha)* (Call a doctor!) – informal

Handling Health Problems

When handling emergency situations, always address doctors, the police and any stranger you're dealing with in formal terms to show your respect for them. Informality is reserved for talking to children, family members and friends. (Go to Chapter 3 to read more on being formal and informal.)

Helping out

If you find yourself in an emergency situation, you'll notice that Polish people are exceptionally helpful and caring and will not hesitate to go out of their way to assist anyone in need of aid.

If all of a sudden you seem to have forgotten all your Polish, try to speak English s-l-o-w-l-y and use simple words.

Master the following phrases that can be helpful in helping out others:

- **Czy mogę jakoś pomóc?** *(chih mo-ge ya-kosh' po-moots)* (Can I help in any way?)
- **Pomóc panu/pani?** *(po-moots pa-noo/pa-n'ee)* (Do you want any help?) – formal to a man/woman
- **Niech mi pan/pani pomoże!** *(n'yeh mee pan/pa-n'ee po-mo-zhe)* (Help me, please!) – formal to a man/woman
- **Zaraz panu/pani pomogę** *(za-ras pa-noo/pa-n'ee po-mo-ge)* (Let me help you) – formal
- **Dziękuję za pomoc** *(dj'yen-koo-ye za po-mots)* (Thank you for your help)

Giving advice

If you encounter a situation in which you can or want to offer advice, you may be able to use one of the following phrases:

- **Powinien pan pójść do lekarza** *(po-vee-n'yen pan pooyz'dj' do le-ka-zha)* (You should go to a doctor) – formal to a man
- **Nie powinnaś tyle siedzieć na słońcu** *(n'ye po-veen-nash' tih-le sh'ye-dj'yech' na swon'-tsoo)* (You shouldn't sit in the sun for so long) – informal to a woman
- **Może powinieneś wziąć coś przeciwbólowego** *(mo-zhe po-vee-n'ye-nez' vz'on'ch' tsosh' pshe-cheev-boo-lo-ve-go)* (Perhaps you should take some painkillers) – informal to a man
- **Powinniśmy to zgłosić na policję** *(po-veen-n'eesh'-mih to zgwo-sh'eech' na po-lee-tsye)* (We should report that to the police)
- **Powinniśmy wykupić ubezpieczenie** *(po-veen-n'eesh'-mih vih-koo-peech' oo-bes-pye-che-n'ye)* (We should take out insurance)

For giving advice you can use the verb **powinienem/powinnam** *(po-vee-n'ye-nem/po-veen-nam)* (man/woman speaking), which translates to *I should*. Remember that different forms exist depending on whether a man or a woman is speaking. See Table 15-1 for the conjugation.

Table 15-1 Present Tense Conjugation of Powinien/Powinna

	Man Speaking	*Woman Speaking*
(ja) *(ya)* I	**powinienem** *(po-vee-n'ye-nem)*	**powinnam** *(po-veen-nam)*
(ty) *(tih)* you	**powinieneś** *(po-vee-n'ye-nesh')*	**powinnaś** *(po-veen-nash')*
on/pan *(on/pan)* he, Mr or you formal	**powinien** *(po-vee-n'yen)*	–
ona/pani *(o-na/pa-n'ee)* she, Mrs or you formal	–	**powinna** *(po-veen-na)*
(my) *(mih)* we	**powinniśmy** *(po-veen-n'eesh'-mih)*	**powinnyśmy** *(po-veen-nihsh'-mih)*
(wy) *(vih)* you informal	**powinniście** *(po-veen-n'eesh'-ch'ye)*	**powinnyście** *(po-veen-nihsh'-ch'ye)*
oni/państwo *(o-n'ee/pan'stfo)* group with at least one man it it	**powinni** *(po-veen-n'ee)*	–
one *(o-ne)* they female	–	**powinny** *(po-veen-nih)*

This verb doesn't have an infinitive form (the one ending in **-ć**). If you want to use it in the past tense, you don't change anything. The context makes clear whether it's 'We should take out insurance' or 'We should have taken out insurance'. How convenient!

When giving advice, you can also use **musieć** *(moo-sh'yech')* (must/have to/need):

- **Musisz jechać do szpitala** *(moo-sh'eesh ye-hadj' do shpee-ta-la)* (You must go to the hospital) – informal
- **Muszą ci/panu/pani założyć szwy** *(moo-shohN ch'ee/pa-noo/pa-n'ee za-wo-zhihch' shfih)* (You need stiches) – informal/formal to a man/woman

Expressing pain when you're hurt

In case you get unlucky and get hurt or simply feel under the weather you may hear the following:

- **Co pana/panią boli?** *(tso pa-na/pa-n'yohN bo-lee)* (What hurts?) – formal to a man/woman
- **Gdzie boli?** *(gdj'ye bo-lee)* (Where does it hurt?)
- **Czy tu boli?** *(chih too bo-lee)* (Does it hurt here?)
- **Co panu/pani dolega?** *(tso pa-noo/pa-n'ee do-le-ga)* (What seems to be the trouble?)
- **Jak się pan/pani czuje?** *(yak sh'ye pan/pa-n'ee choo-ye)* (How are you feeling?) – formal to a man/woman

To answer a question about what hurts, you can say **Boli mnie . . .** *(bo-lee mn'ye)* (. . . hurts me) followed by a singular noun that corresponds to a body part, as shown in Table 15-2.

Table 15-2 Body Parts

English	Polish	Pronunciation
belly	brzuch	*bzhooh*
ear	ucho	*oo-ho*
finger/toe	palec	*pa-lets*

English	Polish	Pronunciation
head	głowa	*gwo-va*
knee	kolano	*ko-la-no*
leg	noga	*no-ga*
liver	wątroba	*von-tro-ba*
stomach	żołądek	*zho-won-dek*
throat	gardło	*gar-dwo*
tooth	ząb	*zomp*

If the part that hurts is a plural noun – and *back* is a plural noun in Polish! – start with **Bolą mnie . . .** (*bo-lohN mn'ye*) and use the nouns in Table 15-3.

Table 15-3 Body Parts (Plural Nouns)

English	Polish	Pronunciation
back	plecy	*ple-tsih*
eyes	oczy	*o-chih*
legs	nogi	*no-gee*
muscles	mięśnie	*myehN-sh'n'ye*
teeth	zęby	*zem-bih*

To get a little more descriptive, use these expressions:

- **Wszystko mnie boli** (*fshih-stko mn'ye bo-lee*) (Everything hurts)
- **Już nie boli** (*joosh n'ye bo-lee*) (The pain has gone)
- **To bardzo boli** (*to bar-dzo bo-lee*) (It hurts a lot)
- **Źle się czuję** (*z'le sh'ye choo-ye*) (I'm not feeling well)
- **Czuję się już lepiej** (*choo-ye sh'ye yoosh le-pyey*) (I feel better now)

To describe where it hurts, what the problem is or to inform a medical person about your health needs, use these sentences:

- **Mam wysokie/niskie ciśnienie** (*mam vih-so-kye/n'ees-kye ch'ee-sh'n'ye-n'ye*) (I have high/low blood pressure)
- **Mam zawroty głowy** (*mam za-vro-tih gwo-vih*) (I feel dizzy)

- **Skaleczyłem się/Skaleczyłam się w palec** *(ska-le-chih-wem sh'ye/ska-le-chih-wam sh'ye fpa-lets)* (I've [man/woman] hurt my finger)
- **Mam coś w oku** *(mam tsosh' vo-koo)* (I've got something in my eye)
- **Leci mi krew z nosa** *(le-ch'ee mee krev zno-sa)* (My nose is bleeding)
- **Złamałem/Złamałam nogę/rękę** *(zwa-ma-wem/zwa-ma-wam no-ge/ren-ke)* (I've broken my leg/arm)
- **Mam biegunkę/rozwolnienie** *(mam bye-goon-ke/roz-vol-n'ye-n'ye)* (I have diarrhoea)
- **Mam gorączkę/wysoką temperaturę** *(mam go-ron-chke/vih-so-kohN tem-pe-ra-too-re)* (I have a high fever)
- **Mam dreszcze** *(mam dresh-che)* (I'm shivering)
- **Mam katar/kaszel** *(mam ka-tar/ka-shel)* (I have a runny nose/cough)
- **Mam alergię na...***(mam a-ler-gye na)* (I'm allergic to . . .)
- **Mam cukrzycę** *(mam tsoo-kshih-tse)* (I'm diabetic)
- **Jestem przeziębiony/przeziębiona** *(yes-tem pshe-z'yem-byo-nih/pshe-z'yem-byo-na)* (I [man/woman] have a cold)
- **Mam grypę** *(mam grih-pe)* (I have flu)
- **Miałem/Miałam zawał serca dwa lata temu** *(mya-wem/mya-wam za-vaw ser-tsa dva la-ta te-moo)* (I had [man/woman] a heart attack two years ago)
- **Wymiotowałem/Wymiotowałam całą noc** *(vih-myo-to-va-wem/vih-myo-to-va-wam tsa-wohN nots)* (I [man/woman] was throwing up/vomiting all night)
- **Jestem w ciąży** *(yes-tem fch'yohN-zhih)* (I'm pregnant)
- **Jest mi niedobrze** *(yest mee n'ye-dob-zhe)* (I feel sick)

Even before you actually sneeze, and certainly right after, you'll hear **Na zdrowie!** *(na zdro-vye)* (Bless you!). Respond with **Dziękuję** *(dj'yen-koo-ye)* (Thank you!). You may be surprised to hear it again when toasting, as in *cheers*. They both mean *To your health.*

Talkin' the Talk

Audio track 32: Anna ate some fast food yesterday and she's been unwell all night. She's at a doctor's surgery now.

Doctor: **Co pani dolega?**
tso pa-n'ee do-le-ga
What seems to be the trouble?

Anna: **Bardzo źle się czuję. Mam gorączkę.**
bar-dzo z'le sh'ye choo-ye mam go-ron-chke
I'm feeling very bad. I have a fever.

Całą noc miałam biegunkę i wymiotowałam trzy razy. Wszystko mnie boli.
tsa-wohN nots mya-wam bye-goon-ke ee vih-myo-to-va-wam tshih ra-zih fshih-stko mn'ye bo-lee
I had diarrhoea all night and I threw up three times. Everything hurts.

Doctor: **Zbadam panią. Proszę głęboko oddychać.**
zba-dam pa-n'yohN pro-she gwem-bo-ko od-dih-hach'
Let me examine you. Please breathe deeply.

Ma pani zatrucie pokarmowe. Czy jest pani uczulona na jakieś leki?
ma pa-n'ee za-troo-ch'ye po-kar-mo-ve chih yest pa-n'ee oo-choo-lo-na na ya-kyesh' le-kee?
You have food poisoning. Are you allergic to any medication?

Anna: **Nie, chyba nie.**
n'ye hih-ba n'ye
No, I don't think so.

Doctor: **Dobrze. Tu są recepty. Proszę to brać trzy razy dziennie po jedzeniu.**
dob-zhe too sohN re-tsep-tih pro-she to brach' tshih ra-zih dj'yen-n'ye po ye-dze-n'yoo
Okay. Here are your prescriptions. Please take this three times a day after meals.

Proszę pić dużo wody. I życzę szybkiego powrotu do zdrowia.
pro-she peedj' doo-zho vo-dih ee zhih-che shihp-kye-go po-vro-too do zdro-vya
Drink lots of water. And I wish you a speedy recovery.

Words to Know

co panu/pani dolega?	tso <u>pa</u>-noo/<u>pa</u>-n'ee do-<u>le</u>-ga	what's troubling you? (formal to a man/woman)
czuć się	chooch' sh'ye	to feel (oneself)
mieć gorączkę	myedj' go-<u>ron</u>-chke	to have a fever
mieć biegunkę	myedj' bye-<u>goon</u>-ke	to have diarrhoea
wymiotować	vih-myo-<u>to</u>-vach'	to throw up
chyba nie	<u>hih</u>-ba n'ye	I don't think so
recepta	re-<u>tsep</u>-ta	prescription
dziennie	<u>dj'yen</u>-n'ye	per day
życzyć szybkiego powrotu do zdrowia	<u>zhih</u>-chihch' shihp-<u>kye</u>-go po-<u>vro</u>-too do <u>zdro</u>-vya	to wish a speedy recovery

Braving the dentist

Dental care is highly professional and relatively inexpensive in Poland. In fact, a growing number of foreigners choose Poland for medical treatment, especially for dental work. Most of the medical staff, in bigger cities in particular, speak good English. However, if you go to a **gabinet dentystyczny** *(ga-<u>bee</u>-ned den-tih-<u>stih</u>-chnih)* (dental surgery) in a smaller place, the following phrases will help you to name your problem with a 'big smile':

- **Potrzebuję dobrego dentysty/stomatologa** *(po-tshe-<u>boo</u>-ye do-<u>bre</u>-go den-<u>tih</u>-stih/sto-ma-to-<u>lo</u>-ga)* (I need a good dentist)
- **Chciałbym/Chciałabym zapisać się na wizytę do doktora . . ./ doktor . . .** *(<u>hch'yaw</u>-bihm/<u>hch'ya</u>-wa-bihm za-<u>pee</u>-sach' sh'ye na vee-<u>zih</u>-te do dok-<u>to</u>-ra/<u>dok</u>-tor)* (I'd like to make an appointment to see Doctor . . . [male name/female name])

- **Boli mnie ząb** *(bo-lee mn'ye zomp)* (I have a toothache)
- **Poproszę o znieczulenie** *(po-pro-she o zn'ye-choo-le-n'ye)* (Can I have anaesthetic?)
- **Trzeba usunąć kamień** *(tshe-ba oo-soo-non'ch' ka-myen')* (The plaque needs to be removed)
- **Ten ząb trzeba leczyć kanałowo** *(ten zomp tshe-ba le-chihch' ka-na-wo-vo)* (This tooth requires a root canal)
- **Wypadła mi plomba** *(vih-pa-dwa mee plom-ba)* (The filling fell out)
- **Jedynka/dwójka/trójka/czwórka na górze po prawej stronie** *(ye-dihn-ka/dvooy-ka/trooy-ka/chfoor-ka na goo-zhe po pra-vey stro-n'ye)* (Top right tooth [number] 1/2/3/4)
- **Piątka/szóstka/siódemka/ósemka po lewej stronie na dole** *(pyon-tka/shoos-tka/sh'yoo-dem-ka/oo-sem-ka po le-vey stro-n'ye na do-le)* (Bottom left tooth [number] 5/6/7/8)
- **Złamał mi się ząb** *(zwa-maw mee sh'ye zomp)* (I've broken my tooth)
- **Trzeba usunąć ten ząb** *(tshe-ba oo-soo-non'ch' ten zomp)* (This tooth needs to be pulled out)
- **Kiedy mogę zapisać się na następną wizytę?** *(kye-dih mo-ge za-pee-sach' sh'ye na nas-temp-nohN vee-zih-te)* (When can I arrange my next appointment for?)

Talkin' the Talk

James has terrible toothache which has ruined the last two days of his holiday in Poland. James has had enough of the pain and makes an appointment to see a dentist.

James: **Chciałbym zapisać się na wizytę do dentysty.**
hch'yaw-bihm za-pee-sach' sh'ye na vee-zih-te do den-tih-stih
I'd like to make an appointment to see a dentist.

Receptionist: **Pasuje panu jutro o dziewiątej rano?**
pa-soo-ye pa-noo yoo-tro o dj'ye-vyon-tey ra-no?
Is tomorrow at 9 a.m. good for you?

James: **Tak. Dziękuję.**
tak dj'yen-koo-ye
Yes. Thank you.

James is now at the dental surgery.

James: **Boli mnie szóstka na górze po prawej stronie.**
(bo-lee mn'ye shoos-tka na goo-zhe po pra-vey stro-n'ye)
The top right sixth tooth hurts.

Dentist: **Tak. Rzeczywiście jest tu ubytek.**
tak zhe-chih-veesh'-ch'ye yest too oo-bih-tek
Yes. Indeed, there is a cavity.

Trzeba też usunąć kamień.
t-she-ba tesh oo-soo-non'ch' ka-myen'
The plaque needs to be removed, too.

Ze znieczuleniem?
ze zn'ye-choo-le-n'yem
Do you want anaesthetic?

James: **Tak, poproszę.**
tak po-pro-she
Yes, please.

Words to Know

umówić się na wizytę	*oo-moo-veech' sh'ye na vee-zih-te*	to make an appointment
pasuje panu/ pani . . .?	*pa-soo-ye pa-noo/ pa-n'ee*	does . . . suit you? (formal to a man/ woman)
rzeczywiście	*zhe-chih-veesh'-ch'ye*	indeed
ubytek	*oo-bih-tek*	cavity
usunąć kamień	*oo-soo-non'ch' ka-m'yen'*	remove the plaque
znieczulenie	*zn'ye-choo-le-n'ye*	anaesthetic

Ensuring that you get reimbursed

Don't forget to sort out **prywatne ubezpieczenie** *(prih-vat-ne oo-bes-pye-che-n'ye)* (individual insurance) before going on holiday. Having insurance means that at least you won't need to worry about money if you have an accident or some other trouble that requires professional help.

These phrases help you talk about insurance:

- **Muszę wykupić ubezpieczenie** *(moo-she vih-koo-peech' oo-bes-pye-che-n'ye)* (I've got to get insurance)
- **Mam pełne ubezpieczenie** *(mam pew-ne oo-bes-pye-che-n'ye)* (I'm fully insured)
- **Czy jest pan ubezpieczony?** *(chih yest pan oo-bes-pye-cho-nih)* (Are you insured?) – formal, to a man
- **Czy moje ubezpieczenie to pokrywa?** *(chih mo-ye oo-bes-pye-che-n'ye to po-krih-va)* (Is that covered by my insurance?)
- **Co pokrywa ubezpieczenie?** *(tso po-krih-va oo-bes-pye-che-n'ye)* (What does the insurance cover?)
- **Poproszę rachunek dla ubezpieczyciela** *(po-pro-she ra-hoo-neg dla oo-bes-pye chih-ch'ye-la)* (Can I have a receipt for my insurer?)

If you come from any European Union (EU) country and plan on visiting Poland, obtain a European Health Insurance Card (in your own country), which entitles you to emergency medical treatment at reduced cost or free of charge in any other EU country. Visit the website at www.ehic.ie.

Dealing with Car Accidents

If you ever get involved in or witness a car accident, always call or ask somebody else to call the **policja** *(po-lee-tsya)* (police) and, in case of casualties, for **karetka** *(ka-ret-ka)* (ambulance). Here's how you do it:

- **Niech pan/pani szybko dzwoni po karetkę/po policję/po straż pożarną!** *(n'yeh pan/pa-n'ee shihp-ko dzvo-n'ee po ka-ret-ke/po po-lee-tsye/po strash po-zhar-nohN)* (Call an ambulance/the police/fire brigade immediately!) – formal, to a man/woman
- **Chciałbym/Chciałabym zgłosić wypadek . . .** *(hch'yaw-bihm hch'ya-wa-bihm zgwo-sh'eedj' vih-pa-dek)* (I'd like [man/woman] to report an accident . . .)
  - **na autostradzie** *(na aw-to-stra-dj'ye)* (on the motorway)

- **na ulicy Mickiewicza** *(na oo-lee-tsih mee-tskye-vee-cha)* (on Mickiewicz Street)
- **na wyjeździe z autostrady A1** *(na vih-yez'-dj'ye z aw-to-stra-dih a ye-den)* (at the exit of the A1 motorway)

- **Są ranni** *(sohN ran-n'ee)* (There are casualties)

The only number you need to call in any emergency situation in Poland is 112. Calling 112 from your mobile allows the police, fire brigade and health services to automatically and instantly determine your position and get to where you're involved in or witness to an emergency situation. Three separate emergency numbers also exist – 999 for an ambulance, 998 for the fire brigade and 997 for the police – but 112 works for all emergencies.

Later, when you talk to the police, you may want to say the following:

- **Drugi kierowca nie zatrzymał się na znaku stop** *(droo-gee kye-rof-tsa n'ye za-tshih-maw sh'ye na zna-koo stop)* (The other driver did not stop at the stop sign)
- **Kierowca TIR-a zjechał na przeciwny pas ruchu** *(kye-rof-tsa tee-ra zye-haw na pshe-ch'eev-nih pas roo-hoo)* (The lorry driver veered into the opposite lane)
- **Wjechał na skrzyżowanie na czerwonym świetle** *(vye-haw na skshih-zho-va-n'ye na cher-vo-nihm sh'fyet-le)* (He went over the crossroads at the red light)
- **Wjechała we mnie** *(vye-ha-wa ve mn'ye)* (She drove into me)
- **To nie moja wina** *(to n'ye mo-ya vee-na)* (It's not my fault)
- **To jego/jej wina** *(to ye-go/yey vee-na)* (It's his/her fault)
- **Kierowca był pijany** *(kye-rof-tsa bihw pee-ya-nih)* (The driver was drunk)
- **Jechał za szybko/za blisko** *(ye-haw za shihp-ko/za blees-ko)* (He drove too fast/close)

Remember to drive with your lights on all year round and 24 hours a day because you risk getting a fine – **mandat** *(man-dat)* – if you don't. Although the blood-alcohol limit is 0.02 per cent, not driving after you've had a drink is safer for both you and other drivers.

If stopped by a police patrol car (a common occurance on Polish roads!), you may hear the following:

- **Proszę prawo jazdy i dowód rejestracyjny pojazdu** *(pro-she pra-vo yaz-dih ee do-voot re-yes-tra-tsihy-nih po-yaz-doo)* (Can I see your, driving licence and car registration documents?)
- **Jechał pan za szybko** *(ye-haw pan za shihp-ko)* (You were driving too fast) – formal, to a man

- **Wyprzedzała pani na zakazie** *(vih-pshe-dza-wa pa-n'ee na za-ka-z'ye)* (You were overtaking illegally) – formal, to a woman
- **Nie ma pan/pani świateł** *(n'ye ma pan/pa-n'ee sh'fya-tew)* (You have your lights off) – formal, to a man/woman

Talkin' the Talk

Audio track 33: Simon has just witnessed a road accident. He calls the 112 emergency line.

Simon: **Na autostradzie był wypadek. Proszę szybko przysłać karetkę.**
na aw-to-stra-dj'ye bihw vih-pa-dek pro-she shihp-ko pshih-swach' ka-ret-ke
There's been an accident on the motorway. Can you send an ambulance quickly, please?

Emergency operator: **Czy są ranni?**
chih sohN ran-n'ee
Are there any casualties?

Simon: **Tak, dwie osoby.**
tak dvye o-so-bih
Yes, two people.

Emergency operator: **W jakim stanie?**
vya-keem sta-n'ye?
What's their condition?

Simon: **Mężczyzna oddycha, ale jest nieprzytomny. Kobieta mówi, że boli ją noga i klatka piersiowa.**
mehNsh-chih-zna od-dih-ha a-le yest n'ye-pshih-tom-nih ko-bye-ta moo-vee zhe bo-lee yohN no-ga ee klat-ka pyer-sh'yo-va
The man is breathing but unconcious. The woman has leg and chest pains.

Emergency operator: **Karetka będzie za dwie minuty.**
ka-ret-ka ben'-dj'ye za dvye mee-noo-tih
An ambulance will be there in two minutes.

Words to Know

na autostradzie	*na aw-to-stra-dj'ye*	on the motorway
wypadek	*vih-pa-dek*	accident
karetka	*ka-ret-ka*	ambulance
ranni	*ran-n'ee*	casualties
nieprzytomny	*n'ye-pshih-tom-nih*	unconcious
boli go/ją . . .	*bo-lee go/yohN*	he/she has a pain in . . .

What Bad Luck! Getting Help with Legal Problems

Being robbed is a nightmare. This event is even more awful when it happens on holiday in a foreign country. Although I hope this won't happen to you, of course (!), it's always good to be prepared in case it does.

Reporting to the police

Ale pech! *(a-le peh)* (What bad luck!). Somebody has stolen your brand new phone! You were robbed! You've lost your passport! Here are some expressions that can help you deal with unpleasant situations:

- **Gdzie mam zgłosić włamanie/kradzież?** *(gdj'ye mam zgwo-sh'eedj' vwa-ma-n'ye/kra-dj'yesh)* (Where should I report the burglary/theft?)
- **Gdzie jest najbliższy posterunek policji?** *(gdj'ye yest nay-blish-shih po-ste-roo-nek po-lee-tsyee)* (Where is the nearest police station?)
- **Chciałabym zgłosić napad** *(hch'ya-wa-bihm zgwo-sh'eech' na-pad)* (I'd like [woman] to report an attack)

- **Zgubiłem/Zgubiłam paszport** *(zgoo-bee-wem/zgoo-bee-wam pash-port)* (I've [man/woman] lost my passport)
- **Ukradziono mi portfel** *(oo-kra-dj'yo-no mee por-tfel)* (My wallet has been stolen)
- **Ktoś ukradł mi telefon** *(ktosh' oo-kradw mee te-le-fon)* (Someone has stolen my phone)
- **Miałem/Miałam włamanie do samochodu** *(mya-wem/mya-wam vwa-ma-n'ye do sa-mo-ho-doo)* (Someone has broken into my car) – a man speaking
- **Widziałem/Widziałam włamywacza** *(vee-dj'ya-wem/vee-dj'ya-wam vwa-mih-va-cha)* (I saw [man/woman] the burglar)
- **To był wysoki, dobrze zbudowany, łysy mężczyzna** *(to bihw vih-so-kee dob-zhe-zboo-do-va-nih wih-sih mehNsh-chih-zna)* (It was a tall, well-built, bald man)
- **To była młoda kobieta** *(to bih-wa mwo-da ko-bye-ta)* (It was a young woman)

And here's what you may hear:

- **Proszę pojechać z nami na komendę** *(pro-she po-ye-hadj' zna-mee na ko-men-de)* (You need to come to the police station with us)
- **Musi pan/pani złożyć zeznanie** *(moo-sh'ee pan/pa-n'ee zwo-zhihdj' ze-zna-n'ye)* (You have to make a statement) – formal, to a man/woman
- **Czy może pan/pani opisać tę osobę?** *(chih mo-zhe pan/pa-n'ee o-pee-sach' te o-so-be)* (Can you describe this person?)
- **Kiedy to się stało?** *(kye-dih to sh'ye sta-wo)* (When did it happen?)
- **Gdzie pan był/pani była w chwili zdarzenia?** *(gdj'ye pan bihw/pa-n'ee bih-wa fhfee-lee zda-zhe-n'ya)* (Where were you at the time of the incident?)
- **Co zginęło?** *(tso zgee-ne-wo)* (What's missing?)

That's a lot of information to take on board and you may need some professional help. Here's how you can request it:

- **Czy mogę prosić o prawnika, który mówi po angielsku?** *(chih mo-ge pro-sh'eech' o prav-n'ee-ka ktoo-rih moo-vee po an-gyel-skoo)* (Can I have an English-speaking lawyer?)
- **Muszę skontaktować się z konsulatem** *(moo-she skon-tak-to-vach' sh'ye skon-soo-la-tem)* (I need to contact the consulate)

- **Przepraszam, nic nie rozumiem** *(pshe-pra-sham n'eets n'ye ro-zoo-myem)* (I'm sorry, I don't understand anything)
- **Czy mogę prosić o tłumacza?** *(chih mo-ge pro-sh'eech' o twoo-ma-cha)* (Can I have a translator, please?)

Dealing with Domestic Emergencies

In this section, I help you deal with some domestic emergencies – be it a water leak, problems with the Internet or an electricity failure. Here are some expressions that may come in handy when something at home doesn't work:

- **Nie działa klimatyzacja** *(n'ye dj'ya-wa klee-ma-tih-za-tsya)* (The air-conditioning is not working)
- **Zepsuła się pralka** *(ze-psoo-wa sh'ye pral-ka)* (The washing machine broke)
- **(Jest) awaria prądu** *(yest a-va-rya pron-doo)* (There's been a power failure)
- **(Jest) awaria windy** *(yest a-va-rya veen-dih)* (The lift has broken down)
- **Leje się w łazience** *(le-ye sh'ye vwa-z'yen-tse)* (There's a water leak in the bathroom)
- **Mam problem z internetem** *(mam pro-blem zeen-ter-ne-tem)* (I have a problem with the Internet)
- **Chciałbym zgłosić awarię instalacji gazowej** *(hch'yaw-bihm zgwo-sh'eech' a-va-rye een-sta-la-tsyee ga-zo-vey)* (I'd like [man] to report a gas leak)
- **Trzeba zawołać fachowca** *(tshe-ba za-vo-wach' fa-hof-tsa)* (You need to call a specialist)
- **Potrzebuję dobrego hydraulika** *(po-tshe-boo-ye dob-re-go hih-draw-lee-ka)* (I need a good plumber)
- **Nie ma wody** *(n'ye ma vo-dih)* (There's no water)
- **Proszę przyjechać jak najszybciej** *(pro-she pshih-ye-hach' yak nay-shihp-ch'yey)* (Please come as soon as possible)
- **Da się to naprawić dzisiaj?** *(da sh'ye to na-pra-veedj' dj'ee-sh'yay)* (Is it possible to fix it today?)

Fun & Games

Some words relating to a theft have escaped! See if you can find a place for them in the dialogue between Mrs Jones and the police officer:

konsulatem, dokumenty, osobę, zeznanie, ktoś, kradzież, gdzie

Mrs Jones:	Dzień dobry. Chciałabym zgłosić ....
Officer:	Co zginęło?
Mrs Jones:	Pieniądze i ....
Officer:	Kiedy i .... to się stało?
Mrs Jones:	Godzinę temu jechałam autobusem i .... ukradł mi torbę.
Officer:	Czy może pani opisać tę .... ?
Mrs Jones:	Niestety, nie. Było dużo ludzi.
Officer:	Musi pani złożyć ....
Mrs Jones:	Dobrze. W torbie miałam też paszport. Muszę skontaktować się z ....

Answer key:

kradzież, dokumenty, gdzie, ktoś, osobę, zeznanie, konsulatem

Part IV

Polish in the Workplace

"This may be my first time in Poland, but you don't have to explain to me what the 'office brown nose' means."

In this part . . .

Not all foreign travels are for pure pleasure. This part transports you to the world of the Polish business, office and worksite cultures and their specialised language. You discover how to talk about your job, plan your day, arrange meetings, go on business trips as well as how to make your workplace safe or even how to quit your job.

Chapter 16

Using Polish in the Office

In This Chapter

- Getting around the office
- Scheduling your day
- Organising business trips
- Bidding farewell

This chapter takes you through the world of Polish business and office work culture and its specialised language.

Finding Your Way around the Office

Some offices in Poland are luxurious, spacious, modern and light while others still remember Communist times and are a little older and dingier. Wherever you work, you need to be able to find your way to the locations in Table 16-1.

Table 16-1 Locations in the Office

English	*Polish*	*Pronunciation*
conference room	sala konferencyjna	*sa-la kon-fe-ren-tsihy-na*
customer service	dział obsługi klienta	*dj'yaw op-swoo-gee klee-yen-ta*
director's office	gabinet dyrektora	*ga-bee-net dih-re-kto-ra*
emergency exit	wyjście ewakuacyjne	*vihy-sh'ch'ye e-va-koo-a-tsihy-ne*
female/male/disabled toilet	toaleta damska/męska/dla niepełnosprawnych	*to-a-le-ta dam-ska/mehN-ska/dla n'ye-pew-no-sprav-nihh*
human resource department	dział personalny	*dj'yaw per-so-nal-nih*
kitchen	kuchnia	*koo-hn'ya*

(continued)

Table 16-1 (continued)

English	*Polish*	*Pronunciation*
lift	winda	*veen-da*
marketing and advertising department	dział marketingu i reklamy	*dj'yaw mar-ke-teen-goo ee re-kla-mih*
meeting room	sala spotkań	*sa-la spot-kan'*
reception desk	sekretariat/recepcja	*se-kre-ta-ryat/re-tse-ptsya*
technical support department	dział techniczny	*dj'yaw te-hn'ee-chnih*

Go to Chapter 7 to practise stating on which floor your office is located and to Chapter 11 for how to give directions.

Office furniture and accessories

To be able to ask for a pen or a file, you need to be familiar with their Polish names. Table 16-2 contains the terms for some useful office furniture and accessories.

Table 16-2 Office Furniture and Equipment

English	*Polish*	*Pronunciation*
bin	kosz	*kosh*
binder	segregator	*se-gre-ga-tor*
calendar	terminarz/kalendarz	*ter-mee-nash/ka-len-dash*
computer	komputer	*com-poo-ter*
pen	długopis	*dwoo-go-pees*
desk	biurko	*byoor-koh*
files	dokumenty	*do-koo-men-tih*
keyboard	klawiatura	*kla-vya-too-ra*
mouse	myszka	*mih-shka*
(printer) paper	papier do drukarki	*pa-pyer do droo-kar-kee*
photocopier	ksero	*kse-ro*
printer	drukarka	*droo-kar-ka*
(computer) screen	monitor	*mo-n'ee-tor*
swivel chair	krzesło obrotowe	*kshe-swo o-bro-to-ve*
USB stick	pendrive	*pen-drayf*

Dealing with faulty office equipment

Imagine you're trying to print out some documents just minutes before a meeting but your printer refuses to cooperate! Or you're working on an important business plan when your computer crashes. **Koszmar!** *(kosh-mar)* (Nightmare!). Here's how you can talk about and deal with your office problems:

- **Ciągle zawiesza mi się komputer** *(ch'yon-gle za-vye-sha mee sh'ye kom-poo-ter)* (My computer freezes all the time)
- **Nie działa faks** *(n'ye dj'ya-wa faks)* (The fax machine isn't working)
- **Nie działa drukarka/ksero** *(n'ye dj'ya-wa droo-kar-ka/kse-ro)* (The printer/photocopier isn't working)
- **Zepsuł się ekspres do kawy** *(ze-psoow sh'ye eks-pres do ka-vih)* (The coffee machine has broken down)
- **Czy możesz sprawdzić, dlaczego nie mam internetu?** *(chih mo-zhesh sprav-dj'yeech' dla-che-go n'ye mam een-ter-ne-too)* (Can you check why I don't have Internet access?)
- **Nie mogę się zalogować do systemu** *(n'ye mo-ge sh'ye za-lo-go-vadj' do sih-ste-moo)* (I can't log in to the system)
- **Czy mamy kopię zapasową?** *(chih ma-mih ko-pye za-pa-so-vohN)* (Do we have a back-up copy?)
- **Skończył się toner** *(skon'-chiw sh'ye to-ner)* (We've run out of toner)
- **Zadzwoń po pomoc techniczną!** *(za-dzvon' po po-mots te-hn'ee-chnohN)* (Call technical support!) – informal
- **Rozładował mi się telefon** *(roz-wa-do-vaw mee sh'ye te-le-fon)* (My phone battery has died)
- **Nie działa mi myszka** *(n'ye dj'ya-wa mee mih-shka)* (My mouse doesn't work)
- **Trzeba zrestartować komputer** *(tshe-ba zre-star-to-vach' kom-poo-ter)* (You need to restart the computer)

Talkin' the Talk

Audio track 34: Anna *(an-na)* is struggling to print out a file. She's tried everything already and now she asks Marek *(ma-rek)* for help.

Anna: **Marek, możesz mi pomóc?**
ma-rek mo-zhesh mee po-moots
Marek, can you help me, please?

Marek:	**Co się stało?** *tso sh'ye sta-wo* What's wrong?
Anna:	**Mam problem z drukarką. Chcę wydrukować ten dokument, ale nie mogę.** *mam pro-blem zdroo-kar-kohN htse vih-droo-ko-vach' ten do-koo-ment a-le n'ye mo-ge* I have a problem with the printer. I want to print out this file but I can't.
Marek:	**Może trzeba zrestartować komputer.** *mo-zhe tshe-ba zre-star-to-vach' kom-poo-ter* Maybe you need to restart your computer.
Anna:	**Już to zrobiłam, ale nie pomogło.** *yoosh to zro-bee-wam a-le n'ye po-mo-gwo* I've tried that already but it didn't help.
Marek:	**Może papier się skończył?** *mo-zhe pa-pyer sh'ye skon'-chihw* Maybe we've run out of paper?
Anna:	**Papier jest.** *pa-pyer yest* There is some paper left.
Marek:	**To zadzwoń po pomoc techniczną.** *to za-dzvon' po po-mots te-hn'ee-chnohN* Call technical support, then.

Business people

You should always be formal when dealing with Polish business people, especially those of the older generation. Younger managers tend to be less formal, but you should still refrain from calling them by their first name unless invited to. Your best bet is to follow their example and if they call you by your first name, feel free to take that path.

Don't get discouraged when you find your Polish business partners to be distant and formal at first. Polish people like to get to know their business associates before engaging in a closer business relationship. Be patient; with time you can expect a more personal and open approach.

Words to Know

co się stało?	tso sh'ye *sta*-wo	what's wrong/ what's happened?
problem z drukarką	*pro*-blem zdroo-*kar*-kohN	problem with the printer
wydrukować	vih-droo-*ko*-vach'	to print out
zrestartować komputer	zre-star-*to*-vach' kom-*poo*-ter	to restart the computer
już	yoosh	already
nie pomogło	n'ye po-*mo*-gwo	it didn't help
skończyć się	*skon'*-chihch' sh'ye	to finish (run out of)
zadzwonić po	za-*dzvo*-n'eech' po	call (for)
pomoc techniczna	*po*-mots te-*hn'ee*-chna	technical support

Planning Your Day

Good planning is the key to being successful in business. This section helps you to plan your business schedule.

- **Musimy skończyć ten projekt do piątku** *(moo-sh'ee-mih skon'-chihch' ten pro-yegd do pyon-tkoo)* (We have to finish this project by Friday)
- **Rano mamy spotkanie** *(ra-no ma-mih spot-ka-n'ye)* (We have a meeting in the morning)
- **Po południu jest prezentacja nowej strategii firmy** *(po po-woo-dn'yoo yest pre-zen-ta-tsya no-vey stra-te-gyee feer-mih)* (The new company strategy will be presented this afternoon)
- **Na kiedy to ma być gotowe?** *(na kye-dih to ma bihdj' go-to-ve)* (When does this need to be ready?)

- **Trzeba przygotować ofertę na przyszły tydzień** *(tshe-ba pshih-go-to-vach' o-fer-te na pshih-shwih tih-dj'yen')* (We need to prepare the offer for next week)
- **Jaki mamy plan na dzisiaj?** *(ya-kee ma-mih plan na dj'ee-sh'yay)* (What's the plan for today?)
- **Musi pan/pani potwierdzić rezerwację do czwartku** *(moo-sh'ee pan/pa-n'ee pot-fyer-dj'eech' re-zer-va-tsye do chfar-tkoo)* (You need to confirm your reservation by Thursday) – formal, to a man/woman
- **Dzisiaj pracuję nad cennikiem** *(dj'ee-sh'yay pra-tsoo-ye nat tsen-n'ee-kyem)* (I'm working on the price list today)
- **Jutro przychodzi nowy pracownik** *(yoo-tro pshih-ho-dj'ee no-vih pra-tsov-n'eek)* (The new employee is coming tomorrow)
- **Mam rozmowę kwalifikacyjną** *(mam roz-mo-ve kfa-lee-fee-ka-tsihy-nohN)* (I have a job interview)
- **Nowy budżet musi być gotowy na czwartek** *(no-vih bood-zhet moo-sh'ee bihch' go-to-vih na chfar-tek)* (The new budget needs to be ready for Thursday)
- **W ten weekend jadę służbowo do Polski** *(ften wee-kent ya-de swoozh-bo-vo do pol-skee)* (I'm going on a business trip to Poland this weekend)
- **Kiedy masz spotkanie z klientem?** *(kye-dih mash spot-ka-n'ye sklee-yen-tem)* (When are you meeting the client?)
- **Do kiedy mamy termin?** *(do kye-dih ma-mih ter-meen)* (When is the deadline?)
- **Biorę bezpłatny urlop** *(byo-re bes-pwat-nih oor-lop)* (I'm taking an unpaid holiday)

Arranging a meeting

No work is safe from meetings. Arranging business meetings in Poland is done in pretty much the same way as it's done in the UK. The first meeting is always preceded by a number of phone calls or an exchange of emails in which you set up a date and decide on the topic to discuss. The best time to schedule a meeting is late morning or afternoon. The following questions help you schedule a meeting:

- **Proszę mnie umówić na spotkanie z dyrektorem** *(pro-she mn'ye oo-moo-veech' na spot-ka-n'ye zdih-re-kto-rem)* (Can you set up a meeting for me with the director, please?)
- **Kiedy możemy się spotkać?** *(kye-dih mo-zhe-mih sh'ye spot-kach')* (When can we meet?)

- **Kiedy jest pan wolny/pani wolna?** *(kye-dih yest pan vol-nih/pa-n'ee vol-na)* (When are you free?) – formal, to a man/woman
- **Czy pasuje ci/panu/pani trzecia?** *(chih pa-soo-ye ch'ee/pa-noo/pa-n'ee t-she-ch'ya)* (Does 3 p.m. suit you?) – informal/formal, to a man/woman
- **W jakim terminie panu/pani pasuje?** *(vya-keem ter-mee-n'ye pa-noo/pa-n'ee pa-soo-ye)* (What date works for you?) – formal, to a man/woman
- **Masz czas jutro?** *(mash chas yoo-tro)* (Are you free tomorrow?) – informal
- **Ma pan/pani czas w środę o 10:00?** *(ma pan/pa-n'ee chas fsh'ro-de o dj'ye-sh'yon-tey)* (Do you have time on Wednesday at 10 a.m.?) – formal, to a man/woman
- **Chciałbym/Chciałabym się spotkać o wpół do drugiej** *(hch'yaw-bihm/hch'ya-wa-bihm sh'ye spot-kach' o fpoow do droo-gyey)* (I'd like to meet at half past one) – a man/woman speaking
- **Może w przyszłym tygodniu?** *(mo-zhe fpshih-shwihm tih-god-n'yoo)* (How about next week?)

If you're trying to set up a meeting with someone in a government institution, remember that in Poland government workers tend to start work at 7 or 8 a.m. and finish earlier at 3 or 4 p.m.

Business lunches and dinners are gaining in popularity in Poland but all the details of deals are still being discussed in boardrooms. When it comes to agreeing to or refusing to attend a meeting, these phrases come into play:

- **Wtorek mi pasuje** *(fto-rek mee pa-soo-ye)* (Tuesday suits me)
- **Mogę w poniedziałek** *(mo-ge fpo-n'ye-dj'ya-wek)* (I can [make it] on Monday)
- **Może być** *(mo-zhe bihch')* (That's fine)
- **Pasuje mi** *(pa-soo-ye mee)* (That suits me)
- **Niestety, nie mogę** *(n'ye-ste-tih n'ye mo-ge)* (Unfortunately, I can't)
- **Przepraszam, ale mam wtedy inne spotkanie** *(pshe-pra-sham a-le mam fte-dih een-ne spot-ka-n'ye)* (I'm sorry but I have another meeting then)
- **We wtorek mi nie pasuje, ale mogę w środę** *(ve fto-rek mee n'ye pa-soo-ye a-le mo-ge fsh'ro-de)* (I can't make Tuesday but can do Wednesday)
- **Przykro mi, ale jestem (wtedy) zajęty/zajęta** *(psih-kro mee a-le yes-tem fte-dih za-yen-tih/za-yen-ta)* (I'm sorry but I'm busy then) – a man/woman speaking

Make your way to Chapter 9 for tips on arranging meetings over the phone, to Chapter 7 to learn days of the week, parts of the day and the Polish clock and to Chapter 3 for greetings and how to introduce yourself.

Some expressions you may hear or use before and during a meeting include:

- **Jestem umówiony/umówiona na spotkanie z panem Nowakiem/panią Łakomą** *(yes-tem oo-moo-vyo-nih/oo-moo-vyo-na na spot-ka-n'ye spa-nem no-va-kyem/spa-n'yohN wa-ko-mohN)* (I have a meeting with Mr Nowak/ Mrs Łakoma)

  (Go to Chapter 8 for information on how to put a name in the instrumental case.)

- **Przepraszam za spóźnienie** *(pshe-pra-sham za spooz'-n'ye-n'ye)* (Sorry I'm late)
- **Spóźnię się chwilę** *(spooz'-n'ye sh'ye hfee-le)* (I'll be a bit late)
- **Proszę, to moja wizytówka** *(pro-she to mo-ya vee-zih-toof-ka)* (Here is my business card)
- **Czy ma pan/pani wizytówkę?** *(chih ma pan/pa-n'ee vee-zih-toof-ke)* (Can I have your business card, please?) – to a man/woman; literally: Do you have a business card?
- **Czy mogę prosić o tłumacza?** *(chih mo-ge pro-sh'eech' o twoo-ma-cha)* (Can I have an interpreter, please?)
- **Czy mogę prosić o przesłanie dokumentacji mailem?** *(chih mo-ge pro-sh'eech' o pshe-swa-n'ye do-koo-men-ta-tsyee mey-lem)* (Could you send the documentation by email, please?)
- **Proszę chwilę poczekać** *(pro-she hfee-le po-che-kach')* (One moment, please)
- **Proszę usiąść** *(pro-she oo-sh'yon'sh'ch')* (Please, have a seat)

Shaking hands and exchanging business cards with business colleagues are customary in Poland.

Polish manners are fairly formal, perhaps even old-fashioned. If you're a man dealing with a woman, wait for her to extend her hand first. Likewise, let older people and those higher in a company's hierarchy be the first to offer a hand to shake. Again, if you're a man, avoid standing with hands in your pockets and always get up when a woman is standing. If you're a woman meeting Polish businessmen, especially those from the older generation, don't feel patronised when they bow slightly to kiss your hand. To that generation, such a gesture shows that they're perfect gentlemen! Polish men will hold doors open for you, help you with your coat and offer you a seat on buses and trams.

Talkin' the Talk

Simon is arranging to meet the director to show him an offer he's put together for a client.

Simon: **Dzień dobry, panie dyrektorze. Czy możemy się spotkać jutro rano?**
(dj'yen' dob-rih pa-n'ye dih-re-kto-zhe chih mo-zhe-mih sh'ye spot-kach' yoo-tro ra-no)
Good morning. Can we meet tomorrow morning?

Director: **W jakiej sprawie?**
vya-kyey spra-vye
With regards to what?

Simon: **Mamy już gotową ofertę dla klienta i chcielibyśmy ją panu przedstawić.**
ma-mih yoozh go-to-vohN o-fer-te dla klee-yen-ta ee hch'ye-lee-bih-sh'mih yohN pa-noo pshet-sta-veech'
The offer for the client is ready and we would like to present it to you.

Director: **Niestety, jutro jestem zajęty cały dzień.**
n'ye-ste-tih yoo-tro yes-tem za-yen-tih tsa-wih dj'yen'
Unfortunately, I'm busy all day tomorrow.

Simon: **To może dzisiaj po południu?**
to mo-zhe dj'ee-sh'yay po po-wood-n'yoo
How about this afternoon?

Director: **Tak, mam czas. Może być o drugiej?**
tak mam chas mo-zhe bihch' o droo-gyey
Yes, I'm free. What about 2 p.m.?

Simon: **Tak, pasuje nam.**
tak pa-soo-ye nam
Yes, that suits us.

Words to Know

spotkać się	spot-kach' sh'ye	to meet
w jakiej sprawie?	vya-kyey spra-vye	with regards to what?
oferta dla klienta	o-fer-ta dla klee-yen-ta	offer for a client
przedstawić	pshet-sta-veech'	to present
zajęty	za-yen-tih	busy
cały dzień	tsa-wih dj'yen'	all day
może . . . ?	mo-zhe	what about . . .?
mam czas	mam chas	I'm available
pasuje mi	pa-soo-ye mee	(that) suits me

Setting a date

Whether arranging business meetings, booking a hotel or making medical appointments, knowing how to set Polish dates helps you do it right. Here are some useful questions:

- **Którego jest konferencja?** *(ktoo-re-go yest kon-fe-ren-tsya)* (When [on what date] is the conference?)
- **Kiedy jest spotkanie?** *(kye-dih yest spot-ka-n'ye)* (When is the meeting?)
- **W jakim terminie masz wyjazd służbowy?** *(vya-keem ter-mee-n'ye mazh vih-yast swoozh-bo-vih)* (When [literally: on what dates] is your business trip?)

When setting dates, you use ordinal numbers in the genitive case. This is pretty straightforward, so don't worry. (Go to Chapter 7 for a refresher on ordinals.) To change ordinal numbers to the genitive case, simply add the ending **-ego** to the ordinal number and your date is nearly ready. Just add a month in the genitive case, as in the examples below, and it's all done:

- **pierwszego stycznia** *(pyer-fshe-go stih-chn'ya)* (on the 1st of January)
- **drugiego lutego** *(droo-gye-go loo-te-go)* (on the 2nd of February)
- **trzeciego marca** *(t-she-ch'ye-go mar-tsa)* (on the 3rd of March)
- **czwartego kwietnia** *(chfar-te-go kfye-tn'ya)* (on the 4th of April)
- **piątego maja** *(pyon-te-go ma-ya)* (on the 5th of May)
- **szóstego czerwca** *(shoo-ste-go cher-ftsa)* (on the 6th of June)
- **siódmego lipca** *(sh'yoo-dme-go leep-tsa)* (on the 7th of July)
- **ósmego sierpnia** *(oo-sme-go sh'yer-pn'ya)* (on the 8th of August)
- **dziewiątego września** *(dj'ye-vyon-te-go vzhe-sh'n'ya)* (on the 9th of September)
- **dziesiątego października** *(dj'ye-sh'yon-te-go paz'-dj'yer-n'ee-ka)* (on the 10th of October)
- **jedenastego listopada** *(ye-de-na ste-go lee-sto-pa-da)* (on the 11th of November)
- **dwunastego grudnia** *(dvoo-na-ste-go groo-dn'ya)* (on the 12th of December)

Check your calendar to see if you've got everything up to date:

- **Konferencja zaczyna się dwunastego kwietnia** *(kon-fe-ren-tsya za-chih-na sh'ye dvoo-na-ste-go kfye-tn'ya)* (The conference starts on the 12th of April)
- **Urlop planuję od pierwszego sierpnia** *(oor-lop pla-noo-ye ot pyer-fshe-go sh'yer-pn'ya)* (I'm planning my holiday from the 1st of August)
- **Nie ma mnie w biurze od drugiego do siódmego grudnia** *(n'ye ma mn'ye vbyoo-zhe od droo-gye-go do sh'yoo-dme-go groo-dn'ya)* (I'm out of the office from the 2nd to the 7th of December)
- **Zaczynam nową pracę piętnastego maja** *(za-chih-nam no-vohN pra-tse pye-tna-ste-go ma-ya)* (I'm starting a new job on the 15th of May)
- **Projekt ma być gotowy na jedenastego lipca** *(pro-yekt ma bihdj' go-to-vih na ye-de-na-ste-go leep-tsa)* (The project needs to be ready for the 11th of July)

As you can see in the above sentences, to say 'from [a date] to [a date]' you use **od** *(ot)* . . . **do** *(do)* . . .

Na *(na)* . . . means 'for [a date]'.

Go to Chapter 14 if you want to know how to say in January, in February and so on and how the endings change, again.

Cancelling meetings and apologising

No matter how well-organised you are, things come up and you may need to cancel or reschedule a business meeting, sometimes at very short notice. These expressions help you to do so politely:

- **Bardzo mi przykro, ale muszę odwołać nasze spotkanie** *(bar-dzo mee pshih-kro a-le moo-she od-vo-wach' na-she spot-ka-n'ye)* (I'm very sorry but I need to cancel our meeting)
- **Niestety, nie mogę być na spotkaniu** *(n'ye-ste-tih n'ye mo-ge bihch' na spot-ka-n'yoo)* (Unfortunately, I can't make it to the meeting)
- **Czy możemy przełożyć spotkanie?** *(chih mo-zhe-mih pshe-wo-zhihch' spot-ka-n'ye)* (Can we reschedule the meeting?)
- **Przepraszam, ale coś pilnego mi wypadło** *(pshe-pra-sham a-le tsosh' peel-ne-go mee vih-pa-dwo)* (I'm sorry but something urgent has come up)
- **Możemy umówić się na inny termin?** *(mo-zhe-mih oo-moo-veech' sh'ye na een-nih ter-meen)* (Can we arrange another date?)
- **Muszę sprawdzić w kelendarzu/w terminarzu** *(moo-she sprav-dj'eech' fka-len-da-zhoo/fter-mee-na-zhoo)* (I need to check my calendar)
- **Oczywiście, nie ma problemu** *(o-chih-veesh'-ch'ye n'ye ma pro-ble-moo)* (Certainly, no problem)

Remember that being punctual is a sign of respect for the other party, so if you're running late, make sure you notify your business partner or client.

Getting Down to Business with Business Travelling

Not every foreign trip is purely for pleasure. A **delegacja** *(de-le-ga-tsya)* (business trip) requires a lot of preparation, language-wise, too. Here are some expressions that can come in handy when travelling on business:

- **Wyjeżdżam służbowo do Polski** *(vih-yezh-djam swoozh-bo-vo do pol-skee)* (I'm going on a business trip to Poland)
- **Muszę załatwić kilka formalności** *(moo-she za-wa-tfeech' keel-ka for-mal-nosh'-ch'ee)* (I've got to sort out a couple of formalities)

- **Proszę wypełnić formularz delegacji** *(pro-she vih-pew-n'eech' for-moo-lazh de-le-ga-tsyee)* (Please fill out the business trip form)
- **Mam szkolenie** *(mam shko-le-n'ye)* (I have a training course)
- **Muszę zarezerwować hotel/pokój w hotelu** *(moo-she za-re-zer-vo-vach' ho-tel/po-kooy fho-te-loo)* (I have to book a hotel/a room in a hotel)
- **Proszę mi zamówić taksówkę na lotnisko** *(pro-she mee za-moo-veech' tak-soof-ke na lot-n'ee-sko)* (Can you call a taxi to the airport for me, please?)
- **Proszę mi wynająć samochód** *(pro-she mee vih-na-yon'ch' sa-mo-hoot)* (Can you rent a car for me, please?)
- **Jadę na konferencję do Warszawy** *(ya-de na kon-fe-ren-tsye do var-sha-vih)* (I'm going to Warsaw for a conference)
- **Mam kilka spotkań biznesowych w Polsce** *(mam keel-ka spot-kan' bee-zne-so-vihch fpol-stse)* (I have a couple of business meetings in Poland)
- **Muszę przygotować prezentację** *(moo-she pshih-go-to-vach' pre-zen-ta-tsye)* (I have to prepare a presentation)
- **Szukam partnerów biznesowych w Europie Wschodniej** *(shoo-kam par-tne-roof bee-zne-so-vih ve-oo-ro-pye fs-hod-n'yey)* (I'm looking for business partners in Eastern Europe)
- **Chciałbym/Chciałabym potwierdzić spotkanie** *(hch'yaw-bihm/hch'ya-wa-bihm pot-fyer-dj'eech' spot-ka-n'ye)* (I'd like [man/woman] to confirm the meeting)
- **Mam samochód firmowy** *(mam sa-mo-hoot feer-mo-vih)* (I have a company car)

Leaving for Good

No matter how exciting a job is, everyone gets to the point when they say: **Odchodzę z pracy** *(ot-ho-dze spra-tsih)* (I'm quitting my job). The reason for this move may be one of the following:

- **Chcę więcej zarabiać** *(htse vyen-tsey za-ra-byach')* (I want to earn more)
- **Mam problemy z szefem** *(mam pro-ble-mih sshe-fem)* (I have problems with my boss)
- **Moja praca jest stresująca** *(mo-ya pra-tsa yest stre-soo-yon-tsa)* (My work is stressful)
- **Nie rozwijam się** *(n'ye roz-vee-yam sh'ye)* (I'm not developing)
- **W pracy jest zła atmosfera** *(fpra-tsih yezd zwa a-tmo-sfe-ra)* (The atmosphere at work is bad)

- **Idę na emeryturę** *(ee-de na e-me-rih-too-re)* (I'm retiring)
- **Idę na urlop macierzyński** *(ee-de na oor-lop ma-ch'ye-zhihn'-skee)* (I'm taking maternity leave)
- **Robię nadgodziny** *(ro-bye nad-go-dj'ee-nih)* (I'm working overtime)
- **Chcę założyć własną firmę** *(htse za-wo-zhihch' vwa-snohN fee-rme)* (I want to set up my own business)
- **Nie dostaję pensji na czas** *(n'ye dos-ta-ye pen-syee na chas)* (I'm not getting paid on time)
- **Boję się, że mnie zwolnią** *(bo-ye sh'ye zhe mn'ye zvol-n'yohN)* (I'm worried they'll fire me)

After you quit your job, you can say: **Szukam pracy** *(shoo-kam pra-tsih)* (I'm looking for a job). **Powodzenia!** *(po-vo-dze-n'ya)* (Good luck!).

Figure 16-1 shows your desk in your office in Poland. Try to name in Polish all the objects you can see in the figure.

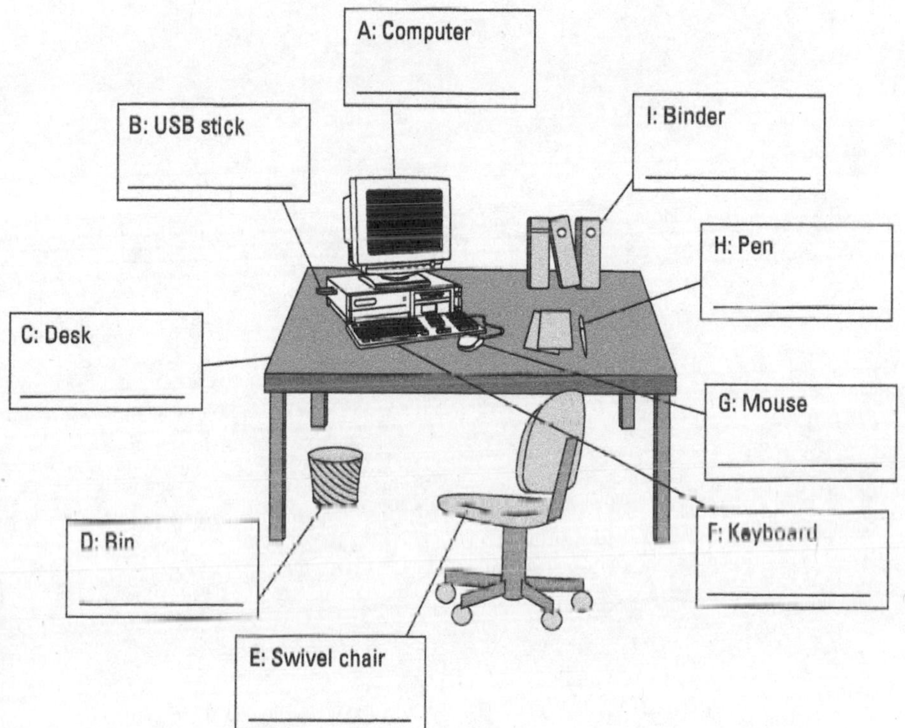

Figure 16-1: Your desk in your office in Poland.

Answer key: A: komputer, B: pendrive, C: biurko, D: kosz, E: krzesło obrotowe, F: klawiatura, G: myszka, H: długopis, I: segregator

Chapter 17

Polish on the Worksite

In This Chapter

- Talking hiring and firing
- Dealing with professionals and their tools
- Paying attention to Health and Safety
- Responding to an accident at work

If you're a builder, plumber or electrician – or if you need to deal with a professional in one of these fields – this chapter helps you speak their language. This chapter also focuses on hiring or firing employees and workplace health and safety.

Go to Chapters 16 and 18 for other Polish-at-work situations.

Getting Hired and Getting Fired

When talking about hiring people you use the verb **zatrudniać** *(za-troo-dn'yach')* (to employ) or the more English-like **rekrutować** *(re-kroo-to-vach')* (to recruit). **Zatrudniać** follows the **-m/-sz** type of conjugation, while **rekrutować** uses the **-uję/-ujesz** type in the present tense. Read more about types of conjugation in Chapter 2.

Table 17-1 Conjugating Zatrudniać and Rekrutować

Zatrudniać			*Rekrutować*		
English	***Polish***	***Pronunciation***	***English***	***Polish***	***Pronunciation***
I hire	(ja) zatrudniam	*(ya) za-troo-dn'yam*	I recruit	(ja) rekrutuję	*(ya) re-kroo-too-ye*

(continued)

Table 17-1 *(continued)*

Zatrudniać			***Rekrutować***		
English	***Polish***	***Pronunciation***	***English***	***Polish***	***Pronunciation***
you hire	(ty) zatrudniasz	*(tih) za-troo-dn'yash*	you recruit	(ty) rekrutujesz	*(tih) re-kroo-too-yesh*
he/she/it hires	on/ona/ono zatrudnia	*on/o-na/o-no za-troo-dn'ya*	he/she/it recruits	on/ona/ono rekrutuje	*on/o-na/o-no re-kroo-too-ye*
we hire	(my) zatrudniamy	*(mih) za-troo-dn'ya-mih*	we recruit	(my) rekrutujemy	*(mih) re-kroo-too-ye-mih*
you hire	(wy) zatrudniacie	*(vih) za-troo-dn'ya-ch'ye*	you recruit	(wy) rekrutujecie	*(vih) re-kroo-too-ye-ch'ye*
they hire	oni/one zatrudniają	*o-n'ee/o-ne za-troo-dn'ya-yohN*	they recruit	oni/one rekrutują	*o-n'ee/o-ne re-kroo-too-yohN*

You may hear or use the following sentences when hiring people or being hired yourself:

- **Będziemy zatrudniać nowych pracowników** *(ben'-dj'ye-mih za-troo-dn'yach' no-vihh pra-tso-vn'ee-koof)* (We will be hiring new employees)
- **Daliśmy ofertę do biura pośrednictwa pracy** *(da-lee-sh'mih o-fer-te do byoo-ra po-sh're-dn'ee-tstfa pra-tsih)* (We advertised in the job centre)
- **Szukamy osoby na stanowisko kierownika budowy** *(shoo-ka-mih o-so-bih na sta-no-vee-sko kye-ro-vn'ee-ka boo-do-vih)* (We are looking for a person for a construction executive position)
- **Nie zatrudniamy na czarno** *(n'ye za-troo-dn'ya-mih na char-no)* (We do not hire illegally)
- **Zatrudniamy doświadczonych pracowników budowlanych** *(za-troo-dn'ya-mih do-sh'fyat-cho-nihh pra-tso-vn'ee-koof boo-do-vla-nihh)* (We're hiring experienced construction workers)
- **Oferujemy pełne ubezpieczenie zdrowotne i emerytalne** *(o-fe-roo-ye-mih pew-ne oo-bes-pye-che-n'ye zdro-vot-ne ee e-me-rih-tal-ne)* (We offer full health insurance and pension)

- **Proszę przeczytać i podpisać umowę** *(pro-she pshe-chih-tach' ee pot-pee-sach' oo-mo-ve)* (Please read and sign the contract)

Talkin' the Talk

Mr Morgan has applied for a job at a well-known construction company. He is now having a job interview.

Employer: **Dzień dobry. Bardzo proszę się przedstawić.**
dj'yen' dob-rih bar-dzo pro-she sh'ye pshet-sta-veech'
Good morning. Can you introduce yourself, please.

Mr Morgan: **Nazywam się James Morgan. Jestem inżynierem budownictwa.**
na-zih-vam sh'ye djeyms mor-gan yes-tem een-zhih-n'ye-rem boo-do-vn'ee-tstfa
My name is James Morgan. I'm a construction engineer.

Employer: **Ile ma pan lat doświadczenia w branży budowlanej?**
ee-le ma pan lat do-sh'fyat-che-n'ya vbran-zhih boo-do-vla-ney
How many years of experience do you have in the construction industry?

Mr Morgan: **15 lat. Pracowałem w kilku krajach w Europie i w Azji jako menedżer projektów.**
pyet-nash'-ch'ye lat pra-tso-va-wem fkeel-koo kra-yah vew-ro-pye ee va-zyee ya-ko me-ne-djer pro-ye-ktoof
15 years. I worked in a few countries in Europe and Asia as a project manager.

Employer: **Czy ma pan jakieś referencje?**
chih ma pan ya-kyesh' re-fe-ren-tsye
Do you have any references?

Mr Morgan: **Oczywiście. Proszę bardzo.**
o-chih-veesh'-ch'ye pro-she bar-dzo
Of course. Here they are.

Employer: **Jest pan dyspozycyjny w weekendy?**
yest pan dih-spo-zih-tsihy-nih vwee-ken-dih
Are you available at weekends?

Mr Morgan: **Tak.**
tak
Yes. [I am]

Employer: **Mamy pracowników z różnych krajów. Często słabo mówią po angielsku.**
ma-mih pra-tso-vn'ee-koov zroo-zhnihh kra-yoof chehN-sto swa-bo moo-vyohN po an-gyel-skoo
We have employees from different countries. They often speak little English.

Mr Morgan: **To nie problem, bo znam kilka języków. Poza tym już wcześniej pracowałem z obcokrajowcami.**
to n'ye pro-blem bo znam keel-ka yehN-zih-koof po-za tihm yoosh fche-sh'n'yey pra-tso-va-wem zob-tso-kra-yof-tsa-mee
That's not a problem because I speak several languages. Besides, I've previously worked with foreigners.

Employer: **Skontaktujemy się z panem w ciągu kilku dni.**
skon-ta-ktoo-ye-mih sh'ye spa-nem fch'yon-goo keel-koo dn'ee
We will get in touch with you within the next few days.

Words to Know

przedstawić (się)	*pshet-sta-veech' (sh'ye)*	to introduce (oneself)
inżynier budownictwa	*een-zhih-n'yer boo-do-vn'ee-tstfa*	construction engineer
doświadczenie	*do-sh'fyat-che-n'ye*	experience
w branży budowlanej	*vbran-zhih boo-do-vla-ney*	in the construction industry
legalnie	*le-gal-n'ye*	legally
dyspozycyjny	*dih-spo-zih-tsihy-nih*	available
pracownik/pracownik fizyczny	*pra-tso-vn'eek/pra-tso-vn'eek fee-zih-chnih*	employee/labour worker
w ciągu kilku dni	*fch'yon-goo keel-koo dn'ee*	within the next couple of days

Talking about how much you work

When you get a job, you may work full-time, part-time or do shift work. Table 17-2 shows you how to tell people **Pracuję** *(pra-tsoo-ye)* (I work/I'm working).

Table 17-2 Job Talk

English	*Polish*	*Pronunciation*
shifts	na zmiany	*na zmya-nih*
morning shift	na porannej zmianie	*na po-ran-ney zmya-n'ye*
afternoon shift	na popołudniowej zmiane	*na po-po-wood-n'yo-vey zmya-n'ye*
night shift	na nocnej zmianie	*na nots-ney zmya-n'ye*
full-time	na pełny etat	*na pew-nih e-tat*
half-time	na pół etatu	*na poow e-ta-too*
part-time	na niepełny etat	*na n'ye-pew-nih e-tat*

You can also tell people about your job status:

- **Jestem na okresie próbnym** *(yes-tem na o-kre-sh'ye proo-bnihm)* (I'm in my probationary period)
- **Jestem zatrudniony/zatrudniona na stałe** *(yest-tem za-troo-dn'yo-nih/ za-troo-dn'yo na na sta-we)* (I was hired for a permanent position) a man/ woman speaking
- **Pracuję dorywczo** *(pra-tsoo-ye do rihf-cho)* (I do odd jobs)
- **Pracuję w sektorze prywatnym** *(pra-tsoo-ye fse-kto-zhe prih-vat-nihm)* (I work in the private sector)
- **Mam nadgodziny** *(mam nad-go-dj'ee-nih)* (I work overtime)

Getting fired

If you're unlucky and the company you work for has **problemy finansowe** *(pro-ble-mih fee-nan-so-ve)* (financial problems), you may be made redundant, in which case the following expressions help you say it in Polish:

- **Zwolnili mnie z pracy** *(zvol-n'ee-lee mn'ye spra-tsih)* (They fired me from my job)

- **Straciłem/Straciłam pracę** *(stra-ch'ee-wem/stra-ch'ee-wam pra-tse)* (I've [man/woman] lost my job)
- **Dostałem wypowiedzenie z pracy** *(do-sta-wem vih-po-vye-dze-n'ye spra-tsih)* (I [man] got a redundancy letter)
- **Muszę przejść na wcześniejszą emeryturę** *(moo-she psheysh'ch' na fche-sh'n'yey-shohN e-me-rih-too-re)* (I need to take early retirement)
- **Jestem bezrobotny/bezrobotna** *(yes-tem bez-ro-bot-nih/bez-ro-bot-na)* (I'm [man/woman] unemployed)
- **Szukam pracy** *(shoo-kam pra-tsih)* (I'm looking for a job)
- **Jestem na zasiłku** *(yes-tem na za-sh'eew-koo)* (I'm on unemployment benefit)

Getting Familiar with Workers and their Tools

Polish builders have a reputation for being hardworking and trustworthy specialists, **fachowcy** *(fa-hof-tsih)*. Whether you work alongside native Polish-speakers or employ them to work in your own company, mastering a few basic expressions isn't a bad idea. This section helps build up your building site-related vocabulary.

You can start with the names of the people who work at a building site, which is called **plac budowy** *(plats boo-do-vih)* or **budowa** *(boo-do-va)*, as shown in Table 17-3.

Table 17-3 Construction Professions

English	*Polish*	*Pronunciation*
bricklayer	murarz	*moo-rash*
carpenter	stolarz	*sto-lash*
electrician	elektryk	*e-lek-trihk*
labourer	pomocnik budowlany	*po-mo-tsn'eek boo-do-vla-nih*
painter	malarz	*ma-lash*
plasterer	tynkarz	*tihn-kash*
plumber	hydraulik	*hih-draw-leek*
security guard	stróż/ochroniarz	*stroosh/o-hro-n'yash*
welder	spawacz	*spa-vach*

You can now practise these expressions:

- **Pracuję na budowie** *(pra-tsoo-ye na boo-do-vye)* (I work at a building site)
- **Szukam pracy jako pracownik budowlany** *(shoo-kam pra-tsih ya-ko pra-tso-vn'eek boo-do-vla-nih)* (I'm looking for a job as a builder)
- **Jestem wykwalifikowanym pracownikiem budowlanym** *(yes-tem vih-kfa-lee-fee-ko-va-nihm pra tso-vn'ee-kyem boo-do-vla-nihm)* (I'm a skilled construction worker)
- **To pracownik tymczasowy** *(to pra-tso-vn'eek tihm-cha-so-vih)* (He's a temporary employee)
- **Mam pozwolenie na budowę** *(mam po-zvo-le-n'ye na boo-do-ve)* (I have planning permission)
- **Potrzebuję dobrego elektryka** *(po-tshe-boo-ye dob-re-go e-lek-trih-ka)* (I need a good electrician)
- **Czy zna się pan na hydraulice?** *(chih zna sh'ye pan na hih-draw-lee-tse)* (Are you well-versed in plumbing?)

Talkin' the Talk

Audio track 35: Simon wants to build an extension to his house. A good Polish builder was recommended to him. They are talking about the project.

Builder: **Czy ma pan pozwolenie na przebudowę?**
chih ma pan po-zvo-le-n'ye na pshe-boo-do-ve
Do you have planning permission for the extension?

Simon: **Tak. Chcemy dobudować pokój o wymiarach sześć na osiem metrów.**
tak htse-mih do-bo-do-vach' po-kooy o vih-mya-rah shesh'ch' na o-sh'yem met-roof
Yes, we have it. We want to build a 6 by 8 metre-extension.

Builder: **Robimy malowanie reszty domu?**
ro-bee-mih ma-lo-va-n'ye resh-tih do-moo
Shall we paint the rest of the house?

Simon: **Oczywiście. I jeszcze w łazience trzeba położyć płytki.**
o-chih-veesh'-ch'ye ee yesh-che vwa-z'yen-tse tshe-ba po-wo-zhihch' pwih-tkee
Indeed. And we also need to tile the bathroom.

Builder: **Świetnie! Przygotuję wycenę za robociznę i dam panu wstępny kosztorys materiałów budowlanych.**
sh'fyet-n'ye pshih-go-too-ye vih-tse-ne za ro-bo-ch'ee-zne ee dam pa-noo fstem-pnih kosh-to-rihs ma-te-rya-woov boo-do-vla-nihh
Great. I'll prepare the quote for the labour and will give you an estimate for the building materials.

Words to Know

pozwolenie na przebudowę	*po-zvo-le-n'ye na pshe-boo-do-ve*	planning permission
płytki	*pwih-tkee*	tiles
wycena	*vih-tse-na*	quote
za robociznę	*za ro-bo-ch'ee-zne*	for labour
kosztorys	*ko-shto-rihs*	calculation
materiały budowlane	*ma-te-rya-wih boo-do-vla-ne*	building materials

Getting down to tools and construction equipment

If you happen to work at a building site with Polish builders, you may need to familiarise yourself with the **maszyny i narzędzia budowlane** *(ma-shih-nih ee na-zhen'-dj'ya boo-do-vla-ne)* (construction equipment and tools) listed in Table 17-4.

Table 17-4 Building Tools and Equipment

English	*Polish*	*Pronunciation*
brush	pędzel	*pen-dzel*
chisel	dłuto	*dwoo-to*
crane	dźwig	*dj'veek*
drill/hammer drill	wiertarka/wiertarka udarowa	*vyer-tar-ka/vyer-tar-ka oo-da-ro-va*
grinder	szlifierka	*shlee-fyer-ka*
hacksaw	piła do metalu	*pee-wa do me-ta-loo*
hammer	młotek	*mwo-tek*
ladder	drabina	*dra-bee-na*
measuring tape	miarka	*myar-ka*
mixer	betoniarka	*be-to-n'yar-ka*
nail/nails	gwóźdź/gwoździe	*gvoosh'ch'/gvoz'-dj'ye*
pincers	obcęgi	*op-tsen-gee*
planer	heblarka	*he-blar-ka*
plasterboard	płyta gipsowo-kartonowa	*pwih-ta gee-pso-vo kar-to-no-va*
pliers	kombinerki	*kom-bee-ner-kee*
scaffolding	rusztowania	*roo-shto-va-n'ya*
screwdriver	śrubokręt	*sh'roo-bo-kront*
spirit level	poziomica	*po-z'yo-mee-tsa*
tool box	skrzynka z narzędziami	*skshihn-ka zna-zhen'-dj'ya-mee*
soldering iron	spawarka	*spa-var-ka*

Dealing with problems at home

Fachowiec *(fa-ho-vyets)* is the name for a handyman, electrician, plumber or any other person who can help you with a domestic problem. Whether you work as a **hydraulik** *(hih-draw-leek)* (plumber) or an **elektryk** *(e-lek-trihk)* (electrician) or need one, the following expressions can be help you deal with pipes and sockets:

- **Trzeba zawołać elektryka** *(tshe-ba za-vo-wach' e-lek-trih-ka)* (You need to call an electrician)
- **Spalił się bezpiecznik** *(spa-leew sh'ye bes-pye-chn'eek)* (The fuse has blown)
- **Trzeba wymienić ten kabel** *(tshe-ba vih-mye-n'eech' ten ka-bel)* (This wire needs to be replaced)
- **Gdzie mają iść kable?** *(gdj'ye ma-yohN eesh'ch' ka-ble)* (Where do you want the cables placed?)
- **Nie ma prądu** *(n'ye ma pron-doo)* (There is no electricity)
- **Trzeba sprawdzić instalację gazową** *(tshe-ba sprav-dj'eech' een-sta-la-tsye ga-zo-vohN)* (The gas pipe needs to be inspected)
- **Musi pan/pani wymienić całą instalację elektryczną** *(moo-sh'ee pan/pa-n'ee vih-mye-n'eech' tsa-wohN een-sta-la-tsye e-lek-trih-chnohN)* (You need to replace all the electrical wiring) – formal, to a man/woman
- **Nie działa światło** *(n'ye dj'ya-wa sh'fya-two)* (The lighting is not working)
- **Dzisiaj nie uda się tego naprawić** *(dj'ee-sh'yay n'ye oo-da sh'ye te-go na-pra-veech')* (It won't be possible to fix that today)
- **Mogę przyjechać dopiero jutro** *(mo-ge pshih-ye-hadj' do-pye-ro yoo-tro)* (I can only come tomorrow)

Chapter 15 talks extensively about emergency situations.

Health and Safety

Bezpieczeństwo i Higiena Pracy *(bes-pye-chen'-stfo ee hee-gye-na pra-tsih)*, which you commonly hear abbreviated to **BHP** *(be ha pe)*, is the Polish version of the British Health and Safety regulations. Following are expressions that help you keep your workplace safe:

- **Przeszedłem/Przeszłam szkolenie z udzielania pierwszej pomocy** *(pshe-she-dwem/pshe-shwam shko-le-n'ye zoo-dj'ye-la-n'ya pyer-fshey po-mo-tsih)* (I've taken first aid training) man/woman talking
- **Przestrzegamy przepisów BHP** *(pshe-stshe-ga-mih pshe-pee-soov be ha pe)* (We keep an eye on Health and Safety regulations)
- **Ta firma łamie przepisy BHP** *(ta feer-ma wa-mye pshe-pee-sih be ha pe)* (This company breaks the Health and Safety regulations)

- **Idę na szkolenie z BHP** *(ee-de na shko-le-n'ye zbe ha pe)* (I'm taking Health and Safety training)
- **To jest niezgodne z kodeksem pracy** *(to yest n'ye-zgod-ne sko-de-ksem pra-tsih)* (This breaks the employment regulations)
- **Na terenie budowy trzeba nosić kask ochronny** *(na te-re-n'ye boo-do-vih tshe-ba no-sh'eech' kask o-hron-nih)* (You have to wear a hard hat on a building site)
- **Proszę założyć maskę pyłową** *(pro-she za-wo-zhihch' ma-ske pih-wo-vohN)* (You need to put on a dust mask)
- **Gdzie znajdę rękawice ochronne?** *(gdj'ye znay-de ren-ka-ve-tse o-hron-ne)* (Where can I find protective gloves?)
- **Jest hałas. Trzeba mieć zatyczki do uszu** *(yest ha-was tshe-ba myech' za-tih-chkee do oo-shoo)* (It's noisy. You need ear plugs)
- **Potrzebujesz okularów ochronnych** *(po-tshe-boo-yesh o-koo-la-roof o-hron-nihh)* (You need safety glasses)
- **Gdzie jest moje ubranie ochronne** *(gdj'ye yest mo-ye oo-bra-n'ye o-hron-ne)* (Where is my protective clothing?)

Watch out for the following warning signs:

- **Uwaga!** *(oo-va-ga)* (Attention!)
- **Prace na wysokości** *(pra-tse na vih-so-kosh'-ch'ee)* (Workers overhead)
- **Wysokie napięcie** *(vih-so-kye na-pyen'-ch'ye)* (High voltage)
- **Roboty budowlane** *(ro-bo-tih boo-do-vla-ne)* (Construction works)
- **Roboty drogowe** *(ro-bo-tih dro-go-ve)* (Road works)
- **Wyjazd z budowy** *(vih-yazd zboo-do-vih)* (Construction site exit)
- **Wyjście ewakuacyjne** *(vihy-sh'ch'ye e-va-koo-a-tsihy-ne)* (Emergency exit)
- **W czasie pożaru nie korzystać z windy** *(fcha-sh'ye po-zha-roo n'ye ko-zhih-stadj' zveen-dih)* (In case of fire, do not use the lift)
- **W razie niebezpieczeństwa . . .** *(vra-z'ye n'ye-bes-pye-chen'-stfa)* (In case of emergency . . .)

Reporting Accidents

Hopefully you'll never need to use vocabulary related to accidents at work. Just in case you do witness an accident, though, here are some expressions that help you call for help:

- **Doszło do wypadku** *(do-shwo do vih-pat-koo)* (There's been an accident)
- **Dwie osoby uległy wypadkowi** *(dvye o-so-bih oo-le-gwih vih-pat-ko-vee)* (Two people have had an accident)
- **Miałem wypadek w pracy** *(mya-wem vih-pa-dek fpra-tsih)* (I had an accident at work)
- **Gdzie jest apteczka?** *(gdj'ye yest a-pte-chka)* (Where is the first aid kit?)
- **Trzeba zadzwonić po karetkę** *(tshe-ba za-dzvo-n'eech po ka-ret-ke)* (We need to call an ambulance)
- **Należy mi się odszkodowanie** *(na-le-zhih mee sh'ye ot-shko-do-va-n'ye)* (I'm entitled to compensation)
- **Dostałem odszkodowanie za wypadek w miejscu pracy** *(do-sta-wem ot-shko-do-va-n'ye za vih-pa-dek vmyey-stsoo pra-tsih)* (I [man] got compensation for an accident at my workplace)
- **Poszkodowany w wypadku został odwieziony do szpitala** *(po-shko-do-va-nih vvih-pat-koo zos-taw od-vye-z'yo-nih do shpee-ta-la)* (The person injured in the accident has been taken to hospital)

Fun & Games

You work in a tool shop in Poland and need to label the following tools in Figure 17-1. Match the names of tools with their pictures.

Figure 17-1: Label the tools shown.

Labels

gwoździe
wiertarka
młotek
miarka
poziomica
śrubokręt
skrzynka z narzędziami
piłka do metalu
drabina

Answer key:

nails – gwoździe; drill – wiertarka; hammer – młotek; measuring tape – miarka; spirit level – poziomica; screwdriver – śrubokręt; tool box – skrzynka z narzędziami; hacksaw – piłka do metalu; ladder – drabina

Chapter 18

Polish for Public Servants and Professionals

In This Chapter

- Describing what you do
- Working in the health services
- Talking about the police and fire services
- Selling telecommunications products

If you're thinking about (or you already have) a career in public services, **służby publiczne** *(swoo-zhbih poo-blee-chne)*, or you work in a profession, this chapter helps you talk about it in Polish.

Talking About Your Job

If you don't really know what to talk about, work is always a good (and safe) topic. Here's how you can ask someone about their work:

- **Czym się zajmujesz?** *(chihm sh'ye zay-moo-yesh)* (What do you do for a living?) – informal
- **Czym się pan/pani zajmuje?** *(chihm sh'ye pan/pa-n'ee zay-moo-ye)* (What do you do for living?) – formal, to a man/woman
- **Co pan/pani robi (zawodowo)?** *(tso pan/pa-n'ee ro-bee (za-vo-do-vo))* (What do you do (professionally)?) – formal, to a man/woman
- **Gdzie pan/pani pracuje?** *(gdj'ye pan/pa-n'ee pra-tsoo-ye)* (Where do you work?) – formal, to a man/woman

If you talk about your job you can use the phrase **Pracuję jako . . .** *(pra-tsoo-ye ya-ko)* (I work as . . .) followed by the nominative (no change in the ending) or **Jestem . . .** *(yes-tem)* (I'm a . . .) or **Zajmuję się . . .** *(zay-moo-ye sh'ye)* (I deal with . . .) followed by the instrumental case (the ending **-em** for masculine and neuter nouns and **-ą** for feminine). (If you need more work on those two cases, make your way to Chapter 2 for the nominative and Chapter 8 for the instrumental.)

Some of the jobs you may hear about are:

- **Jestem doradcą finansowym** *(yes-tem do-rat-tsohN fee-nan-so-vihm)* (I'm a financial advisor)
- **Pracuję w branży farmaceutycznej** *(pra-tsoo-ye vbran-zhih far-ma-tsew-tih-chney)* (I work in the pharmaceutical industry)
- **Jestem pracownikiem budowlanym** *(yes-tem pra-tsov-n'ee-kyem boo-do-vla-nihm)* (I'm a construction worker)
- **Uczę angielskiego w szkole językowej** *(oo-che an-gyel-skye-go fshko-le yen-zih-ko-vey)* (I teach English in a language school)
- **Jestem menedżerem projektu** *(yes-tem me-ne-dje-rem pro-ye-ktoo)* (I'm a project manager)
- **Pracuję w szpitalu jako lekarz/lekarka** *(pra-tsoo-ye fshpee-ta-loo ya-ko le-kash/le-kar-ka)* (I work in a hospital as a [male/female] doctor)
- **Projektuję strony internetowe** *(pro-ye-ktoo-ye stro-nih een-ter-ne-to-ve)* (I'm a website designer) – literally: I design websites
- **Jestem kucharzem** *(yes-tem koo-ha-zhem)* (I'm a cook)
- **Jestem kelnerem/kelnerką** *(yes-tem kel-ne-rem/kel-ner-kohN)* (I'm a waiter/waitress)
- **Zajmuję się marketingiem i reklamą** *(zay-moo-ye sh'ye mar-ke-teen-gyem ee re-kla-mohN)* (I work in [literally: deal with] marketing and advertising)
- **Jestem programistą** *(yes-tem pro-gra-mee-stohN)* (I'm a programmer)

You may also hear about different states of employment:

- **Jestem samozatrudniony/samozatrudniona** *(yes-tem sa-mo-za-trood-n'yo-nih/sa-mo-za-trood-n'yo-na)* (I'm self-employed) – man/woman
- **Teraz nie pracuję** *(te-ras n'ye pra-tsoo-ye)* (I'm not working at the moment)
- **Jestem bezrobotny/bezrobotna** *(yes-tem bez-ro-bo-tnih/bez-ro-bo-tna)* (I'm unemployed) – man/woman

Dressing up or down

You may be surprised to see all the colours Polish people wear in the workplace. The attitude is that if you don't have face-to-face meetings with clients, wearing uncomfortable suits or high heels is pointless. However, those working in western-style companies have to dress smartly all week long and only the lucky ones have the luxury of casual Fridays!

If you have a business meeting or want to sort out something with local authorities, formal business dress is the norm. And remember, you'll be judged on your appearance! For Poles, dressing well is a sign of your respect for them.

The verb pracować (to work)

The verb **pracować** *(pra-tso-vach')* (to work) is the most important tool when you want to describe what you do. It belongs to the **-ę/-esz** type of conjugation.

For verbs that end in **-ować** in the infinitive (the basic dictionary form) – such as **pracować** – you take off the **-ować** and replace it with **-uję**, **-ujesz**, **-uje**, **-ujemy**, **-ujecie**, **-ują** *(oo-ye oo-yesh oo-ye oo-ye-mih oo-ye-ch'ye oo-yohN)*, as shown in Table 18-1.

Table 18-1 Conjugation of Pracować (to work)

Personal Pronoun	Conjugation	Pronunciation
ja (I)	prac**uję**	*pra-tsoo-ye*
ty (you)	prac**ujesz**	*pra-tsoo-yesh*
on/ona/ono/pan/pani (he/she/it/'you' formal to a man/woman	prac**uje**	*pra-tsoo-ye*
my (we)	prac**ujemy**	*pra-tsoo-ye-mih*
wy (you)	prac**ujecie**	*pra-tsoo-ye-ch'ye*
oni/one/państwo (they men or mixed group/female/'you' formal	prac**ują**	*pra-tsoo-yohN*

To talk about your work, you may use these sentences:

- **Moja praca jest ciekawa** *(mo-ya pra-tsa yest ch'ye-ka-va)* (My work is interesting)
- **Pracuję jako kierowca** *(pra-tsoo-ye ya-ko kye-rof-tsa)* (I work as a [bus/lorry/car] driver)
- **Pracuję na umowę zlecenie** *(pra-tsoo-ye na oo-mo-ve zle-tse-n'ye)* (I'm a contractor)
- **Już (tu) nie pracuję** *(yoosh (too) n'ye pra-tsoo-ye)* (I don't work [here] any more)

Industries and departments

To indicate what industry or department you work in, start with **Pracuję w branży . . .** *(pra-tsoo-ye vbran-zhih)* and add the appropriate industry from Table 18-2 to say *I work in the . . . industry*.

Table 18-2 Industries

English	*Polish*	*Pronunciation*
advertising	reklamowej	*re-kla-mo-vey*
banking	bankowej	*ban-ko-vey*
building	budowlanej	*boo-do-vla-ney*
catering	gastronomicznej	*ga-stro-no-mee-chney*
education	edukacyjnej	*e-doo-ka-tsihy-ney*
energy	energetycznej	*e-ner-ge-tih-chney*
finance	finansowej	*fee-nan-so-vey*
food	spożywczej	*spo-zhih-fchey*
hotel	hotelarskiej	*ho-te-lar-skyey*
insurance	ubezpieczeniowej	*oo-bes-pye-che-n'yo-vey*
IT (information technology)	komputerowej/ informatycznej	*kom-poo-te-ro-vey/een-for-ma-tih-chney*
marketing	marketingowej	*mar-ke-teen-go-vey*
sales	handlowej	*han-dlo-vey*
technical	technicznej	*te-hn'ee-chney*
telecommunications	telefonicznej	*te-le-fo-n'ee-chney*
tourism	turystycznej	*too-rih-stih-chney*

Table 18-3 lists some departments, many of which are similar to their counterpart in Table 18-2. In this instance, start by saying, **Pracuję w dziale/w departamencie . . .** *(pra-tsoo-ye vdj'ya-le/vde-par-ta-men'-ch'ye)* and add a department to say, 'I work in the . . . department'.

Table 18-3 Departments

English	*Polish*	*Pronunciation*
advertising	reklamy	*re-kla-mih*
customer services	obsługi klienta	*op-swo-gee klee-yen-ta*
finance	finansowym	*fee-nan-so-vihm*
human resources (HR)	personalnym/HR	*per-so-nal-nihm/ha er*
information technology (IT)	komputerowym/ informatycznym	*kom-poo-te-ro-vihm/een-for-ma-tih-chnihm*
legal	prawnym	*pra-vnihm*
marketing	marketingu	*mar-ke-teen-goo*
sales	handlowym	*han-dlo-vihm*
technical	techniczym	*te-hn'ee-chnihm*

Talkin' the Talk

Krystyna *(krih-stih-na)* and Ignacy *(ee-gna-tsih)* have met at a conference in Warsaw and they engage in a conversation about their work:

Krystyna: **Czym się pan zajmuje?**
chihm sh'ye pan zay-moo-ye
What do you do for a living?

Ignacy: **Jestem przedstawicielem handlowym firmy farmaceutycznej. Szukam nowych klientów. A pani?**
yes-tem pshet-sta-vee-ch'ye-lem han-dlo-vihm feer-mih far-ma-tsew-tih-chney shoo-kam no-vihh klee-yen-toof a pa-n'ee
I'm a sales representative for a pharmaceutical company. I'm looking for new clients. And you?

Krystyna: **Pracuję w branży finansowej. Jestem doradcą finansowym dla firm.**
pra-tsoo-ye vbran-zhih fee-nan-so-vey yes-tem do-rat-tsohN fee-nan-so-vihm dla feerm
I work in the finance industry. I'm a financial advisor for companies.

Ignacy: **To chyba niełatwe w czasie kryzysu finansowego.**
to hih-ba n'ye-wat-fe fcha-sh'ye krih-zih-soo fee-nan-so-ve-go
That's probably not so easy in the financial crisis.

Krystyna: **Nie jest tak źle.**
n'ye yest tak z'le
It's not so bad.

Words to Know

przedstawiciel handlowy	*pshet-sta-vee-ch'yel han-dlo-vih*	sales representative
firma farmaceutyczna	*feer-ma far-ma-tsew-tih-chna*	pharmaceutical company
szukać	*shoo-kach'*	to look for
w branży finansowej	*vbran-zhih fee-nan-so-vey*	in the finance industry
doradca finansowy	*do-rat-tsa fee-nan-so-vih*	financial advisor
kryzys	*krih-zihs*	crisis

Working in a Hospital or Pharmacy

Chapter 15 explains how to deal with a personal health problem or an emergency. But if you work in the health field, you may need to know the phrases in the following list:

- **Pan/pani doktor przyjmuje od poniedziałku do piątku od ósmej do piętnastej** *(pan/pa-n'ee dok-tor pshihy-moo-ye ot po-n'ye-dj'yaw-koo do pyon-tkoo ot oo-smey do pyet-nas-tey)* (The doctor [male/female] sees patients from Monday to Friday from 8 a.m. to 3 p.m.)

- **Mamy wolny termin pierwszego marca o dziewiątej rano** *(ma-mih vol-nih ter-meen pyer-fshe-go mar-tsa o dj'ye-vyon-tey ra-no)* (We have the 1st of March at 9 a.m. available)
- **Ma pan/pani Europejską Kartę Pacjenta?** *(ma pan/pa-n'ee ew-ro-pey-skohN kar-te pa-tsyen-ta)* (Do you have a European Health Insurance Card?)
- **Czy jest pan ubezpieczony/pani ubezpieczona?** *(chih yest pan oo-bes-pye-cho-nih/pa-n'ee oo-bes-pye-cho-na)* (Do you have insurance?) formal, to a man/woman
- **Proszę chwilę poczekać** *(pro-she hfee-le po-che-kach')* (Wait a moment, please) formal
- **Dam panu/pani skierowanie na badania** *(dam pa-noo/pa-n'ee skye-ro-va-n'ye na ba-da-n'ya)* (I'll give you a referral for tests) – formal, to a man/woman
- **Zapraszam na kontrolę za miesiąc** *(za-pra-sham na kon-tro-le za mye-sh'yonts)* (Please come back for a check-up in a month)
- **To jest silny lek przeciwbólowy** *(to yest sh'eel-nih lek pshe-ch'eev-boo-lo-vih)* (This is a strong painkiller)
- **Dam panu/pani coś na biegunkę i gorączkę** *(dam pa-noo/pa-n'ee tsosh' na bye-goon-ke ee go-ron-chke)* (I'll give you something for diarrhoea and fever)
- **Ten lek jest tylko na receptę** *(ten lek yest tihl-ko na re-tse-pte)* (You need a prescription for this medicine)
- **Trzeba zrobić prześwietlenie** *(tshe-ba zro-beech' pshe-sh'fye-tle-n'ye)* (We need to take an X-ray)
- **Czy bierze pan/pani jakieś leki?** *(chih bye-zhe pan/pa-n'ee ya-kyesh' le-kee)* (Are you on any medication?) formal, to a man/woman
- **Czy ma pan/pani na coś alergię?** *(chih ma pan/pa-n'ee na tsosh' a-ler-gye)* (Do you have any allergies?) formal, to a man/woman
- **Już wysyłam karetkę** *(yoozh vih-sih-wam ka-ret-ke)* (The ambulance is on its way)

Talkin' the Talk

Dr Jones works in a hospital and he's just been called to a patient who has been hit by a car. This conversation is formal.

Dr Jones: **Poproszę kartę pacjenta. Co się stało?**
po-pro-she kar-te pa-tsyen-ta tso sh'ye sta-wo
Can I have the patient's chart? What's happened?

Nurse:	**Pacjent został potrącony przez samochód na przejściu dla pieszych. Jest przytomny.** *pa-tsyent zos-taw po-tron-tso-nih pshes sa-mo-hoot na pshey-sh'ch'yoo dla pye-shih yest pshih-tom-nih* The patient was hit by a car on the zebra crossing. He is conscious.
Dr Jones (to the patient):	**Jak się pan czuje?** *yak sh'ye pan choo-ye* How are you feeling?
Patient:	**Wszystko mnie boli, ale najbardziej lewa ręka i noga.** *fshih-stko mn'ye bo-lee a-le nay-bar-dj'yey le-va ren-ka ee no-ga* Everything hurts but my left arm and leg hurt the most.
Dr Jones:	**Noga powinna być w porządku, ale ręka jest złamana. Trzeba założyć gips.** *no-ga po-veen-na bihch' fpo-zhont-koo a-le ren-ka yezd zwa-ma-na tshe-ba za-wo-zhihch' geeps* Your leg looks okay but your arm is broken. We need to put it in plaster.
Patient:	**Kręci mi się w głowie i jest mi niedobrze.** *kren'-ch'ee mee sh'ye vgwo-vye ee yest mee n'ye-dob-zhe* I feel dizzy and sick.
Dr Jones:	**Zrobimy badania i prześwietlenie ręki i nogi. Damy panu coś przeciwbólowego.** *zro-bee-mih ba-da-n'ya ee pshe-sh'fye-tle-n'ye ren-kee ee no-gee da-mih pa-noo tsosh' pshe-ch'eev-boo-lo-ve-go* We will run some tests and X-ray your arm and leg. And we will give you some painkillers. **Czy bierze pan jakieś lekarstwa?** *chih bye-zhe pan ya-kyesh le-kar-stfa* Are you on any medication now?
Patient:	**Nie, nie biorę.** *N'ye, n'ye byo-re* No, I'm not.

Service with a smile

You may notice that some Poles working in public service jobs or for local authorities are not as polite or keen on helping you as you might expect. This attitude reaches back to the time of Communism when you had to have contacts in the right place to be able to gain access to information, services or goods in short supply. Your best bet when dealing with local authorities or public servants is to let a wide smile help you **załatwić sprawę** *(za-wat-feech' spra-ve)*, which is colloquial for *sort out your matter* smoothly.

Words to Know

przytomny	*pshih-tom-nih*	conscious
wszystko mnie boli	*fshih-stko mn'ye bo-lee*	everything hurts
gips	*geeps*	plaster
prześwietlenie	*pshe-sh'fye-tle-n'ye*	X-ray
zrobić badania	*zro-beedj' ba-da-n'ya*	to run tests
brać lekarstwa	*brach' le-kar-stfa*	to take medicine

Working for the Police and Fire Department

In this section you can read expressions that can be useful if you work for the police or fire services.

Practise these phrases if you're a police officer:

- **Jest pan aresztowany/Jest pani aresztowana pod zarzutem . . .** *(yest pan a-resh-to-va-nih/yest pa-n'ee a-resh-to-va-na pod za-zhoo-tem)* (You're being arrested on suspicion of . . .) – formal, to a man/woman
- **Musi pan/pani złożyć zeznanie** *(moo-sh'ee pan/pa-n'ee zwo-zihdj' ze-zna-n'ye)* (You need to make a statement) formal, to a man/woman
- **Proszę z nami na komendę** *(pro-she zna-mee na ko-men-de)* (Please come with us to the police station)
- **Poproszę dokumenty** *(po-pro-she do-koo-men-tih)* (Can I see some ID, please?)
- **Zabieramy pana na izbę wytrzeźwień** *(za-bye-ra-mih pa-na na eez-be vih-tshe-z'vyen')* (We're taking you to the drunk tank [a cell where the person can sober up])
- **Gdzie doszło do incydentu?** *(gdj'ye do-shwo do een-tsih-den-too)* (Where did the incident happen?)

You can read more about police emergencies in Chapter 15.

If you're a firefighter, the following phrases are part of your vocabulary:

- **Pracuję w straży pożarnej** *(pra-tsoo-ye fstra-zhih po-zhar-ney)* (I work for the fire service)
- **Przyjąłem/Przyjęłam zgłoszenie pożaru w centrum** *(psih-yo-wem/pshih-ye-wam zgwo-she-n'ye po-zha-roo ftsen-troom)* (We've had a fire reported in the city centre) – a man/woman speaking
- **Gdzie jest pożar?** *(gdj'ye yest po-zhar)* (Where's the fire?)
- **Czy ktoś jest w budynku?** *(chih ktosh' yest vboo-dihn-koo)* (Is there anyone in the building?)
- **Przyczyną pożaru była awaria instalacji gazowej** *(pshih-chih-nohN po-zha-roo bih-wa a-va-rya een-sta-la-tsyee ga-zo-vey)* (The cause of the fire was a broken gas installation)
- **Nikt nie ucierpiał** *(n'eekt n'ye oo-ch'yer-pyaw)* (Nobody was hurt)
- **Strażacy będa na miejscu za pięć minut** *(stra-zha-tsih ben-dohN na myey-stsoo za pyen'ch' mee-noot)* (The fire brigade will be there in five minutes)
- **Mam dzisiaj dyżur** *(mam dj'ee-sh'yay dih-zhoor)* (I'm on duty today)

Talkin' the Talk

One of the residents in a block of flats on ul. Polna *(oo-lee-tsa pol-na)* has woken up and noticed that there is a fire in the building on the other side of the street. He calls the fire service on 998.

Fire service: **Straż pożarna, słucham?**
strash po-zhar-na swoo-ham
Fire service, how can I help?

Resident: **W bloku na przy ulicy Polnej wybuchł pożar.**
vblo-koo na pshih oo-lee-tsih pol-ney vih-boohw po-zhar
There is fire in a block of flats on Polna street.

Fire service: **Czy ktoś jest w budynku?**
chih ktosh' yezd vboo-dihn-koo
Is there anyone in the building?

Resident: **Chyba tak.**
hih-ba tak
I think so.

Fire service: **Już jedziemy.**
yoosh ye-dj'ye-mih
We're on the way.

Words to Know

straż pożarna	*strash po-zhar-na*	fire service
pożar	*po-zhar*	fire
ktoś	*ktosh'*	someone
chyba tak	*hih-ba tak*	I think so
już jedziemy	*yoosh ye-dj'ye-mih*	we're on the way

Connecting People

In Chapter 9 I talk in depth about making phone calls, but in this section, I present the Polish you need to know to sell telecommunication products:

- **W czym mogę pomóc?** *(fchihm mo-ge po-moots)* (How can I help you?)
- **To jest najnowszy model** *(to yest nay-nof-shih mo-del)* (This is a brand new model)
- **Czy to będzie telefon prywatny czy na firmę?** *(chih to ben'-dj'ye te-le-fon prih-vat-nih chih na feer-me)* (Is it going to be a personal or business phone?)
- **Mamy teraz atrakcyjną ofertę** *(ma-mih te-ras a-trak-tsihy-nohN o-fer-te)* (We currently have a special offer)
- **Dla stałych klientów mamy zniżki** *(dla sta-wihh klee-yen-toof ma-mih zn'yeesh-kee)* (We have discounts for our regular customers)
- **Będzie pan/pani mieć dwieście minut wliczonych w abonament** *(ben'-dj'ye pan/pa-n'ee myech' dvyesh'-ch'ye mee-nood vlee-cho-nihh va-bo-na-ment)* (You have two hundred minutes included) – formal, to a man/woman
- **Abonament wynosi 40 zł na miesiąc** *(a-bo-na-ment vih-no-sh'ee chter-dj'yesh'-ch'ee zwo-tihh na mye-sh'yonts)* (The monthly fee/line rental is 40 PLN)
- **Umowa jest na dwa lata** *(oo-mo-va yest na dva la-ta)* (The contract is for two years)
- **Można później zmienić taryfę** *(mo-zhna pooz'-n'yey zmye-n'eech' ta-rih-fe)* (You will be able to change your tariff later)
- **Mamy telefony na abonament i na kartę** *(ma-mih te-le-fo-nih na a-bo-na-ment ee na kar-te)* (We have phones on contract or on a pay-as-you-go basis)
- **Ma pan/pani 100 mega danych** *(ma pan/pa-n'ee sto me-ga da-nihh)* (You have 100 megabytes of data) – formal, to a man/woman
- **W telefonie jest też Internet** *(fte-le-fo-n'ye yest tesh een-ter-net)* (The phone has Internet access too)
- **Mam słaby zasięg** *(mam swa-bih za-sh'yenk)* (The reception is bad)

Fun & Games

The words in the following sentences have become all mixed up. Put each sentence in the correct order.

1. się, zajmuje, czym, pan, ?
2. dam, gorączkę, na, pani, coś, biegunkę, i
3. czy, lekarstwa, bierze, pan, jakieś, ?
4. na, pracuję, etatu, pół
5. nami, na, proszę, z, komendę
6. branży, pracuję, w, farmaceutycznej
7. pracuję, w, jako, lekarz, szpitalu
8. jest, pożar, gdzie, ?
9. będzie, za, karetka, pięć, minut

Answer key:

1. Czym się pan zajmuje? (What do you do for a living?)
2. Dam pani coś na biegunkę I gorączkę or Dam pani coś na gorączkę i biegunkę (I'll give you something for diarrhoea and fever) or (I'll give you something for fever and diarrhoea)
3. Czy bierze pan jakieś lekarstwa? (Are you on any medication now?)
4. Pracuję na pół etatu (I work part-time)
5. Proszę z nami na komendę (Please come with us to the police station)
6. Pracuję w branży farmaceutycznej (I work In the pharmaceutical industry)
7. Pracuję w szpitalu jako lekarz (I work as a doctor in a hospital)
8. Gdzie jest pożar? (Where's the fire?)
9. Karetka będzie za 5 minut (The ambulance will be 5 minutes)

Part V
The Part of Tens

"Common phrases you'll hear Polish people speak to foreigners are 'Welcome to our country,' 'Have a good visit,' 'Yes, we've heard the jokes,' and 'No, we don't think they're funny.'"

In this part . . .

If you're looking for small, easily digestible pieces of information about Polish, this part is for you. Here, you can find ways to speak Polish quickly; useful Polish expressions to know; and celebrations worth joining in.

Chapter 19

Ten Ways to Pick Up Polish Quickly

In This Chapter

- Dipping into the written word
- Listening to the spoken word
- Exchanging language skills

Learning a new language, especially if the language happens to be Polish, can be challenging at first – phrases seem like tongue twisters and the grammar can give you a real headache. But that's just the first impression and with good guidance (hopefully you'll find your *Polish For Dummies* counts!), you'll find diving into the language enjoyable and easy in no time.

This chapter shares a few secrets of the best approach on how to effectively learn the Polish language.

Reading Polish Magazines and Easy Books

If you find reading magazines or articles too advanced, you can always try easy Polish books, which are simplified versions of well-known novels, plays, short stories and so on and usually have vocabulary boxes with English translations so you don't have to use your Polish–English dictionary so often. You can check out www.2ndlanguage.co.uk/ebooks.

Watching Polish Films

This is probably one of the most enjoyable ways of picking up the language. Check out foreign bookshops or the Internet for excellent Polish films with English subtitles and learn the language while still enjoying the film. You can play the film a couple of times. Use the pause button to stop the film while you write down interesting phrases.

Using Stickers or Flashcards

Write words or expressions you find useful, interesting or difficult to remember on the pages of a sticky pad or on flashcards. You can post the sticky pages on the wall next to your computer, on the items they identify or wherever you like. Just by looking at them, you can't help but learn the phrases fast. Use the flashcards to quiz yourself on your bus ride to work or on the treadmill at the gym.

Listening to Polish Music and Radio

Buy yourself some Polish songs and look up the lyrics on the Internet. You're bound to find yourself singing along! When doing some housework, put on a Polish radio station or turn on a Polish TV channel (available online too!) and be immersed in the sound of the Polish language. Even just passive listening helps your ear to get used to the word and sentence intonation and improves your pronunciation!

Surfing the Internet

The Internet is, undoubtedly, the richest source of material of all kinds that can help you build up your mental Polish library. Just type 'Polish language' in your search engine and let yourself dive into whatever interests you.

Using Language CDs and Computer Programs

You'll easily find a number of CDs or computer programs that can help you to pick up and polish your Polish. The audio tracks that come with your *Polish For Dummies* give you the opportunity to get a better idea of what Polish sounds like. Interactive programs not only enable you to listen to the pronunciation and practise the spelling but also to record your voice . . . and some even correct you!

Looking Up Words in the Dictionary

Whenever you come across a new word, look it up in a dictionary and try to memorise a sentence with it. With so many online dictionaries and phone applications (many of which are free or very cheap), you can check the meaning of new words instantly. Of course, having a traditional printed dictionary is always a good thing.

Visiting Poland

The best way by far to pick up a language is to visit the country where it's spoken. Visiting Poland, even if just for a short weekend, can hugely improve your speaking and listening comprehension. You'll be exposed to the language all day long, surrounded by the sound of Polish and, wherever you turn your head, you'll see signs in Polish. Bring a pocket notebook and jot down all the new or interesting expressions you don't understand so that you can look them up in a dictionary – or ask a Pole to translate.

Mingling with Poles

You may be lucky enough to live in an area with a Polish community or work with Polish people. Check out if there's anyone who would like to practise Polish with you in exchange for English. Interacting with native speakers helps you to learn the spoken language naturally and to get to know the people.

Taking Polish Classes

Search the Internet or local newspapers for Polish courses or one-to-one lessons. Regular classes help you to learn the language in a structured way, and with the help of an experienced teacher, you'll easily get through the labyrinth of Polish endings, pronunciation and sentence structure. Most language classes include some cultural training too so that you can familiarise yourself with the dos and don'ts of everyday (Polish) life.

Chapter 20

Ten Everyday Polish Expressions

In This Chapter

- Using **no** to say *yes*
- Expressing appreciation for food and drink
- Emphasising your feelings

This chapter provides ten Polish expressions frequently used in everyday life.

No

(no)

No, ***no*** does not equal the English word *no* at all. To add to your confusion, it actually means quite the opposite! You can use this word in a variety of situations to mean a variety of things.

- It's colloquial for **tak** *(tak)* meaning *yes*.
- It emphasises an order: **Chodź no tutaj!** *(hoch' no too-tay)* (Come here!)
- It expresses impatience, uncertainty, amazement and warnings:
  - **No, no, i co się stało?** *(no no ee tso sh'ye sta-wo)* (Well, come on. What happened next?) – impatience.
  - **No, nie wiem** *(no n'ye vyem)* (Well, I don't know) – uncertainty.
  - [Two people speaking] **Mam pytanie. No?** *(mam pih-ta-n'ye no)* (I have a question. Well, what is it?) – uncertainty.
  - **No, to jest świetne!** *(no to yest sh'fyet-ne)* (Well, that's really good!) – amazement.
  - **No, ale bez żartów!** *(no a-le bez zhar-toof)* (Don't you dare play any jokes!) – warning.
- It expresses finality: **No, to cześć!** *(no to chesh'ch')* (Goodbye then!)

Pa/Pa, pa

(pa/pa pa)

This expression is a very cute way of saying *bye bye* to little children. You may also hear it frequently at the end of conversations between friends or family members. As it's completely unsuitable for formal situations, don't use it in shops, banks or with your managers or clients. Go to Chapter 3 if you want to read more on formal and informal situations and other greetings and goodbyes.

Smacznego!

(sma-chne-go)

Imagine you're just about to take the first bite of your favourite Polish **pierogi** *(pye-ro-gee)* (dumplings). In order to sound like a native speaker, you can say **Smacznego**! *(sma-chne-go)*, much like the English *Enjoy*! or the French *Bon appetit*! If someone has outpaced you and said it first, you can reply by simply repeating **Smacznego** or saying **Nawzajem** *(na-vza-yem)* (you too), which literally means *one another* or *mutually*.

Na zdrowie!

(na zdro-vye)

If you already go out drinking with Polish friends or have read Chapter 7 of *Polish For Dummies*, you know that **Na zdrowie!** *(na zdro-vye)* is a common toast that accompanies drinking vodka or other alcohol and is the equivalent of *cheers*. It literally means *to your health*. If used after someone's sneezed, however, it turns into *bless you*.

You may frequently hear **Sto lat** *(sto lat)* instead of **Na zdrowie** and that means *100 years*, implying that you should live to be 100 years old!

To niemożliwe!

(to n'ye-mo-zhlee-ve)

This phrase is used to express your astonishment or disbelief at something. It translates to *impossible* or *this can't be true*.

Chyba

(hih-ba)

You use **chyba** to express assumptions, pretty strong suppositions and guesses, as in the following sentences:

- **To chyba idzie Agata** *(to hih-ba ee-dj'ye a-ga-ta)* (That must be Agata coming.)
- **Chyba tego nie zrobisz?** *(hih-ba te-go n'ye zro-beesh)* (You surely won't do it?)
- **Chyba nie mogę** *(hih-ba n'ye mo-ge)* (I don't think I can.)
- **Chyba tak** *(hih-ba tak)* (I think so.)
- **Chyba nie** *(hih-ba n'ye)* (I don't think so.)

Chyba isn't a verb, a noun or an adjective, so you never need to change its form – a big relief, huh?

Naprawdę

(na-pra-vde)

One of the words that has a number of equivalents in English, **naprawdę** can mean *really, truly, indeed, honestly* and so on. You use it as a question to express surprise or in a statement to emphasise the facts.

Dokładnie

(do-kwa-dn'ye)

This word translates to *exactly* or *indeed* and is used to show agreement with what someone else is saying. When someone tells you that they live in Warsaw, you can say **Gdzie dokładnie?** *(gdj'ye do-kwa-dn'ye)* (Whereabouts?) to find out which part of Warsaw it is, as you may happen to be neighbours!

Masz rację

(mash ra-tsye)

You can use this phrase to express your agreement with someone you're on informal terms with. It means *You're right.* The formal version would be **Ma pan/pani rację** *(ma pan/pa-n'ee ra-tsye).*

Palce lizać!/Pycha!/Mniam, mniam!

(pal-tse lee-zach'/pih-ha/mn'yam mn'yam)

If invited to a Polish dinner at your friend's house or to visit your future mother-in-law, you can expect the meal to be prepared in your honour. In order to express your appreciation of the excellent cooking, you can stick to the simple **Bardzo smaczne** *(bar-dzo sma-chne)* (very tasty) or go a bit crazy and say that something is **Palce lizać!** *(pal-tse lee-zach')* (finger-licking) or **Pycha!** *(pih-ha)* (good!). Children say **Mniam, mniam!** *(mn'yam mn'yam)* (Yummy!).

Chapter 21

Ten Polish Holidays to Remember

In This Chapter

- Celebrating with family and friends
- Honouring religious holidays

Polish people are well known for their enthusiasm for celebrations, festivities and cultivation of national and religious customs. Some rituals date back to pagan times, which gives them a unique flavour and magical character. Whether you have an opportunity to witness a national or religious holiday or are invited to a Polish wedding, you'll soon notice that the Poles are masters of entertaining. This chapter aims to bring at least some of the Polish holidays, **święta** *(sh'fyen-ta)*, closer.

Polish Weddings

Polish weddings – **wesela** *(ve-se-la)* – are famous for their intensity and duration. Nowadays, they usually start on Saturday afternoon and last until the early hours of Sunday and, after a short break to rest up and gather strength, restart around lunch time and continue until the last guest leaves. This may seem to be a bit excessive, but if you happen to take part in a wedding in the Tatra Mountains, be prepared for an entire week of constant celebrations!

Name Days

Most Poles have Christian names and celebrate their **imieniny** *(ee-mye-n'ee-nih)* (name day) on the feast day of the saint they're named for. The word **imieniny** comes from **imię** *(ee-mye)*, which means first name.

Imieniny are celebrated at work with the boss and colleagues or at home with family and friends. If you're invited to celebrate **imieniny**, remember to take a small gift, a bottle of good wine or a bunch of flowers. Turning up empty-handed is impolite.

Focusing on your **imieniny** is a great way out if you don't feel like celebrating yet another 29th birthday! After all, nobody needs to know how old you really are!

Fat Thursday

Fat Thursday – **Tłusty Czwartek** *(twoo-stih chfar-tek)* – opens the last week of carnival before Lent. This is the day when Poles stuff themselves with **pączki** *(pon-chkee)* (doughnuts) or **faworki** *(fa-vor-kee)* (French dough fingers served with lots of icing sugar), as the next opportunity for excessive eating won't be until Easter, theoretically at least, when Lent is over.

Easter

The religious holiday of Easter is called **święta Wielkiej Nocy** *(sh'fyen-ta vyel-kyey no-tsih)*, or the shorter **Wielkanoc** *(vyel-ka-nots)*, and is even more important than Christmas in Poland. The Easter season begins with Palm Sunday, **Niedziela Palmowa** *(n'ye-dj'ye-la pal-mo-va)*, which is the first day of the Holy Week, called **Wielki Tydzień** *(vyel-kee tih-dj'yen')* (the Great Week).

The village of Łyse *(wih-se)* in the Kurpie *(koor-pye)* region attracts tourists from all over the world during the Easter period to witness a competition involving making the tallest, most colourful and most amazingly designed palm trees. These trees bear no resemblance to those you see in the tropics. They're made with branches from hazel or young pine trees, juniper, mosses, boxwood and yew and are decorated with flowers and hand-crafted ribbons. It takes a number of people months of hard work to make one palm tree and seeing hundreds of them all in one place is absolutely spectacular.

The observance of Easter goes on for several days:

- **Good Friday – Wielki Piątek** *(vyel-kee pyon-tek)*: On the evening of this Friday before Easter, you can witness processions carrying crosses from one church to another.

- **Holy Saturday – Wielka Sobota** *(vyel-ka so-bo-ta)*: A day for traditional and charming festitivities when families colour and decorate eggs (see the cover of your *Polish For Dummies* book for how the eggs look when finished!), place them in beautifully decorated wicker baskets, then take them to church to place on a huge table where, next to hundred of similar baskets, they wait to be blessed.
- **Easter Sunday – Wielka Niedziela** *(vyel-ka n'ye-dj'ye-la)*: Lent finishes on Easter Sunday, and after attending morning Mass, those who have been depriving themselves for the last 40 days start eating their favourite foods again in a celebration that continues until the following day.
- **Easter Monday – Śmigus Dyngus** *(sh'mee-goos dihn-goos)* or **Lany Poniedziałek** *(la-nih po-n'ye-dj'ya-wek)*: On this day, young boys and teenagers run through the streets with buckets filled with water in search of a 'victim'. So, if you don't fancy getting wet, especially on a cold April day, you should really stay at home. This spring custom originates from pagan times when Poles would pour each other with water to make themselves clean, pure and worthy of awakening nature and the coming year.

Prima Aprilis

April Fools' Day is celebrated on 1 April, and people play all kinds of jokes on family members, friends, neighbours, work colleagues and anyone else they feel like. Even on TV and radio you may hear ridiculous information presented in a deadpan manner. And you may not even know you've just been fooled until you hear **Prima Aprilis**! *(prih-ma a-prih-lees)*.

Constitution Day – 3 May 1791

Not many people are aware that the Polish constitution was the first in Europe and the second oldest written constitution in the world. Ironically, it was only a year later when Russia, Austria and Prussia took over a large part of the Polish territory, followed by two further partitions, the effect of which was that Poland lost its territory for 123 years.

Official ceremonies and parades are held on Constitution Day, but for most people, the day is simply a part of the long May weekend, **długi weekend majowy** *(dwoo-gee wee-kent ma-yo-vih)*, starting on 1 May (Labour Day), when they go away and simply enjoy the beautiful weather.

All Saints' Day

All Saints' Day, **Wszystkich Świętych** *(fshih-stkeeh sh'fyen-tihh)*, falls on 1 November and is devoted to remembering dead family members and friends. Poles from all over Poland and those living abroad make their way to the cemeteries, where they clean their relatives' graves, light candles, lay flowers and gather together in remembrance. Cemeteries are covered with a colourful blanket of flowers, and at night the warm glow from countless candles makes the scenery surreal and absolutely magical.

Independence Day

A key national holiday (**święto państwowe**) is 11 November when Poles commemorate Independence Day, **Święto Odzyskania Niepodległości** *(sh'fyen-to od-zih-ska-n'ya n'ye-po-dle-gwo-sh'ch'ee)*. This day commemorates 1918 when Poland regained its independence after 123 years of non-existence on the map of Europe, when its territory was partitioned between Russia, Prussia and Austria. Lots of official ceremonies take place on that day and patriots fly flags from their windows.

St Andrew's Day

St Andrew's Day falls on 29 November and gives everyone called **Andrzej** *(an-dzhey)* (Andrew) a chance to celebrate their name day. Traditionally, the eve of this day – **Andrzejki** *(an-dzhey-kee)* – is a day of fortune telling. For example, children at school and home gather together and pour melted wax through the hole of an old key into a bucket of water. After that, they take out the biggest piece and hold it in front of a lamp and, from the shadow cast against the wall, try to read their future.

Christmas

You may not be familiar with the way Poles celebrate Christmas, **Święta Bożego Narodzenia** *(sh'fyen-ta bo-zhe-go na-ro-dze-n'ya)*. The most important day for the family celebration falls on **Wigilia** *(vee-gee-lya)*, Christmas Eve. Although this isn't an official holiday, most people take a day off or simply leave work early in order to make all the necessary preparations, which include decoration of **choinka** *(ho-yeen-ka)* (a Christmas tree) and cooking the 12 traditional courses. When all is ready, the family gathers around the table, where an extra place is set for an unexpected guest, and shares **opłatek** *(o-pwa-tek)*, Holy Bread, wishing each other **wesołych świąt** *(ve-so-wihh sh'fyont)*, Merry Christmas. After dinner, they sing traditional Christmas carols. And only then comes the fun part, at least for the children. **Święty Mikołaj** *(sh'fyen-tih mee-ko-way)*, Father Christmas (usually an uncle dressed in costume) comes along and, in exchange for a short song or poem, gives presents to good boys or girls. Those who have misbehaved that year are threatened with a birch rod, but only for a short moment, until they promise to always listen to their parents! At midnight, people go to church to take part in a Christmas Mass called **pasterka** *(pa-ster-ka)* and admire marvellous nativity displays called **szopka** *(shop-ka)*.

Superstitions add a special flavour to the evening, like the one that, at midnight, animals can speak. However, as everyone is at the Mass, there's no one to hear them.

Unlike in the UK, 25 December (**Pierwszy Dzień Świąt**) *(pyer-fshih dj'yen' sh'fyont)* and 26 December (**Drugi Dzień Świąt**) *(droo-gee dj'yen' sh'fyont)* are rather quiet affairs. People mostly spend them at home or possibly take off for a skiing holiday.

Chapter 22

Ten Phrases That Make You Sound Fluent in Polish

In This Chapter

- Casual assurances
- Thoughtful expressions

Knowing the right expressions and using them at the right place and moment can convince Polish native speakers that you speak fluent Polish. In this chapter, you can master ten expressions that will impress your Polish friends when you use them. Ready?

Nie ma mowy!

(n'ye ma mo-vih)

(No way!) If translated literally this expression means something like 'No speaking/saying'. Use it when you want to clearly express your disagreement with something and end the discussion. A similar expression is **W żadnym wypadku!** *(vzha-dnihm vih-pat-koo)* (In no case!).

Nie ma sprawy

(n'ye ma spra-vih)

(No problem.) If somebody asks you for a favour and you're happy to help, you can simply say **Nie ma sprawy** *(n'ye ma spra-vih)* meaning *No problem.*

You can also use this colloquial expression when someone apologises to you for something, as in this example:

Przepraszam, że nie oddzwoniłem *(pshe-pra-sham zhe n'ye od-dzvo-n'ee-wem)* (I apologise for not calling you back) – a man speaking

Nie ma sprawy *(n'ye ma spra-vih)* (That's fine/No problem/No big deal)

Być może and Może być

(bihch' mo-zhe) (mo-zhe bihch')

(Perhaps) (Yes, that's fine) These two are very Polish and quite confusing expressions as they mean different things. **Być może** *(bihch' mo-zhe)* translates to *perhaps*, *maybe*, *possibly*, as in:

Być może w tym roku zmienię pracę *(bihch' mo-zhe ftihm ro-koo zmye-n'ye pra-tse)* (Perhaps I'll change my job this year)

Być może masz rację *(bihch' mo-zhe mash ra-tsye)* (Maybe you're right)

Może być *(mo-zhe bihch')*, however, is used for agreeing with something:

Napijesz się kawy? *(na-pee-yesh sh'ye ka-vih)* (Would you like some coffee?)

Może być *(mo-zhe bihch')* (Yes, that's fine)

Może być trochę więcej? *(mo-zhe bihch' tro-he vyen-tsey)* (Is a little bit more okay?)

Tak, może być *(tak mo-zhe bihch')* (Yes, that's fine)

Wszystko (mi) jedno

(fshih-stko mee ye-dno)

(I don't mind/I don't really care) You can use this phrase to express that you don't mind if it's one way or another or that you really couldn't care less.

Nie mam (zielonego/bladego) pojęcia

(n'ye mam (z'ye-lo-ne-go/bla-de-go) po-yen'-ch'ya)

(I have no idea) This expression literally translates to *I don't have the green/pale idea* and naturally you use it to say that you know nothing about the matter.

O co chodzi?

(o tso ho-dj'ee)

(What's going on?/What's the matter?/What's the problem?) Use this phrase if your friend is in some kind of trouble and you don't actually know what it is but want to find out, or your child is in a bad mood for some reason unknown to you. To get answers, simply ask **O co chodzi?**

Szkoda!/Jaka szkoda!

(shko-da/ya-ka shko-da)

(That's a pity!/What a shame!) You can use this phrase to express your regret that something won't happen or can't be done, such as your friends can't join you for your birthday party or you won't be in town when they visit.

Co za pech!

(tso za peh)

(What bad luck!) Some days everything seems to go wrong and nothing works in your favour. You lose your keys, miss your train and your wife's birthday just slips your mind. **Co za pech!**

Pozdrów go/ją ode mnie

(po-zdroov go/yohN o-de mn'ye)

(Say 'hello' to him/her) Polish people like to keep in touch with their friends and never forget to send regards to their friends' friends or relatives. Master this phrase as a friendly way to show you care.

Udanej zabawy!

(oo-da-ney za-ba-vih)

(Have fun!/Enjoy!) You say this phrase to someone who's going to a party or on a date.

Part VI
Appendixes

"Good, but still not authentic Polish. Let's try it with a sock in the other cheek."

In this part . . .

In this last but not least part, you can find important information that you can use for reference. I give you a mini-dictionary in both Polish-to-English and English-to-Polish formats and provide some brief facts about Poland. I include verb tables that show you how to conjugate a regular verb and how to conjugate those verbs that stubbornly refuse to fit the pattern. I also provide a listing of the audio tracks so that you can find out where in the book those dialogues are and follow along.

Polish-English Mini-Dictionary

A

a (a): and, yet

abonament (a-bo-*na*-ment) m: subscription, fee

albo (*al*-bo): or

ale (*a*-le): but

aleja (a-*le*-ya) f: avenue

alergia (a-*ler*-gya) f: allergy

alkohol (al-*ko*-hol) m: alcohol

ambasada (am-ba-*sa*-da) f: embassy

apteczka (a-*pte*-chka) f: first aid kit

apteka (a-*pte*-ka) f: pharmacy

autobusem (aw-to-*boo*-sem) m: by bus

B

babcia (*bap*-ch'ya) f: grandmother

bagaż (*ba*-gash) m: luggage

banan (*ba*-nan) m: banana

banknot (*ban*-knot) m: note

bankomat (ban-*ko*-mat) m: cash machine

baranina (ba-ra-*n'ee*-na) f: lamb

basen (*ba*-sen) m: swimming pool

bezrobotny (bez-ro-*bo*-tnih) m: unemployed

BHP (be ha pe): Health and Safety

biegunka (bye-*goon*-ka) f: diarrhoea

bilet (*bee*-let) m: ticket

biurko (*byoor*-ko) n: desk

biuro podróży (*byoo*-ro po-*droo*-zhih) n: travel agents

blisko (*blee*-sko): near, close by

boleć (*bo*-lech') perf. **zaboleć** (za-*bo*-lech'): hurt, ache

ból (bool) m: ache, pain

branża (*bran*-zha) f: industry

brat (brat) m: brother

bratowa (bra-*to*-va) f: sister-in-law

brokuły (bro-*koo*-wih) pl: broccoli

brudny (*broo*-dnih) m: dirty

budowa (boo-*do*-va) f: construction

butelka (boo-*tel*-ka) f: bottle

być (bihch'): be

C

cena (*tse*-na) f: price

cebula (tse-*boo*-la) f: onion

chcieć (hch'yech'): want, wish

chętnie (*hen*-tn'ye): gladly, willingly

chleb (hlep) m: bread

chodzić (*ho*-dj'eech'): go, walk, attend

chyba nie (*hih*-ba n'ye): I don't think so

chyba tak (*hih*-ba tak): I think so

cielęcina (chye-len'-*ch'ee*-na) f: veal

ciemny (*ch'yem*-nih) m: dark

ciepły (*ch'ye*-pwih) m: warm

cieszyć się (*ch'ye*-shihch' sh'ye) perf. **ucieszyć się** (oo-*ch'ye*-shihch' sh'ye): be happy, look forward to, enjoy

ciocia (*ch'yo*-ch'ya) f: auntie

cło (tswo) n: customs

co (tso): what

codziennie (tso-*dj'yen*-n'ye): everyday, daily

coś (tsosh'): something

coś jeszcze (tsosh' *yesh*-che): anything, something else

córka (*tsoor*-ka) f: daughter

cukiernia (tsoo-*kyer*-n'ya) f: pastry shop

cześć (chesh'ch'): hello, hi, bye [informal]

czy (czih): whether, or

czytać (*chih*-tach') perf. **przeczytać** (pshe-*chih*-tach'): read

czas (chas) m: time

czekać (*che*-kach') perf. **poczekać, zaczekać** (po-*che*-kach' za-*che*-kach'): wait

czerwiec (*cher*-vyets) m: June

często (*chehN*-sto): often

czosnek (*chos*-nek) m: garlic

cztery (*chte*-rih): four

czwartek (*chfar*-tek) m: Thursday

czysty (chih-stih) m: clean

D

daleko (da-*le*-ko): far, far away

danie (*da*-n'ye) n: dish

deser (*de*-ser) m: dessert

deszcz (deshch) m: rain

dla (dla): for

dlaczego (dla-*che*-go): why

dlatego (dla-*te*-go): therefore, so

dobranoc (dob-*ra*-nots): good night [formal]

dobry wieczór (*dob*-rih *vye*-choor): good evening [formal]

dobrze (*dob*-zhe): well, fine, correct

dochodzić (do-*ho*-dj'eech') perf. **dojść** (doysh'ch'): get to, reach

dokąd (*do*-kont): where to

dokładnie (do-*kwa*-dn'ye): exactly, whereabouts, precisely

dokument (do-*koo*-ment) m: document

doświadczenie (do-sh'fyat-*che*-n'ye) n: experience

do widzenia (do vee-*dze*-nya): goodbye [formal]

dowód osobisty (*do*-voot o-so-*bees*-tih) m: ID

do zobaczenia (do zo-ba-*che*-n'ya): see you later

drobne (*dro*-bne) pl: small change

drób (droop) m: poultry

drukarka (droo-*kar*-ka) f: printer

drugie danie (*droo*-gye *da*-n'ye) n: main course

dużo (*doo*-zho): much, a lot, many

duży (*doo*-zhih) m: big, large

dwa (dva): two

dworzec (*dvo*-zhets) m: station

dziadek (*dj'ya*-dek) m: grandfather

dziecko (*dj'ye*-tsko) n: child

dzień dobry (dj'yen' *dob*-rih): hello [formal]

dziesięć (*dj'ye*-sh'yen'ch'): ten

dziewięć (*dj'ye*-vyen'ch'): nine

dziękować (dj'yen-*ko*-vach') perf. **podziękować** (po-dj'yen-*ko*-vach'): thank

dzwonić (*dzvo*-n'eech') perf. **zadzwonić** (za-*dzvo*-n'eech'): call, ring, phone

E

elegancki (e-le-*gan*-tskee) m: elegant, smart

e-mail (ee-meyl) m: email

F

fachowiec (fa-*ho*-vyets) m: handyman, specialist, professional

fasola (fa-*so*-la) f: bean

filiżanka (fee-lee-*zhan*-ka) f: cup

formularz (for-*moo*-lash) m: form

funt (foont) m: pound

G

gabinet (ga-*bee*-net) m: office

gdzie (gdj'ye): where

głodny (*gwod*-nih) m: hungry

głowa (*gwo*-va) f: head

godzina (go-*dj'yee*-na) f: hour, time

gorąco (go-*ron*-tso): hot

gorączka (go-*ron*-chka) f: fever

gotować (go-*to*-vach') perf. **ugotować** (oo-go-*to*-vach'): cook

gotówka (go-toof-ka) f: cash

grudzień (*groo*-dj'yen') m: December

gruszka (*groo*-shka) f: pear

H

hala odlotów (*ha*-la od-*lo*-toof) f: departure hall

hala przylotów (*ha*-la pshih-*lo*-toof) f: arrival hall

herbata (her-*ba*-ta) f: tea

I

i (ee): and

ile (*ee*-le): how much, how many

imię (*ee*-mye) n: first name

impreza (eem-*pre*-za) f: party

informacja turystyczna (een-for-*ma*-tsya too-rih-*stih*-chna) f: tourist information

interesować się (een-te-re-*so*-vach' sh'ye): be interested

owoce (o-*vo*-tse) pl: fruits

iść (eesh'ch') *perf.* **pójść** (pooysh'ch'): go, walk [single action]

J

jabłko (yap-ko) n: apple

jajecznica (ya-yech-*n'ee*-tsa) f: scrambled eggs

jajko (*yay*-ko) n: egg

jak (yak): how, what, as

jak długo (yag *dwoo*-go): how long

jaki (*ya*-kee) m: what type, what like

jasny (*ya*-snih) m: light

jechać (*ye*-hach') perf. **pojechać** (po *ye*-hach'): go [by means of transportation, single action]

jeden (*ye*-den): one

jedzenie (ye-*dze*-n'ye) n: food

jesień (*ye*-sh'yen') f: autumn

jeszcze (*yesh*-che): yet, still, even, more, else

jeść (yesh'ch') perf. **zjeść** (zyesh'ch'): eat

jeździć (*yez'*-dj'eech'): go [by means of transportation, repeated action]

język obcy (*yehN*-zihk *op*-tsih) m: foreign language

jutro (*yoo*-tro): tomorrow

K

kaczka (*ka*-chka) f: duck

kalafior (ka-*la*-fyor) m: cauliflower

kalendarz (ka-*len*-dash) m: calendar

kanapka (ka-*nap*-ka) f: sandwich

kantor (*kan*-tor) m: exchange bureau
karetka (ka-*re*-tka) f: ambulance
karta (*kar*-ta) f: menu, card
karta pokładowa (*kar*-ta po-kwa-*do*-va) f: boarding card
kasa (*ka*-sa) f: checkout
kasjer (*ka*-syer) m: cashier
katar (*ka*-tar) m: runny nose
kaszel (*ka*-shel) m: cough
kawa (*ka*-va) f: coffee
kawałek (ka-*va*-wek) m: piece
kawiarenka internetowa (ka-vya-*ren*-ka een-ter-ne-*too*-va) f: Internet café
kawiarnia (ka-*vyar*-n'ya) f: coffee shop
kiełbasa (kyew-*ba*-sa) f: sausage
kilka (*keel*-ka): a few
kino (*kee*-no) n: cinema
klawiatura (kla-vya-*too*-ra) f: keyboard
klimatyzacja (klee-ma-tih-*za*-tsya) f: air-conditioning
kolacja (ko-*la*-tsya) f: dinner, supper
kolega (ko-*le*-ga) m: male friend, colleague, mate
koleżanka (ko-le-*zhan*-ka) f: female friend, colleague
komórka (ko-*moor*-ka) f: mobile phone
komputer (kom-*poo*-ter) m: computer
koncert (*kon*-tsert) m: concert
konsulat (kon-*soo*-lat) m: consulate
konto (*kon*-to) n: account
kończyć się (*kon'*-chihch' sh'ye) perf. **skończyć się** (*skon'*-chihch' sh'ye): finish, end
kosztorys (ko-*shto*-rihs) m: estimate
kosztować (kosh-*to*-vach'): cost
kotlet schabowy (*kot*-let s-ha-*bo*-vih) m: pork cutlet
komenda policji (ko-*men*-da po-*lee*-tsyee) f: police station
kraj (kray) m: country
krew (kref) f: blood
kropka (*krop*-ka) f: dot, full stop
ksero (*kse*-ro) n: photocopier
książka (*ksh'yohN*-shka) f: book
kto (kto): who
który (*ktoo*-rih) m: which
kurczak (*koor*-chak) m: chicken
kurs (koors) m: course, exchange rate
kuzyn (*koo*-zihn) m: male cousin
kuzynka (koo-*zihn*-ka) f: female cousin
kwiecień (*kfye*-ch'yen') m: April

L

laptop (*lap*-top) m: laptop computer
lato (*la*-to) n: summer
lądować (lon-*do*-vach') perf. **wylądować** (vih-lon-*do*-vach'): land, touch down
legalnie (le-*gal*-n'ye): legally
lekarz (*le*-kash) m: doctor
lek przeciwbólowy (lek pshe-ch'eef-boo-*lo*-vih) m: painkiller
literować (lee-te-*ro*-vach') perf. **przeliterować** (pshe-lee-te-*ro*-vach'): spell
lipiec (*lee*-pyets) m: July
listopad (lee-*sto*-pad) m: November
lot (lot) m: flight
lotnisko (lo-*tn'ee*-sko) n: airport
lubić (*loo*-beech') perf. **polubić** (po-*loo*-beech'): like
luty (*loo*-tih) m: February

Ł

ładowarka (wa-do-*var*-ka) f: charger
łatwy (*wat*-fih) m: easy, simple
łazienka (wa-*z'yen*-ka) f: bathroom

łóżko (*woosh*-ko) n: bed
łyżeczka (wih-*zhe*-chka) f: teaspoon
łyżka (*wih*-shka) f: spoon

M

maj (may) m: May
mało (*ma*-wo): a little, a bit, small amount
małpa (*maw*-pa) f: monkey, @-sign
mały (*ma*-wih) m: small, little
mapa (*ma*-pa) f: map
marchewka (mar-*hef*-ka) f: carrot
marzec (*ma*-zhets) m: March
materiały budowlane (ma-te-*rya*-wih boo-do-*vla*-ne) pl: building materials
matka (*mat*-ka) f: mother
mąż (mohNsh) m: husband
mecz (mech) m: football match
metrem (*me*-trem) n: by tube, underground
mężatka (mehN-*zhat*-ka) f: married woman
miasto (*mya*-sto) n: city
mieć (myech'): have
miejsce (*myey*-stse) n: place, space
miesiąc (*mye*-sh'yonts) m: month
mieszkać (*myesh*-kach'): live
mieszkanie (mye-*shka*-n'ye) n: flat
mięso (*myehN*-so) n: meet
miło mi (*mee*-wo mee): nice to meet you
mleko (*mle*-ko) n: milk
masło (*ma*-swo) n: butter
młodszy (*mwot*-shih) m: younger
moim zdaniem (*mo*-yeem *zda*-n'yem): in my opinion
moneta (mo-*ne*-ta) f: coin
może (*mo*-zhe): maybe, perhaps
móc (moots): can, be able to, be capable
mówić (*moo*-veech') perf. **powiedzieć** (po-*vye*-dj'yech'): speak, say, tell
myszka (*mih*-shka) f: computer mouse, little mouse
myślnik (*mih*sh'l-n'eek) m: dash

N

nad (nat): above
najlepszy (nay-*lep*-shih) m: best
na (na): on, at, in, to, for [time]
naprawdę (na-*pra*-vde): really, truly, honestly
nauczyć się see **uczyć się**: study, learn
na wprost (na *fprost*): opposite
nawzajem (na-*vza*-yem): mutually, you too
na zasiłku (na za-*sh'eew*-koo): on benefits
na zdrowie (na *zdro*-vye): cheers, bless you
nazwisko (na-*zvee*-sko) n: surname
nazywać się (na-*zih*-vach' sh'ye): be called
nie (n'ye): no
niedziela (n'ye-*dj'ye*-la) f: Sunday
niemożliwe (n'ye-mo-*zhlee*-ve): impossible
niestety (n'yes-*te*-tih): unfortunately
nigdy (*n'ee*-gdih): never
no (no): well, yes [colloquial]
noga (*no*-ga) f: leg
nóż (noosh) m: knife

O

o (o): about, relating to, at [a time]
obiad (*o*-byat) m: lunch
oczywiście (o-chih-*veesh'*-ch'ye): certainly, of course
odpowiadać (ot-po-*vya*-dach') perf. **odpowiedzieć** (ot-po-*vye*-dj'yech'): answer, reply
odpowiedź (ot-*po*-vyech') f: answer

odprawa bagażowa (ot-*pra*-va ba-ga-*zho*-va) f: check-in

odszkodowanie (ot-shko-do-*va*-n'ye) n: compensation

ogórek (o-*goo*-rek) m: cucumber

ojciec (*oy*-ch'yets) m: father

oko (*o*-ko) n: eye

osiedle (o-*sh'ye*-dle) n: estate

osiem (*o*-sh'yem): eight

otwarte (o-*tfar*-te): open

o wpół do (o *fpoow* do): at half past

P

pa (pa): bye-bye [very informal]

pacjent (*pa*-tsyent) m: patient

paczka (*pach*-ka) f: packet

państwo (*pan'*-stfo): ladies and gentlemen, country

paragon (pa-*ra*-gon) m: receipt

parking (*par*-keenk) m: car park

parter (*par*-ter) m: ground floor

paszport (*pash*-port) m: passport

październik (paz'-*dj'yer*-n'eek) m: October

pensja (*pen*-sya) f: salary

piątek (*pyon*-tek) m: Friday

pić (peech') perf. **wypić** (*vih*-peech'): drink

piekarnia (pye-*kar*-n'ya) f: bakery

pieniądze (pye-*n'yon*-dze) pl: money

pieprz (pyepsh) m: pepper [condiment]

pierogi (pye-*ro*-gee) pl: dumplings

pięć (pyen'ch'): five

piętro (*pyen*-tro) n: floor

piwo (*pee*-vo) n: beer

plac (plats) m: square

plaża (*pla*-zha) f: beach

plecy (*ple*-tsih) pl: back

płacić (*pwa*-ch'eech') perf. **zapłacić** (za-*pwa*-ch'eech'): pay

pochmurno (po-*hmoo*-rno): cloudy

pociąg (*po*-ch'yonk) m: train

poczekać see **czekać**: wait

poczta (*po*-chta) f: post office

podkreślenie (pot-kre-*sh'le*-n'ye) n: underscore

podobać się (po-*do*-bach' sh'ye) perf. **spodobać się** (spo-*do*-bach' sh'ye): like, appeal to

podpisywać (pot-pee-*sih*-vach') perf. **podpisać** (pot-*pee*-sach'): sign

podróżować (po-droo-*zho*-vach'): travel

pod (pot): under, below

podziękować see **dziękować**: thank

pogoda (po-*go*-da) f: weather

pojechać see **jechać**: go

pojutrze (po-*yoo*-tshe): the day after tomorrow

pokój (*po*-kooy) m: room

polecać (po-*le*-tsach') perf. **polecić** (po-*le*-ch'eech'): recommend

policjant (po-*lee*-tsyant) m: police officer

policja (po-*lee*-tsya) f: police

polubić see **lubić**: like

pomagać (po-*ma*-gach') perf. **pomóc** (*po*-moots): help

pomarańcza (po-ma-*ran'*-cha) f: orange

pomidor (po-*mee*-dor) m: tomato

pomocy (po-*mo*-tsih): help!

pomóc see **pomagać**: help

poniedziałek (po-n'ye-*dj'ya*-wek) m: Monday

po polsku (po *pol*-skoo): in Polish

po południu (po po-*woo*-dn'yoo): in the afternoon

poprosić see **prosić**: ask, request

posłuchać see **słuchać**: listen

potwierdzać (po-*tfyer*-dzach') perf. **potwierdzić** (po-*tfyer*-dj'eech'): confirm

powiedzieć see **mówić**: speak, say, tell
powodzenia (po-vo-*dze*-n'ya): good luck
powtarzać (pof-*ta*-zhach') perf. **powtórzyć** (pof-*too*-zhihch'): repeat
pożar (*po*-zhar) m: fire
pójść see **iść**: go, walk [single action]
pół (poow): half
praca (*pra*-tsa) (noun) f: work
pracować (pra-*tso*-vach'): work
prawo jazdy (*pra*-vo *yaz*-dih) n: driving licence
prosić (*pro*-sh'eech') perf. **poprosić** (po-*pro*-sh'eech'): ask, request
prosto (*pro*-sto): straight ahead
prowizja (pro-*vee*-zya) f: commission
przejściówka (pshey'-*sh'ch'yoof*-ka) f: adaptor
przeliterować see **literować**: spell
przepraszać (pshe-*pra*-shach') perf. **przeprosić** (pshe-*pro*-sh'eech'): apologise, say sorry
przez (pshes): through, across, by
przyjazd (*pshih*-yast) m: arrival [train, bus]
przyjeżdżać (pshih-*yezh*-djach') perf. **przyjechać** (pshih-*ye*-hach'): to arrive
przykro mi (*pshih*-kro mee): I'm sorry
przylot (*pshih*-lot) m: arrival [plane]
przymierzać (pshih-*mye*-zhach') perf. **przymierzyć** (pshih-*mye*-zhihch'): try on
przystanek (pshih-*sta*-nek) m: bus, tram stop
puszka (*poosh*-ka) f: tin, can
pycha (*pih*-ha): yummy
pytać (*pih*-tach') perf. **zapytać** (za-pih-tach'): ask, inquire
pytanie (pih-*ta*-n'ye) n: question

R

rachunek (ra-*hoo*-nek) m: bill
rano (*ra*-no): in the morning
recepcja (re-*tse*-ptsya) f: reception desk
recepta (re-*tse*-pta) f: prescription
referencje (re-fe-*ren*-tsye) pl: references
remont (*re*-mont) m: redecoration, refurbishment
restauracja (re-staw-*ra*-tsya) f: restaurant
reszta (*resh*-ta) f: change
rezerwacja (re-zer-*va*-tsya) f: booking, reservation
rezerwować (re-zer-*vo*-vach') perf. **zarezerwować** (za-re-zer-*vo*-vach'): reserve, book
ręka (*ren*-ka) f: arm, hand
rodzeństwo (ro-*dzen'*-stfo) n: siblings
rodzice (ro-*dj'ee*-tse) pl: parents
rok (rok) m: year
rozmawiać (roz-*ma*-vyach') perf. **porozmawiać** (po-roz-*ma*-vyach'): talk, speak
rozmiar (*roz*-myar) m: size
rozmowa kwalifikacyjna (roz-*mo*-va kfa-lee-fee-ka-*tsihy*-na) f: job interview
rozumieć (ro-*zoo*-myech') perf. **zrozumieć** (zro-*zoo*-myech'): understand
również (*roov* n'yesh): also, too
ryba (*rih*-ba) f: fish
rzadko (*zhat*-ko): rarely, seldom

S

sala (*sa*-la) f: room
sałatka (sa-*wat*-ka) f: salad
samochód (sa-*mo*-hoot) m: car
samozatrudniony (sa-mo-za-trood-*n'yo*-nih) m: self-employed
schody (s-*ho*-dih) pl: stairs
ser (ser) m: cheese
siedem (*sh'ye*-dem): seven
sierpień (*sh'yer*-pyen') m: August

siostra (*sh'yo*-stra) f: sister
skąd (skont): from where
sklep (sklep) m: shop
skończyć się see **kończyć się**: finish, end
skrzyżowanie (skshih-zho-*va*-n'ye) n: junction
słabo (*swa*-bo): poorly, weakly
słonecznie (swo-*nech*-n'ye): sunny
słońce (*swon'*-tse) n: the sun
słuchać (*swoo*-hach') perf. **posłuchać** *(po-swoo-hach')*: listen
słyszeć (*swih*-shech') perf. **usłyszeć** (oo-*swih*-shech'): hear
smacznego (sma-*chne*-go): enjoy your meal
sobota (so-*bo*-ta) f: Saturday
sól (sool) f: salt
spodobać się see **podobać się**: like, appeal to
spotkanie (spo-*tka*-n'ye) n: meeting
spotykać się (spo-*tih*-kach' sh'ye) perf. **spotkać się** (*spot*-kach' sh'ye): meet
spóźniać się (*spooz'*-n'yach' sh'ye) perf. **spóźnić się** (*spooz'*-n'eech' sh'ye): be late
stan konta (stan *kon*-ta) m: balance
starszy (*star*-shih) m: older
stawka (*staf*-ka) f: rate
sto (sto): hundred
stolik (*sto*-leek) m: table at a restaurant
straż pożarna (strash po-*zhar*-na) f: fire services
styczeń (*stih*-chen') m: January
synowa (sih-*no*-va) f: daughter-in-law
syn (sihn) m: son
sześć (shesh'ch'): six
szkolenie (shko-*le*-n'ye) n: training
szkoła językowa (*shko*-wa yehN-zih-*ko*-va) f: language school
szpinak (*shpee*-nak) m: spinach
szpital (*shpee*-tal) m: hospital
sztućce (*shtooch'*-tse) pl: cutlery
szybko (*shihp*-ko): quickly, hurry up
szynka (*shihn*-ka) f: ham

Ś

śledź (sh'lech') m: herring
śniadanie (sh'n'ya-*da*-n'ye) n: breakfast
śnieg (sh'n'yek) m: snow
środa (*sh'ro*-da) f: Wednesday
świetnie (*sh'fyet*-n'ye): great, excellent
święto (*sh'fyen*-to) n: holiday [national or religious]

T

tak (tak): yes
taksówką (ta-*ksoo*-fkohN) f: by taxi
teraz (*te*-ras): now, at the moment
termin (*ter*-meen) m: date
teściowa (tesh'-*ch'yo*-va) f: mother-in-law
teść (tesh'ch') m: father-in-law
też (tesh): also
tłumacz (*twoo*-mach) m: translator, interpreter
tramwaj (*tram*-vay) m: tram
trochę (*tro*-he): a little, some
trudny (*troo*-dnih) m: difficult, hard, tough
truskawka (troos-*kaf*-ka) f: strawberry
trzymaj się (*t-shih*-may sh'ye): take care
trzy (t-shih): three
tu (too): here
tutaj (*too*-tay): in here
tydzień (*tih*-dj'yen') m: week
tylko (*tihl*-ko): only
tysiąc (*tih*-sh'yonts) m: thousand

U

ubezpieczenie (oo-bes-pye-*che*-n'ye) n: insurance

ucho (*oo*-ho) n: ear

ucieszyć see **cieszyć się:** be happy, look forward to, enjoy

uczulony (oo-choo-*lo*-nih) m: allergic

uczyć się (*oo*-chihch' sh'ye) perf. **nauczyć się** (na-*oo*-chihch' sh'ye): study, learn

ugotować see **gotować**: cook

ulica (oo-*lee*-tsa) f: street, road

umawiać się (oo-*ma*-vyach' sh'ye) perf. **umówić się** (oo-*moo*-veech' sh'ye): arrange to meet, make an appointment

umowa (oo-*mo*-va) f: agreement, contract

urlop (*oor*-lop) m: holiday [time off]

usłyszeć see **słyszeć**: hear

uwaga (oo-*va*-ga) f: attention, caution, look out

W

w (v) : in, at, on, into

warzywa (va-*zhih*-va) pl: vegetables

ważny (*va*-zhnih) m: valid, important

wczoraj (*fcho*-ray): yesterday

wegetarianin (ve-ge-ta-*rya*-n'een) m: vegetarian [man]

wegetarianka (ve-ge-ta-*ryan*-ka) f: vegetarian [woman]

wejście (vey-sh'ch'ye) n: entrance

wędliny (ven-*dlee*-nih) pl: cold meet

wiadomość (vya-*do*-mosh'ch') f: message, news, text message

widelec (vee-*de*-lets) m: fork

wieczorem (vye-*cho*-rem): in the evening

wiedzieć (*vye*-dj'yech'): know [a fact]

wieprzowina (vye-psho-*vee*-na) f: pork

winda (*veen*-da) f: lift

wiosna (*vyo*-sna) f: spring

wizytówka (vee-zih-*toof*-ka) f: business card

w lewo (*vle*-vo): to the left

wliczony (vlee-cho-nih) m: included

włosy (*vwo*-sih) pl: hair

w nocy (*vno*-tsih): at night

wnuczka (*vnoo*-chka) f: granddaughter

wnuk (*vnoo*k) m: grandson

w ogóle (vo-*goo*-le): at all

woleć (*vo*-lech'): prefer

wolniej (*vol*-n'yey): more slowly

wołowina (vo-wo-*vee*-na) f: beef

w prawo (*fpra*-vo): to the right

wrzesień (*vzhe*-sh'yen') m: September

wszyscy (*fshih*-stsih): everyone, all

wszystko (*fshih*-stko): everything, all

wtorek (*fto*-rek) m: Tuesday

wujek (*voo*-yek) m: uncle

wycieczka (vih-*ch'ye*-chka) f: trip, excursion

wyjście (*vihy*-sh'ch'ye) n: exit

wylądować see **lądować**: land, touch down

wymieniać (vih-*mye*-n'yach') perf. **wymienić** (vih-*mye*-n'yeech'): exchange, replace

wypadek (vih-*pa*-dek) m: accident

wypić see **pić**: drink

wyżywienie (vih-zhih-*vye*-n'ye) n: board, feeding

Z

z (z): from, with, of

zaboleć see **boleć**: hurt, ache

zadowolony (za-do-vo-*lo*-nih) m: content satisfied, pleased

zaczynać (za-*chih*-nach') perf. **zacząć** (*za*-chon'ch'): begin, start

zadzwonić see **dzwonić**: call, ring, phone

za granicą (za gra-*n'ee*-tsohN): abroad

zajęty (za-*yen*-tih) m: busy

zajmować się (zay-mo-vach' sh'ye) perf. **zająć się** (za-yon'ch' sh'ye): deal with, take care of

zakupy (za-*koo*-pih) pl: shopping

zakwaterowanie (za-kfa-te-ro-*va*-n'ye) n: accommodation

zamknięte (zam-*kn'yen*-te) n: closed

zapłacić see **płacić**: pay

zapytać see **pytać**: ask, inquire

zarabiać (za-*ra*-byach') perf. **zarobić** (za-ro-beech'): earn, make money

zarezerwować see **rezerwować**: reserve, book

zasięg (*za*-sh'yenk) m: reception, range, scope

zatrudniać (za-*troo*-dn'yach') perf. **zatrudnić** (za-*troo*-dn'eech'): employ, hire

zawsze (*zaf*-she): always, forever, ever

ząb (zomp) m: tooth

zero (*ze*-ro) n: zero

z góry (zgoo-rih): in advance, from upstairs

zima (*z'ee*-ma) f: winter

zimno (*z'ee*-mno): [it's] cold

zimny (*z'ee*-mnih) m: cold

zjeść see **jeść**: eat

złodziej (*zwo*-dj'yey) m: thief

złotówki (zwo-*toof*-kee) pl: Polish currency

zmęczony (zmen-*cho*-nih) m: tired

znaczyć (zna-chihch'): mean

znać (znach'): know [a person or place]

znakomity (zna-ko-*mee*-tih) m: superb

znieczulenie (zn'ye-choo-*le*-n'ye) n: anaesthetic

znowu, znów (*zno*-voo znoof): again

z przyjemnością (spshih-yem-*nosh'*-ch'yohN): with pleasure

zrozumieć see **rozumieć**: understand

zupa (*zoo*-pa) f: soup

Ź

źle (z'le): incorrect, wrongly, badly

Ż

żonaty (zho-*na*-tih) m: married man

żona (*zho*-na) f: wife

English-Polish Mini-Dictionary

A

about: **o** (o), **z** (z), **około** (o-*ko*-wo)

above: **nad** (nat)

abroad: **za granicą** (za gra-*n'ee*-tsohN)

accident: **wypadek** (vih-*pa*-dek) m

accommodation: **zakwaterowanie** (za-kfa-te-ro-*va*-n'ye) n

account: **konto** (*kon*-to) n

ache: **ból** (bool) m

ache: **boleć** (*bo*-lech') perf. **zaboleć** (za-*bo*-lech')

adaptor: **przejściówka** (pshey'-*sh'ch'yoof*-ka) f

a few: **kilka** (*keel*-ka)

again: **znowu, znów** (*zno*-voo znoof)

agreement: **umowa** (oo *mo*-va) f

air-conditioning: **klimatyzacja** (klee-ma-tih-*za* tsya) f

airport: **lotnisko** (lo-*tn'ee*-sko) n

alcohol: **alkohol** (al-*ko*-hol) m

a little: **trochę** (*tro*-he)

all: **wszyscy** (*fshih*-stsih)

allergic: **uczulony** (oo-choo-*lo*-nih) m

allergy: **alergia** (a-*ler*-gya) f

a lot: **dużo** (*doo*-zho)

also: **również** (*roov*-n'yesh)

also: **też** (tesh)

always: **zawsze** (*zaf*-she)

ambulance: **karetka** (ka-*re*-tka) f

anaesthetic: **znieczulenie** (zn'ye-choo-*le*-n'ye) n

and: **i** (ee)

answer: **odpowiadać** (ot-po-*vya*-dach') perf. **odpowiedzieć** (ot-po-*vye*-dj'yech')

answer: **odpowiedź** (ot-*po*-vyech') f

apologise: **przepraszać** (pshe-*pra*-shach') perf. **przeprosić** (pshe-*pro*-sh'eech')

apple: **jabłko** (*yap*-ko) n

April: **kwiecień** (*kfye*-ch'yen') m

arm: **ręka** (*ren*-ka) f

arrange to meet: **umawiać się** (oo-*ma*-vyach' sh'ye) perf. **umówić się** (oo-*moo*-veech' sh'ye)

arrive [train, bus]: **przyjeżdżać** (pshih-*yezh*-djach') perf. **przyjechać** (pshih-*ye*-hach')

arrival [plane]: **przylot** (*pshih*-lot) m

arrival [train, bus]: **przyjazd** (*pshih*-yast) m

arrival hall: **hala przylotów** (*ha*-la pshih-*lo*-toof) f

ask, inquire: **pytać** (*pih*-tach') perf. **zapytać** (za-*pih*-tach')

ask, request: **prosić** (*pro*-sh'eech') perf. **poprosić** (po-*pro*-sh'eech')

at [place]: **w** (v), **na** (na)

at [time]: **o** (o)

at all: **w ogóle** (vo-*goo*-le)

at half past: **o wpół do** (o *fpoow* do)

at night: **w nocy** (*vno*-tsih)

attention: **uwaga** (oo-*va*-ga) f

August: **sierpień** (*sh'yer*-pyen') m

auntie: **ciocia** (*ch'yo*-ch'ya) f

autumn: **jesień** (*ye*-sh'yen') f

avenue: **aleja** (a-*le*-ya) f

B

back: **plecy** (*ple*-tsih) pl

badly: **źle** (z'le)

bakery: **piekarnia** (pye-*kar*-n'ya) f

balance: **stan konta** (stan *kon*-ta) m

banana: **banan** (*ba*-nan) m

bathroom: **łazienka** (wa-*z'yen*-ka) f

be: **być** (bihch')

beach: **plaża** (*pla*-zha) f

bean: **fasola** (fa-*so*-la) f

be called: **nazywać się** (na-*zih*-vach' sh'ye)

bed: **łóżko** (*woosh*-ko) n

beef: **wołowina** (vo-wo-*vee*-na) f

beer: **piwo** (*pee*-vo) n

begin: **zaczynać** (za-*chih*-nach') perf. **zacząć** (*za*-chon'ch')

be happy: **cieszyć się** (*ch'ye*-shihch' sh'ye) perf. **ucieszyć się** (oo-*ch'ye*-shihch' sh'ye)

be interested: **interesować się** (een-te-re-*so*-vach' sh'ye)

be late: **spóźniać się** (*spooz'*-n'yach' sh'ye) perf. **spóźnić się** (*spooz'*-n'eech' sh'ye)

below: **pod** (pot)

best: **najlepszy** (nay-*lep*-shih) m

big: **duży** (*doo*-zhih) m

bill: **rachunek** (ra-*hoo*-nek) m

bless you: **na zdrowie** (na *zdro*-vye)

blood: **krew** (kref) f

board: **wyżywienie** (vih-zhih-*vye*-n'ye) n

boarding card: **karta pokładowa** (*kar*-ta po-kwa-*do*-va) f

book: **książka** (*ksh'yohN*-shka) f

book: **rezerwować** (re-zer-*vo*-vach') perf. **zarezerwować** (za-re-zer-*vo*-vach')

booking: **rezerwacja** (re-zer-*va*-tsya) f

bottle: **butelka** (boo-*tel*-ka) f

bread: **chleb** (hlep) m

breakfast: **śniadanie** (sh'n'ya-*da*-n'ye) n

broccoli: **brokuły** (bro-*koo*-wih) pl

brother: **brat** (brat) m

building materials: **materiały budowlane** (ma-te-*rya*-wih boo-do-*vla*-ne) pl

business card: **wizytówka** (vee-zih-*toof*-ka) f

busy: **zajęty** (za-*yen*-tih) m

but: **ale** (*a*-le)

butter: **masło** (*ma*-swo) n

by bus: **autobusem** (aw-to-*boo*-sem) m

bye-bye [very informal]: **pa** (pa)

by taxi: **taksówką** (ta-*ksoo*-fkohN) f

by tube, underground: **metrem** (*me*-trem) n

C

calendar: **kalendarz** (ka-*len*-dash) m

call: **dzwonić** (*dzvo*-n'eech') perf. **zadzwonić** (za-*dzvo*-n'eech')

can: **puszka** (*poosh*-ka) f

can: **móc** (moots)

car: **samochód** (sa-*mo*-hoot) m

car park: **parking** (*par*-keenk) m

carrot: **marchewka** (mar-*hef*-ka) f

cash: **gotówka** (go-*toof*-ka) f

cashier: **kasjer** (*ka*-syer) m

cash machine: **bankomat** (ban-*ko*-mat) m

cauliflower: **kalafior** (ka-*la*-fyor) m

certainly: **oczywiście** (o-chih-*veesh'*-ch'ye)

change [money]: **reszta** (*resh*-ta) f

charger: **ładowarka** (wa-do-*var*-ka) f

check-in: **odprawa bagażowa** (ot-*pra*-va ba-ga-*zho*-va) f

checkout: **kasa** (*ka*-sa) f

cheers: **na zdrowie** (na *zdro*-vye)

cheese: **ser** (ser) m

chicken: **kurczak** (*koor*-chak) m

child: **dziecko** (*dj'ye*-tsko) n

cinema: **kino** (*kee*-no) n

city: **miasto** (*mya*-sto) n

clean: **czysty** (*chih*-stih) m

close by: **blisko** (*blee*-sko)

closed: **zamknięte** (zam-*kn'yen*-te) n

cloudy: **pochmurno** (po-*hmoo*-rno)

coffee: **kawa** (*ka*-va) f

coffee shop: **kawiarnia** (ka-*vyar*-n'ya) f

coin: **moneta** (mo-*ne*-ta) f

cold: **zimny** (*z'ee*-mnih) m

[it's] cold: **zimno** (*z'ee*-mno)

cold meat: **wędliny** (ven-*dlee*-nih) pl

colleague [female]: **koleżanka** (ko-le-*zhan*-ka) f

colleague [male]: **kolega** (ko-*le*-ga) m

commission: **prowizja** (pro-*vee*-zya) f

compensation: **odszkodowanie** (ot-shko-do-*va*-n'ye) n

computer: **komputer** (kom-*poo*-ter) m

computer mouse: **myszka** (*mih*-shka) f

concert: **koncert** (*kon*-tsert) m

confirm: **potwierdzać** (po-*tfyer*-dzach') perf. **potwierdzić** (po-*tfyer*-dj'eech')

construction: **budowa** (boo-*do*-va) f

consulate: **konsulat** (kon-*soo*-lat) m

content, satisfied, pleased: **zadowolony** (za-do-vo-*lo*-nih) m

contract: **umowa** (oo-*mo*-va) f

cook: **gotować** (go-*to*-vach') perf. **ugotować** (oo-go-*to*-vach')

cost: **kosztować** (kosh-*to*-vach')

cough: **kaszel** (*ka*-shel) m

country: **państwo** (*pan'*-stfo), **kraj** (kray) m

course: **kurs** (koors) m

cousin [female]: **kuzynka** (koo-*zihn*-ka) f

cousin [male]: **kuzyn** (*koo*-zihn) m

cucumber: **ogórek** (o-*goo*-rek) m

cup: **filiżanka** (fee-lee-*zhan*-ka) f

customs: **cło** (tswo) n

cutlery: **sztućce** (*shtooch'*-tse) pl

D

dark: **ciemny** (*ch'yem*-nih) m

dash: **myślnik** (*mih*-sh'l-n'eek) m

date: **termin** (*ter*-meen) m

daughter: **córka** (*tsoor*-ka) f

deal with: **zajmować się** (zay-*mo*-vach' sh'ye) perf. **zająć się** (*za*-yon'ch' sh'ye)

December: **grudzień** (*groo*-dj'yen') m

departure hall: **hala odlotów** (*ha*-la od-*lo*-toof) f

dessert: **deser** (*de*-ser) m

desk: **biurko** (*byoor*-ko) n

diarrhoea: **biegunka** (bye-*goon*-ka) f

difficult: **trudny** (*troo*-dnih) m

dinner: **kolacja** (ko-*la*-tsya) f

dirty: **brudny** (*broo*-dnih) m

dish: **danie** (*da*-n'ye) n

doctor: **lekarz** (*le*-kash) m

document: **dokument** (do-*koo*-ment) m

dot: **kropka** (*krop*-ka) f

daughter-in-law: **synowa** (sih-*no*-va) f

drink: **pić** (peech') perf. **wypić** (*vih*-peech')

driving licence: **prawo jazdy** (*pra*-vo *yaz*-dih) n

duck: **kaczka** (*ka*-chka) f

dumplings: **pierogi** (pye-*ro*-gee) pl

E

ear: **ucho** (*oo*-ho) n

earn: **zarabiać** (za-*ra*-byach') perf. **zarobić** (za-*ro*-beech')

easy: **łatwy** (*wat*-fih) m

eat: **jeść** (yesh'ch') perf. **zjeść** (zyesh'ch')

egg: **jajko** (*yay*-ko) n

eight: **osiem** (*o*-sh'yem)

elegant: **elegancki** (e-le-*gan*-tskee) m

email: **e-mail** (*ee*-meyl) m

embassy: **ambasada** (am-ba-*sa*-da) f

employ: **zatrudniać** (za-*troo*-dn'yach') perf. **zatrudnić** (za-*troo*-dn'eech')

end: **kończyć się** (*kon'*-chihch' sh'ye) perf. **skończyć się** (*skon'*-chihch' sh'ye)

enjoy your meal: **smacznego** (sma-*chne*-go)

entrance: **wejście** (*vey*-sh'ch'ye) n

estate: **osiedle** (o-*sh'ye*-dle) n

estimate: **kosztorys** (ko-*shto*-rihs) m

everyday: **codziennie** (tso-*dj'yen*-n'ye)

everyone: **wszyscy** (*fshih*-stsih)

everything: **wszystko** (*fshih*-stko)

exactly: **dokładnie** (do-*kwa*-dn'ye)

exchange, replace: **wymieniać** (vih-*mye*-n'yach') perf. **wymienić** (vih-*mye*-n'yeech')

exchange bureau: **kantor** (*kan*-tor) m

exchange rate: **kurs** (koors) m

excuse me: **przepraszam** (pshe-*pra*-sham)

exit: **wyjście** (*vihy*-sh'ch'ye) n

experience: **doświadczenie** (do-sh'fyat-*che*-n'ye) n

eye: **oko** (o-ko) n

F

far, far away: **daleko** (da-*le*-ko)

father: **ojciec** (*oy*-ch'yets) m

father-in-law: **teść** (tesh'ch') m

February: **luty** (*loo*-tih) m

fever: **gorączka** (go-*ron*-chka) f

finish: **kończyć się** (*kon'*-chihch' sh'ye) perf. **skończyć się** (*skon'*-chihch' sh'ye)

fire: **pożar** (*po*-zhar) m

fire services: **straż pożarna** (strash po-*zhar*-na) f

first aid kit: **apteczka** (a-*pte*-chka) f

first name: **imię** (*ee*-mye) n

fish: **ryba** (*rih*-ba) f

five: **pięć** (pyen'ch')

flat: **mieszkanie** (mye-*shka*-n'ye) n

flight: **lot** (lot) m

floor: **piętro** (*pyen*-tro) n

food: **jedzenie** (ye-*dze*-n'ye) n

football match: **mecz** (mech) m

for: **dla** (dla)

foreign language: **język obcy** (*yehN*-zihk *op*-tsih) m

fork: **widelec** (vee-*de*-lets) m

form: **formularz** (for-*moo*-lash) m

four; **cztery** (*chte*-rih)

Friday: **piątek** (*pyon*-tek) m

friend [female]: **koleżanka** (ko-le-*zhan*-ka) f

friend [male]: **kolega** (ko-*le*-ga)

from: **z** (z)

from where: **skąd** (skont)

fruits: **owoce** (o-*vo*-tse) pl

full stop: **kropka** (*krop*-ka) f

G

garlic: **czosnek** (*chos*-nek) m

get to [on foot]: **dochodzić** (do-*ho*-dj'eech') perf. **dojść** (doysh'ch')

gladly: **chętnie** (*hen*-tn'ye)

go [on foot, repeated action]: **chodzić** (*ho*-dj'eech')

go [on foot, single action]: **iść** (eesh'ch') perf. **pójść** (pooysh'ch')

go [by means of transportation, repeated action]: **jeździć** (*yez'*-dj'eech')

go [by means of transportation, single action]: **jechać** (*ye*-hach') perf. **pojechać** (po-*ye*-hach')

goodbye [formal]: **do widzenia** (do vee-*dze*-nya)

good evening [formal]: **dobry wieczór** (*dob*-rih *vye*-choor)

good luck: **powodzenia** (po-vo-*dze*-n'ya)

good night [formal]: **dobranoc** (dob-*ra*-nots)

granddaughter: **wnuczka** (*vnoo*-chka) f

grandfather: **dziadek** (*dj'ya*-dek) m

grandmother: **babcia** (*bap*-ch'ya) f

grandson: **wnuk** (*vnook*) m

great: **świetnie** (*sh'fyet*-n'ye)

ground floor: **parter** (*par*-ter) m

H

hair: **włosy** (*vwo*-sih) pl

half: **pół** (poow)

hand: **ręka** (*ren*-ka) f

ham: **szynka** (*shihn*-ka) f

handyman, specialist, professional: **fachowiec** (fa-*ho*-vyets) m

have: **mieć** (myech')

head: **głowa** (*gwo*-va) f

Health and Safety: **BHP** (be ha pe)

hear: **słyszeć** (*swih*-shech') perf. **usłyszeć** (oo-*swih*-shech')

hello, hi [informal]: **cześć** (chesh'ch')

hello [formal]: **dzień dobry** (dj'yen' *dob*-rih)

help: **pomagać** (po-*ma*-gach') perf. **pomóc** (*po*-moots)

help: **pomocy** (po-*mo*-tsih)

here: **tu** (too)

herring: **śledź** (sh'lech') m

hire: **zatrudniać** (za-*troo*-dn'yach') perf. **zatrudnić** (za-*troo*-dn'eech')

holiday [national, religious]: **święto** (*sh'fyen*-to) n

holiday [time off]: **urlop** (*oor*-lop) m

honestly: **naprawdę** (na-*pra*-vde)

hospital: **szpital** (*shpee*-tal) m

hot: **gorąco** (go-*ron*-tso)

hour: **godzina** (go-*dj'yee*-na) f

how, what: **jak** (yak)

how long: **jak długo** (yag *dwoo*-go)

how much, how many: **ile** (ee-le)

hundred: **sto** (sto)

hungry: **głodny** (*gwod*-nih) m

hurt: **boleć** (*bo*-lech') perf. **zaboleć** (za-*bo*-lech')

hurry up: **szybko** (*shihp*-ko)

husband: **mąż** (mohNsh) m

I

ID: **dowód osobisty** (*do*-voot o-so-*bees*-tih) m

I don't think so: **chyba nie** (*hih*-ba n'ye)

important: **ważny** (*va*-zhnih) m

impossible: **niemożliwe** (n'ye-mo-*zhlee*-ve)
in: **w** (v), **na** (na), **z** (z)
in advance: **z góry** (*zgoo*-rih)
included: **wliczony** (vlee-*cho*-nih) m
incorrect: **źle** (z'le)
industry: **branża** (*bran*-zha) f
in here: **tutaj** (*too*-tay)
in my opinion: **moim zdaniem** (*mo*-yeem *zda*-n'yem)
in Polish: **po polsku** (po *pol*-skoo)
insurance: **ubezpieczenie** (oo-bes-pye-*che*-n'ye) n
Internet café: **kawiarenka internetowa** (ka-vya-*ren*-ka een-ter-ne-*too*-va) f
in the afternoon: **po południu** (po po-*woo*-dn'yoo)
in the evening: **wieczorem** (vye-*cho*-rem)
in the morning: **rano** (*ra*-no)
inquire: **pytać** (*pih*-tach') perf. **zapytać** (za-*pih*-tach')
I think so: **chyba tak** (*hih*-ba tak)
I'm sorry: **przykro mi** (*pshih*-kro mee)

J

January: **styczeń** (*stih*-chen') m
job interview: **rozmowa kwalifikacyjna** (roz-*mo*-va kfa-lee-fee-ka-*tsihy*-na) f
July: **lipiec** (*lee*-pyets) m
junction: **skrzyżowanie** (skshih-zho-*va*-n'ye) n
June: **czerwiec** (*cher*-vyets) m

K

keyboard: **klawiatura** (kla-vya-*too*-ra) f
knife: **nóż** (noosh) m
know [a fact]: **wiedzieć** (*vye*-dj'yech')
know [a person or place]: **znać** (znach')

L

ladies and gentlemen: **państwo** (*pan'*-stfo)
lamb: **baranina** (ba-ra-*n'ee*-na) f
land: **lądować** (lon-*do*-vach') perf. **wylądować** (vih-lon-*do*-vach')
language school: **szkoła językowa** (*shko*-wa yehN-zih-*ko*-va) f
laptop computer: **laptop** (*lap*-top) m
large: **duży** (*doo*-zhih) m
learn: **uczyć się** (*oo*-chihch' sh'ye) perf. **nauczyć się** (na-*oo*-chihch' sh'ye)
leg: **noga** (*no*-ga) f
legally: **legalnie** (le-*gal*-n'ye)
lift: **winda** (*veen*-da) f
light: **jasny** (*ya*-snih)
like [appeal to somebody]: **podobać się** (po-*do*-bach' sh'ye) perf. **spodobać się** (spo-*do*-bach' sh'ye)
like: **lubić** (*loo*-beech') perf. **polubić** (po-*loo*-beech')
listen: **słuchać** (*swoo*-hach') perf. **posłuchać** *(po*-swoo-*hach')*
live: **mieszkać** (*myesh*-kach')
look out: **uwaga** (oo-*va*-ga) f
luggage: **bagaż** (*ba*-gash) m
lunch: **obiad** (o-byat) m

M

main course: **drugie danie** (*droo*-gye *da*-n'ye) n
map: **mapa** (*ma*-pa) f
March: **marzec** (*ma*-zhets) m
married man: **żonaty** (zho-*na*-tih) m
married woman: **mężatka** (mehN-*zhat*-ka) f
May: **maj** (may) m
maybe: **może** (*mo*-zhe)
mean: **znaczyć** (*zna*-chihch')

meet: **mięso** (*myehN*-so) n
meet: **spotykać się** (spo-*tih*-kach' sh'ye) perf. **spotkać się** (*spot*-kach' sh'ye)
meeting: **spotkanie** (spo-*tka*-n'ye) n
menu: **karta dań** (*kar*-ta dan') f
message: **wiadomość** (vya-*do*-mosh'ch') f
milk: **mleko** (*mle*-ko) n
mobile phone: **komórka** (ko-*moor*-ka) f
Monday: **poniedziałek** (po-n'ye-*dj'ya*-wek) m
money: **pieniądze** (pye-*n'yon*-dze) pl
monkey, @-sign: **małpa** (*maw*-pa) f
month: **miesiąc** (*mye*-sh'yonts) m
more slowly: **wolniej** (*vol*-n'yey)
mother: **matka** (*mat*-ka) f
mother-in-law: **teściowa** (tesh'-*ch'yo*-va) f
much, many: **dużo** (*doo*-zho)
mutually, you too: **nawzajem** (na-*vza*-yem)

N

near: **blisko** (*blee*-sko)
never: **nigdy** (*n'ee*-gdih)
nice to meet you: **miło mi** (*mee*-wo mee)
nine: **dziewięć** (*dj'ye*-vyon'ch')
no: **nie** (n'ye)
note: **banknot** (*ban*-knot) m
November: **listopad** (lee-*sto*-pad) m
now: **teraz** (*te*-ras)

O

October: **październik** (paz'-*dj'yer*-n'eek) m
of course: **oczywiście** (o-chih-*veesh'*-ch'ye)
office: **gabinet** (ga-*bee*-net) m
often: **często** (*chehN*-sto)
older: **starszy** (*star*-shih) m
on: **na** (na), **w** (v), **o** (o), **po** (po)
on benefits: **na zasiłku** (na za-*sh'eew*-koo)
one: **jeden** (*ye*-den)
onion: **cebula** (tse-*boo*-la) f
only: **tylko** (*tihl*-ko)
open: **otwarte** (o-*tfar*-te)
opposite: **na wprost** (na *fprost*)
or: **albo** (*al*-bo)
orange: **pomarańcza** (po-ma-*ran'*-cha) f

P

packet: **paczka** (*pach*-ka) f
pain: **ból** (bool) m
painkiller: **lek przeciwbólowy** (lek pshe-ch'eev-boo-*lo*-vih) m
parents: **rodzice** (ro-*dj'ee*-tse) pl
party: **impreza** (eem-*pre*-za) f
passport: **paszport** (*pash*-port) m
pastry shop: **cukiernia** (tsoo-*kyer*-n'ya) f
patient: **pacjent** (*pa*-tsyent) m
pay: **płacić** (*pwa*-ch'eech') perf. **zapłacić** (za-*pwa*-ch'eech')
pear: **gruszka** (*groo*-shka) f
pepper [condiment]: **pieprz** (pyepsh) m
pharmacy: **apteka** (a-*pte*-ka) f
photocopier: **ksero** (*kse*-ro) n
piece: **kawałek** (ka-*va*-wek) m
place, space: **miejsce** (*myey*-stse) n
police: **policja** (po-*lee*-tsya) f
police officer: **policjant** (po-*lee*-tsyant) m
police station: **komenda policji** (ko-*men*-da po-*lee*-tsyee) f
Polish currency: **złotówki** (zwo-*toof*-kee) pl
poorly: **słabo** (*swa*-bo)
pork: **wieprzowina** (vye-psho-*vee*-na) f
pork cutlet: **kotlet schabowy** (*kot*-let s-ha-*bo*-vih) m
post office: **poczta** (*po*-chta) f
poultry: **drób** (droop) m

pound: **funt** (foont) m
prefer: **woleć** (*vo*-lech')
prescription: **recepta** (re-*tse*-pta) f
price: **cena** (*tse*-na) f
printer: **drukarka** (droo-*kar*-ka) f
question: **pytanie** (pih-*ta*-n'ye) f
quickly: **szybko** (*shihp*-ko)

R

rain: **deszcz** (deshch) m
rarely: **rzadko** (*zhat*-ko)
rate: **stawka** (*staf*-ka) f
read: **czytać** (*chih*-tach') perf. **przeczytać** (pshe-*chih*-tach')
really: **naprawdę** (na-*pra*-vde)
receipt: **paragon** (pa-*ra*-gon) m
reception, range, scope: **zasięg** (*za*-sh'yenk) m
reception desk: **recepcja** (re-*tse*-ptsya) f
recommend: **polecać** (po-*le*-tsach') perf. **polecić** (po-*le*-ch'eech')
redecoration: **remont** (*re*-mont) m
references: **referencje** (re-fe-*ren*-tsye) pl
repeat: **powtarzać** (pof-*ta*-zhach') perf. **powtórzyć** (pof-*too*-zhihch')
reply: **odpowiadać** (ot-po-*vya*-dach') perf. **odpowiedzieć** (ot-po-*vye*-dj'yech')
reservation: **rezerwacja** (re-zer-*va*-tsya) f
reserve: **rezerwować** (re-zer-*vo*-vach') perf. **zarezerwować** (za-re-zer-*vo*-vach')
restaurant: **restauracja** (re-sta-oo-*ra*-tsya) f
request: **prosić** (*pro*-sh'eech') perf. **poprosić** (po-*pro*-sh'eech')
room: **pokój** (*po*-kooy) m
runny nose: **katar** (*ka*-tar) m

S

salad: **sałatka** (sa-*wat*-ka) f
salary: **pensja** (*pen*-sya) f
salt: **sól** (sool) f
sandwich: **kanapka** (ka-*nap*-ka) f
Saturday: **sobota** (so-*bo*-ta) f
sausage: **kiełbasa** (kyew-*ba*-sa) f
say: **mówić** (*moo*-veech') perf. **powiedzieć** (po-*vye*-dj'yech')
scrambled eggs: **jajecznica** (ya-yech-*n'ee*-tsa) f
see you later: **do zobaczenia** (do zo-ba-*che*-n'ya)
self-employed: **samozatrudniony** (sa-mo-za-trood-*n'yo*-nih) m
September: **wrzesień** (*vzhe*-sh'yen') m
seven: **siedem** (*sh'ye*-dem)
shop: **sklep** (sklep) m
shopping: **zakupy** (za-*koo*-pih) pl
siblings: **rodzeństwo** (ro-*dzen'*-stfo) n
sign: **podpisywać** (pot-pee-*sih*-vach') perf. **podpisać** (pot-*pee*-sach')
simple: **łatwy** (*wat*-fih) m
sister: **siostra** (*sh'yo*-stra) f
sister-in-law: **bratowa** (bra-*to*-va) f
six: **sześć** (shesh'ch')
size: **rozmiar** (*roz*-myar) m
small: **mały** (*ma*-wih) m
small amount: **mało** (*ma*-wo)
small change: **drobne** (*dro*-bne) pl
snow: **śnieg** (sh'n'yek) m
some: **trochę** (*tro*-he)
something: **coś** (tsosh')
something else: **coś jeszcze** (tsosh' *yesh*-che)
son: **syn** (sihn) m

soup: **zupa** (*zoo*-pa) f
speak: **mówić** (*moo*-veech') perf. **powiedzieć** (po-*vye*-dj'yech')
spell: **literować** (lee-te-*ro*-vach') perf. **przeliterować** (pshe-lee-te-*ro*-vach')
spinach: **szpinak** (*shpee*-nak) m
spoon: **łyżka** (*wih*-shka) f
spring: **wiosna** (*vyo*-sna) f
square: **plac** (plats) m
stairs: **schody** (s-*ho*-dih) pl
start: **zaczynać** (za-*chih*-nach') perf. **zacząć** (*za*-chon'ch')
station: **dworzec** (*dvo*-zhets) m
still: **jeszcze** (*yesh*-che)
[bus, tram] stop: **przystanek** (pshih-*sta*-nek) m
straight ahead: **prosto** (*pro*-sto)
strawberry: **truskawka** (troos-*kaf*-ka) f
street, road: **ulica** (oo-*lee*-tsa) f
study: **uczyć się** (*oo*-chihch' sh'ye) perf. **nauczyć się** (na-*oo*-chihch' sh'ye)
subscription: **abonament** (a-bo-*na*-ment) m
summer: **lato** (*la*-to) n
[the] sun: **słońce** (*swon'*-tse) n
Sunday: **niedziela** (n'ye-*dj'ye*-la) f
sunny: **słonecznie** (swo-*nech*-n'ye)
superb: **znakomity** (zna-ko-*mee*-tih) m
supper: **kolacja** (ko-*la*-tsya) f
surname: **nazwisko** (na-*zvee*-sko) n
swimming pool: **basen** (*ba*-sen) m

T

table [at a restaurant]: **stolik** (*sto*-leek) m
take care: **trzymaj się** (*tshih*-may sh'ye)
take care of: **zajmować się** (zay-*mo*-vach' sh'ye) perf. **zająć się** (*za*-yon'ch' sh'ye)
talk: **rozmawiać** (roz-*ma*-vyach') perf. **porozmawiać** (po-roz-*ma*-vyach')
tea: **herbata** (her-*ba*-ta) f
teaspoon: **łyżeczka** (wih-*zhe*-chka) f
tell: **mówić** (*moo*-veech') perf. **powiedzieć** (po-*vye*-dj'yech')
ten: **dziesięć** (*dj'ye*-sh'yen'ch')
the day after tomorrow: **pojutrze** (po-*yoo*-tshe)
therefore: **dlatego** (dla-*te*-go)
thief: **złodziej** (*zwo*-dj'yey) m
thousand: **tysiąc** (*tih*-sh'yonts) m
three: **trzy** (t-shih)
through, across, by: **przez** (pshes)
Thursday: **czwartek** (*chfar*-tek) m
ticket: **bilet** (*bee*-let) m
time: **czas** (chas) m
tin: **puszka** (*poosh*-ka) f
tired: **zmęczony** (zmen-*cho*-nih) m
tomato: **pomidor** (po-*mee*-dor) m
tomorrow: **jutro** (*yoo*-tro)
too: **również** (*roov*-n'yesh)
tooth: **ząb** (zomp) m
to the left: **w lewo** (*vle*-vo)
to the right: **w prawo** (*fpra*-vo)
tourist information: **informacja turystyczna** (een-for-*ma* tsya too-rih-*stih*-chna) f
train: **pociąg** (*po*-ch'yonk) m
training: **szkolenie** (shko-*le*-n'ye) n
tram: **tramwaj** (*tram*-vay) m
translator: **tłumacz** (*twoo*-mach) m
travel: **podróżować** (po-droo-*zho*-vach')
travel agents: **biuro podróży** (*byoo*-ro po-*droo*-zhih) n
trip: **wycieczka** (vih-*ch'ye*-chka) f
try on: **przymierzać** (pshih-*mye*-zhach') perf. **przymierzyć** (pshih-*mye*-zhihch')

Tuesday: **wtorek** (*fto*-rek) m

two: **dwa** (dva)

U

uncle: **wujek** (*voo*-yek) m

under: **pod** (pot)

underscore: **podkreślenie** (pot-kre-*sh'le*-n'ye) n

understand: **rozumieć** (ro-*zoo*-myech') perf. **zrozumieć** (zro-*zoo*-myech')

unemployed: **bezrobotny** (bez-ro-*bo*-tnih) m

unfortunately: **niestety** (n'yes-*te*-tih)

V

valid: **ważny** (*va*-zhnih) m

veal: **cielęcina** (ch'ye-len'-*ch'ee*-na) f

vegetables: **warzywa** (va-*zhih*-va) pl

vegetarian [man]: **wegetarianin** (ve-ge-ta-*rya*-n'een) m

vegetarian [woman]: **wegetarianka** (ve-ge-ta-*ryan*-ka) f

W

wait: **czekać** (*che*-kach') perf. **poczekać** (po-*che*-kach')

walk [repeated action]: **chodzić** (*ho*-dj'eech')

walk [single action]: **iść** (eesh'ch') perf. **pójść** (pooysh'ch')

want: **chcieć** (hch'yech')

warm: **ciepły** (*ch'ye*-pwih) m

weather: **pogoda** (po-*go*-da) f

Wednesday: **środa** (*sh'ro*-da) f

week: **tydzień** (*tih*-dj'yen') m

well, fine, correct: **dobrze** (*dob*-zhe)

what: **co** (tso)

what type, what like: **jaki** (*ya*-kee) m

where: **gdzie** (gdj'ye)

whereabouts: **gdzie dokładnie** (gdj'ye do-*kwa*-dn'ye)

where to: **dokąd** (*do*-kont)

whether, or: **czy** (czih)

what time: **która godzina** (*ktoo-ra go-dj'yee-na*)

which: **który** (*ktoo*-rih) m

who: **kto** (kto)

why: **dlaczego** (dla-*che*-go)

wife: **żona** (*zho*-na) f

winter: **zima** (*z'ee*-ma) f

with pleasure: **z przyjemnością** (spshih-yem-*nosh'*-ch'yohN)

work: **praca** (*pra*-tsa) f

work: **pracować** (pra-*tso*-vach')

Y

year: **rok** (rok) m

yes: **tak** (tak)

yes [colloquial]: **no** (no)

yesterday: **wczoraj** (*fcho*-ray)

yet: **jeszcze** (*yesh*-che)

younger: **młodszy** (*mwot*-shih) m

yummy: **pycha** (*pih*-ha)

Z

zero: **zero** (*ze*-ro) n

Appendix B
Verb Tables

The verb tables in this appendix use the following abbreviations: *m* indicates masculine, *f* feminine, *n* neuter (which exists in the third person singular only) and *a* all genders. The following table lists the personal pronouns along with their translations. Because the Polish itself takes up so much space, I provide just the pronouns without the translations with the verb tables. Remember to include the future form of the verb **być** *(bihch')* (to be), before the masculine, feminine and neuter forms of imperfective verbs. I just include it once at the start of the conjugations in the tables. And don't be surprised that you can't find the present tense of perfective verbs: they simply don't have it.

Personal Pronouns	English Translation
ja	I
ty	you – singular informal
on	he
ona	she
ono	it
my	we
wy	you – plural informal
oni	they – a group with at least one man in it
one	they – a group with no man in it

Unlike English, Polish uses formal forms to address people in official situations. (I write more about addressing people formally and informally in Chapter 3.) So, the *you* form has the following formal equivalents in Polish:

- **pan, pani: pan** *(pan)* is the formal *you* to address a man and **pani** *(pa-n'ee)* is the formal *you* to address a woman.
- **państwo, panowie, panie** *(pan'-stfo pa-no-v'ye pa-n'ye)*: the formal, plural *you* form to address a mixed group, a group of men and a group of women, respectively; be aware that **państwo** also means *ladies and gentlemen*, **panowie** are *gentlemen* and **panie** translates as *ladies*.

When reading verb tables or conjugating verbs, remember that **pan** takes the same verb form as **on** (he) and **pani** the same verb form as **ona** (she): the third-person singular. In the present tense, the plural **państwo, panowie** and

panie take on a verb in the third-person plural (the same as **oni** [*they* male or mixed] and **one** [*they* female]). However, in the past tense and the future that uses past tense forms, **państwo** and **panowie** follow **oni**, while **panie** follows **one** in a choice of verb form. (I explain all formal forms of addressing people in the Introduction to this book.)

Polish verbs have both imperfective and perfective forms, depending on whether the verb's action is ongoing or completed. This very general explanation is fully covered in Chapter 2.

Regular Polish Verbs

Conjugation of -m/-sz Verbs
pytać (imperfective) and zapytać (perfective) (to ask)

	pytać (imperfective)			zapytać (perfective)	
	Present	**Past m/f/n**	**Future a//m/f/n**	**Past m/f/n**	**Future**
ja	pytam	pytałem/ pytałam	będę pytać//pytał/ pytała	zapytałem/-łam	zapytam
ty	pytasz	pytałeś/ pytałaś	będziesz pytać// pytał/pytała	zapytałeś/-łaś	zapytasz
on/ona/ ono	pyta	pytał/pytała/ pytało	będzie pytać//pytał/ pytała/pytało	zapytał/-ła/-ło	zapyta
my	pytamy	pytaliśmy/ pytałyśmy	będziemy pytać// pytali/pytały	zapytaliśmy/ -łyśmy	zapytamy
wy	pytacie	pytaliście/ pytałyście	będziecie pytać// pytali/pytały	zapytaliście/ -łyście	zapytacie
oni/one	pytają	pytali/pytały	będą pytać//pytali/ pytały	zapytali/-ły	zapytają

oglądać (imperfective) and obejrzeć (perfective) (to watch)

	oglądać (imperfective)			obejrzeć (perfective)	
	Present	Past m/f/n	Future a//m/f/n	Past m/f/n	Future
ja	oglądam	oglądałem/-łam	będę oglądać// oglądał/oglądała	obejrzałem/ obejrzałam	obejrzę
ty	oglądasz	oglądałeś/-łaś	będziesz oglądać// oglądał/oglądała	obejrzałeś/ obejrzałaś	obejrzysz
on/ona/ ono	ogląda	oglądał/-ła/-ło	będzie oglądać// oglądał/oglądała/ oglądało	obejrzał/ obejrzała/ obejrzało	obejrzy
my	oglądamy	oglądaliśmy/ -łyśmy	będziemy oglądać// oglądali/oglądały	obejrzeliśmy/ obejrzałyśmy	obejrzymy
wy	oglądacie	oglądaliście/ -łyście	będziecie oglądać// oglądali/oglądały	obejrzeliście/ obejrzałyście	obejrzycie
oni/one	oglądają	oglądali/-ły	będą oglądać// oglądali/oglądały	obejrzeli/ obejrzały	obejrzą

Conjugation of -ę/-isz Verbs

robić (imperfective) and zrobić (perfective) (to do)

	robić (imperfective)			zrobić (perfective)	
	Present	Past m/f/n	Future a//m/f/n	Past m/f/n	Future
ja	robię	robiłem/ robiłam	będę robić//robił/robiła	zrobiłem/ -łam	zrobię
ty	robisz	robiłeś/ robiłaś	będziesz robić//robił/ robiła	zrobiłeś/-łaś	zrobisz
on/ona/ ono	robi	robił/robiła/ robiło	będzie robić//robił/ robiła/robiło	zrobił/-ła/-ło	zrobi
my	robimy	robiliśmy/ robiłyśmy	będziemy robić//robili/ robiły	zrobiliśmy/ -łyśmy	zrobimy
wy	robicie	robiliście/ robiłyście	będziecie robić//robili/ robiły	zrobiliście/ -łyście	zrobicie
oni/one	robią	robili/robiły	będą robić//robili/robiły	zrobili/-ły	zrobią

mówić (imperfective) and powiedzieć (perfective) (to speak, to say, to tell)

	mówić (imperfective)			powiedzieć (perfective)	
	Present	**Past m/f/n**	**Future a//m/f/n**	**Past m/f/n**	**Future**
ja	mówię	mówiłem/ mówiłam	będę mówić//mówił/ mówiła	powiedziałem/-łam	powiem
ty	mówisz	mówiłeś/ mówiłaś	będziesz mówić// mówił/mówiła	powiedziałeś/-łaś	powiesz
on/ona/ ono	mówi	mówił/mówiła/ mówiło	będzie mówić// mówił/mówiła/ mówiło	powiedział/-ła/ło	powie
my	mówimy	mówiliśmy/ mówiłyśmy	będziemy mówić// mówili/mówiły	powiedzieliśmy/ powiedziałyśmy	powiemy
wy	mówicie	mówiliście/ mówiłyście	będziecie mówić// mówili/mówiły	powiedzieliście/ powiedziałyście	powiecie
oni/one	mówią	mówili/mówiły	będą mówić//mówili/ mówiły	powiedzieli/ powiedziały	powiedzą

Conjugation of -ę/-ysz Verbs

tańczyć (imperfective) and zatańczyć (perfective) (to dance)

	tańczyć (imperfective)			zatańczyć (perfective)	
	Present	**Past m/f/n**	**Future a//m/f/n**	**Past m/f/n**	**Future**
ja	tańczę	tańczyłem/ tańczyłam	będę tańczyć// tańczył/tańczyła	zatańczyłem/ -łam	zatańczę
ty	tańczysz	tańczyłeś/ tańczyłaś	będziesz tańczyć// tańczył/ tańczyła	zatańczyłeś/-łaś	zatańczysz
on/ona/ ono	tańczy	tańczył/ tańczyła/ tańczyło	będzie tańczyć// tańczył/tańczyła/ tańczyło	zatańczył/-ła/ło	zatańczy
my	tańczymy	tańczyliśmy/ tańczyłyśmy	będziemy tańczyć// tańczyli/tańczyły	zatańczyliśmy/ -łyśmy	zatańczymy
wy	tańczycie	tańczyliście/ tańczyłyście	będziecie tańczyć// tańczyli/tańczyły	zatańczyliście/ -łyście	zatańczycie
oni/one	tańczą	tańczyli/ tańczyły	będą tańczyć// tańczyli/tańczyły	zatańczyli/-ły	zatańczą

Conjugation of -ę/-esz Verbs

pisać (imperfective) and napisać (perfective) (to write)

	pisać – to write (imperfective)			napisać (perfective)	
	Present	**Past m/f/n**	**Future a//m/f/n**	**Past m/f/n**	**Future**
ja	piszę	pisałem/pisałam	będę pisać//pisał/ pisała	napisałem/ -łam	napiszę
ty	piszesz	pisałeś/pisałaś	będziesz pisać//pisał/ pisała	napisałeś/ -łaś	napiszesz
on/ona/ ono	pisze	pisał/pisała/ pisało	będzie pisać//pisał/ pisała/pisało	napisał/-ła/ło	napisze
my	piszemy	pisaliśmy/ pisałyśmy	będziemy pisać// pisali/pisały	napisaliśmy/ -łyśmy	napiszemy
wy	piszecie	pisaliście/ pisałyście	będziecie pisać// pisali/pisały	napisaliście/ -łyście	napiszecie
oni/one	piszą	pisali/pisały	będą pisać//pisali/ pisały	napisali/-ły	napiszą

Conjugation of -ować Verbs

studiować (no perfective form) (to study, to be a student)

	Present	**Past m/f/n**	**Future a//m/f/n**
ja	studiuję	studiowałem/studiowałam	będę studiować//studiował/ studiowała
ty	studiujesz	studiowałeś/studiowałaś	będziesz studiować//studiował/ studiowała
on/ona/ ono	studiuje	studiował/studiowała/ studiowało	będzie studiować//studiował/ studiowała/studiowało
my	studiujemy	studiowaliśmy/ studiowałyśmy	będziemy studiować//studiowali/ studiowały
wy	studiujecie	studiowaliście/ studiowałyście	będziecie studiować//studiowali/ studiowały
oni/one	studiują	studiowali/studiowały	będą studiować//studiowali/ studiowały

Irregular Verbs

The following tables show conjugations of some of the commonly used irregular verbs.

brać (imperfective) and wziąć (perfective) (to take)

	Present	Past m/f/n	Future a//m/f/n	Past m/f/n	Future
ja	biorę	brałem/brałam	będę brać//brał/ brała	wziąłem/ wzięłam	wezmę
ty	bierzesz	brałeś/brałaś	będziesz brać// brał/brała	wziąłeś/ wzięłaś	weźmiesz
on/ona/ ono	bierze	brał/brała/ brało	będzie brać//brał/ brała/brało	wziął/wzięła/ wzięło	weźmie
my	bierzemy	braliśmy/ brałyśmy	będziemy brać// brali/brały	wzięliśmy/ wzięłyśmy	weźmiemy
wy	bierzecie	braliście/ brałyście	będziecie brać// brali/brały	wzięliście/ wzięłyście	weźmiecie
oni/one	biorą	brali/brały	będą brać//brali/ brały	wzięli/wzięły	wezmą

jeść (imperfective) and zjeść (perfective) (to eat)

	Present	Past m/f/n	Future a//m/f/n	Past m/f/n	Future
ja	jem	jadłem/jadłam	będę jeść//jadł/jadła	zjadłem/zjadłam	zjem
ty	jesz	jadłeś/jadłaś	będziesz jeść//jadł/ jadła	zjadłeś/zjadłaś	zjesz
on/ona/ ono	je	jadł/jadła/ jadło	będzie jeść//jadł/ jadła/jadło	zjadł/zjadła/ zjadło	zje
my	jemy	jedliśmy/ jadłyśmy	będziemy jeść//jedli/ jadły	zjedliśmy/ zjadłyśmy	zjemy
wy	jecie	jedliście/ jadłyście	będziecie jeść//jedli/ jadły	zjedliście/ zjadłyście	zjecie
oni/one	jedzą	jedli/jadły	będą jeść//jedli/jadły	zjedli/zjadły	zjedzą

pić (imperfective) and wypić (perfective) (to drink)

	Present	Past m/f/n	Future a//m/f/n	Past m/f/n	Future
ja	piję	piłem/piłam	będę pić//pił/piła	wypiłem/wypiłam	wypiję
ty	pijesz	piłeś/piłaś	będziesz pić//pił/ piła	wypiłeś/wypiłaś	wypijesz
on/ona/ ono	pije	pił/piła/piło	będzie pić//pił/ piła/piło	wypił/wypiła/ wypiło	wypije
my	pijemy	piliśmy/ piłyśmy	będziemy pić// pili/piły	wypiliśmy/ wypiłyśmy	wypijemy
wy	pijecie	piliście/ piłyście	będziecie pić// pili/piły	wypiliście/ wypiłyście	wypijecie
oni/one	piją	pili/piły	będą pić//pili/piły	wypili/wypiły	wypiją

myć (imperfective) and umyć (perfective) (to wash, to clean)

	Present	Past m/f/n	Future a//m/f/n	Past m/f/n	Future
ja	myję	myłem/ myłam	będę myć//mył/myła	umyłem/umyłam	umyję
ty	myjesz	myłeś/myłaś	będziesz myć//mył/ myła	umyłeś/umyłaś	umyjesz
on/ona/ ono	myje	mył/myła/ myło	będzie myć//mył/ myła/myło	umył/umyła/ umyło	umyje
my	myjemy	myliśmy/ myłyśmy	będziemy myć//myli/ myły	umyliśmy/ umyłyśmy	umyjemy
wy	myjecie	myliście/ myłyście	będziecie myć//myli/ myły	umyliście/ umyłyście	umyjecie
oni/one	myją	myli/myły	będą myć//myli/ myły	umyli/umyły	umyją

iść (imperfective) and pójść (perfective) (to go, to walk [a single action])

	Present	Past m/f/n	Future m/f/n	Past m/f/n	Future
ja	idę	szedłem/szłam	będę szedł/szła	poszedłem/ poszłam	pójdę
ty	idziesz	szedłeś/szłaś	będziesz szedł/szła	poszedłeś/ poszłaś	pójdziesz
on/ona/ ono	idzie	szedł/szła/szło	będzie szedł/szła/ szło	poszedł/poszła/ poszło	pójdzie
my	idziemy	szliliśmy/ szłyśmy	będziemy szli/szły	poszliśmy/ poszłyśmy	pójdziemy
wy	idziecie	szliście/ szłyście	będziecie szli/szły	poszliście/ poszłyście	pójdziecie
oni/one	idą	szli/szły	będą szli/szły	poszli/poszły	pójdą

chodzić (imperfective – no perfective form) (to go, to walk, to attend [a repeated action])

	Present	Past m/f/n	Future a//m/f/n
ja	chodzę	chodziłem/chodziłam	będę chodzić//chodził/chodziła
ty	chodzisz	chodziłeś/chodziłaś	będziesz chodzić//chodził/ chodziła
on/ona/ ono	chodzi	chodził/chodziła/chodziło	będzie chodzić//chodził/chodziła/ chodziło
my	chodzimy	chodziliśmy/chodziłyśmy	będziemy chodzić//chodzili/ chodziły
wy	chodzicie	chodziliście/chodziłyście	będziecie chodzić//chodzili/ chodziły
oni/one	chodzą	chodzili/chodziły	będą chodzić//chodzili/chodziły

jechać (imperfective) and pojechać (perfective)
(to go [in a vehicle, a single action])

	Present	Past m/f/n	Future a//m/f/n	Past m/f/n	Future
ja	jadę	jechałem/-łam	będę jechać// jechał/jechała	pojechałem/ -łam	pojadę
ty	jedziesz	jechałeś/-łaś	będziesz jechać// jechał/ jechała	pojechałeś/-łaś	pojedziesz
on/ona/ ono	jedzie	jechał/-ła/-ło	będzie jechać// jechał/jechała / jechało	pojechał/-ła/-ło	pojedzie
my	jedziemy	jechaliśmy/ -łyśmy	będziemy jechać// jechali/jechały	pojechaliśmy/ -łyśmy	pojedziemy
wy	jedziecie	jechaliście/ -łyście	będziecie jechać// jechali/ jechały	pojechaliście/ -łyście	pojedziecie
oni/one	jadą	jechali/-ły	będą jechać// jechali/ jechały	pojechali/-ły	pojadą

jeździć (imperfective – no perfective form)
(to go [in a vehicle, repeated action])

	Present	Past m/f/n	Future a//m/f/n
ja	jeżdżę	jeździłem/jeździłam	będę jeździć//jeździł/jeździła
ty	jeździsz	jeździłeś/jeździłaś	będziesz jeździć//jeździł/jeździła
on/ona/ ono	jeździ	jeździł/jeździła/jeździło	będzie jeździć//jeździł/jeździła/ jeździło
my	jeździmy	jeździliśmy/jeździłyśmy	będziemy jeździć//jeździli/jeździły
wy	jeździcie	jeździliście/jeździłyście	będziecie jeździć//jeździli/jeździły
oni/one	jeżdżą	jeździli/jeździły	będą jeździć//jeździli/jeździły

Verbs with No Perfective Form

Some verbs don't have perfective forms as they describe constant states that can't be completed.

wiedzieć (to know [a fact])

	Present	Past m/f/n	Future a//m/f/n
ja	wiem	wiedziałem/wiedziałam	będę wiedzieć//wiedział/wiedziała
ty	wiesz	wiedziałeś/wiedziałaś	będziesz wiedzieć//wiedział/ wiedziała
on/ona/ono	wie	wiedział/wiedziała/ wiedziało	będzie wiedzieć//wiedział/ wiedziała/wiedziało
my	wiemy	wiedzieliśmy/wiedziałyśmy	będziemy wiedzieć//wiedzieli/ wiedziały
wy	wiecie	wiedzieliście/wiedziałyście	będziecie wiedzieć//wiedzieli/ wiedziały
oni/one	wiedzą	wiedzieli/wiedziały	będą wiedzieć//wiedzieli/wiedziały

być (to be)

	Present	Past m/f/n	Future
ja	jestem	byłem/byłam	będę
ty	jesteś	byłeś/byłaś	będziesz
on/ona/ono	jest	był/była/było	będzie
my	jesteśmy	byliśmy/byłyśmy	będziemy
wy	jesteście	byliście/byłyście	będziecie
oni/one	są	byli/były	będą

mieć (to have)

	Present	Past m/f/n	Future a//m/f/n
ja	mam	miałem/miałam	będę mieć//miał/miała
ty	masz	miałeś/miałaś	będziesz mieć//miał/miała
on/ona/ono	ma	miał/miała/miało	będzie mieć//miał/miała/miało
my	mamy	mieliśmy/miałyśmy	będziemy mieć//mieli/miały
wy	macie	mieliście/miałyście	będziecie mieć//mieli/miały
oni/one	mają	mieli/miały	będą mieć//mieli/miały

Modal verbs

Modal verbs modify the verb they're followed by (which is why they're also called *helping verbs* and *auxiliary verbs*). They have no perfective form.

chcieć (to want)

	Present	Past m/f/n	Future m/f/n
ja	chcę	chciałem/chciałam	będę chciał/chciała
ty	chcesz	chciałeś/chciałaś	będziesz chciał/chciała
on/ona/ono	chce	chciał/chciała/chciało	będzie chciał/chciała/chciało
my	chcemy	chcieliśmy/chciałyśmy	będziemy chcieli/chciały
wy	chcecie	chcieliście/chciałyście	będziecie chcieli/chciały
oni/one	chcą	chcieli/chciały	będą chcieli/chciały

musieć (to have to, must)

	Present	Past m/f/n	Future m/f/n
ja	muszę	musiałem/musiałam	będę musiał/musiała
ty	musisz	musiałeś/musiałaś	będziesz musiał/musiała
on/ona/ono	musi	musiał/musiała/musiało	będzie musiał/musiała/musiało
my	musimy	musieliśmy/musiałyśmy	będziemy musieli/musiały
wy	musicie	musieliście/musiałyście	będziecie musieli/musiały
oni/one	muszą	musieli/musiały	będą musieli/musiały

móc (can, to be able to, to be capable)

	Present	Past m/f/n	Future m/f/n
ja	mogę	mogłem/mogłam	będę mógł/mogła
ty	możesz	mogłeś/mogłaś	będziesz mógł/mogła
on/ona/ono	może	mógł/mogła/mogło	będzie mógł/mogła/mogło
my	możemy	mogliśmy/mogłyśmy	będziemy mogli/mogły
wy	możecie	mogliście/mogłyście	będziecie mogli/mogły
oni/one	mogą	mogli/mogły	będą mogli/mogły

umieć (can, to know how to)

	Present	Past m/f/n	Future m/f/n
ja	umiem	umiałem/umiałam	będę umiał/umiała
ty	umiesz	umiałeś/umiałaś	będziesz umiał/umiała
on/ona/ono	umie	umiał/umiała/umiało	będzie umiał/umiała/umiało
my	umiemy	umieliśmy/umiałyśmy	będziemy umieli/umiały
wy	umiecie	umieliście/umiałyście	będziecie umieli/umiały
oni/one	umieją	umieli/umiały	będą umieli/umiały

woleć (to prefer)

	Present	Past m/f/n	Future m/f/n
ja	wolę	wolałem/wolałam	będę wolał/wolała
ty	wolisz	wolałeś/wolałaś	będziesz wolał/wolała
on/ona/ono	woli	wolał/wolała/wolało	będzie wolał/wolała/wolało
my	wolimy	woleliśmy/wolałyśmy	będziemy woleli/wolały
wy	wolicie	woleliście/wolałyście	będziecie woleli/wolały
oni/one	wolą	woleli/wolały	będą woleli/wolały

Conditional mood

Conditional forms express a wish or possibility. The tables below show probably the most frequently used verbs in the conditional Polish: **chcieć** and **móc**.

chciałbym (would like)

	Masculine	Feminine	Neuter
ja	chciałbym	chciałabym	–
ty	chciałbyś	chciałabyś	–
on/ona/ono	chciałby	chciałaby	chciałoby
my	chcielibyśmy	chciałybyśmy	–
wy	chcielibyście	chciałybyście	–
oni/one	chcieliby	chciałyby	–

mógłbym (could)

	Masculine	Feminine	Neuter
ja	mógłbym	mogłabym	–
ty	mógłbyś	mogłabyś	–
on/ona/ono	mógłby	mogłaby	mogłoby
my	moglibyśmy	mogłybyśmy	–
wy	moglibyście	mogłybyście	–
oni/one	mogliby	mogłyby	–

The following examples show you some of the 'conditions' in which you can use the conditional mood:

- **Chciałbym pojechać na urlop** *(hch'yaw-bihm po-ye-hach' na oor-lop)* (I'd like to go on holiday) – a man speaking.
- **Czy mógłbyś mi pomóc?** *(chih moogw-bihsh' mee po-moots)* (Could you help me, please?) – speaking to a man informally.

Appendix C

Polish Facts

Here are some facts about Poland and the Polish language:

- The Republic of Poland is the ninth-largest country in Europe and a member of the European Union, NATO (North Atlantic Treaty Organisation) and the United Nations. Its population totals over 38 million citizens.
- Poland's long history covers more than 1,000 years. Its borders have changed throughout the centuries:
  - In the fourteenth century Poland, together with Lithuania, formed the Polish–Lithuanian Commonwealth whose territory extended right up to the gates of Muscovy (Russia), including most of today's Ukraine and Belarus. The alliance that lasted for more than two centuries made the country one of the most powerful and largest in Europe.
  - At the end of the eighteenth century, Poland was partitioned between the three neighbouring countries of Russia, Prussia and Austria, effectively disappearing from the map of Europe for 123 years. Poland regained its status as a free country in 1918, after the First World War.
  - After the end of the Second World War, despite having fought arm in arm with the Allied Powers, Poland lost about 20 per cent of its eastern territory to the Soviet Union and struggled under the Communist regime for 44 years.
- As a result of the political repression experienced during Communist times, many Poles were forced to leave the country and settle down in other parts of the world. At the moment, some 15 to16 million Poles live outside of the Polish borders so your chance of meeting a Polish person in the UK, US, Canada, Australia, France, Germany, Greece and many other countries all over the world is pretty high.

  Poland's borders have remained stable since the 1940s; its current borders and neighbours are shown in the map in Figure C-1 and you can see some of Poland's larger cities in Figure C-2.

Figure C-1: Poland's current borders and neighbours.

Figure C-2: Poland's cities.

- In 1989 the world-renowned Solidarity movement brought down Communism in Poland and re-established democracy. Soon after, other countries from the Eastern bloc, including Germany, followed Poland's example in peacefully removing the Communist order.

- With many other European languages, Polish is part of the Indo-European group and, together with Czech and Slovak, belongs to the West Slavic group of languages. If you already happen to speak any other Slavic language, such as Czech, Slovak, Russian, Ukrainian or Slovenian, learning Polish will be a piece of cake (**bułka z masłem**) (*boow-ka zma-swem*).

  Polish is based on Latin, yet it has a number of 'additional' letters and letter combinations that are unfamiliar to the English tongue.

- Polish is the main language of Poland, where nearly all citizens declare Polish to be their mother tongue.

  Poles love their native tongue and appreciate your attempt to speak even a few words. Any language or cultural mistakes are easily forgiven; what counts is your making an effort to learn and speak the language. You need never feel at all embarrassed to speak it.

- Polish grammar may seem a little daunting with its ever-changing nouns, adjectives, pronouns and different verb forms for each person. I admit, Polish is not the easiest language to learn, but it's certainly not impossible. In fact, a rapidly growing number of foreigners fall in love with the Polish language and actually speak it well. Surely, you'll join that group shortly (if you haven't already!).

Appendix D

Audio Tracks

Polish For Dummies comes packed to bursting with audio tracks – indicated in the chapters by the 'Play This!' icon – that provide conversations between Polish speakers.

In this appendix, I provide a complete track listing.

Discovering What's On the Audio Tracks

Table D-1 lists all the tracks along with a description, so you can quickly look up any conversation.

Table D-1 ***Polish For Dummies* Audio Tracks**

Track	*Description*
1	Pronunciation guide.
2	Adam and Magda have just bumped into each other.
3	Mr Tomasz Wiśniewski demonstrates how Polish people introduce themselves formally.
4	Simon and Michelle chat on a train.
5	Ola and Tomek sit next to each other on a plane
6	Martha shows Ela a photo of her family.
7	Arek phones a restaurant to make a reservation.
8	Arek and Anna arrive at the Wesele restaurant.
9	Arek and Anna place their order.
10	Arek and Anna enjoy their Polish food.
11	Asking for the bill.
12	Asking where the toilets are.

(continued)

Table D-1 (continued)

Track	*Description*
13	Simon is shopping at the market.
14	Shopping for a dress.
15	Marek calls Agata to ask her to join him to see a film.
16	Organising a house-warming party.
17	Buying theatre tickets.
18	Dominika is reading a book. Her new class mate, Marek, wants to get to know her better.
19	Emilia calls her friend Patrycja on the phone.
20	Mrs Lewis leaves a message about a meeting.
21	Mr Kowalik calls the 'Lingua' school and speaks to the school secretary.
22	Simon asks if he can use a credit card.
23	Changing currency.
24	Asking for directions to the Old Town.
25	Asking for directions to the pharmacy.
26	Booking a hotel room.
27	Anna arrives at the hotel.
28	Anna checks out of her hotel.
29	Anna checks in at the airport.
30	Buying a train ticket.
31	Booking a flight to Poland with a travel agent.
32	At the doctor's surgery.
33	Reporting a motorway accident.
34	Asking for help with the printer in the office.
35	Simon talks to his builder about an extension to his house.

Index

• A •

• B •

• C •

• D •

• E •

• F •

• G •

• H •

• I •

• J •

• K •

• O •

• P •

• Q •

• R •

• S •

• U •

• V •

• W •

• Y •

• Z •